'GLUM HEROES'

# 'GLUM HEROES'

*Hardship, Fear and Death – Resilience and Coping in the British Army on the Western Front 1914-1918*

Wolverhampton Military Studies No.22

Peter E. Hodgkinson

Helion & Company Limited

Helion & Company Limited
26 Willow Road
Solihull
West Midlands
B91 1UE
England
Tel. 0121 705 3393
Fax 0121 711 4075
Email: info@helion.co.uk
Website: www.helion.co.uk
Twitter: @helionbooks
Visit our blog http://blog.helion.co.uk/

Published by Helion & Company 2016. Reprinted in paperback 2018
Designed and typeset by Mach 3 Solutions Ltd (www.mach3solutions.co.uk)
Cover designed by Paul Hewitt, Battlefield Design (www.battlefield-design.co.uk)
Printed by Lightning Source Ltd, Milton Keynes, Buckinghamshire

Text © Peter E. Hodgkinson 2016

Front cover: Men of a Labour Battalion at dinner; Ancre sector, October 1916.
(© Imperial War Museum IWM Q1600).

Every reasonable effort has been made to trace copyright holders and to obtain their permission for the use of copyright material. The author and publisher apologize for any errors or omissions in this work, and would be grateful if notified of any corrections that should be incorporated in future reprints or editions of this book.

Pbk ISBN is 978-1-912174-74-4

British Library Cataloguing-in-Publication Data.
A catalogue record for this book is available from the British Library.

All rights reserved. No part of this publication may be reproduced, stored in a retrieval system, or transmitted, in any form, or by any means, electronic, mechanical, photocopying, recording or otherwise, without the express written consent of Helion & Company Limited.

For details of other military history titles published by Helion & Company Limited contact the above address, or visit our website: http://www.helion.co.uk.

We always welcome receiving book proposals from prospective authors.

# Contents

| | |
|---|---|
| Series Editor's Preface | vi |
| Preface | viii |
| Acknowledgements | ix |
| Abbreviations | x |
| Introduction | xi |
| 1  'The Very Limit of Endurance' – Coping in the Great War | 21 |
| 2  'I Will be Glad When I Can See Your Dear Face Again' – Family and Home | 53 |
| 3  'A Warm Fraternity' – Pals, Chums and Mates | 76 |
| 4  'Here I am Doing a Man's Work' – Stoicism, Manliness and Coping | 93 |
| 5  'We Must Go on Trusting in God' – Faith, Fatalism and Superstition | 106 |
| 6  'Depths of Terror Hitherto Undiscovered' – Fear in the Trenches | 137 |
| 7  'It Isn't Natural to be Brave' – Courage and Cowardice | 164 |
| 8  'Literally We are Living Amongst the Dead' | 187 |
| 9  'A Momentary Pang of Regret' – Loss and Burial | 222 |
| Conclusion | 244 |
| Bibliography | 256 |
| Index | 275 |

# The Wolverhampton Military Studies Series
## Series Editor's Preface

As series editor, it is my great pleasure to introduce the *Wolverhampton Military Studies Series* to you. Our intention is that in this series of books you will find military history that is new and innovative, and academically rigorous with a strong basis in fact and in analytical research, but also is the kind of military history that is for all readers, whatever their particular interests, or their level of interest in the subject. To paraphrase an old aphorism: a military history book is not less important just because it is popular, and it is not more scholarly just because it is dull. With every one of our publications we want to bring you the kind of military history that you will want to read simply because it is a good and well-written book, as well as bringing new light, new perspectives, and new factual evidence to its subject.

In devising the *Wolverhampton Military Studies Series*, we gave much thought to the series title: this is a *military* series. We take the view that history is everything except the things that have not happened yet, and even then a good book about the military aspects of the future would find its way into this series. We are not bound to any particular time period or cut-off date. Writing military history often divides quite sharply into eras, from the modern through the early modern to the mediaeval and ancient; and into regions or continents, with a division between western military history and the military history of other countries and cultures being particularly marked. Inevitably, we have had to start somewhere, and the first books of the series deal with British military topics and events of the twentieth century and later nineteenth century. But this series is open to any book that challenges received and accepted ideas about any aspect of military history, and does so in a way that encourages its readers to enjoy the discovery.

In the same way, this series is not limited to being about wars, or about grand strategy, or wider defence matters, or the sociology of armed forces as institutions, or civilian society and culture at war. None of these are specifically excluded, and in some cases they play an important part in the books that comprise our series. But there are already many books in existence, some of them of the highest scholarly standards, which cater to these particular approaches. The main theme of the *Wolverhampton Military Studies Series* is the military aspects of wars, the preparation for wars or their prevention, and their aftermath. This includes some books whose main theme is the technical details of how armed forces have worked, some books on wars and battles, and some books that re-examine the evidence about the existing stories, to show in a different light what everyone thought they already knew and understood.

As series editor, together with my fellow editorial board members, and our publisher Duncan Rogers of Helion, I have found that we have known immediately and almost by instinct the kind of books that fit within this series. They are very much the kind of well-written and challenging books that my students at the University of Wolverhampton would want to read. They are books which enhance knowledge, and offer new perspectives. Also, they are books for anyone with an interest in military history and events, from expert scholars to occasional readers. One of the great benefits of the study of military history is that it includes a large and often committed section of the wider population, who want to read the best military history that they can find; our aim for this series is to provide it.

Stephen Badsey
University of Wolverhampton

# Preface

The phrase 'glum heroes' comes from the poem 'Base Details' by Siegfried Sassoon, written in March 1917.[1] The late Bob Bushaway of the University of Birmingham had intended to write a book about the British soldier with this title when his untimely death intervened. This is undoubtedly not the book that he would have written, yet it seems important that the simple yet rich evocation of the infantryman of the Great War that these two words imply remains before us.

This book acts as a testimony to the extraordinary powers of endurance of those who fought in the Great War. It is dedicated to three such men – my grandfather, Private Peter Rimmer, 168093 ASC (27 Motorised Ambulance Convoy); my great-uncle, Private William R. Moxey, 206165 ASC; and my great-uncle, Corporal Henry J. Boyd, 14004 and 113481, 12th Battalion 'Bristol's Own' Gloucestershire Regiment and RE (Special Brigade). Without these men's stories in my childhood, my passion for the Great War would have been the less.

The book has its origins in MA research conducted for the degree of Master of Arts in British First World Studies at the University of Birmingham, entitled 'Human Remains on the Great War Battlefield – Coping with Death in the Trenches' (2006), and supervised by Rob Thompson. This was where the journey of attempting to understand the psychological experience of the First World War from the standpoint of soldiers themselves began.

Dr Peter E Hodgkinson<br>
Framfield<br>
August 2015

---

1   S. Sassoon, *Counter-Attack and Other Poems*, p.25.

# Acknowledgements

Thanks are due to Professor Peter Simkins and Michael Stewart for their comments on specific chapters. Also to Nikki Oatham, Consultant Clinical Psychologist – the most trenchant (and nearly always correct) critic of my writing – for both reading much of the manuscript and its revisions, and many conversations on the psychological topics. Thanks similarly go to Duncan Rogers of Helion for so readily offering the opportunity for publication.

Further thanks are due to the Imperial War Museum for access; and the Documents Collection, Sound Archive, and individual copyright holders for permission to quote from the private papers etc. of H.R. Butt, H.M.B. de Sales la Terriere, W.B. Henderson, C.K. McKerrow, A. Griffin, J.L. Hall, L.J. Ounsworth, S.H. Raggett, D. Railton, A.C. Razell and H.C. Rees. Every effort has been made to contact the copyright holders of the papers of E.F. Chapman, W. Clarke, H.T. Clements, H.H. Cooper, E.C. Crosse, R.G. Dixon, C.H. Dudley-Ward, R. Gwinnell, A.J. Heraty, T.A. Jennings, H.J. Knee, J.T. Lawton, E.B. Lord, J. McCauley, J.B. Mackenzie, T Macmillan, E.L. Marchant, F.E. Packe, C.S. Rawlins, W.B. St Leger, A.E. Wrench, and H.Y. Yoxall. The author and the Imperial War Museum would be grateful for any information which might help to trace these whose identities or addresses are not currently known.

# Abbreviations

| | |
|---|---|
| ANZAC | Australian and New Zealand Army Corps |
| ASC | Army Service Corps |
| BEF | British Expeditionary Force |
| C of E | Church of England |
| CO | Commanding Officer |
| CWGC | Commonwealth War Graves Commission |
| DAH | Disordered Action of the Heart |
| GHQ | General Headquarters |
| HQ | Headquarters |
| IWM | Imperial War Museum |
| LRB | London Rifle Brigade |
| NAM | National Army Museum |
| NCO | Non-Commissioned Officer |
| OR | Other ranks |
| PTSD | Post-Traumatic Stress Disorder |
| RAMC | Royal Army Medical Corps |
| RC | Roman Catholic |
| RE | Royal Engineers |
| RFC | Royal Flying Corps |
| RSM | Regimental Sergeant Major |
| RWOCESS | Report of the War Office Committee of Enquiry into Shell Shock |
| SRD | Supply Reserve Depot |
| TNA | The National Archives |
| VC | Victoria Cross |
| VDH | Valvular Disease of the Heart |
| YMCA | Young Men's Christian Association |

# Introduction

Our vision of the Great War soldier is often suffused with sentimentality – an exaggerated and self-indulgent tenderness, sadness, or nostalgia.[1] This is typified by the response to the discovery of a mass grave at Point du Jour, Arras, in 2001. It contained the bodies of 20 soldiers, buried in a line. Archaeologist Alain Jacques remarked: 'Can you imagine the friendship and dedication of those who went about laying down the remains in this way? To go and get a leg and position it in the line – what a remarkable act'.[2] Jacques took the view from the position of the arms of the tightly-packed corpses, bent at the elbow, that the dead were actually 'arm in arm'. *The Guardian* took up this theme with a headline: 'Arm in arm, soldiers lie in their grave'.[3] Several shoulder titles of the Lincolnshire Regiment were found. The 10th Battalion Lincolnshire Regiment, a locally-raised unit known as the 'Grimsby Chums', had indeed fought in the area during April 1917. It was even suggested that one burial, fractionally further apart from the others, might be a missing officer.[4] A self-supporting argument developed. The burial in a line supposedly indicated an act of 'friendship and dedication'. Only real chums would bury their dead pals with their arms linked, comrades in death as well as life. Hence the burials *must* be lost 'Grimsby Chums'.

Let us consider the simple features of the burial. Firstly, such a grave would likely be dug as a trench and filled over the days, the bodies perforce laid in a line. Secondly, as Major-General Dick Gerrard-Wright noted: 'Men were usually laid with their arms crossed over their chest, and as the bodies decayed and the weight of the earth pressed down, the arms often dropped down'.[5] The arms were therefore linked only in illusion. Both aspects of the burial were likely acts of pragmatism rather than ones of 'friendship and dedication'. Thirdly, the Lincolns had been in line with the 15th Royal Scots. Not only was the grave close to another Royal Scots burial, but soldiers of that regiment also numbered amongst the battle's missing. It could not be safely assumed that all the remains were Lincolns. Lastly, with 700 casualties in 1916 and subsequent rebuilding with reinforcements that had no Grimsby connection, the 10th Lincolns

---

1 http://www.oxforddictionaries.com/definition/english/sentimentality.
2 *The Times*, 20 June 2001, 'Grimsby Chums are found in war grave'.
3 *The Guardian*, 20 June 2001, 'Arm in arm, soldiers lie in their grave'.
4 Lieutenant Wyllard Cocks – see http://battlefields1418.50megs.com/point_du_jour.htm.
5 *The Yorkshire Post*, 21 March 2002.

no longer had their friendship 'Pals Battalion' identity by the time of the Battle of Arras. A desire to give identity back to lost 'Grimsby Chums', even to the extent of potentially naming an individual burial based on the most spurious of grounds, had become conflated with a romantic notion of 'palship'. The requirement to adopt the simplest explanation which fitted the evidence was thus obscured.

How have we come to have such an emotive view of the Great War soldier? Attitudes towards the First World War and our understanding of the experience of those who fought it have developed over time. The first period of interest during the late 1920s and early 1930s was marked by the publishing of a host of memoirs. As this lost steam, disinterest asserted itself. With the triumphant conclusion of the Second World War, its predecessor which had solved nothing became the 'bad war'. Interest waned further. The position changed with the approach of the 50th anniversary of the war in the 1960s and the BBC's screening of its documentary *The Great War* in 1963-4. In his obituary of the associate producer and principal scriptwriter John Terraine, the eminent historian Brian Bond noted Terraine's mission to change the predominant view of the war from one of 'mud, blood and futility', to one which put the 'British army's achievement in the wider context of modern industrialised warfare'.[6] In keeping with the increasingly introspective decade, the producer Tony Essex had an alternative vision. He 'wanted an intensely personal piece of television that would try to portray the experience of war'.[7] Essex succeeded, and Terraine's purpose was subverted. The series only served to reinforce the perception of the war's appalling and futile nature. The opening sequence said it all. A crucifix marking a lone grave was silhouetted against the skyline, followed by a sequence of imagery tumbling as if into an abyss, finally coming to rest on a famous image of skeletal remains. Viewers' perceptions were frozen before they had a chance to make up their own minds. It was all about death. John Bourne draws our attention to 'the unprecedented and unique' level of British casualties during the war which are 'difficult to reconcile ... with the rest of British history'.[8] Even the Prince of Wales had written in *The Times* in 1928: 'It is not easy to grasp the meaning of the words "A Million Dead". No one has ever seen – or could see – an assemblage of that number of living'.[9] The volume of death increasingly became the defining feature of the war – a 'lost generation'.

This all occurred within a decade of societal change. In the face of increasing prosperity and technological change, the importance of shared norms diminished as people were freed more and more from mutual interdependence. One particular aspect of the individualism that flourished was the increasing value placed on introspection and expression of emotion over repression and non-expression. This waxing

---

6   *The Guardian*, 1 January 2004.
7   E. Hanna, *The Great War on the Small Screen*, p.49.
8   J.M. Bourne, 'The BEF's Generals of 29 September 1918: An Empirical Portrait with Some British and Australian Comparisons', in P. Dennis and J. Grey (eds), *Defining Victory 1918*, p.97.
9   *The Times*, 10 November 1928, 'War Graves Issue'.

impetus to self-analysis enhanced interest in those greatest of First World War introspectors, the war poets. A presumption developed that in some way they represented the unspoken musings of all soldiers. 'Tommy Atkins' had therefore fought sharing Siegfried Sassoon and Wilfred Owen's expressed sense of futility in his efforts. This mistaken view coincided happily with the stronger sense of pacifism that had threaded itself through the weave of society.

Quite separately during this period psychologists were coming to understand more and more about human experience, particularly about the emotional effects of negative life events. By the 1970s and 1980s the concept of grief was well researched, and the concept of trauma or post-traumatic stress was becoming established. Science was providing conceptual vehicles to look back at and recast the experience of the soldier of 1914-18. Surely therefore, in a war so terrible, the universal experience must have been one of grief and trauma? As John Bourne and Bob Bushaway have noted, however: 'It is a modern conceit that soldiers must necessarily be traumatised by war'.[10]

At the same time, historical writing had begun to turn to using veterans' memoirs. The advent of the cassette recorder had given oral historians the ability to conduct what constituted a smash-and-grab raid on veterans' memories before it became too late. Martin Middlebrook's seminal *The First Day on the Somme*, published in 1971 and based on a raft of soldiers' accounts, was the first to personalise battle in this way.[11] Popular histories of the 'Pals Battalions' followed over the ensuing decades, the notion of chums setting off to fight together further encouraging romantic fascination. The growing volume of foreign travel meant that battlefield touring became more common, yet the focus was often on the 'cities of the dead' rather than the battlefields themselves. The cemeteries were the one concrete reminder and obvious connection with those who fought. Many people had failed to discuss the experience of the war with elderly relatives. The growing interest in the study of family history and the increasing availability of records on-line at the turn of the millenium thus spurred many to research their combatant ancestors. There was therefore in motion a growing impetus to 'make a connection' with the soldiers of the Great War, one which accelerated as the 100th anniversary of the war's outbreak approached. The presumed experience of suffering, death, futility and trauma thus became increasingly personalised.

The experience of the trenches has thus been brought into distorted focus through the prism of modern preoccupation. It is in this light that the interpretation of the Point du Jour burials was created. As a discovery, it epitomised our central preoccupation with the war – mass death. In our need to make a connection we aspired to give back an identity to all the uncovered based on mere shreds of evidence. Modern attitudes towards friendship, mourning and burial coloured our view of the uncovered corpses beyond all fact. It was *our* need, as bystanders to the discovery of their bodies,

10   G.R. Husbands, *Joffrey's War*, p.20.
11   M. Middlebrook, *The First Day on the Somme*.

to make these soldiers friends in death as well as supposed longstanding friends in life and the recipients of lovingly conducted ritual.

Modern eyes thus perceive the soldiers of the Great War and their experiences through a glass darkly. Yet we commonly acknowledge that in some way they were different to us. This recognition is often voiced in the question: 'How did they stick it?' The observation that follows close upon its heels is that 'people just wouldn't do it today'. So, how did these individuals with their seeming particular power of endurance differ from their modern counterparts? They were the same flesh and blood, yet their values were very different. Whilst the age in which they lived was increasingly modern in some respects, it seems very distant from our own. Alexander Watson sets out a number of ways in which the soldiers of 1914-1918 existed in a different cultural milieu.[12] He begins with the view of Peter Simkins that most historians 'are in broad agreement that the nature of British society in 1914-18 provided a bedrock of social cohesion'.[13] The social cohesion which kept the British army together under the strain of war is much less evident today. A discourse has developed concerning the supposed alienation of the soldier on the Western Front from civilian life.[14] Yet the discontinuity may be less than believed. For the volunteers and conscripts that made up the bulk of that army soldiering was another, if temporary, job. As John Bourne has noted, the British male who went to war 'was shaped by the workplace', and 'soldiering was, after all, a form of work'. That celebrated painter of the Great War battlefield, Sir William Orpen, referred to the images of soldiers in the paintings of his equally celebrated counterpart, Christopher Nevinson, as 'the British workman in disguise'.[15] The first unemployment benefits had only been introduced three years before the outbreak of war,[16] and workers were used to sticking with tough, demanding jobs in order to keep their families fed. Further, the industrial unrest of 1911-12 aside, Jay Winter has argued that Britain had the 'most highly disciplined industrial labour force in the world'.[17] This discipline was undoubtedly demonstrated on the battlefield. Despite the rise of trade unionism, much of the character of the employer-employee relationship was based on the paternalism-deference exchange that Gary Sheffield has shown governed officer-ranker relationships during the war.[18] Workers were used to being told what to do as long as they felt looked after, an exchange which has long since vanished.

---

12  A. Watson, *Enduring the Great War*, pp.3-4.
13  P. Simkins, 'Everyman at War', in B. Bond (ed.), *The First World War and British Military History*, pp. 289-313.
14  See E.J. Leed, *No Man's Land*.
15  W. Orpen, *The Outline of Art*, p.374.
16  In the National Insurance Act of 1911.
17  J. Winter, *The Experience of World War I*, p.159.
18  G. Sheffield, *Leadership in the Trenches*, pp.72-3.

Of the experience of being at war itself, 'tedium, regimentation, subordination and physical hardship were the common lot of the British working man',[19] and so it was in the trenches of France and Flanders. One hundred years on, this is difficult for us to grasp. In the present age of electronic stimulation, tedium is a horror not to be tolerated. Regimentation and subordination are anathema to the spirit of individualism. In terms of the war's brutal nature, Richard Holmes goes further to suggest that many of the soldiers who fought in the armies of the First World War had simply exchanged 'one harsh and violent environment for another'.[20] Although true for some jobs and living environments, this was not accurately the lot of all the pre-war working class. The notion sells short the unique terror and horror of the direct hit of a howitzer shell on men in the close confines of a trench. Yet these soldiers undoubtedly had civilian lives which required impassivity in the face of hardship. In facing this they had fostered the skill of making-do. They were able to achieve this because 'working-class values did not encourage morbid introspection'.[21] This fact is so contrary to the modern experience that it is particularly difficult for us to comprehend. It is a central platform of the argument of this book.

Other aspects of life in the working class community of a century ago were radically different. Sharing was the norm. People shared space and possessions in a way that is unfamiliar to us, their descendants. A 'group solidarity and mutuality' existed at work, home and in leisure that was readily transferred to the trenches.[22] Sleeping en masse in farms and barns came easily to soldiers unused to privacy. Without romanticising the era, there was a 'loyalty to community and comrades'.[23] This focussed and local loyalty was based on survival, not sentiment. The individuals who went off to fight between 1914 and 1918 thus possessed qualities and attitudes which have largely disappeared in a richer, more comfortable and materialistic culture.

One of the major differences between the modern world and that of 100 years ago is the issue of individualism. The centrality of the individual has become a dominant aspect of Western culture. As the sociologist Emile Durkheim noted in the 1950s: 'Today (the individual) has acquired a kind of dignity which places him above himself as well as above society'.[24] People brought up in an era of individualism 'owe no man anything ... they form the habit of thinking of themselves in isolation and imagine that their whole destiny is in their hands'.[25] And, as we have seen in our discussion of introspection, it was not simply a focus *on* the individual but *within* the individual. Yet for many centuries an individual's life had held little importance. The only thing

19 J. Bourne, 'The British Working Man in Arms', in H. Cecil & P.H. Liddle (eds), *Facing Armageddon*, p.345.
20 R. Holmes, *Acts of War*, p.133.
21 Bourne, op. cit. p.347.
22 Bourne, op. cit. p.347.
23 Bourne, op. cit. p.349.
24 E. Durkheim, *Suicide*, p.333.
25 R. Bellah, *Habits of the Heart*, p.37.

that mattered was fit into the predominant group, religious or work, to survive. At the time of the Great War, many of the working class were still in a state of economic collectivism and their social conditions were intimately tied to this. Individualism was not something that was aspired to or prized. It was the group of the neighbourhood, the workplace, the trade union and the working men's club that mattered. It was the economic cooperation of the Friendly and Co-Operative societies that was the norm. The New Armies were a massive act of collectivism into which working men entered with a sense of familiarity.

We thus misperceive the response of Great War soldiers to what they underwent unless we consider how the cultural norms of the late Victorian era and early 20th century shaped how they thought. What truly sustained them? How did they view fear and death? What rules governed how they expressed their thoughts and emotions? Did these rules channel their experience in a protective way, or did it leave them emotionally vulnerable? It is these issues that this book seeks to consider. It attempts a measured and unsentimental portrayal of the confrontation between those who fought the First World War and the stresses of the battlefield and the ways in which they coped within the constraints of the era in which they lived.

At the time of the Great War, modern psychology was in its infancy. Exactly a century later, the situation could hardly be more different. Psychological explanation permeates both home and workplace, and psychological terminology is commonplace in everyday conversation. Freud published the first study of bereavement in 1917. It is rare now for a news bulletin to pass without the notion of 'coming to terms' with a loss being mentioned.[26] Clinical psychology as a profession developed in the post-Second World War period, pioneering the understanding of human conditions such as anxiety and depression in the 1960s and 70s. Such concepts are now a part of everyday life. The word 'stress' is commonplace. People speak of being 'anxious' when they are simply concerned, and of being 'depressed' when they are merely 'down'. The study of human responses to traumatic events gained momentum following the end of the Vietnam War in 1975 as psychologically damaged veterans required and demanded help. The diagnosis of Post-Traumatic Stress Disorder (PTSD) first appeared in 1980.[27] Over three decades on, matters are referred to in everyday conversation as 'traumatic' which do not remotely correspond to the notion of serious threat. The cult of the primacy of individual experience almost demands the deployment of such language to describe the supposed richness of modern experience. Yet the soldiers of 1914-1918 were not introspective. They resorted to examination of their reactions infrequently. Indeed, they had little of such vocabulary to grace any self-examination. When they did reflect, they did so through particular filters which it is our task to attempt to describe.

---

26  S. Freud, 'Mourning and Melancholia', *International Journal for Medical Psychoanalysis*, p.288.
27  American Psychiatric Association, *Diagnostic and Statistical Manual*.

It would be a simple exercise to catalogue the awfulness of trench warfare. This book accepts this as given. We will seek here to understand not simply how the soldier reacted but how he coped. In its earlier years psychological research demonstrated the negative effects of stressful life events. Identifying what protects individuals against such effects moved more slowly. It was during the 1980s that the concept of hardiness was established.[28] Hardiness, resilience, or existential courage as it is variously called, involves attitudes and strategies that through mental processing turn stressful circumstances into growth opportunities. Specifically, this coping style involves three 'Cs', which necessarily come together. The first is 'challenge', the acceptance that life is stressful but that this offers natural opportunities for development, the individual learning and changing to their advantage. The second is 'commitment', active engagement in activities, sharing effort and learning, not sinking into detachment. The third is 'control', the belief that one *can* influence events and try to turn things to one's advantage. Being high in hardiness is known to be a good predictor of an individual's positive performance and health. More recently, considerable research has been directed at the issue of resilience in the military. High hardiness positively predicted mental health at the end of a four month combat training program with the Israeli military;[29] and in an American study, proved to be negatively related to depression and anger.[30]

Common sense though these observations may be, there is something that does not quite fit about the detailed concept of hardiness in the context of the age that contained the First World War. It is anachronistic. It far more accurately reflects characteristics honed by the modern world of individualism and education-based opportunity. The idea of personal growth, welcoming change and growing from it, and a sense of having control over events would have in many ways been alien to the individuals of 1914. Yet resilience and endurance were the keystones of coping of the British soldier. What therefore is a more appropriate template for understanding this? It is the concept of Stoicism that emerges as a better fit to the mental processing of the Edwardian age. This formed the bedrock of attitudes towards coping which permeated British society from top to bottom. Indeed, the more developed concepts of hardiness have evolved from it. Stoicism will be a major theme running though the deliberations of the following pages.

The historiography of the subject of the soldier's coping is relatively slim. The literature of the 1970s, such as Paul Fussell's *The Great War and Modern Memory*, and Eric Leed's *No Man's Land*, produced a vision of the soldier's supposed alienation. In tune with the zeitgeist of mud, blood and horror they were more concerned with damage

---

28  S.C. Kobasa, 'Stressful life events, personality, and health', *Journal of Personality and Social Psychology*, p.1.
29  V. Florian, M. Milkulincer & O. Taubman, 'Does Hardiness Contribute to Mental Health During a Stressful Real Life Situation?', *Journal of Personality and Social Psychology*, p.687.
30  S.R. Maddi, M. Brow, D.M. Khoshaba, & M. Viatkus, 'Relationship of Hardiness and Religiousness to Depression and Anger', *Consulting Psychology Journal*, p.148.

than accounting for coping. Indeed, they emphasised an inevitable failure of adaptation. One of the problems with addressing this field is that it crosses disciplinary boundaries – history, sociology, and psychology. Michael Roper, a sociologist, has come closest to grasping many of the issues in his sensitive book, *The Secret Battle*, published in 2009.[31] Roper takes a broad sweep, examining a series of 80 sets of letters. His enthusiasm for psychoanalytic thinking is openly displayed in his emphasis on the mother-son relationship as developed in correspondence as a vehicle of support.[32] In contrast, the historian Alexander Watson in his thorough work on morale develops the concept of functional 'self-deception' as a coping mechanism.[33] Both authors fail, however, to place their interesting assertions within any broad and widely-accepted psychological theory, and only partially succeed in placing their observations within era-appropriate cultural norms.

In attempting to move away from sentimental preoccupation and see the combatants of the Great War in the perspective of their own era, the chapters that follow will tread a path between two major aims. The first is to identify the nature of the coping mechanisms available to the soldiers of the time. These include both external resources, particularly the support of people; and inner resources, the attitudes which helped contain and structure experiences and provided models for how to behave. The second aim is to explore coping with two particular stresses of warfare, fear and death. The era-specific attitudes to dealing with these prove very different to our own.

The journey of understanding falls into a number of steps. Chapter One approaches the notion of coping in a general way. The stresses of war as presented in individual accounts are elaborated. Soldiers' motivations to keep fighting and the basic ways in which they described themselves as coping are examined. The central concept of endurance is introduced. Without attempting to force a fit between modern psychology and the soldier's experience, Abraham Maslow's theory of human needs and motivation is set out. This model describes a hierarchy of needs, from basic physiological needs, to safety needs, to the need for love and belonging, to the need for esteem, and finally to the need for self-actualization. The chapter considers how these first two needs could be fulfilled in a 'just enough' way in a hostile environment. Chapters Two and Three concern the need for a sense of belonging and love. They review the soldier's two sources of external support. Chapter Two introduces the first source, the family. It seeks to understand how the soldier dealt with the loss of the home environment yet used the memory of it to maintain a sustaining sense of caring and being cared for. It examines how this was achieved, sometimes imperfectly, in the twin activities of letter writing and leave. Chapter Three considers the opportunity for developing an alternative sense of supportive belongingness on active service. Friends had partly to take

---

31  M. Roper, *The Secret Battle*.
32  In particular the theories of Melanie Klein.
33  A. Watson, op. cit. and 'Self Deception and Survival', *Journal of Contemporary History*, p.247.

the place that the family had been forced to abdicate. The notion of friendship prevalent at the time, however, proves to be different from modern notions. A de-romanticised vision of 'pals, chums and mates' is crucial to truly understanding both the limitations of friendship and the lifeline it offered in coping at the front. Chapters Four and Five concentrate on internal sources of support. Chapter Three introduces Stoicism, its influence on Western thinking, and its impact on attitudes to life. It also examines the prevalent concept of manliness. Stoicism and manliness formed the bedrock of the soldier's endurance. Chapter Five considers the sustaining role of faith in its very broadest sense in facing existential threat. Finally, the last four chapters examine two main threats to the soldier's equilibrium, the twin companions of fear and death. Chapter Six attempts to understand both the roots of fear in the trenches and contemporary attitudes towards its expression and control. Chapter Seven examines brave acts and the conceptions of courage of the age that offered a model for dealing with fear. Lastly, Chapters Eight and Nine concern coping with death in the form of the presence of human remains, and the way the loss of comrades was negotiated. A detailed analysis is carried out to grasp the coping mechanisms that soldiers constructed to distance themselves from the reality of death. The legacy of Victorian attitudes towards death and grief and the use of mourning ritual is then examined to understand how these assisted soldiers to deal both practically and emotionally with the loss of their fellows.

This book is based on a rich volume of evidence in the written and spoken accounts of Great War soldiers. Letters, diaries and memoirs, published and unpublished, contemporaneous or written later, are employed. In respect of the latter, Jessica Meyer has concluded that the narratives of memoirs published both during the memoir boom of 1928-1931 and in the 1960s and 1970s 'bear strong relations to earlier written records of war experience such as letters and diaries'.[34] Ian Beckett has noted, however, that: 'If history in any form rarely comes value-free' then autobiography, memoir, and biography are arguably the historical genres most susceptible to conscious (or unconscious) manipulation by their authors'.[35] We are not, however, concerned here with reputation or the analysis of strategy or tactics, where distortion is a critical issue. We are instead largely concerned with soldiers' reported thoughts and attitudes about the things that happened to them. And in this area, as Michael Roper has observed, 'retrospective accounts are generally more reflective about the emotional experience of war than the letter or diary'. Indeed, the soldier needed to be at a distance from the events to digest and reflect raw impressions – 'time was needed before a coherent narrative could be constructed'.[36] The fact remains that veterans misremember and sometimes lie. Their accounts are however, warts and all, our only means of examining the personal experience of the war. Some memoirs are individual restatements

---

34  J. Meyer, *Men of War*, p.129.
35  I. Beckett, 'Frocks and Brasshats,' in Bond, op. cit. pp. 89-112.
36  M. Roper, op. cit. p.21.

of events. A few are, in parts, deeply analytic of the writer's experience. In rejecting A.J.P. Taylor's patronising distaste for oral history: 'In this matter I am an almost total sceptic …. Old men drooling about their youth – No';[37] a far more positive view of personal accounts will be adopted. In understanding the social psychology of trench life, soldiers' voices are both the prime material and data open to analysis.

The personal accounts examined are solely those of men. This is not to indicate that the service of women and their courage during the war is of any less interest. It is simply that this book concerns coping at the teeth end of the Great War, and this was the province of men. As Lieutenant Charles Carrington remarked, the world of the trenches was 'entirely a man's world'.[38] Thus, using the words 'he', 'him' or 'men' is simply reflective of the gendered reality of the warfare of 1914-1918.

---

37  A.J.P. Taylor, quoted in B. Harrison, 'Oral History and Recent Political History', *Oral History*, p.46.
38  C. Carrington, in M. Arthur, *Forgotten Voices of the Great War*, p.169.

# 1

## 'The Very Limit of Endurance' – Coping in the Great War

The popular image of the Great War is of mud, blood and horror. Undoubtedly there were a plethora of times when it was so. At other times the war was simply uncomfortable. As war becomes increasingly 'smart' and remotely controlled, the Great War has attained a particular place in the history of conflict. The opposing combatants lived a partly troglodyte existence in such close proximity to each other for so long, under constant threat and in execrable conditions. Its worst moments lived in the memories of those who endured it. Corporal William Andrews evocatively entitled his memoirs *Haunting Years*, describing how: 'The War pressed down on some of us like a doom after the last shot was fired'.[1] On the other hand, perhaps surprisingly, some found the experience of the war to have uplifting aspects.

### Uplifted by War

Captain the Honourable Julian Grenfell wrote to his mother from Flanders on 24 October 1914: 'I adore War. It is like a big picnic without the objectlessness of a picnic. I have never been so well or so happy'.[2] This letter became infamous when it was published, with Grenfell accused of naivety and providing pro-war propaganda. A letter ten days later to both parents claimed:

> It is all *the* best fun. I have never never felt so well, or so happy, or enjoyed anything so much. It just suits my stolid health, and stolid nerves, and barbaric disposition. The fighting-excitement vitalizes everything, every sight and word and action. One loves one's fellow man so much more when one is bent on killing him.[3]

---

1  W.L. Andrews, *Haunting Years*, p.5.
2  J. Grenfell, quoted in L. Housman, *War Letters of Fallen Englishmen*, p.117.
3  J. Grenfell, quoted in Housman, op. cit. p.118 (italics in original).

Grenfell was a man of outstanding bravery who had won his Distinguished Service Order for stalking and despatching German snipers. He rejected a staff post to remain in the trenches, and was mortally wounded by a shell splinter to the head, dying 13 days later on 26 May 1915. Within days, his poem 'Into Battle' was published in *The Times*. It is a classical glorification of war where for the soldier in action: 'Joy of Battle only takes Him by the throat'.[4]

Was Grenfell simply naïve, caught up in an outdated vision of the glory of war? Was he writing home in this vein to mollify his parents, as many tried to? Or did war simply suit his nature? An aggressive and athletic young man, he was schooled at Eton and Oxford. A poet who would attack aesthetes with his horse whip, he rowed, boxed, and hunted. He was commissioned in a cavalry regiment in 1910. The probable truth is that indeed, despite being a committed Christian with a love of the works of the monk Thomas à Kempis, 'fighting made life more vivid'. He simply 'enjoyed hunting human beings' as an extension of his pre-war competitive disposition.[5] As John (later Lord) Reith claimed for himself, Grenfell manifestly 'had war in (his) bones'.[6] Reith's own experience of war was that he was 'happy and absolutely thrilled with it all'.[7] He was not alone. Corporal Thomas Dyson wrote to a pal serving in a different unit: 'What a game war is. There are more thrills in one second than at a dozen footer matches'. He and his comrades, he stated, were 'very happy and jolly for the most part'.[8] Lieutenant Stuart Cloete took up Grenfell's theme: 'If the weather was fine and there was not much shelling, nothing could have been nicer'. He concluded romantically that 'it was a boy's dream of an endless picnic on an unprecedented scale'.[9]

There were others less martial who would reflect positively on their wartime experience, both during and after, but who did not see the excitement of fighting as the key positive experience. Lieutenant Sidney Rogerson made the balanced observation that the war years were 'sometimes' terrifying and 'often' uncomfortable, but claimed that they would 'stand out in the memories of vast numbers of those who fought as the happiest period of their lives'. In his opinion, war 'let loose the worst' but also 'brought out the finest qualities in men'.[10] Part of this personal development was related, as Second-Lieutenant Alec Dawson concluded, to sense of purpose. He 'never felt happier'. He believed that war made it 'worthwhile to be alive and fit; more worthwhile than it ever was in civil life'.[11] Captain Francis Buckley never regretted joining up although he acknowledged that it had brought him 'great troubles and anguish', but

---

4   J. Grenfell, 'Into Battle', https://movehimintothesun.wordpress.com.
5   G.M. Griffiths, https://movehimintothesun.wordpress.com.
6   J. Reith, *Wearing Spurs*, p.15.
7   Reith, op. cit. p.68.
8   T. Dyson, quoted in P. Liddle, 'British Loyalties: The Evidence of an Archive', in. H. Cecil & P.H. Liddle (eds), *Facing Armageddon*, p.524.
9   S. Cloete, *A Victorian Son*, pp.218-9.
10  S. Rogerson, *Twelve Days on the Somme*, p.59-60.
11  A.J. Dawson, *A 'Temporary Gentleman' in France*, p.228.

from the positive point of view it provided 'peace of mind and the satisfaction of using to the full such energy as I possess'.[12] Private George Coppard echoed Julian Grenfell, describing the first few months of trench life in 1915 as 'a kind of dangerous fun to me'. In terms of development, he saw it as part of his path to manhood: 'Although only a boy I had lived with grown men, sharing their fears and dangers'.[13]

Stuart Cloete denied worries, explaining that 'though there is danger ... there is also security'. This came from being a member of a 'great brotherhood of men and, like a monk in a curious monastery, (you) lead a very sheltered if dangerous life'.[14] Lieutenant Harold Macmillan also felt the importance of this great brotherhood. In addition to an 'extraordinary thrill', war brought for him 'a sense of comradeship – a sense of teamship and a sense of triumph'.[15] Captain Alfred Pollard, a private in 1914, described how: 'There was something almost Divine in the comradeship of those early days'. An office-worker, he felt that: 'There was romance, too, in those long nights spent in the open air'.[16] For men who had been the captives of factory or office, the outdoor life indeed had attractions. Speaking for many who emerged from urban industrialised Britain, Francis Buckley described how: 'It took me out of the stifling heat of the town and gave me at least four years of an open-air life'. As with Rogerson and Macmillan, not least, 'it brought the friendship of real men'.[17] Captain Rowland Feilding also relished the outdoor life. He wrote home in May 1915: 'It is a healthy life and I have never felt better'. Like Stuart Cloete, he believed 'it is worry that kills, and we have no worry here'.[18] Writing home as a lieutenant-colonel in 1918, when the war of movement diminished the personal closeness of positional warfare, he claimed that 'there was a good deal to be said in favour of the old trench life'. Noting the tendency for those not as yet demobilised to create an idealistic vision of pre-war Britain he stated of the war-time life: 'There were none of the mean haunting fears of poverty'. Taking flight into hyperbole, he described an egalitarian atmosphere where rich and poor stood 'solely upon their individual merits' within 'an atmosphere of selflessness'. He extolled the 'spirit of camaraderie' claiming it 'the like of which has probably not been seen in the world before'. He concluded that 'there was no humbug in the trenches', and that the 'better kind of men' would look back upon such times with 'something like affection'.[19]

Similarly countering any view that the war represented wasted years, Second-Lieutenant Douglas Gillespie wrote home: 'I shall never regret the time spent in the

---

12 F. Buckley, *Q.6.a*, p.3.
13 G. Coppard, *With a Machine Gun to Cambrai*, p.62.
14 Cloete, op. cit. pp.218-9.
15 H. Macmillan, *Winds of Change*, p.99.
16 A.O. Pollard, *Fire-Eater*, p.43.
17 Buckley, op. cit. p.3.
18 R. Feilding, *War Letters to a Wife*, p.8.
19 Feilding, op. cit. p.208.

trenches', the hours he endured there being 'as well spent as most in peace time'.[20] Invalided, Captain G.B. Manwaring wistfully recorded that he would 'always be thankful' that he had experienced the war: 'For in these months I have had years of educational value, and have gained experience that will be useful to me throughout my life'.[21] Lieutenant Arthur Dugmore denied that war brutalised men and claimed not only intellectual but personal improvement. He took the view that the 'very finest that is in a man is developed *out there*. The callous gain hearts'.[22] Gassed and sent home, despite having experienced fully the fighting on the Somme in 1916, he wrote almost with a sense of loss: 'There is a fascination about the life over there that cannot be described'.[23]

Some men enjoyed war for the excitement. An exhausted Rowland Feilding would still write after battle in 1918: 'It is a cursed war ... yet I love it: it has been the breath of life to me'.[24] Some valued the change from a previous humdrum, claustrophobic urban existence, and savoured war for the sense of purpose and personal development it provided. Others relished the sense of comradeship. Most, however, were not immune from its stresses.

## The Grinding Stress of Trench Life

Whatever the positives that might be taken at leisure from an overview of war experience, as Second-Lieutenant Stephen Hewett wrote home, in the trenches one moment was 'never quite the same as another, but one is either getting killed or wounded or honoured or experienced or brutalised'.[25] Sergeant Ben Keeling noted dryly in a letter dated June 1915, that 'this is not a life for any one with anything like nerves'.[26] Just prior to his death in September 1916, Captain Evelyn Southwell described that whilst he experienced 'excitement', it took 'the form of a fearful strain on the nerves without any of the exhilaration one usually associates with danger'.[27] The experiences that energised Julian Grenfell depleted Southwell. Second-Lieutenant Arthur Adam similarly indicated the unrelenting pressure: 'The strain in the trenches is continuous'.[28] One central aspect of this strain, as Second-Lieutenant Raymond Lodge wrote, was anticipation: 'Being on tenterhooks is quite the worst part'.[29] Second-Lieutenant Ernest Routley agreed in a letter in desperate vein to his brother, due to come out to

---

20 A.D. Gillespie, *Letters from Flanders*, p.255.
21 G.B. Manwaring, *If We Return*, p.149.
22 A.R. Dugmore, *When the Somme Ran Red*, p.237 (italics in original).
23 Dugmore, op. cit. p.281.
24 Feilding, op. cit. p.186.
25 S. Hewett, *A Scholar's Letters*, p.55.
26 F.H. Keeling, *Letters*, p.228.
27 H.E.E. Howson, *Two Men*, p.36.
28 A.M. Adam, *A Record Founded on His Letters*, p.164.
29 O.J. Lodge, *Raymond*, p.42.

the Western Front: 'It isn't being killed that worries you; it's the waiting for it'.[30] Lodge saw the degree of strain as directly related to the time an individual was exposed to it, and indeed most reported a wearing down of resources over time. Rifleman Aubrey Smith, who had been out since early 1915, was admitted to hospital in mid-1917. He had had no leave for 18 months and had worked every day since. At rest: 'Only now could I realise the extent of the tension at which we had been working'. He was released from 'apprehension'.[31] Captain Douglas Bell returned to the Western Front after four months' wound convalescence in May 1916, and whilst he stated that his nerves were 'under control', he found that 'I am feeling the strain in a way I used not to do'. In particular, he found himself irritable, a classic symptom of increased physical arousal.[32] In biological terms, two things happen under prolonged and traumatic stress. The body's 'fight or flight' mechanism, the sympathetic branch of the autonomic nervous system (ANS), the spinal nervous system that works automatically, outside of our conscious control, produces excessive neurotransmitters called catecholamines. It is these, notably adrenalin, which generate normal, necessary bodily and psychological arousal. Under protracted stress, however, the body's system that acts as a brake on this, the parasympathetic ANS, comes to produce less of the hormone cortisol which acts as its brake fluid. The body remains in a state of arousal, its engine racing like that of car with the driver's foot pressing hard on the accelerator.[33]

Doctor A.F. Hurst, who had served on Lemnos during the Gallipoli campaign, gave evidence to the War Office Committee of Enquiry into 'Shell-Shock' in 1922 and stated that: 'The fatigue, strain and responsibility of long service' eventually led to the psychological breakdown of many men who had previously withstood the stress of battle and responsibility.[34] Human resources, he clearly believed, were finite. He and other witnesses believed that the burden of responsibility that was the lot of officers was particularly corrosive of coping over time. William Andrews, writing in 1917 when he had been at the front for two years, felt sorry for new arrivals 'often sent straight into the most frightful experiences'. He viewed his own introduction to war in 1915 as easier, having been 'trained by a gradual process into self-control under stress'.[35] Andrews was correct. Stress inoculation, where a gradual introduction to a stressful situation allows coping skills to develop, is known to reduce longer term stress and anxiety.[36] The exigencies of war often denied this to others.

Soldiers could recognise that they were reaching the end of their tether. Lieutenant James Hyndson, who had fought at Mons, the Aisne and First Ypres, wrote on 7

30  E. Routley, quoted in B. MacArthur (ed.), *For King and Country*, p.230.
31  A Rifleman (A.Smith), *Four Years on the Western Front*, pp.247-8.
32  D.H. Bell, *A Soldier's Diary*, p.152.
33  Symptoms of this include problems sleeping, irritability, concentration difficulties, hypervigilance and exaggerated startle.
34  *Report of the War Office Committee of Enquiry into 'Shell-Shock'* (RWOCESS), p.24.
35  Andrews, op. cit. p.243.
36  D. Meichenbaum, *Stress Inoculation Training*.

February 1915: 'The strain of the fighting is beginning to tell ... I am near breaking point'.[37] He was correct. Thirteen days later he was evacuated, writing of 'those pestilential trenches, and the unceasing strain of noise by day and vigilance by night'.[38] Taking part in two actions in successive days at Second Ypres in 1915, Captain Edward Venning 'came near to blowing my own head off with my revolver', but was saved by the distraction of assisting another wounded officer.[39] He was reprieved for approximately three months before being killed. After thirteen months at the front, Lieutenant Bernard Adams started 'wondering how much longer my nerves would hold out'. He had just returned from his second leave, and thought 'I couldn't expect a third leave'.[40] He lasted longer than he might have expected, but on his final day on the Somme described constant physical and mental arousal in which 'my nerves were all jangled, and my brain would not rest a second. We were all like that at times'.[41] He was wounded that day and was taken to the casualty clearing station at Heilly. Even here 'my mind was working so fast and hard that it seemed to make the skin tight over my forehead'.[42] It took another five days and arrival on English soil until he reached the state where 'my body relaxed: the tension suddenly melted away'. He 'was out of the grip of war'.[43] Adams was lucky – for some veterans of war, these biological symptoms of arousal remained indefinitely. Tank commander Captain Wilfred Bion was profoundly worn out in the early months of 1918, and fell victim to despair rather than hyperarousal. 'I found myself looking forward to getting killed', he wrote, for then, at least, he would be rid of 'this intolerable misery'.[44] Second-Lieutenant Charles Douie met an old schoolfellow who similarly had fallen victim to despair. He 'told me that he had hardly known a happy hour', and 'cared very little whether he lived or died'. Douie was shocked to realise 'how much of unhappiness the laughter of a brave man may conceal'.[45]

The constant stress manifested its physical effects in different ways. Second-Lieutenant Edmund Blunden was with his unit at Cuinchy in 1916 and was subject to enemy mining. He noted simply: 'The strain of this sector made everyone exceedingly tired'.[46] For Private Henry Clapham, after six months in the Salient, stress played havoc with his stomach: 'My inside seems to have gone wrong and I cannot eat'. Describing his fellows as prey to the same symptoms he concluded that they were

---

37   J.G.W. Hyndson, *From Mons to the First Battle of Ypres*, Kindle edition location 1373.
38   Hyndson, op. cit. location 1380.
39   E. Venning, quoted in Housman, op. cit. p.281.
40   J.B.P. Adams, *Nothing of Importance*, p.141.
41   Adams, op. cit. p.268.
42   Adams, op. cit. p.277.
43   Adams, op. cit. p.293.
44   W.R. Bion, *War Memoirs 1917-19*, p.94.
45   C. Douie, *The Weary Road*, p.84.
46   E. Blunden, *Undertones of War*, p.32.

victim of 'nervous exhaustion'. They were all 'fed up with life'.[47] Soldiers could differentiate between the state of their physical health and mental exhaustion. Captain Geoffrey Dugdale endured both Third Ypres and the Battle of Cambrai in the second half of 1917. By December that year he would write that: 'My nerves were in a state of exhaustion, although my general health was excellent'. He understood that he could not go on much longer in this state as he was 'now getting to the end of my tether' and 'needed a rest badly'.[48] This he got. Gassed a few days later, he was sent to the south of France, and then on a month's home leave. On leave, he slept badly, wanted to stay indoors and had fits of 'acute depression'. Granted a further three months leave by a medical board, he felt perfectly well. Others, however, detected the continuing psychological effects and he was appointed a lecturer to home service units.[49] Captain Robert Graves also recognised in early 1916 that his breaking point was 'near now, unless something happened to stave it off'. With characteristic dry humour he foresaw 'tears and twitchings and dirtied trousers'.[50] He, too, was saved by a period of leave lengthened by an operation and a short period with the Reserve Battalion in the UK.

Sidney Rogerson could speak positively of war on one hand but noted on the other that: 'It was a compound of many things; fright and boredom, humour, comradeship, tragedy, weariness, courage and despair'.[51] Second-Lieutenant Huntly Gordon wrote of a hierarchy of stressors. 'First one has to endure the lack of sleep'; secondly there was 'the inescapable fear of being hit'; whilst thirdly one had to endure 'the continued effort of masking one's real feelings'.[52] Captain Gerald Burgoyne described the cost of this effort in December 1914: 'I hear "brain strain" has accounted for a few suicides among our officers'. In the front-line himself he declared that 'human nature cannot stand it'.[53] Only routine sustained. 'Man ... acts, as a horse does in harness, more or less mechanically'.[54] Charles Carrington described on the first day of the Battle of the Somme (when actually not in action) how he had: 'Never been so excited in my life, this was like a boy going to the play for the first time'.[55] His enthusiasm was, however, also subject to the process of constant wearing down. By early 1917, when he had been in France for over a year, he reported that fighting had 'entirely ceased to be fun. He no longer recounted his adventures 'with gusto' in long letters to his mother. On a training course supposedly away from the immediacy of front line stresses he was 'bored and nervy and irritable'. He too had clearly fallen victim to chronic hyperarousal. He found himself hating the war yet at the same time 'longing to be back with

---

47 H.S. Clapham, *Mud and Khaki*, p.165.
48 G. Dugdale, *'Langemarck' and 'Cambrai'*, pp.121-2.
49 Dugdale, op. cit. p.128.
50 R. Graves, *Goodbye To All That*, p.175.
51 Rogerson, op. cit. p. xxxi.
52 H. Gordon, *The Unreturning Army*, Kindle edition locations 1527-1534.
53 C. Davison, *The Burgoyne Diaries*, p.6.
54 Davison, op. cit. p.14.
55 C. Carrington, quoted in M. Arthur, *Forgotten Voices of the Great War*, p.156.

the regiment'.[56] Reunited with his unit in the Ypres Salient, however, an 'insensible numbness' descended upon him, and he was overcome by 'the presentiment that this was the end'.[57] Bernard Adams understood this too, writing of the stress of the omnipresence of death. Sometimes 'forgotten', sometimes faced directly, the threat to existence was always hovering 'with its relentless overhanging presence, dulling our spirits, wearing out our lives'.[58] This sustained sense of threat to life and limb had a corrosive effect on coping. Ralph Scott described a mounting series of stressors. In August 1918 he was subjected to particularly vicious machine gun fire and took his marked reaction to be 'another indication that my nerves are slowly giving out'.[59] A month or so later, when shells landed amongst a working party, he wrote that the 'suddenness of the shock has knocked my nerves to pieces and even as I write my hand trembles'.[60] Yet, the very next day he had to lead his men through a German barrage, the experience of which was 'great ... after that I felt we could do anything'.[61] He had merely been lifted by an adrenalin-driven euphoria, for after another few days he conceded that he was 'worn out' having been living 'for months ... on my will power', with his body and nerves 'exhausted a year ago'.[62] He knew he was due to attack again on the morrow, and for the first time in France his 'nerves gave way completely'. He lay in a chair for two hours 'actually shivering with fear and apprehension'.[63] He considered reporting sick and pretending to faint. These moment he called 'black fits', and as October 1918 progressed they occurred more frequently.[64]

Private Hugh Quigley described how the impetus of army life sustained him on the Somme: 'The Army so inures one that, even if the mud had risen neck-high, one would have struggled on'. His physical exhaustion interplayed with psychological factors: 'You can have no idea how tired I felt', his nerves 'wearing to a very fine edge'. Another victim of constant bodily arousal, 'Irritability took the place of resignation'. Interestingly, however, he claimed that it was 'monotony' that was the key negative element.[65] A fiercely intelligent man, Quigley continued this theme: 'Intellect sleeps. The brain descends to sordid trivialities'.[66] Second-Lieutenant Denis Garstin agreed with Quigley, describing how 'at the best of times it is the boredom of war that is its chief quality'.[67] Gerald Burgoyne described trench work as 'tedious, uninteresting'.[68]

56  Edmonds, op. cit. pp.100-101.
57  Edmonds, op. cit. pp.104-5.
58  Adams, op. cit. pp. 115-6.
59  R. Scott, *A Soldier's Diary*, p.75.
60  Scott, op. cit. p.129.
61  Scott, op. cit. p.132.
62  Scott, op. cit. p.162.
63  Scott, op. cit. p.164.
64  Scott, op.cit. p.176.
65  H. Quigley, *Passchendaele and the Somme*, pp.76-7.
66  Quigley, op. cit. p.136.
67  D. Garstin, *The Shilling Soldiers*, p.72.
68  Davison, op. cit. p.48.

Second-Lieutenant Siegfried Sassoon similarly viewed war as 'tedious and repetitional',[69] and in Corps reserve found his whole platoon 'bored and apathetic'.[70] Second-Lieutenant Max Plowman agreed, viewing boredom as 'the trench-dweller's worst enemy'.[71] Private Arthur Lambert described one day in the front line at Gheluvelt during Third Ypres being dominated by 'the painful crawl of the hours ... the dull apathy of the mind and nerves'.[72] Second-Lieutenant Llewellyn Griffith similarly noted that 'the greatest burden of all is enforced inactivity'.[73] Second-Lieutenant Graham Greenwell described being somewhat depressed. Avoiding shelling he had been sitting in a 'miserable dug-out with nothing to do' for a 12 hour period.[74] Stephen Hewett found a way to cope, writing to his sister: 'War is a fearfully boring business at the best' and how he was able to 'keep the spirit in me alive' by constant reading.[75] Sidney Rogerson, struggling in the final stages of the 1916 Somme campaign, found activity, however monotonous, a relief. He wrote of his platoon: 'Better by far that they should be made to busy their brains and their bodies' by moving about 'on some trivial task'.[76] Major James Jack was second-in-command of 2nd Scottish Rifles with 'not enough responsible occupation' during the Somme period which brought the loss of friends. He found he had 'too much time to think about it'.[77] There was a balance between the need to keep busy so as not to fall into dwelling, against the need to rest from sheer physical exhaustion. Private Frederic Manning took care to guard against extreme tiredness, noting that when 'strain had finally been released', in the physical exhaustion which followed there could come a collapse, 'in which one's emotional nature was no longer under control'.[78] For some, inaction could indeed have catastrophic results. On 2 January 1917, Lieutenant Robert Mackay noted in his diary: 'Major A died – had too little to do. (Suicide)'.[79]

The worst stress experienced was therefore of an extended background nature. Remorseless anticipation and responsibility led to perpetual arousal of the body and added to exhaustion. Boredom ground at the soul, giving soldiers too much time to think unless they could achieve distraction. Indeed, experts giving evidence to the shell-shock enquiry repeatedly asserted that it was this background stress that disposed men to break down, rather than traumatic stress. Edward Mapother, the most influential psychiatrist of the age, stated the case simply: 'Prolonged stress was much

---

69  S. Sassoon, *The Complete Memoirs of George Sherston*, p.407.
70  Sassoon, op. cit. p.409.
71  Mark VII (M. Plowman), *A Subaltern on the Somme*, p.51.
72  A. Lambert, *Over the Top*, p.85.
73  L.W. Griffith, *Up to Mametz*.
74  G.H. Greenwell, *An Infant in Arms*, p.92.
75  S. Hewett, quoted in Housman, op. cit. p.133.
76  Rogerson, op. cit. p.20.
77  J. Terraine (ed.), *General Jack's Diary*, p.158.
78  F. Manning, *The Middle Parts of Fortune*, Kindle edition location 58.
79  R. L. Mackay, Diary, http://www.firstworldwar.com/diaries/rlm1.htm.

more important than specific incidents'.[80] Many men hoped for a 'Blighty' wound that would take them home and remove them from strain and threat.[81] Second-Lieutenant Charles Carrington went into action at Third Ypres in the hope of one such. When he was suddenly exposed to a perfect wound, an arm sliced open to the bone, and observed the victim's pain: 'The sight of it cured me of hoping for a "blighty one"'.[82]

**Motivation and Wellbeing**

This is not a book specifically about morale. This factor is, however, directly related to wellbeing and coping. Alexander Watson's examination of morale in the British army during the Great War concludes that despite the experiences described in the previous section, 'resilience not collapse was the norm'. He concludes that this was due to three things, namely 'societal influences, military factors, and human psychological defence mechanisms'.[83] Men enlisted and fought on out of a sense of patriotic duty, and out of a fear of invasion with the implied threat to their homes and loved ones. Secondly, within the army, it was not the coercion of potential military punishment, but the positive influence of discipline, unit loyalty, comradeship, and personal pride that counted. Negative views about the enemy that were punctuated by spikes of hatred also kept soldiers to task on the basis of the attitude that 'the sacrifices of one's friends had to be justified before fighting could stop'.[84] Men fought because 'their living comrades expected it of them'.[85] The third area, psychological mechanisms, is the subject of this book.

From the psychological point of view, to remain motivated, a person's needs must be met, and they must have a sense of wellbeing. As described in the Introduction, in 1943 Abraham Maslow published an influential paper entitled 'A Theory of Human Motivation'.[86] In it he proposed that there existed a hierarchy of needs that had to be satisfied for individuals to achieve wellbeing. This included basic physiological needs (air, food, water, clothing and shelter); the need for safety; the need for love and belongingness in friendships and family; the need for self-esteem, respect and a sense of pride in what one does; and lastly the need for self-actualization, a sense of mastery and autonomy, reaching one's full potential. This theory came to be represented as a pyramid, with the most basic needs at the bottom and self-actualization at the top.

---

80  RWOCESS, p.28.
81  The word 'Blighty', meaning Britain or England first became common currency during the Second Boer War. Its origins lie in the word 'bilayati', a variant of the Urdu word 'vilayati', meaning foreign, European, or more specifically, British.
82  C. Edmonds (C. Carrington), *A Subaltern's War*, p.117.
83  A. Watson, *Enduring the Great War*, p.232.
84  Watson, op. cit. p.72.
85  J.G. Fuller, *Troop Morale and Popular Culture*, p.66.
86  A. Maslow, 'A Theory of Human Motivation', *Psychological Review*, p.370.

Maslow believed, however, that if the four basic 'deficiency needs' could not be met then the highest level of need, self-actualization, could not be achieved.

The theory has remained popular, although subject to a range of challenges over the years. Some researchers found no evidence for a ranking of needs or hierarchy; others criticised the theory for being ethnocentric, believing needs would be ranked differently in different cultures. However, in a recent study, covering 123 countries, there indeed proved to be the universal needs Maslow described which serve as predictors of wellbeing. As anticipated, people tend to achieve basic physiological and safety needs before they achieve other needs, although in countries where this was very difficult, this did not preclude people achieving higher needs. Half of people who reported low need fulfilment reported no positive feelings. Conversely, fulfilment of needs reduced negative feelings. The lack of basic needs produced particularly low life evaluations; whilst meeting the needs for friendship, love and self-esteem were most strongly related to positive feelings.[87]

This may all seem common sense to the reader, and perhaps psychology is at its best when it confirms that common sense holds water well. The theory gives us an easily understandable framework for identifying and understanding the needs of the Great War soldier, determining what aspects of trench warfare would generate the most stress, and establishing how soldiers went about managing that stress.

*Soldiers' Needs and Coping*
Field Marshall the Earl Wavell described what he called 'the actualities of war' which make a life in the field 'so complicated and difficult'. These included 'the effects of tiredness, hunger, lack of sleep, weather'.[88] Professor G. Roussy, neurologist to the French army, was one of the experts who gave evidence to the War Office shell-shock enquiry. He was particularly aware of the danger of not fulfilling these basic physiological needs. He believed that the 'depressant action of physical or mental fatigue' and temporary food shortages pre-disposed soldiers to shell-shock.[89] Niall Ferguson refers to the 'importance of quite humdrum things in keeping men going'.[90] He lists seven such 'carrots': warm and comfortable clothing; decent accommodation; food; drugs (alcohol and tobacco); rest; leisure; and leave. All these crop up regularly in personal accounts, and fit happily within Maslow's theory.

*Level one – basic needs*
Captain Richard Haigh wrote that war is, above all, 'a reduction to essentials'.[91] In the front line the key basic needs that needed addressing included water, food, clothing

---

87  L. Tay & E. Diener, 'Needs and Subjective Well-Being Around the World', *Journal of Personality and Social Psychology*, p.354.
88  A Wavell, quoted in R. Holmes, *Acts of War*, p.7.
89  RWOCESS, p.19.
90  N. Ferguson, *The Pity of War*, p.350.
91  R. Haigh, *Life in a Tank*, p.132.

and shelter. The physical conditions of the battlefield posed problems for the fulfilment of these. Food and water had to be brought up, and appropriate clothing and shelter were crucial. Like Roussy, Squadron-Leader William Tyrrell linked 'fatigue, mud and blood, wet and cold, misery and monotony, unsavoury cooking and feeding, nauseating environment, etc.' together in predisposing men to shellshock.[92]

Drinking water was generally not a particular issue on the Western Front, even if, delivered in petrol tins, its taste was tainted. Charles Carrington, however, found himself in an exposed position in front of Ovillers in 1916, and found that he and his platoon were beginning to suffer badly from thirst. Nearby corpses were raided for their water bottles. When water finally arrived, 'we swallowed in huge draughts'. It tasted of petrol, but it was 'damp and cool'.[93] Gallipoli was a different matter. Fresh water had to the brought ashore from ships, and in the intense summer heat of 1915, thirst became a torture. Able Seaman Thomas Macmillan of the Royal Naval Division recorded the aftermath of an attack on 13 July at Helles: 'Our water bottles were now empty and thirst increased with the heat of the day', yet they faced another 24 hours without. At this point water arrived, but there was so little that the men were restricted to two tobacco tins of water each. Those who found moist earth 'stuffed their mouths with it in order to relieve their torment'.[94]

On the Aisne in September 1914, Lieutenant William Synge suffered from having no hot food or drink and 'lived on biscuits and jam for the most part'. Bully beef was available but he found that his 'tongue got so sore from eating it … in an uncooked state' that he 'gave it up altogether'.[95] Supply improved rapidly as the war progressed. Second-Lieutenant Cecil Longley was able to later write home that 'food is plentiful and good, unless on the move'.[96] He eulogized Machonochie's tinned stew: 'Solomon in all his glory never had such a meal'.[97] Not all soldiers were a fan, but Conningsby Dawson noted that pragmatism overcame absence of choice. He and his men were existing mostly on tinned food, but 'our appetites make anything taste palatable'.[98] Henry Clapham found that a little cheffing could lead to improvement. A tin of curried Maconochie was 'far better than that the somewhat sickly article in its native state', with jam as a substitute for chutney. He described what all soldiers experienced, that out of the line it was possible to supplement the basic diet. 'Pork chops can be bought; eggs are cheap, and soup is generally on tap in our particular estaminet'.[99]

In terms of the basic needs for clothing and shelter, memoirs are full of vivid accounts of challenging physical conditions; hunger, cold (or excessive heat), wet and

---

92  RWOCESS, p.31.
93  Edmonds, op. cit. p.83.
94  T. Macmillan, Private Papers, IWM Docs 11149.
95  W. Synge, quoted in P. Hart, *Fire and Movement*, p.242.
96  C.W. Longley, *Battery Flashes*, p.69.
97  Longley, op. cit. p.97.
98  C. Dawson, *Carry On*, p.56.
99  Clapham, op. cit. p.43.

mud. In addition, there was noise, and associated lack of sleep. Max Plowman on the Somme in 1916 described the physical rigours of trench life: 'Heat, shortage of water, stench, shortage of sleep'.[100] Trooper W. Clarke described how deprivation dulled his senses. His lack of reaction to the deaths or wounding of friends, he thought, was 'because what you really wanted was to go to sleep, get warm, get clean and have a good meal'. It was a matter of practicality – these 'seemed the main priorities'.[101] His statement reflects the hierarchical nature of needs perfectly. The preoccupation with these first two levels is reflected in the comment of Aubrey Smith, who described himself and his comrades as 'living like animals … thinking only of our food and drink, our repose and safety'.[102]

In the terrible winter of 1914-15, Private Frank Richards noted that he and his comrades 'endured enough of physical hardships' sufficient to 'break men that were made of iron'. He described the unavoidable effect on their spirits: 'We suffered more in our morale than in our health', casualties from sickness being few.[103] They stuck it, but suffered. Private Harry Drinkwater, stoical in the face of the deaths of friends wrote in his diary in December 1916 in Flanders that conditions were 'beginning to get hold of me a bit', and he was suffering 'a fit of acute depression'.[104] At Ypres in November 1914, Sergeant John Lucy described terrible physical conditions, unrelievable in that most desperate of fights: 'Snow fell, and our lower limbs half froze while we slept out'.[105] Despite the fact that the army managed to develop a range of clothing more effective in protecting men in the conditions they faced, on the Somme in the early part of the awful winter of 1916, Captain Douglas Cuddeford described: 'Shocking conditions … well-nigh inconceivable', and men 'weeping from sheer misery' because of the cold.[106] Max Plowman regarded these particular conditions on the Transloy ridges in November 1916, as 'the very limit of endurance'.[107] In addition to cold there were the twin misfortunes of rain and mud. Major Richard Jeffreys, on the Somme in July 1916, noted that 'I never spent a more miserable 5 hours in my life', up to his waist in 'slushy mud'. Once out of his predicament his sense of humour returned: 'One could not help laughing at one's own misery'.[108] Graham Greenwell, who on the second day of the Somme offensive had written enthusiastically that he was 'awfully glad that I have survived to take part in this show',[109] was soon ground down. Enduring the same weather in the same location as Jeffreys, he told his parents that the ceaseless

100 Plowman, op. cit. p.51.
101 W. Clarke, Private Papers, IWM Docs 1377.
102 Rifleman, op. cit. p.185.
103 F. Richards, *Old Soldiers Never Die*, p.60.
104 J. Cooksey & D. Griffiths (eds), *Harry's War*, p.203.
105 J.F. Lucy, *There's a Devil in the Drum*, p.274.
106 D.W.J. Cuddeford, *And All for What?* p.89.
107 Plowman, op. cit. p.171.
108 R.G.B. Jeffreys, *Collected Letters*, p.18.
109 Greenwell, op. cit. p.134.

rain made 'this is the most depressing time I have ever spent in France'.[110] His ordeal continued. At Martinpuich he declared: 'This is our eighth day up. I am filthy and the cold is bad ... I have had nearly enough of it'; and a month later in front of Ovillers he continued: 'I have seldom felt such a miserable wreck', having had no hot food for thirty-six hours.[111] Five days later he was in hospital. In the misery of Third Ypres in 1917, where the mud became a potential death-trap, Arthur Lambert suffered 'waves of sickness' sweeping over him. In his mid-30s, and with the curious habit of writing about himself in the third person, he described how 'the days of strain, privation and excessive energy had thoroughly exhausted his older system'.[112]

Exhaustion from the physical effort of labour could sap the will. Lambert came under bombardment on his first ammunition carry to the front line in 1917. Shells burst everywhere, 'but he no longer cared or troubled to stop and duck'. His physical endurance seemed to have reached its limits, and he 'hoped that one would hit him and end the misery'.[113] Leading his company back from a spell of front line duty in the final stages of the Somme offensive, Sidney Rogerson described his men as in a 'semiconscious' state, their 'minds tortured by over-exertion and lack of sleep'.[114] Men developed an ability to sleep in discomfort and noise, but as Private David Polley noted: 'Lack of sleep pulls a man down quicker than most things'.[115] Signaller John Palmer noticed a deterioration in his ability to cope from the Somme to Third Ypres which 'absolutely finished me off'. During this battle his negative mood built up: 'I knew for three months before I was wounded that I was going to get it ... I was going to get killed'. Struggling through the mud of the Salient, he was 'so damn tired'. Physical exhaustion and negative mood were thus linked: 'You reached a point where there was no beyond'. One night, crouched in shellhole on his own, he began to wonder how he 'could get out of it'. He thought of putting his leg under the wheel of an oncoming ammunition wagon but had not the courage for it. Two nights later he and a comrade heard a shell coming. His pal dropped to the ground, but Palmer was 'too damned tired even to fall down'. Hit, he sank into the famous Passchendaele mud, experiencing the sensation as 'like a protective blanket'.[116]

Diet and physical conditions bore a direct relationship to health. Fighting since Mons, John Lucy found himself and his comrades in dire straits at Ypres in November 1914: 'Many of us could not now digest bully beef and hard biscuits'.[117] Even after the supply of food improved, however, problems remained. Douglas Cuddeford, in the harsh winter of 1916-17 on the Somme, noted that the 'lack of an occasional hot

---

110 Greenwell, op. cit. p.137.
111 Greenwell, op. cit. p.182.
112 Lambert, op. cit. p.64.
113 Lambert, op. cit. p.46.
114 Rogerson, op. cit. p.95.
115 D.J. Polley, *The Mudhook Machine Gunner*, p.64.
116 J.W. Palmer, quoted in Arthur, op. cit. pp.235-5.
117 Lucy, op. cit. p.274.

meal really told' on his men, and increased their susceptibility to ailments.[118] At Arras in May 1917, Aubrey Smith described men in his transport section as suffering from 'blood trouble as a result of the poor diet'. He claimed that vegetables had been impossible to obtain and it was two months since they had tasted a potato.[119]

Dysentery, trench foot, louse bourn infection – veterans' accounts abound with tales of these additional miseries. In the Ypres Salient in early 1915, Henry Clapham recorded that 'an epidemic of mild diarrhoea has broken out, and nothing seems to stop it'. His misery was amplified by having, several times a night, to step over sleeping comrades and walk down a snowy lane to relieve himself in an open trench.[120] The Gallipoli campaign generated probably the worst challenges to health of the war. Temperatures ranged from very hot to freezing, flies abounded and gastric problems were almost universal. Seaman Joseph Murray described in his diary in July 1915 previously healthy men harrowed by dysentery. 'With drawn faces and staring eyes … most of them should be in hospital. They are cheating death but only just. They are walking corpses'.[121]

John Lucy found a comrade crying in pain. His feet were swollen to 'an extraordinary degree', and when Lucy cut his boots off his feet 'resembled clubs'.[122] After preventative rubbing with whale oil was introduced, such an affliction became an offence. William Andrews, on the Somme in September 1916, recorded: 'I now had trench-fever and neuralgia behind the eyes, and much diarrhoea of blood'.[123] The extraordinarily resilient James Jack, described how physical stresses could coalesce at Ypres in 1914: 'The weather is raw and cold. I have a touch of fever and again fail to get a little sleep'. He felt 'at the end of my tether'.[124]

*Level two – safety needs*
On 1 July 1916, Corporal James Tansley of 9th York and Lancaster was advancing across Nab Valley when he and his comrades were caught by machine-gun fire. His friend was hit twice, and Tansley himself received a serious leg wound. He expected death at any moment. The only and best thing that he could do was to 'lie low, keep quiet'. He had to remain in the open as the nearest shell hole was already full of dead and wounded. For seven and a half hours he lay thus before he could crawl to a trench. He did not bleed to death because instruction in ambulance work had taught him to apply pressure to his groin to stop the bleeding.[125] The desperate seeking of safety in

---

118  Cuddeford, op. cit. p.92.
119  Rifleman, op. cit. p.226.
120  Clapham, op. cit. pp.42-3.
121  J. Murray, *Gallipoli 1915*, p.102.
122  Lucy, op. cit. p.307.
123  Andrews, op. cit. p.198.
124  Terraine, op. cit. p.76.
125  H. Tansley, IWM Sound 13682.

the face of unsuppressed machine gun fire was repeated up and down no-man's land that day.

In other wars, threat to life and limb came in brief peaks as it did that day to James Tansley, with long troughs of comparative safety. The positional warfare of the First World War produced a uniquely prolonged set of threats to safety. Most of such threat came in day-to-day trench duty under shell fire. As we will see later when discussing fear, soldiers could learn to predict shell fall, and could locate snipers that could be avoided. Yet they could only go so far to protect themselves. A dug-out might protect one from everything except a direct hit, but which shell might be the direct hit? Uncertainty and helplessness limited the ability to cope. Max Plowman described trench life as persistently challenging the 'freedom to anticipate', the soldier being 'deprived of reasonable expectation', tried by 'perpetual uncertainty'.[126] At First Ypres, James Hyndson recorded after being trapped in a trench all day by shellfire: 'We are powerless to do anything but sit tight and hope for the best'.[127] A soldier could often increase his safety, but he was powerless to guarantee it. Helplessness, the sense of feeling without control, is a theme we will return to.

### *Meeting basic and safety needs – out of the line*

The place where basic needs could most easily be met and a sense of comparative safety regained, was out of the line. 'It is marvellous to be out of the trenches; it is like being born again', wrote Max Plowman.[128] Joseph Murray described how on Gallipoli as soon as he left the front line he felt 'that time does not matter any more and there is no sense of urgency'. His felt as though a heavy burden had 'mysteriously flitted away and the brain begins to function normally again'.[129]

Trench routine generally comprised four days in the front line, four days in close reserve and finally four at rest. This varied depending on conditions, the fighting situation and the availability of reserve troops for rotation. In principle, therefore, the periods where basic needs were under strain were limited. Charles Carrington analysed his first year at war and found that 28 per cent of his time was spent under fire (12 tours in the trenches ranging from one to 13 days in length), 33 per cent in close reserve, and 20 per cent at rest, with the remainder of time spent in a wide range of activities.[130] Basic and safety needs were thus met on a 'just enough' basis in the periods out of the front line. As well documented in so many personal accounts and unit war diaries, however, periods of so-called rest were merely periods of labour.

Leaving the trenches of the Aisne for the first time in September 1914, James Hyndson recorded that it was 'an immense relief to get away from the strain'.[131]

---

126 Plowman, op. cit. pp.56-7.
127 Hyndson, op. cit. location 917.
128 Plowman, op. cit. p.56.
129 Murray, op. cit. p.148.
130 Edmonds, op. cit. p.95.
131 Hyndson, op. cit. location 655.

Captain Robert Ross described the effect: 'Our bodies were refreshed and our minds tranquillised',[132] giving a good impression of the easing of hyperarousal. But he was also wary of rest, noting 'prolonged leisure, not less than physical exhaustion, tended to enfeeble us'.[133] Second-Lieutenant Patrick Campbell was aware that the respite of being out of the line would be brief: 'We had only escaped for a little. But for the moment we had escaped'.[134] He lost himself in sports, particularly football and riding. Harry Drinkwater listed four important features of being out of the line which accord closely with the fulfilment of basic needs. Firstly, 'real rest' and sleep; secondly, good food and post from home; thirdly, dry and clean clothes; and fourthly, the facility to wash and shave.[135] Arthur Lambert, in the line for 17 days in Italy in 1918, wrote about the fourth of Drinkwater's key aspects of rest. 'It was a terrible hardship for men to be filthy for so long a period', so when baths were arranged there was 'great joy'.[136] Commissioned by 1918, Drinkwater spent a restful time in Italy with 5th Division in the early part of that year. But, returning to France, he noted that these months had not put his nerves 'in good working order again'. Despite rest, the symptoms of stress remained.[137]

Douglas Gillespie summarised that in true rest: 'There is so little for the men to do except eat and sleep, and try to get more beer than they are allowed from the estaminets'.[138] Rest enabled distraction. Lifted from the Battle of Broodseinde at Ypres in 1917, Arthur Lambert described memories as being 'drowned successfully' by being out of the line at Meteren. He noted the pleasure of estaminets and their alcoholic drinks, 'succulent dishes of eggs' served at virtually every house, and confectionery to 'delight the heart that had sickened of bully or stew'. Passes were available to Bailleul, where there were restaurants and shops as well as a cinema, even if what was on show was film of the Battle of Arras.[139] The army organised excursions, there were sports played aplenty, concert parties and, as Lambert indicates, cinemas. When the soldier was released from the boredom of labour and trench duty, there were activities that both relived boredom and duplicated the social activities of normal life.

*Level three – love and belongingness*
On the La Bassée front in 1914, John Lucy had the following dream: 'Loving friends were about me, a smiling valley held my home, and I stood regarding it, full of my happiness'.[140] His dream tells us everything about Maslow's third level of need, that

132 R.B. Ross, *The Fifty-First in France*, p.140.
133 Ross, op. cit. p.158.
134 P.J. Campbell, *In The Cannon's Mouth*, p.100.
135 Cooksey & Griffiths, op. cit. p.154.
136 Lambert, op. cit. p.187.
137 Cooksey & Griffiths, op. cit. p.330.
138 Gillespie, op. cit. p.257.
139 Lambert, op. cit. p.69.
140 Lucy, op. cit. p.231.

for love and belongingness in friendships and family. As Patrick Campbell remarked, the soldier needed 'love and laughter, occasional pleasure, affectionate comradeship always'.[141]

Psychological theory draws our attention to the differences between primary and secondary groups. Primary groups are typically small, their members sharing close, enduring relationships. Secondary groups are often more temporary, their prime reason for existence usually being to perform a task, either work or interest related.[142] War profoundly disrupted the relationship of the soldier with his primary group, his family. As we shall see in Chapter Two, soldiers had to struggle with maintaining a sense of familial love through writing and through infrequent leave. As Chapter Three will show, comradeship therefore assumed much added significance in fulfilling the need for belongingness. The newly created secondary group of the section or platoon, a pool of potential pals, chums and mates, had to become *de facto* the primary group, a proxy family.

Otherwise, the soldier was left to his imagination. On one spell out of the line, Patrick Campbell met a beautiful shop girl. She did not respond to his mild flirting, but he carried her mental image with him, fantasising himself with her every night as he was getting into his sleeping-bag. Far from being a sexual fantasy, he imagined her smiling, 'wanting to console me for the suffering she saw in my eyes'. He concluded: 'My imagination made me very happy'.[143]

### *The higher level – self-esteem and self-actualization*

The highest level of need, self-actualization, concerns achieving a sense of mastery and autonomy, reaching one's full potential. Whether anyone truly reaches their full potential is a moot point. Whether the vast bulk of the population of Edwardian Britain did so with their limited educations and opportunities, is unlikely. But whilst the army was the antithesis of autonomy, men in the trenches did achieve a certain sense of mastery. It was clearly possible to maintain self-esteem. Soldiers developed new skills, and were good at them. Many, at all levels, became effective leaders, whether commissioned or not.

In simple terms, self-esteem encompasses firstly that which is gained from the respect of others, in this case comrades and senior officers. Secondly, it swells though the confidence gained from experience, the knowledge that one is technically performing well. Lastly, it is underwritten by a sense that what one is doing is worthwhile. Thus, Second-Lieutenant Carlos Blacker noted that his own day-to-day morale was affected by 'how useful I felt (my) work was'. He made what on the surface may seem a strange remark, that casualties (and by this he meant wounded) 'could

---

141 P.J. Campbell, op. cit. p.142.
142 The notion of primary and secondary groups was developed by sociologist Charles Horton Cooley, in his work *Social Organization: a Study of the Larger Mind*.
143 P.J. Campbell, op. cit. p.142.

enhance your feelings of satisfaction'.[144] What he meant was that his self-esteem was boosted by the successful performance of a difficult job, and the occurrence of casualties indicated that the job had been difficult. Alfred Pollard, in no-man's land at night, similarly felt that: 'At last I was doing something worthwhile'. Consequently he 'was as happy as a sand boy'.[145] Men revelled in being 'old hands', and the increased emphasis on specialist training cemented a sense of proficiency. Field Marshal Bill Slim believed that morale was based on three foundations; spiritual, intellectual, and material. Of these he viewed the spiritual as most important, and he broke it into four parts. Firstly, 'there must be a great and noble object'; secondly, 'its achievement must be vital'; thirdly, 'the method of achievement must be active, aggressive'; and fourthly, 'the man must feel that what he is and what he does matter directly towards the attainment of the object'.[146]

War concerns the destruction of the enemy. Captain Allan Hanbury-Sparrow wrote that by killing, soldiers 'coarsened and degraded something' in themselves.[147] A sense of shame and guilt did appear in letters, diaries and memoirs, but it seems likely that it was less than that experienced by soldiers of more recent conflicts. Niall Ferguson draws attention to the opposite end of the spectrum occupied by Hanbury-Sparrow. He claims that 'many men simply took pleasure in killing'.[148] Whether 'many' did so is debateable. Julian Grenfell certainly enjoyed hunting men. Fergsuon notes that snipers took pride in their work. For most it was not a matter of pleasure, but a matter of pay-back for dead pals or the frenzy of combat.

It has often been observed that one of the reasons that so much negative psychological aftermath existed for veterans of the Vietnam War was that their sense of purpose of fighting a just 'good war' became eroded. There was a weight of opposition in America to the conflict, and the attention received by the occurrence of atrocities damaged the image of the fighting American. Far from being a returned hero, the image of the American soldier became unwholesome. Undoubtedly at the time, soldiers of the Great War experienced the reassurance that they were fighting a good war. As we will see, religion bolstered this. Frederic Manning set out the following argument: 'What I say is that the Fritzes 'ad to be stopped. If we 'adn't come in, an' they'd got the Frenchies beat, 'twould 'a been our turn next'.[149] His characters argue, but never disagree with the fundamental principal that it was right to be fighting.

What, therefore, were the motivations for fighting? How did motivations change, and in what way did they support self-esteem? There were many reasons for volunteering in 1914. Padre Innes Logan described why he believed men volunteered. First, he described thrill-seekers, men who did things on the spur of the moment, men who

---

144 J. Blacker (ed.), *Have You Forgotten Yet?*, p.146.
145 Pollard, op. cit. p.53.
146 W.J. Slim, *Defeat into Victory*, p.185.
147 A.A.H. Hanbury-Sparrow, *The Land-Locked Lake*, p.91.
148 Ferguson, op. cit. p.363.
149 Manning, op. cit. location 2663.

had not fitted into life previously. Private Frederick Bolwell, a reservist married with two children, may not have exactly been a thrill-seeker, but wrote that: 'I was only too pleased to be able to leave a more or less monotonous existence for something more exciting and adventurous'.[150] Secondly, Logan described those who were 'passionately patriotic'.[151] Second-Lieutenant Bernard Martin described 'a just war ... a righteous war, a great and glorious adventure, patriotic and God on our side, too'.[152] Patriotism was allied to the concepts of duty and honour. Private Norman Gladden, 15 months into his war noted two prongs to his motivation. Firstly, the 'feeling that we were with those who were doing their duty'. Secondly, 'that we were suffering for those whom we had left behind, and for the ideals and future of our country'.[153] In joining up, 17 year-old Private Ernest Parker 'decided where I thought my duty lay', and believed that all who volunteered with him were conscious of threat to their country.[154] Francis Buckley, attesting in May 1915 did so in the spirit of 'better death and ruin than dishonour'.[155] Lieutenant Eric Lubbock wrote to his mother with a simple analogy for fighting: 'An individual pledged to defend a friend would not receive any sympathy if he allowed his friend to be attacked and did not defend him'.[156] Reginald Davis similarly found that the declaration of war sent a particular call to him: 'I knew my duty was to fight'. He was conscious of a sense of personal responsibility: 'I wouldn't let another man do *my* fighting for me'.[157] For many there was a genuine sense of protecting their families. When Katie Morter protested at her husband joining up she received the response: 'There has to be men to go and fight for the women, otherwise where should we be?'[158] Impetuousness and thrill-seeking was therefore balanced by the protection of loved-ones, patriotism, duty, and honour. In our modern world fighting for the last three reasons is less easy to grasp.

Despite war-weariness, for some these motivations did not alter in intensity as the war ground on. Even after being wounded in 1916 and denouncing the vileness of war, Bernard Adams still felt driven to write: 'We did not start, we did not want this war. We have gone into it, fighting for the better cause'.[159] The day before his death on 1 July 1916, Second-Lieutenant John Engall wrote to his parents that 'the day has almost dawned when I shall really do my little bit in the cause of civilization'.[160] In July 1917, four days before his death, Lieutenant Henry Jones sent a letter to his brother

---

150 F.A. Bolwell, *With a Reservist in France*, p.3.
151 I. Logan, *On the King's Service*, pp.7-8.
152 B. Martin, *Poor Bloody Infantry*, p.3.
153 N. Gladden, *Ypres 1917*, p.115.
154 E.W. Parker, *Into Battle*, p.1.
155 Buckley, op. cit. p.1.
156 E. Lubbock, quoted in Housman, op. cit. p.177.
157 E. Hodder-Williams, *One Young Man*, Kindle edition locations 140-7 (italics in original).
158 K. Morter, BBC 'The Great War Interviews'.
159 Adams, op. cit. p.305.
160 J. Engall quoted in Housman, op. cit. pp.106-7.

about the possibility of death: 'You have the satisfaction of knowing that you have "pegged out" in the attempt to help your country'.[161] Huntly Gordon could similarly state in 1917: 'We are rightly fighting – for our freedom'.[162] His view was that his own survival could not be 'the first consideration'.[163] The enemy had to be beaten whatever the cost. As late as August 1918, Lieutenant Hedley Goodyear would write to his mother the day before going into action: 'I shall strike a blow for freedom along with thousands of others', men who like Huntly Gordon 'count personal safety as nothing when freedom is at stake'.[164] Many thus had persisting lofty motivations that maintained self-esteem.

Captain David Campbell, however, denied 'lofty motives' in joining up. He wanted 'to escape from the drab life I was then leading', studying for the clergy and the social round.[165] Second-Lieutenant Guy Chapman similarly had 'no romantic illusions' and his 'heart gave back no answering throb to the thought of England'.[166] Private Francis Vaughan enlisted in the Sheffield City Battalion because 'my pals were going, chaps I had kicked about with in the street'.[167] Major Arthur Gibbs joined up on the basis that if he did not, 'could I ever call myself a man again?'[168] Otherwise he concluded: 'God knows why most of us went'.[169] Private Evelyn Fryer could not decide whether he attested out of 'boredom or patriotism'.[170] Alfred Pollard did not claim patriotism. Watching men march to war in August 1914, he simply thought: 'How could I be left behind?'[171] Below the moral high ground of patriotism and duty there was therefore a range of personal motivations.

Some remained in possession of the moral high ground. For others, war-weariness bit hard, eating into motivation. Douglas Gillespie described in a letter home that territorials fresh from home were with his unit for instruction. With the insouciance of the old-hand he observed: 'Their enthusiasm will soon wear off, I'm afraid'.[172] Arthur Gibbs served in France from the end of 1914 into 1915 and then, commissioned, went to Salonika. By 1916 his mental attitude towards the war had changed. 'Whatever romance and glamour there may have been' had worn off. He viewed it all as 'just one long bitter waste of time'.[173] During the second winter of the war, Jeffery Jeffery wrote that the conflict to which he had set out 'so light-heartedly' had proved itself to be 'not

161  H. Jones, quoted in Housman, op. cit. p.159.
162  Gordon, op. cit. location 1427.
163  Gordon, op. cit. location 1540.
164  H. Goodyear, quoted in Housman, op. cit. p.113.
165  D. Campbell, *Forward the Rifles*, p.10.
166  G. Chapman, *A Passionate Prodigality*, p.8.
167  F.B. Vaughan, quoted in Arthur, op. cit. p.18.
168  A.H. Gibbs, *Gun Fodder*, p.5.
169  Gibbs, op. cit. p.46.
170  E.R.M. Fryer, *Reminiscences of a Grenadier*, p.2.
171  Pollard, op. cit. p.22.
172  Gillespie, op. cit. p.90.
173  Gibbs, op. cit. p.141.

the "greatest of games", but the greatest of all ghastly horrors'.[174] On Gallipoli, Major George Davidson wrote in the latter stages of stalemate that 'the monotony lately has been very trying', and for the first time he 'felt astonished I had been able "to stick it"' so long.[175] Wesleyan chaplain Thomas Westerdale wrote that after six months soldiers settled down with a 'dogged determination to see the thing through'. They would develop 'a more or less "fed up" feeling', with few thinking 'very deeply now of the great principles for which they came out to fight'.[176] For most, therefore, patriotism ebbed away. George Coppard may have joined up for this very reason, but observed that by 1917 'that had burned itself out long ago'.[177] Rowland Feilding noted a concert party joke which went down well with a front-line audience: '"What is a Patriot?" Answer: "A man who sheds your blood for his country!"'[178] By mid-1917, Lieutenant Burgon Bickersteth noted that the average British soldier 'resents the highly patriotic tone, except when presented in a sentimental song at a "smoker"'.[179]

If patriotism diminished, did hatred of the enemy replace it, maintaining a sense of superiority and purpose? Richard Holmes claims that 'the fighting man rarely felt a high degree of hostility' towards his opponents.[180] This is not entirely true. Many memoirs reveal the negative attitudes generally held towards the enemy. Edward Spiers describes in Scottish units a 'real sense of enmity towards the Germans'.[181] Private Stephen Graham described the attitude towards the enemy that they were 'a sort of vermin like plague-rats that had to be exterminated'.[182] Indeed, two officers of the Berkshire Regiment used exactly these words in conversation, describing the enemy as 'unutterable vermin'.[183] A ranker, responding to a German prisoner simply stated: 'We just looks on you as vomit'.[184] Second-Lieutenant Norman Taylor noted 'the genuine hatred of Germans one gets after a year or so of this'.[185] Even well-educated soldiers did not escape the perception of the German as brute. Memoirs abound with disgust at descriptions of alleged German atrocities, nearly always recounted second-hand. Soldiers clearly wanted the justification of believing their enemy to be morally inferior. More powerful was personally motivated enmity. Private Arthur Lambert wrote of receiving bad news from home of German air-raids 1917 and how this motivated him to want to kill the enemy.[186] Most frequently, the enmity was that experienced by

---

174 J.E. Jeffery, *Servants of the Guns*, p.4.
175 G. Davidson, *With the Incomparable 29th*, p.210.
176 T.L.B. Westerdale, *Messages from Mars*, pp.86-7.
177 Coppard, op. cit. p.107.
178 Feilding, op. cit. p.184.
179 Bickersteth, op. cit. p.169.
180 R. Holmes, *Tommy*, p.536.
181 E. Spiers, 'The Scottish Soldier at War', in Cecil & Liddle, op. cit. p.326.
182 S. Graham, *A Private in the Guards*, p.217.
183 Quoted in A. Simpson, *Hot Blood and Cold Steel*, p.168.
184 Quoted in D. Winter, *Death's Men*, p.211.
185 N. Taylor, quoted in J. Lewis-Stempel, *Six Weeks*, 225.
186 Lambert, op. cit. pp.49-50.

Frank Brent, an Australian NCO. He described how going into action: 'There was a feeling of exultation that once again you were going to be able to ... extract retribution from the fellows who'd killed your mates'.[187]

Others, of course, were able to hold the view of 'my enemy like me'. Ben Keeling was definite that 'I will not hate Germans to the order of any bloody politician'.[188] He admired Nurse Edith Cavell, but thought the Germans within their rights to execute her. For him, it was no war crime. The Reverend Julian Bickersteth, a veteran of the Western Front and a devotee of the idea of crushing Germany early in the war, wrote in September 1917 of a general lack of enthusiasm for killing. In his view soldiers 'know little and care less about the great Prussian Evil', and that 'the supply of rations and the getting out alive' were far more important motivations.[189] In June 1918 he continued: 'Men don't and won't hate the Germans – they only hate the war'.[190] The picture is almost certainly not a simple one. Men who were able to respect 'live and let live' in trench warfare were also capable at other times of shooting dead a German who had surrendered out of simple distrust or out of revenge for the death of a mate. Lieutenant-Colonel Ralph Hamilton looked at the matter simply: 'The more we kill the sooner it will be over. After all, they have done this sort of thing to us'.[191]

Motivation as demonstrated in a sense of worthwhile purpose was therefore varied, and changed over time, from the public to the personal. Second-Lieutenant Arthur West, as he slipped further into pacifism considered that soldiers simply accepted that the war was 'necessary and inevitable'.[192] He remarked that most men fought, 'if not happily, at any rate patiently', sure of the 'necessity and usefulness of their work'.[193] Gerald Burgoyne simply remarked that the war was 'stern duty'.[194] It was a matter of finishing the job. In the end most were fighting because there was no alternative, and because their friends were fighting by their side. The main motivation that had been distilled was very probably the need to finish a job started in the company of friends. Siegfried Sassoon wrote by the opening of the Battle of Arras in April 1917 that he had lost his 'faith' in the war and 'there was nothing left to believe in except "the Battalion spirit"'.[195] By the early months of 1918, Wilfred Bion 'didn't care tuppence whether we held the "line" or not.' He would, however, 'do my job by my men as well as I could'.[196] William Andrews confided to his dairy in early 1917: 'We had to fight

---

187 F. Brent, BBC 'The Great War Interviews'.
188 Keeling, op. cit. p.259.
189 Bickersteth, op. cit. p.149.
190 Bickersteth, op. cit. p.257.
191 R.G. Hamilton, *The War Diary of the Master of Belhaven*, p.70.
192 A.G. West, *Diary of a Dead Officer*, p.56.
193 West, op. cit. p.57.
194 Davison, op. cit. p.65.
195 Sassoon, op. cit. p.421.
196 Bion, op. cit. p.94.

this War, and we must win it. We must not be disloyal to our dead'.[197] Conningsby Dawson probably summed up what most thought when he wrote: 'We "carry on" because, if we don't, we shall let other men down and put their lives in danger'.[198]

**Endurance and Coping**

Guy Chapman, in collecting together over 700 pages of the writings of British soldiers in 1937 in his book *Vain Glory*, expressed the opinion that: 'The Englishman ... appears to be the most serious fighter'. Within the meaning of the title of his book he took the view that the British soldier 'does not believe in war', that he looked on it 'without enthusiasm', but that he dealt with it 'as a dirty job to be carried out'.[199] The 'British workman in disguise' was used to such. For the private soldier, endurance was to varying extents the key to his everyday pre-war life, and now he had to dig deep in this resource. Conningsby Dawson declared: 'For sheer hardness and discomfort there's nothing in the life of the poorest worker in England to compare with it', yet he claimed that 'the level of their spirits is far higher than you'd find it in any model factory or workshop at home'.[200] In digging deep, as George Coppard wrote, the British soldier utilised the 'ingrained sense of duty and obedience, in keeping with the times'.[201] Stephen Graham was of the view that endurance was a self-fulfilling prophecy: 'Such habits of patience under suffering have been formed as could not be exhausted'.[202] Lieutenant Sidney Rogerson similarly recognised the 'grim determination' of the British soldier.[203] Second-Lieutenant Billie Nevill enjoyed the 'marvellous feeling all the time of the (men) sticking it out'.[204] Bernard Adams celebrated 'the sheer power of will conquering the body and "carrying on"'.[205] Huntly Gordon noted of his artillery battery that they possessed not only 'a wonderful spirit and loyalty to each other', but also 'a good-humoured endurance that seemingly nothing can break down'.[206] Max Plowman expressed the inherent contradiction: 'I am fit. I shall go on, even gladly. But it is hell'.[207] Some, described earlier, feared that their endurance could not persist, but few would have questioned Plowman's statement of stoic perseverance. They did not see themselves as the victims of the title of Henry Russell's wartime

---

197 Andrews, op. cit. p.213.
198 C. Dawson, op. cit. p.88.
199 G. Chapman, *Vain Glory*, p.x.
200 C. Dawson, op. cit. p.178.
201 Coppard, op. cit. p.77.
202 Graham, op. cit. p.7.
203 Rogerson, op. cit. p.14.
204 R.E. Harris, *Billie – The Nevill Letters: 1914-1916*, p.68.
205 Adams, op. cit. p.299.
206 Gordon, op. cit. location 2183.
207 Plowman, op. cit. p.124.

autobiography, *Slaves of the War Lords*. They were simply acting within the spirit of duty of the age.

### *Humour*

The grumbling of the British soldier has become totemic. Alec Dawson described of his men how 'grousing is one of the passions of their lives'. He undoubtedly got it right that this was nothing negative, noting that it would be truer to say that it was 'a favourite form of recreation'. He added that it was 'absolutely forbidden to growl when there's anything to growl about', true miseries being met with 'a lot of chaffing and joke-cracking and apparent merriment'.[208] Harry Drinkwater similarly observed the inverse relationship between grumbling and hardship. Grumbling only 'applied to the petty things of army life', more serious discomforts being stoically endured.[209] Frederic Manning concurred: 'The greater the hardships they had to endure … the less they grumbled'.[210]

Equally totemic was the reverse side of the coin that was grousing – the cheerfulness of the British soldier. Captain Robert Manion described the 'drollery' of soldiers confronted with both narrow escapes from death and the myriad of inconveniences of trench life. Drollery was sometimes 'good-natured, sometimes ill-tempered and critical', but was 'ever present'.[211] Bernard Adams celebrated that: 'It is great that Tommy's laughter has been immortalised' but reminded us that its greatness lay in the fact that it was 'uttered beneath the canopy of ever-impending Death'.[212] Robert Graves similarly observed that 'the men are much afraid but always joking'.[213]

Lord Moran was convinced of the central role of humour in coping. 'Only humour helped', a humour that laughed at life 'and scoffed at our own frailty'.[214] Moran believed it was crucial in dealing with the threat of death. 'We simply could not afford to allow death to hover in the offing' – it had to be dealt with directly, 'brought to earth and robbed of its disturbing influence, by rough jibes and the touch of ridicule'. If the threat of death was 'firmly grasped like a nettle soon there was no sting left in it.[215] By and large, psychological research supports what both Moran and common sense suggests. Humour relieves tension and anxiety. A good sense of humour is related to 'muscle relaxation, control of pain and discomfort, positive mood states, and overall psychological health including a healthy self-concept'.[216] The stress-moder-

---

208 A.J. Dawson, op. cit. pp.173-4.
209 Cooksey & Griffiths, op. cit. p.155.
210 Manning, op. cit. location 3232.
211 R.J. Manion, *A Surgeon in Arms*, p.143.
212 Adams, op. cit. p.116.
213 Graves, op. cit. p.104.
214 Lord Moran, *The Anatomy of Courage*, p.140.
215 Moran, op. cit. p.144.
216 M.H. Abel, 'Humor, Stress and Coping Strategies', *Humor: International Journal of Humor Research*, p.366.

ating effects of humour appear to operate, at least in part, 'through more positive appraisals and more realistic cognitive processing of environmental information'.[217] A sense of humour allows one to reinterpret, to see things more clearly and positively, without the magnifying cloak of negative thinking. It allows both 'distancing oneself from the stressor' yet eases efforts toward confronting and dealing with the problems causing stress.[218] Humour therefore allows one to move away from or move closer to the stressor to deal with it. A study of the humour of American troops in the Second World War suggested that it helped troops achieve a state of mind where they could 'endure and accept what could not be avoided'. Humour allowed a 'safe discharge of dangerous tensions'.[219] There is, however, a difference between positive (good-natured) humour and negative (mean-spirited) humour. Positive humour is the most effective in 'up-regulating positive and down-regulating negative emotions'.[220] Positive humour may help reappraisal, negative humour may simply recycle the stress in an unhelpful way. Thus police officers displaying greater levels of humour actually proved at increased risk for cardiovascular disease, greater body mass, and increased smoking.[221] The people who work in such organisations have traditionally been very wary of demonstrating distress and consequently been masters of black humour. There are thus indications that when humour is used very extensively or exclusively to avoid dealing with stress, the results may not be positive. The role of humour in combatting stress is therefore not simple – it cannot be the only strategy deployed.

As J.G. Fuller has noted, trench journals often used humour to present grievances in a light-hearted way, and there was no 'detectable darkening' as the war proceeded.[222] Similarly, the ever-popular concert parties were characterised by the themes of the British music hall tradition: 'Fatalism, political scepticism, the evasion of tragedy or anger, and a stance of comic stoicism'.[223] The display of muted grievances in such performances was well cloaked in humour. Fuller records that 'The Very Lights' song 'Living in the Trenches' drew the following response from one ranker: 'Somehow making a joke of it when you knew you had to go back to it made it all just bearable'.[224] The evidence suggests that the humour was largely not of the negative, avoidant nature. It was gently escapist, reframing stress. The concert parties reinforced

---

217 N.A. Kuiper, & R.A. Martin, 'Is Sense of Humor a Positive Personality Characteristic?', in W. Ruch, *The Sense of Humor*, p.162.
218 Abel, op. cit. p.376.
219 S.A. Stouffer, *The American Soldier*, p.190.
220 A.C. Samson & J.J. Gross, 'Humour as Emotion Regulation: The Differential Consequences of Negative Versus Positive Humour', *Cognition & Emotion*, p.381.
221 P. Kerkkänen, N.A. Kuiper, & R.A. Martin, R. A. 'Sense of Humor, Physical Health, and Well-being at Work: A Three-year Longitudinal Study of Finnish Police Officers', *Humor: International Journal of Humor Research*, p.21.
222 Fuller, op. cit. pp.13-14.
223 G.S. Jones, 'Working Class Culture and Working Class Politics in London, 1879-1900', *Journal of Social History*, pp.478-9.
224 Fuller, op. cit. p.109.

positivity: 'Cheerfulness … was a constant music hall theme'.[225] 'What's the use of worrying, it never was worthwhile', went the chorus of *Pack up Your Troubles in Your Old Kit Bag*. Bruce Bairnsfather's famous cartoon characters, 'Old Bill', 'Bert' and 'Alf', were anti-heroes who grumbled with sardonic humour at the miseries of trench life. This served as a popular model. Bairnsfather's most famous cartoon, 'A Better 'Ole', where two characters have their heads exposed in a shell hole during a bombardment, one saying to the other 'Well, if you knows of a better 'ole, go to it', thus tackles humorously the reality of a soldier's helplessness under shellfire. It names the problem, it does not avoid it.

Lieutenant-Colonel William Malone, whose Wellington Battalion of New Zealanders remained perilously unrelieved for days on Walker's Ridge, Gallipoli, informed his wife: 'Sang froid, is our moto, also "cheeriness". Everybody jokes, smiles and laughs'.[226] Richard Jeffreys wrote home soon after arrival in France in June 1916: 'Everyone is very cheery out here', all managing to see 'the humour in the disagreeable part of the business'.[227] James Hyndson, in the very first trenches of the war on the Aisne in 1914, noted the 'many amusing stories' which relieved both 'the strain of the fighting' and the 'monotony' of trench life.[228] Commanding a company of 2nd West Yorkshire on the Somme in 1916, Sidney Rogerson similarly described himself and his fellow officers as 'possessors of a sense of humour which persisted in rising equally above the various forms of boredom which beset us and the many manifestations of "frightfulness"'.[229] Douglas Cuddeford described a shell burst which toppled a brick wall on top of an Irish officer whose response on being dug out caused howls of laughter. Cuddeford noted later that 'there really could have been nothing very funny about it', and viewed it as an indication of 'how perverted our idea of humour had become'.[230] He recognised however that it was generally a 'case of laugh or cry … and most chose to laugh', for anything was 'looked upon as a diversion and a relief for the moment'.[231] He estimated that there was at least one 'bright and irresponsible' individual in each platoon 'whose good humour and lively wit provided the leaven that kept the majority cheerful even under the most trying conditions'.[232]

Charles Douie may have hit the nail on the head in thinking that laughter was 'born of defiance'.[233] Richard Haigh described a tank commander during the 1918 Hundred Days advance being carried past, both legs blown off below the knees, 'joking with

---

225 Fuller, op. cit. p.126.
226 J. Crawford, *No Better Death*, Kindle edition location 2880.
227 Jeffreys, op. cit. p.8.
228 Hyndson, op. cit. location 648.
229 Rogerson, op. cit. p.4.
230 Cuddeford, op. cit. p.67.
231 Cuddeford, op. cit. p.148.
232 Cuddeford, op. cit. p.167.
233 Douie, op. cit. p.85.

everyone' as he was carried on a stretcher.[234] Whether this was defiance or simply the euphoria generated by adrenalin which precedes full realisation of what has happened is difficult to determine. But by laughing at discomfort or danger, a soldier was, at least for the moment, not its victim. There were times, however, when humour was ineffective. Scout Joe Cassells, waiting to go into action related that occasionally a man would joke or tell a funny story: 'Those who heard him either looked as if they hadn't heard or laughed rather thinly'.[235]

Humour was in varying degrees an international coping strategy. Walter Ludwig's study of the coping strategies of wounded German soldiers found it used by 15 per cent in moments of extreme stress, the seventh most used strategy.[236] Was there some particular nature to British humour, which some believed different to the observed taciturn nature of the French soldier?[237] Was it cynicism, sarcasm or irony? The difference is worth teasing out. 'Cynicism' and 'sarcasm' are both used with the intention of mocking or hurting another person. Cynicism has a strong element of contempt, sarcasm has a bitterness and caustic nature. 'Irony' is not malevolent, involving the use of words to express something other than and especially the opposite of the literal meaning. This is not to say that the British soldier was not cynical and sarcastic – but it was irony that dominated his humour. Irony and its reversals made discomfort, boredom, threat and horror more manageable. And 'British humour was to many the war-winning quality'.[238]

### *Distraction and avoidance*

Soldiers naturally had their own opinions on what constituted coping. Stephen Graham's tool-kit of 'mental relief' for most soldiers included 'Bumble and Buck,[239] cards, cigarettes, and when out of the line beer, vin blanc, and flirtation with French girls'.[240] These were all mechanisms of distraction. Chaplain Maurice Ponsonby listed four principal coping strategies, all representing distraction or avoidance. Firstly, ironic humour in 'calling a terrible thing by a pleasant or comic name'. Thus being killed famously became 'nah poohed', from the French *il n'y a plus* – no more. Secondly, as we shall see later when discussing fear, 'making yourself appear quite unconcerned' in the not unrealistic belief that how one behaved would positively affect how one felt inside. Thirdly, fatalism, a way of easing anxiety about the threat of death; and fourthly, distraction though alcohol.[241] Private Giles Eyre agreed: 'Eat, drink and be

---

234 Haigh, op. cit. p.87.
235 Cassells, op. cit. pp.163-4.
236 Watson, op. cit. p.237.
237 Fuller, op. cit. p.148.
238 Fuller, op. cit. p.148.
239 Another name for the board game Crown & Anchor.
240 Graham, op. cit. p.190.
241 M. Ponsonby, *Visions and Vignettes of War*, pp.31-3.

merry, for to-morrow you may die – the philosophy of the fighting man, a jolly sound one, for who dare say it is wrong?'[242]

Alcohol is a time-honoured means of relieving stress. George Coppard's view was that: 'Carousing was the best medicine for battle-weary soldiers',[243] although most found local drinks unsatisfactory. Even the army itself recognised the fortifying role of alcohol, issuing 1/16th of a pint of dark rum per man per day. Amidst his privations on the Aisne, William Synge noted that 'rum was our one expedient'.[244] Max Plowman described it as 'our chief great good', the moment of its serving becoming a 'moment of religious worship'.[245] It was not generously dispensed, but Private Henry Russell noted that the 'three tablespoons' each were sufficient to 'warm starved bodies and steady shattered nerves'.[246] The temporary warming effect was valued by all – Frank Richards described in similar circumstances that rum 'helped keep the cold out of our bodies'. Henry Clapham claimed that 'it revives one when soaked to the skin. It revives one at one's worst'.[247] Douglas Cuddeford thought the same, believing that the morning rum ration after a freezing night 'saved many a life'.[248] Gerald Burgoyne did not 'want rum in the cold, or for the cold'; he and his men wanted it 'just as a "pick me up" when we are "done to the wide"'.[249] The rum jar was marked SRD, Supply Reserve Depot, transposed by its recipients as 'Seldom Reaches Destination'. Private Henry Williamson described one sad catastrophe associated with the rum ration in December 1914. 'One poor chap ... took a first sip of the rum and gave a shriek and dropped the jar'.[250] The rum had been stolen and replaced with Condy's fluid, a disinfectant. Its constituent being potassium permanganate, poisonous in sufficient strength, the unfortunate victim died.

Frank Richards claimed that he saw non-commissioned officers and men drunk in action and thought that this was very dangerous as it 'made one reckless'.[251] Men certainly drank both before and during battle. John Lucy, commissioned from the rank of sergeant, admitted that when about to go over the top: 'At two minutes to zero, I took a good swig of neat whisky'.[252] Evelyn Fryer, also now commissioned, was with his platoon in the middle of the summer of 1916 in Sanctuary Wood, Ypres. They lay in the bottom of a trench for 19 hours a day under shellfire. He considered that 'our morale would have entirely departed' had it not been for two convenient bottles of

242 G.E.M. Eyre, *Somme Harvest*, p.19.
243 Coppard, op. cit. p.117.
244 W. Synge, quoted in Hart, op. cit. p.242.
245 Plowman, op. cit. p.174.
246 H. Russell, *Slaves of the War Lords*, p.38.
247 Clapham, op. cit. p.440.
248 Cuddeford, op. cit. p.92.
249 Davison, op. cit. pp.131-2.
250 H. Williamson, quoted in Arthur, op. cit. p.54.
251 Richards, op. cit. pp.100-101.
252 Lucy, op. cit. p.372.

port.²⁵³ For many, however, alcohol's effects were used to combat the general grinding nature of stress. Having drunk three-quarters of a bottle of red wine, Arthur West, by no means a drinker, and profoundly miserable about his experience of the army found himself 'perfectly happy physically'. The feeling lasted for the duration of a march: 'The intensity of perpetual wellbeing doesn't even leave my remotest finger-tips'.²⁵⁴ As 1918 ground on, Lieutenant-Colonel Howard de Sales la Terriere confided how he used drink to mitigate stress: 'I was so utterly worn out both physically and nervously that without some form of dope I could not possibly have carried on'.²⁵⁵ Drinking of course inspires legends and David Campbell alleged of the GHQ vessel, *Aragon*, anchored in Mudros harbour during the Gallipoli campaign: 'When first they tried to move her they found that she was aground on champagne bottles'.²⁵⁶

Robert Graves, who claimed that he only had eight hours sleep in a ten day period, described that 'I kept myself awake and alive by drinking about a bottle of whisky a day'.²⁵⁷ He later asserted that many officers surviving in the trenches for two years became 'dipsomaniacs'.²⁵⁸ Gerald Burgoyne viewed drink as 'a regular curse' in his Royal Irish Rifles company. He described a sergeant who lay asleep in a trench for two days, having drunk 'nearly half a jar of rum', whilst in billets 'a pig of a man took a jar of rum to bed with him, and was found dead next morning'.²⁵⁹ Lieutenant Angus Grieve similarly described his unit, 4th Highland Light Infantry, as possessing a 'marvellous talent for getting drunk'.²⁶⁰ Being drunk on duty was a court-martial offence. Many must have avoided being so caught. Robert Graves noted that the temporary CO of his unit, James Cuthbert, 'felt the strain badly and took a lot of whisky', and was relieved.²⁶¹ Huntly Gordon, whose first contact with his colonel was finding him insensible through drink noted another occasion where he remained drunk and alone in a cellar for two days and nights. He concluded 'perhaps his nerve was going'.²⁶²

Temporary distraction through substance use is both age-old and very familiar to us. Smoking was similarly another release. Henry Russell was of the opinion that cigarettes 'played a big part' in making the war 'endurable';²⁶³ and Norman Gladden noted that 'under the stresses of the battlefield a smoker could become desperate and risk anything'. He would chance the possibility of the cigarette's glow giving away his location in exchange for 'release from tension'.²⁶⁴ Yet such temporary distraction was

253 Fryer, op. cit. p.97.
254 West, op. cit. p.75.
255 H.M.B. de Sales la Terriere, Private Papers, IWM Docs 14737.
256 D. Campbell, op. cit. p.37.
257 Graves, op. cit. p.148.
258 Graves, op. cit. p.154.
259 Davison, op. cit. p.34.
260 A.A. Macfarlane Grieve, quoted in Spiers, op. cit. p.321.
261 Graves, op. cit. p.211.
262 Gordon, op. cit. location 1856.
263 Russell, op. cit. p.48.
264 Gladden, op. cit. p.36.

only the tip of a broad seam of avoidance. This, as we shall see, was far from a bad thing. And if avoidance was the norm, then it is understandable that by and large the one coping method that was not used was talking. As will become abundantly clear, this introspective and essentially modern form of coping was not part of the spirit of the age. Experiences were mostly not processed in this way. Revealing stress and resulting emotions was indicative of weakness, contrary to the code of manliness. Thus, Arthur West talked in depth to other officers he had never met before when on a course: 'We talk of ourselves, of our natures and moods, of what we would do if we were home … (of) what we were doing before the war … We confided our dreams'.[265] Their talk was essentially escapist. Avoidance of unnecessary stirring of thoughts and feelings was the bedrock of maintaining mental stability.

Naturalist come temporary gentleman Arthur Dugmore speculated as to whether the 'average soldier does much thinking'. He concluded that as long as basic needs, 'immediate bodily comforts' were satisfied, that he did not. 'It is better so', Dugmore observed.[266] He had hit on a truism. For the soldier on active duty, over-thinking can be disabling. Charles Douie was in full agreement, writing a letter home on his 21st birthday on the Yser in 1917 which concluded: 'At the front the only thing to do is to live well and forget while you can. The most fatal mistake is to think at all'.[267] Second-Lieutenant Alan Thomas was advised 'live from day to day – and don't think'.[268] Captain Harry Yoxall similarly noted: 'If you did ruminate much on the real meaning of the things you do and the things that are done to you, your nerves would crack in no time'.[269] Arriving to join his unit on the Somme in 1916, Alan Thomas noted the attitude of his company commander, Captain Hodgson-Smith, towards death to be one of 'utter indifference … the natural indifference of a man who isn't interested'.[270] Many soldiers simply avoided looking ahead. Captain Cecil Brownlow summed the matter up succinctly: 'To-morrow you may be dead. And so the absorbing interest is the present: in the present you laugh and live and die'.[271]

## Conclusion

The British soldier endured the dirty and dangerous job of trench warfare on a 'just enough' principle. If basic human needs had to be fulfilled for the soldier to maintain motivation and bear the stress, then being out of the line allowed just enough time for the need for water, food, warmth, shelter and safety to be topped up. Companionship provided a good enough temporary substitute for the love and sense of belongingness

---

265 West, op. cit. p.76.
266 Dugmore, op. cit. p.77.
267 Douie, op. cit. p.201.
268 A. Thomas, *A Life Apart*, p.41.
269 H.W. Yoxall, Private Papers, IWM Docs 22290.
270 Thomas, op. cit. p.53.
271 C.A.L. Brownlow, *The Breaking Storm*, p.105.

that was normally provided by family. Whilst the average soldier did not glory in war, if loftier motives had faded, a very local sense of purpose was maintained, bolstering self-esteem. Tommy Atkins fought for those about him because they continued to fight, just as his pre-war loyalties had been very local. Coping, however, was not a once and for all time matter. Moods fluctuated. Bruce Bairnsfather wrote that: 'One's mental outlook, I find, varies very much from day to day'. Some days he felt 'quite merry and bright', and at other times 'thoroughly depressed and weary'.[272] The sheer length of the war and the grinding repetitive threat and deprivation drove some to the brink, a brink from whose environs most, however, were able to return.

Eric Leed, as we have seen, presents us with an image of the alienation of the First World War soldier caused by the radical discontinuity of the disparate worlds of soldier and civilian, and the dehumanising effects of *materialschlacht*, industrial warfare.[273] J.G. Fuller gives us an alternative view. The war carried over from civilian life 'many institutions and attitudes which helped them to adjust to, and to humanize, the new world in which they found themselves'.[274] The popular, press-born image of the absurdly cheerful Tommy was a caricature, but the working class British soldier had learned from long experience that it was better to concentrate on pleasures rather than on hardships. He had absorbed this lesson in peacetime and took it to war, a lesson which enabled him to use jokes and social activity 'to render tolerable the worst of conditions'.[275]

To those familiar with J.R.R. Tolkien's *Lord of the Rings*, the Great War imagery is unmistakable. Tolkien, commissioned into the 13th Lancashire Fusiliers acknowledged that the nightmare landscape of Mordor had its origin in his experience of the Somme battlefield. But it is one particular character who expresses the nature of the British Tommy as Tolkien perceived it. This is Sam Gamgee, Frodo Baggins' trusted manservant on his increasingly purgatorial journey across Mordor to Mount Doom and victory over evil. Tolkien stated that he was a 'portrait of the English soldier, of the private and batman I knew in the 1914 war and recognized as so superior to myself'.[276] The image is of a man of courage, endurance and steadfastness, whose limited vision only strengthened his loyalty. Romantic vision this may be, parody it is not.

---

272 B. Bairnsfather, *Bullets and Billets*, p.219.
273 E.J. Leed, *No Man's Land*.
274 Fuller, op. cit. p.175.
275 Fuller, op. cit. p.180.
276 H. Carpenter, *J.R.R. Tolkien: A Biography*, p.89.

# 2

## 'I Will be Glad When I Can See Your Dear Face Again' – Family and Home

In June 1915, a certain Mrs Philip Snowden reported the comments of a British officer concerning the most painful aspect of the battlefield to the Women's Peace Congress in San Francisco. 'It is not the shrieks of the wounded as they fall,' he allegedly told her. Rather, it was the fact that 'they may say, "mother" … in their agony all those boys call for the one who has given them the greatest care all their lives'.[1] The truth of this is not to be doubted. Seaman Joe Murray described the shooting of a fellow ranker, 'young Horton', at the Second Battle of Krithia in May 1915: 'Poor Horton, he kept crying for his mother'. The normally phlegmatic Murray added, 'I can hear him now'.[2] Private Harry Patch, celebrated as the 'Last Fighting Tommy', described a similar occurrence on the Pilckem Ridge on 31 July 1917. In his case, the dying soldier 'just said one word: "Mother" … I shall always remember that cry'.[3] The notion of soldiers calling for their mothers *in extremis* speaks volumes to the importance of the nurturing family in the soldier's mind.

The 'primary' group that is the family of origin, crucial in the development of personal identity, is the first such group a person experiences. When as adults we create our own families with a partner and, very likely, children, our primary group expands. Identity develops further as we now become carer as well as cared for. These groups are the main places where Maslow's third level need for love and belonging is met. A soldier's family was both a source of support and a source of loss. Loved ones were a comfort in the midst of war through both memory and contact, maintained through letter-writing. Combatants held out the hope of being re-united both finally and in occasional leave. Private Hugh Quigley wrote of the sustaining power of thinking of family: 'Every man exulted in the hope of seeing loved ones again'.[4] Men were thus enabled to look beyond the bleakness immediately in front of them.

---

1   *The New York Times*, 27 June 1915.
2   J. Murray, quoted in M. Arthur, *Forgotten Voices of the First World War*, p.117.
3   http://www.bbc.co.uk/history/worldwars/wwone/last_tommy_gallery_03.shtml.
4   H. Quigley, *Passchendaele and the Somme*, p.3.

Captain Alfred Pollard's favourite letters were those of a nurse who had begun to write to him. These letters gave him 'hope', enabling him to fantasise a future beyond the conflict's end.[5] The relationship came to nothing, but for a period Pollard was able to nourish himself with such thoughts. Walter Ludwig's study of wounded German soldiers found that 'memories of home' were spontaneously listed as the second most popular coping strategy when under significant stress, utilised by a third of soldiers.[6] Rifleman Aubrey Smith in a desperate and helpless state in action at St Julien in May 1915 fortified himself by re-reading his last letters from home, finding them 'full of courage and hope'.[7] Michael Roper suggests on the basis of several soldiers who variously directed their thoughts in difficult and threatening moments to home scenes such as the garden in the family home, or having tea accompanied by a sibling's antics, that: 'The more stressful the situation, the greater was the urge to construct home as a haven'.[8] Thoughts that connected the soldier to his primary group were therefore powerfully sustaining. On the other hand, there was a potential sense of loss. Firstly, there was the enforced separation from loved ones themselves. Secondly, the volunteer or conscript had been displaced from his various roles within the family – son, husband, father, the ever-present protector and provider that the image of domestic manliness demanded. There were therefore loss-related stresses of both relationships and previous identities, stresses that had to be endured in their own right on top of those of war itself.

### *Letters from home*

The Army Post Office was one of the organisational triumphs of the war, 12.5 million letters being sent weekly over its course.[9] Letters from home were a major boost to morale. Lieutenant Ronald Poulton stated: 'It is THE great thing to get the mail in the evening in the trenches'.[10] Lieutenant-Colonel William Malone was emphatic that 'it is the one thing above all that we want, our mail'.[11] Second-Lieutenant Graham Greenwell, on the Somme in 1916, wrote home how 'your letters continue to arrive regularly … which cheers me up tremendously'.[12] Private Henry Clapham described such letters as 'the only connecting thread' to civilisation.[13] Private Eric Marchant use the same words, the value of letters being not 'so much the news', but 'just the connection with home'.[14] Their absence was keenly felt. When his unit was transferred

---

5   A.O. Pollard, *Fire-Eater*, p.49.
6   W. Ludwig, cited in A. Watson, *Enduring the Great War*, pp.236-7.
7   A Rifleman, *Four Years on the Western Front*, p.51.
8   M. Roper, *The Secret Battle*, pp.70-2.
9   P.B. Boyden, *Tommy Atkins' Letters*, p.5.
10  E.B. Poulton, *The Life of Ronald Poulton*, p.357.
11  J. Crawford, *No Better Death*, Kindle edition location 3531.
12  G.H. Greenwell, *An Infant in Arms*, p.159.
13  H.S. Clapham, *Mud and Khaki*, p.89.
14  E.L. Marchant, Private Papers, IWM Docs 12054.

to Italy in 1917 Private Arthur Lambert felt as if he was 'cut off like the dead' as no mail arrived for weeks, 'the longing for home' thus being intensified.[15] Similarly, in early 1918 Corporal Geoffrey Husbands experienced 'some depression' due to a 'famine' of letters from home.[16] Gunner Cecil Longley's view was that: 'One naturally gets very fed up at times, and then in comes the post with the best tonic in the world'.[17] He described how letters could transport the reader away from the realities of war amidst which they were read. Avidly consuming one selection of letters about a trip through the English countryside, he demonstrated the power of positive mental imagery. Directing his gaze away from the evidence of war about him, he lay on the ground looking at the sky and 'imagined I had just got off my bike by Kenilworth Castle'. Others used letters to conjure up comforting images of loved ones. Lieutenant Patrick Campbell described himself on one morning in 1917 as 'as happy as I had ever been'. His night's work with his battery was behind him, and he was thinking of his home, 'which letters brought so clearly before me'. He mentally made contact with those he loved: 'I could picture them – my father, my mother, and my sister'.[18] Such imagery was not just visual. Second-Lieutenant Hedley Payne actually experienced the sensation of 'hearing dad's voice again', when reading his letters.[19] One hundred years ago simple words from loved ones on paper were powerful enough to provide distraction and transportation away from the immediacy of war. No wonder letters were read and re-read many times.

A 'linking object' is an item which has a particular connection with another person which channels intense thoughts and emotions.[20] William Malone expounded the importance of the photograph that the letter from home might enclose, writing to his wife from Gallipoli in May 1915, sitting in his shelter in the rain, that the 'longing to be with you again or at least to see you is ... endurable' because of having received 'those beautiful photographs of your dear, sweet and lovely self'. The photo became a channel for his love: 'I sit and lie and gaze and gaze and devour you'. He even helpfully set out the psychological process: 'The coming to me of the photo completes the connection and almost renders it physical'.[21] Second-Lieutenant Roland Leighton disclosed to Vera Brittain how her picture became a momentary physical substitute. 'I have just been kissing your photograph', he declared without embarrassment.[22] Major Reggie Trench had a different linking object to his wife Clare. She had sent him one of her scarves after he had been away for three months. He slept in it every night,

---

15   A. Lambert, *Over the Top*, p.103.
16   G.R. Husbands, *Joffrey's War*, p.522.
17   C.W. Longley, *Battery Flashes*, p.68.
18   P.J. Campbell, *In The Cannon's Mouth*, pp.42-3.
19   H.S. Payne, Private Papers, IWM Docs 196.
20   P.E. Hodgkinson & M. Stewart, *Coping with Catastrophe*, p.193.
21   Crawford, op. cit. location 3531.
22   A. Bishop & M. Bostridge (eds), *Letters from a Lost Generation*, p.80.

winding it round his head, the scarf creating a sense of her presence in bed with him.[23] *In extremis* the memory of a loved one might be the last thought a fatally wounded soldier might enjoy. Sergeant Jack Dorgan described two of his men having their legs blown off at Second Ypres. One, Private Bob Young, remained conscious until the last and asked Dorgan to get his wife's photograph from his breast pocket. 'He couldn't move, he couldn't lift a hand, he couldn't lift a finger, but he somehow held his wife's photograph on his chest'.[24] In his mind, therefore, he did not die alone, separate from the ones he loved.

Letters could also contain bad news. Lieutenant Robert Graves noted that such news in a missive from home might have two possible effects. Firstly, it might seem trivial in comparison with the reality facing the soldier and be shrugged off. Secondly, it might drive the individual to 'suicide (or recklessness amounting to suicide)'.[25] Sometimes letters could generate distress rather than comfort because they were simply too dissonant with the reader's surroundings. On the Aisne in September 1914, Sergeant John Lucy described the arrival of post. Some letters were 'read in misery', their readers 'at a loss to reconcile fond messages, warm and homely, with the bitter conditions' that surrounded them.[26]

Similarly, parcels were sent to the trenches, often in response to specific requests. The Army Post Office handled 60,000 each day, and 4.5 million at Christmas 1916.[27] When Henry Clapham went out of the line in March 1915: 'Thirty bags of parcels were waiting for the battalion, so we lived on the fat of the land'. His own section dined gloriously on 'tongue, pork pie, cake, pineapple, pears, peaches, white wine and Kümmel' as a result.[28] Cecil Longley informed his family that the most useful things to receive were 'papers, writing paper and envelopes, and chocolate and cigarettes[29]. Officers often requested a more exotic range of goods, a matter which reflected both their backgrounds and their financial circumstances. Second-Lieutenant Wilbert Spencer in 19 letters from the front line asked for a camera, a cardigan waistcoat, pyjamas, gum boots, cigarettes, cocoa, soup tabloids, Oxo cubes, condensed milk, a tobacco pouch, a method of making lemonade, and toilet paper; and recorded receiving a Christmas tree and pudding, chocolate, cigarettes, tobacco, mittens, a scarf, medicines, and a Sam Browne belt.[30] Second-Lieutenant Billie Nevill was so inundated by goods that he had to ask that nothing more be sent ('except the Nestle's

23  A. Fletcher, *Life, Death and Growing Up on the Western Front*, p.78.
24  J. Dorgan, quoted in Arthur, op. cit. p.82.
25  R. Graves, *Goodbye to All That*, p.112.
26  J.F. Lucy, *There's a Devil in the Drum*, p.192.
27  D. Winter, *Death's Men*, p.164.
28  Clapham, op. cit. p.77.
29  Longley, op. cit. p.69.
30  M. Tanner (ed.), *War Letters 1914-1918, Volume 1, Wilbert Spencer*, Kindle edition location 280. A Sam Browne belt is a wide belt, usually leather, which is supported by a narrower strap passing diagonally over the right shoulder.

milk & the cigars') until he specifically asked.[31] Lieutenant-Colonel Robert Hermon requested in May 1915 that his wife: 'Arrange with Harrods, or someone like that, to send us a £1 box of stores every week'. Other officers received hampers from the competitor Fortnum & Mason. Hermon's wants were specific: 'Potted meats; soup, sweets, peppermint, Mackintosh's toffee de luxe. The jam is essential & must come without fail'.[32] Perhaps his most inventive request was for two lacrosse bats to catch and return German bombs.[33] Officers often requested either clothing or military equipment, reflecting the patchy supply at certain times, particularly earlier in the war, and the Army & Navy Store no doubt did a roaring trade.

Letters from home contained news and messages of affection which went some way to sustaining the soldier's need for love and belonging. Parcels were a particularly tangible link. Whatever the recipients' backgrounds, and whatever the exotic or basic nature of their requests, wives and mothers at home were able through their parcels to maintain a direct sense of caring for their loved ones. They could feel that they were contributing to their nourishment and safety. Similarly, those at the front were able to feel practically cared for. It was an approximation to former transactions of love absent from their present.

### *Writing home*

We take writing for granted in our well-educated age, and the autobiographical literature of the Great War is studded with collections of officers' letters. Their content ranges between the everyday and the philosophical, but always reflects their education. Rankers' modest letters possessed the limitations imposed by their schooling. The Education Act of 1880 had made education for all aged 5-13 compulsory; and of the six Standards of Education contained in the Revised Code of Regulations (1872), inspectors required schools to achieve between standards four and six, which in terms of writing at standard (iv) meant 'A sentence slowly dictated once, by a few words at a time'; and at standard (v) a 'short ordinary paragraph in a newspaper … slowly dictated once by a few words at a time'. It was only by achieving standard (vi), writing 'A short theme or letter', that a pupil was truly equipped to write their own thoughts of their own volition, and many children schooled in the late Victorian era did not complete all the grades.[34] Michael Roper notes that 'many rankers had probably never even written a letter to a parent before joining the Army'.[35] Indeed, in terms of coping with family separation in World War Two, it has been suggested that even at that point 'letter writing was a flawed and unfamiliar means of communication'.[36]

---

31 R.E. Harris, *Billie – The Nevill Letters: 1914-1916*, p.34.
32 A. Nasson (ed.), *For Love and Courage*, p.15.
33 Nasson, op. cit. p.51.
34 http://www.victorianschool.co.uk/school%20history%20lessons.html.
35 Roper, op. cit. p.55.
36 G. Field, 'Perspectives on the Working-Class Family in Wartime Britain, 1939-1945', *International Labor and Working-Class History*, p.3.

Writing home served a multiplicity of purposes. At a practical level, as Private Henry Russell noted, it was a way of passing spare time. It was thus a distraction, the act being pleasing in itself. He described how immediately after a parade, some would sit and 'write voluminous letters, and seemed to enjoy doing so'.[37] At a psychological level, in contrast to being the hopeful but passive recipient of a letter, it was an active way of reducing isolation from the familiar, momentarily creating the desired sense of belonging. It was also, as we shall see, a way of maintaining the masculine identity of father, husband or son. Lastly, most historians now largely rejecting Eric Leed's 'alienation' hypothesis, contact with family kept the soldier, adrift in the midst of brutality, in touch with the place where his moral compass had been calibrated.

Letters created some possibility of maintaining the identities soldiers had been forced to abdicate. Major Reggie Trench wrote to both his mother and wife. To his mother, 'he was factual and unemotional, like the little boy he had been'; to his wife, 'he was a lover … creating an intimate conversation'.[38] Advising a wife on the daily issues of the home world, the soldier was able to maintain the masculine identity of husband and father, protector and provider. Robert Hermon, preserving the role of father, wrote on 12 December 1915: 'I am enclosing you 30/- to buy the Chugs some small things from Dad for Xmas'.[39] Concerns about health, money and children were frequent topics.

Letter writing has two aspects – to whom and about what. Second-Lieutenant Douglas Gillespie noted that his men wrote as often as they could – 'they do write and write' – and that they did not write to their fathers very often, 'but to mothers and sisters a great deal'.[40] Captain Geoffrey Pollard rather dismissively described the men of his company writing 'mostly rot' in their letters, 'or else a repetition of a few remarks which they could quite easily put on a postcard'. In this he missed the point. It was the act of communicating, not necessarily what was communicated which was the issue. He added somewhat grudgingly: 'But it certainly makes them happy, which is the great thing'.[41] Captain Gerald Burgoyne was another officer dismissive of the content of his rankers' writings, regarding them as 'too illiterate'. They rarely wrote of life at the front, in fact 'from 90% of the letters you would never discover the men were on active service'. The contents of their letters were 'confined to remarks on their own health; questions as to the welfare of those at home, and prayers, so very often, prayers to God to take care of those they have left behind'.[42] Hugh Quigley, when commissioned, described some letters as a 'mere formality, not too careful about facts, and always insisting on the top note'.[43] A transport officer at the front in February 1915

---

37  H. Russell, *Slaves of the War Lords*, p.92.
38  Fletcher, op. cit. p.78.
39  Nasson, op. cit. pp.143-4.
40  A.D. Gillespie, *Letters from Flanders*, p.37.
41  G. Pollard, quoted in L. Housman, *War Letters of Fallen Englishmen*, p.219.
42  C. Davison, *The Burgoyne Diaries*, pp.40-41.
43  Quigley, op. cit. p.104.

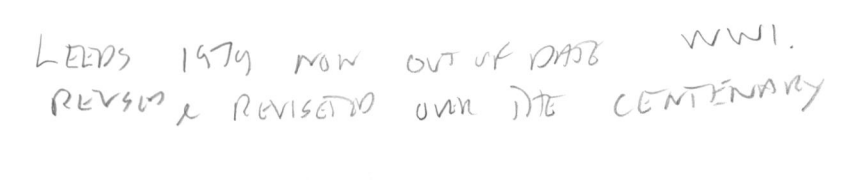

noted: 'Nearly all the letters make you like the writer', their content largely involving 'conjugal affection, and the weather'.[44]

Letters brought loved ones into the 'war world' in a safe way. But to what extent was the *real* 'war world' communicated to them? Two views exist about what was conveyed. John Ellis states that there was 'an enormous disparity between what men were going through and what they were able, or willing, to communicate'.[45] Anthony Fletcher describes the soldier as 'walking a tightrope' between providing 'honest matter-of-fact accounts of performance' yet at the same time 'making light of the worst aspects of trench warfare'.[46] Jessica Meyer maintains that one of the main topics of letters from the front was reassurance that the writer was safe, and hence would return. This involved the deployment of white lies. Captain Edward Chapman wrote home of the physical conditions, notably the cold, but described his layers of clothing and concluded: 'I am probably warmer in the trenches than you are at home'.[47] Private Alec Reader wrote home, palpably untruthfully: 'It sounds silly I know but it is a fact that out here I am as safe as you are at home'.[48] Second-Lieutenant Gerald Garvin gave repeated reassurances of his safety. After a month on the Western Front in August 1915 he described from trenches in the Festubert-Givenchy sector how: 'These trenches expose one to hardly a vestige of risk';[49] and a week later, 'Danger exists hardly to vex one'.[50] The following month he offered the consolation that he was 'perfectly secure' on a working party,[51] and any shells were only 'light noisy harmless ones'.[52]

Lieutenant Paul Jones wrote to his brother in April 1917: 'Don't let the Mater and Pater get the wind up about my personal safety', adding: 'At present I am quite safe; besides, I have wonderful luck'.[53] He was conscious that: 'If I write fully, you may perhaps get the "wind up" about my personal safety'.[54] He was very near to falling off the tightrope. Whilst on one hand offering reassurance that he was safe, he took it away with the other by indicating that he was withholding things that might undermine it. Private Walter Williamson gave the opinion after four months on the Western Front in March 1917 that: 'Talking of the real war, I really don't think it can last long'. This is an oft-repeated theme in letters which has been described by Alex Watson as self-deception.[55] With the idea of a conclusion to hostilities soldiers

---

44 *Yorkshire Evening Post*, 8 February 1915.
45 J. Ellis, *Eye Deep in Hell*, p.139.
46 Fletcher, op. cit. p.89.
47 E.F. Chapman, Private Papers, IWM Docs 1799.
48 B.A. Reader, Private Papers, IWM Docs 4127.
49 M. Pottle & J.G.G. Ledingham, *We Hope to Get Word Tomorrow*, p.49.
50 Pottle & Ledingham, op. cit. p.53.
51 Pottle & Ledingham, op. cit. p.61.
52 Pottle & Ledingham, op. cit. p.66.
53 P. Jones, *War Letters of a Public Schoolboy*, p.241.
54 Jones, op. cit. p.245.
55 A. Watson, 'Self-deception and Survival', *Journal of Contemporary History*, p.247.

may have been heartening themselves by thinking that their chances of survival were improved. Whether Williamson was deceiving himself or simply reassuring those at home is difficult to tell, and his statement: 'Our front line now always feels quite safe',[56] does not help us decide. Whilst there were indeed quiet sectors, the front-line was clearly not a safe place. Major James Jack was selective about whom he reassured about what, describing how he treated his eighty year-old spinster aunt with particular kid gloves, writing as if he 'were always in safety in the rear areas'.[57]

Other observers emphasise that many were prepared to bring aspects of the 'war world' crashing into the 'home world' by sending accounts of discomfort, bloodshed and death. Walter Williamson, the same man who gave dubious assurances about his safety, reported to his wife: 'It is cold, no fire and little light. I have started chilblains now on nearly all my fingers'.[58] Given that life at home for the working classes often included discomfort, freedom with such observations is hardly surprising. Captain Edward Hulse, less familiar with such inconveniences, described to his mother in September 1914 that he had had 'bad dysentery for two days' and the weather was 'pouring rain and cold'. In November 1914 he similarly reported from the snowy front-line that he was standing in 'a freezing cold slush of mud' unable to change socks or boots and that the worst part was 'the cold in one's feet at night'.[59] During the period December 1914 to March 1915, when he was killed, Wilbert Spencer mentioned the appalling weather conditions in the trenches in seven out of 19 letters, writing in January 1915: 'This last time in the trenches was awful … we were flooded out'.[60]

Anthony Fletcher found that: 'Letters home … contain far more material about the deaths of colleagues, their injuries and broken comradeship than about mud or the horrific physical aspects of trench service'.[61] Geoffrey Husbands was quite happy to write home about the grim realities of war, expressing irritation that his officer had censored his letters home from the La Bassée front which made reference to corpses in no-man's land. He could not understand the mindset that sought to hide the fact that in war there would be dead bodies.[62] Helen McCartney similarly notes in her study of the Liverpool Territorials that the nature and circumstances of death in the trenches were frequently detailed.[63] On his first tour of the front line, Wilbert Spencer wrote just before Christmas 1914: 'I wonder how many people realise what hell the trenches can be'.[64] On the occasion of his first shelling he described that one man had been killed and four wounded and that: 'The fellow who was killed lived his last few

---

56 D. Priddey, *A Tommy at Ypres*, Kindle edition location 1466.
57 J. Terraine (ed.), *General Jack's Diary*, p.136.
58 Priddey, op. cit. location 6154.
59 E.H.W. Hulse, *Letters*, p.33.
60 Tanner, op. cit. location 283.
61 Fletcher, op. cit. p.168.
62 Husbands, op. cit. p.204.
63 H.B. McCartney, *Citizen Soldiers*, p.91.
64 Tanner, op. cit. location 218.

minutes with his head on my knee'.[65] When he continued: 'You must try not to worry so much'[66] – a standard platitude perhaps – it is difficult to think that he was unaware that he was giving his parents plenty of material to worry about. Similarly, Second-Lieutenant Billie Nevill told his family that they had 'been so good about not getting nervous about me', and followed this with a description of the blowing of a mine very close to him, and the recovery of buried miners.[67] Thus, letters home were full of the contradictions created by wobbles on the tightrope.

The degree of sanitisation in letters was likely related to the perceived robustness of the reader at home. Michael Roper notes that soldiers were more likely to describe violent events to fathers than to mothers.[68] When Roland Leighton first described finding the body of a dead British soldier in a letter to Vera Brittain, he asked: 'You do not mind my telling you these gruesome things do you?' He reminded her firstly that: 'You asked me to tell you everything', and secondly of the simple reality that 'It is of such things that my new life is made'.[69] Paul Jones wrote home from the Somme: 'I dare not tell you of the ghastly scenes on that historic battlefield; it would give you nightmare for weeks to come if I did'.[70] He thus spoke volumes. Gerald Garvin, so careful to make clear his safety to his parents, described the effectiveness of snipers in a short letter: 'One got my servant this morning with a bullet through the mouth and cheek that narrowly missed killing him'.[71] It had obviously made an impact on him, but he perhaps forgot that his parents might assume his servant was always next to him and his own head had therefore had a very near miss. Private Alec Reader wrote home from the Somme in 1916 describing the wounded and the dead and carrying a mortally wounded man to a dressing station, concluding: 'It was awful'. Realising that he had psychologically leaked, he wrote a few days later: 'Don't take any notice as we all have our rotten moments'.[72] Raymond Lodge grumbled in his letters home, but similarly wrote that 'you mustn't pay any attention to (this) ... it just depends what I feel like'.[73]

Given the mounting casualties reported in the newspapers, it might be thought that any reassurance attempted in letters was only temporary and possibly completely spurious. Indeed, soldiers' letters were forwarded to the local papers for publication, containing details that were far from uplifting. Private W. Davies of the Liverpool Scottish wrote home in April 1915: 'Right facing me was a pair of German's legs sticking out of the earth. I am not exaggerating when I tell you I had to sleep on a body

65  Tanner, op. cit. location 291.
66  Tanner, op. cit. location 275.
67  Harris, op. cit. pp.112-3.
68  Roper, op. cit. p.61.
69  Bishop & Bostridge, op. cit. p.87.
70  Jones, op. cit. p.239.
71  Pottle & Ledingham, op. cit. p.66.
72  Reader, op. cit.
73  O.J. Lodge, *Raymond*, p.44.

covered in about six inches of earth'. His letter was published in the *Liverpool Daily Post*.[74] Similarly, the letter of Lance-Corporal John Molloy of the South Staffordshire regiment appeared in the Wolverhampton *Express and Star*:

> My nerves received a bad shaking the other day. We were just having tea when the Germans started shelling our trenches. After a bit a chap said the Germans were not going to stop him having his tea. The next I heard was the call for stretcher-bearers. The nose of a shell had caught him in the chest. I shall never forget my first experience of shell fire.[75]

Corporal Charles Rushworth's letter to his parents about being in action on 18 April 1915 – 'We have been in Hell for sixteen hours' – was graphic. 'It was a terrible slaughter on top of the hill. Their shrapnel shells were bursting overhead, and men were falling dead at your side'. He concluded: 'We fought like demons; we had lost our minds completely for a time'. His letter was published in the *Yorkshire Evening Post* ten days later,[76] no doubt meant as a stirring tale of bravery, but conveying information that was clearly disturbing. Not only were men writing home about traumatic experiences, these were being made very public. There were other places for public dissemination about the trench experience. The Liverpool Territorials also revealed much 'at their various social and sporting clubs' when on leave.[77] Helen McCartney is of the clear view that: 'Despite the undoubted prevalence of self-censorship, the majority of families … understood the progress of the war from the soldier's point of view'.[78] This view is certainly correct, and Martha Hanna presents evidence from French soldiers to suggest that 'honesty, many wives insisted, was better than dissimulation'.[79]

It is Roland Leighton's statement – 'it is of such things that my new life is made' – that brings us to the reality of the situation. The soldier's 'war world', his everyday experience, often contained profound discomfort and risk. The image of domestic manliness required a man to protect his family in the 'home world', but the reality was that he largely now could not, at any level. The soldier, through his letters, dealt with this dissonance by maintaining his role of carer in the written word as best he could. But in terms of receiving care and support, he was faced with a dilemma. Was the soldier to sustain himself with an image of family and home based on the past, or was he to sustain himself in relationships based on a shared understanding of the reality of the present? It is clear that many chose not to hide the dangerous reality of their 'new lives' from their nearest and dearest. The motivations of those who rejected

---

74 *Liverpool Daily Post*, 5 April 1915.
75 *Express and Star*, 16 April 1915.
76 *Yorkshire Evening Post*, 28 April 1915.
77 McCartney, op. cit. p.101.
78 McCartney, op. cit. p.95.
79 M. Hanna, 'The Couple', in J. Winter (ed.), *The Cambridge History of the First World War*, Vol 3, p.14.

hiding reality no doubt varied, but important reasons will have included the emotional processing that was achieved, the relief of risk shared, and a potential increased sense of bonding. A significant proportion had it both ways, both hiding and revealing. And, of course, those at home would have dipped in and out of the recognition of what they knew of the reality of the war, mentally avoiding at some points and not at others.

*A correspondence explored – Private Frederick Whitham*
To examine these issues further, it is interesting to analyse the detailed content of a set of letters home. Those chosen are the correspondence of Private Frederick Whitham, Yorkshire Regiment, who died during the battle of Loos, on 26 September 1915, aged 32.[80] A married man with four children, Emma (b.1908), Frederick (b.1911), Doris (b.1913), and Sarah Ann (b. 1915), he was working as a shell turner for Vickers Ltd in Sheffield at the outbreak of war. He would never have needed to write to his parents, living in the same street as them when married – Solly Street, Netherthorpe.

Thirty-six letters remain from Fred to Emma, 31 from the Gohelle battlefields. The level of his educational achievement is difficult to gauge. He used little punctuation, erratic capitalisation, unique spellings, and missed words out. He always used the formal opening lines in writing to the world he had left behind: 'I write these few lines to you hoping to find you all in good health as it leaves me at present'; otherwise, he no doubt wrote as he spoke. The topics can be categorised under the headings of 'home' and 'war' worlds. Of the 'home world', there were eight main topics. The five most prolific, in order of importance, were his children, his wife's mood, absence and mechanisms of communications, and photographs. Of the fourteen 'war world' topics, the six most prolific, again in order of importance, were: smoking, money, leave, wounding, goods that he needed/received, and mortality and trauma.

It is no surprise that the most frequently mentioned of the 'home world' topics were his children. He was able to try to maintain the identity of father, for instance, by trying to help in the direction of care for his children: 'Whatever you do look after our Freddie's health and don't forget to take him to the hospital and see what they have to say about him'. In terms of his girls, he mentioned their dolls, hair, and outings. It was of his son Freddie ('Tich') that he wrote most wistfully: 'I would like to see him because I have often pictured him in my mind when I have been running after him', a statement which indicates how he visually constructed in his mind the world he had left behind. A quarter of these references refer to his boy's manliness. In January 1915, for instance, he wrote: 'Tell our Fred he will have to go in training because I am and I will give it to him on the nose'. Four months later he noted approvingly of a photo he had received: 'Our tich has a look on him as if he was going to bust someone'. In June 1915 he revealed the reason for his encouragement of his son's manliness: 'Tell our

---

80  P.E. Hodgkinson, N. Oatham & A. Caisley, 'Identity and Separation – The Letters of Private Frederick Whitham', *Stand To!* p.7.

tich … he does right to claim my chair. When you see him in the chair think that it is me and then you will not get downhearted'. He hoped a strong male presence would give reassurance in his absence.

Photos were an important link as William Malone made clear, and a sense of loss and longing erupts when Fred refers to them. Emma sent him one of her and the children eleven days before he went on active service. He clearly looked at these pictures often, noting in June 1915: 'With pulling your photo out of my pocket it is getting worn out but I have got a case for it'. Yet there were times when the reminder of what was left behind could be too much. On 9 May, a week before the Battle of Festubert, he recorded: 'I pulled out your photo and the children's and I was studying it … you look close'. He continued: 'Memories come to my mind what me and you had gone through. I had to put the photo away because it began to hurt me'. The sense of proximity in the circumstances he was in was too much to bear. In his last letter written six days before his death he wrote of Emma's image: 'I will be glad when I can see your Dear Face again'. The photograph of the new baby in particular brought him much joy: 'You want to know what I think about the child that I have not seen, well she is a little beauty isn't she? And I have put it at the side of your photo and (the) children's. I could not take my eyes of (sic) it last night'. For a moment he could think of being a father, not a soldier.

Keeping up Emma's spirits was the second most prolific topic, and a demonstration of his attempts to maintain the identity of protective husband. He wrote just prior to going to France: 'Don't for God's sake get downhearted lass, will you, and then I shall be better satisfied, lass, and I know that I can go away with a good heart'. It was a topic he returned to repeatedly, his reassurances likely directed at Emma's anxieties expressed in her letters. He offered the ubiquitous encouragement in April 1915: 'You don't want to get downhearted, just think of your children lass, this war cannot last much longer'. He always took care to console her that he was out of the trenches.

But it was often everyday matters that filled the pages. References to not having received letters or promised parcels abound, reflecting their importance as the only means of maintaining the reciprocal nature of their relationship. There are detailed descriptions of the mechanisms of communication – how to address a letter, how to tie a parcel, or why things might be delayed. It was, of course, practicalities that filled everyday life for his family at home. Attempting to maintain the identity of father and husband, Fred was concerned that his family should manage in his absence. He wrote before going to France: 'I have made allowance for you, the amount is 1/- per day lass, so you should receive more money now'. Prior to the birth of Sarah-Anne he advised: 'You want to send the birth certificate of the child to York as soon as possible and then they will put the extra money on your allowance and it will make it better for you'.

Fred's wounding in March 1915 left him particularly emotionally expressive, writing a month later: 'You do not know how much I think of you. They often said that absent (sic) makes the heart grow fonder and it is a true saying too lass. You really cannot imagine what my thoughts are of you'. Six months on, Fred may have worried that absence made Emma's fondness for him less, as he wrote in his last letter before his death:

> Did you read that case about a soldier coming home from the front on leave and finding his wife out carrying on with other men? And his child … He killed his child put it out of its misery. Lass, just fancy a man staring death in the face and coming home on a short leave and thinking what a pleasure it will be to his wife and child and then find when he gets home that his wife is false. I pity that man.

Why Fred should have expressed this so pointedly at this juncture is not clear; he may simply have been expressing fears born out of not having seen his wife for nearly a year. Sadly for his wife Emma, who did not remarry until 1929, these were virtually the last thoughts he expressed.

Many of his 'war world' preoccupations were also of an everyday nature. Tobacco and money (the two often related) were the most prolific topics. In the UK in early November 1914 he noted: 'At this time of night I have not a cig end and if you ask anybody up here they nearly jump down you(r) throat. At the time of writing this letter I have not a cent on me and can't borrow a 1d nowhere'. He was clear about the purpose of smoking, noting it was: 'My only comfort up here … it easy (sic) my mind. I don't get downhearted when I am smoking'. The arrival or non-arrival of promised cigarettes occupied many sentences of his letters. In addition, he recorded the arrival of newspapers, chocolate, 'sharing bread', and toffee, but asked not to be sent 'any more oxo because I cannot make them here', or 'any spice of any kind'. He asked for 'one of Turners 3/11d watches … because a watch is very handy out here'. The item proved less than handy as it unfortunately soon went 'rusty with the sweat from my body'. The traffic of goods was not entirely one-sided. Fred was eternally frustrated in being unable to provide Emma with a photo of himself in uniform, cost and opportunity being the issues. In early June he reassured her that: 'As soon as I come out of the trenches again I will see that you have a photo if I have to go all over France to have it took'. He was sadly unable to provide her with the means to help maintain an image of him. He bought her a crucifix as a keepsake but lost it, instead at the end of July 1915 sending her 'a button off my officer's coat and it is the very same as our badge. It will make you a very nice brooch'. Giving must have created a sense of connection, a thread held between their worlds.

Leave was Fred's third most frequent topic. He never achieved home leave in his 11 months of active service. From Flanders he began to write about the possibility of leave from the start of February, writing at the end of that month: 'I wished I had half a chance of been (sic) at home but it is no good grumbling is it?' In July he returned to the possibility, clearly in response to Emma's expressed hopes:

> Do not build your castle high lass, because God knows when I shall get a chance. It might be when all is over or when I get severely wounded, I don't know. I seem

to be one of the unlucky ones, but never mind. Buck up and don't get downhearted, everything will come right in time.

Fred was one of those soldiers who told his wife very little about trench life. During the bitterly cold winter of 1914-15, when 2nd Yorkshire were spending much of their time removing water from their lines, his sole comment in early January was: 'It is very cold out here, but the Officers see that we get plenty of clothing so we have nothing to grumble at'. He twice, however, wrote euphemistically and with rare flashes of humour about lice. On 11 January 1915 he noted: 'I have got a lot of company but it is on my back. They keep giving me a nip'. On 6 May he reported similar trouble: 'It is very hot out here, the sun is telling a tale on my face, and the gaspers are having a hurdle race over my back', describing his shirt as a 'blood shed battlefield'. He hardly complained at all about the work of being a soldier. Only once in April 1915, when recuperating at the Le Havre base, did he venture the comment: 'I am working from 6 a.m. till 6 p.m. and am tired when I have finished'. He remained largely positive, informing Emma in February 1915, for instance, that when out of the line: 'We can play at football to pass our time away', and noting the following month: 'I get plenty to eat and am as fat as a pig'. It is not difficult to speculate that he included so little detail in order that Emma did not dwell on what he was doing. In February 1915 he wrote about buying his daughter Emma a 'big doll', thus immersing himself momentarily in a world which was so far away, continuing: 'I am putting all this so that I will not bother you with what I have to do in the trenches'. Fred was openly stating that he was avoiding communicating the realities of his life. Perhaps his frequent reassurances to her and his silence on so many matters related to life in France reflect his perception of her as vulnerable. He continued in his role of protective husband.

Yet there were moments when he slipped out of avoidance. His first letter from the combat zone at Fleurbaix four days after arrival is a blurting of shock:

> I am now in the place where they are fighting. I could see the shell burst. Do not fret about me, I'm all right ... You should see the damage they have done here and see the frightened looks on the children faces. It is awful. You over there do not know what it is like, only them that is in it.

Fred was aware of his mortality, and occasionally could not help but refer to it. Before being posted abroad he stated: 'God good and I hope I shall return from the front'. Once in Flanders he wrote: 'I am not getting downhearted lass, but I always say my prayers when I go in the trenches ... but every time we go in there is some one get (sic) knocked over'. Two weeks later he asked Emma to send him 'a lucky horseshoe out because they all seem to be getting them', thus enabling her to feel she could protect him too. He could, however, be direct, even attempting to quantify the risk: 'It is 10 to 1 on a bullet hitting you'. At times he avoided the topic of mortality, at others he almost seemed to be preparing her for the possibility of loss, perhaps sharing the reality in order to master it himself.

Fred was wounded at the Battle of Neuve Chapelle, where he acted as a specialist bomber. As he wrote the following day:

> We had a set to on March 10th and ... I happened to be unlucky same as a good lot of our fellows was. I have seen a thing as I don't want to see again as long as I live. Two of my mates got hit but we daren't stop. We had to keep going. That was about dinnertime when they got hit and we keep going till dark when we got the order to dig ourselves in, but me and a good few round about did not get the chance because the Germans started sending shrapnel and I was hit with a piece.

Maintaining his pursuit of reassurance, he continued: 'You need not be alarmed at this bit of news'. He had been hit in the forehead by shrapnel. Sometime between 11 and 22 March, he was operated on and sent to No 1 Convalescent Depot, Le Havre. Clearly suffering from concussion he wrote 11 days later:

> The hit that I got has left me a bit funny in the head. I cannot describe the feeling to you because it is so funny. I am deaf in the left ear. The noise that I hear is like a steam engine going ... when I am walking about I am like a drunken man, I reel from one side to the other'.

Two weeks later he was still experiencing symptoms: 'My head is not right yet ... The wound that I received was just over the temple so you can guess what it will be like. I don't think that the Doctor has took the shrapnel'.

His first experience of combat left a lasting impression on him. He wrote on 2 April: 'It was awful the last lot I was in. I don't want another do like that I can assure you. It was hell while it lasted and I was in it for about 18 hours'. He seemed, however, to contain himself for Emma's sake thereafter. Even though his company was under heavy shellfire at the Battle of Festubert on 18 May he did not mention it in his letters. Soon after on 2 June, in protective husband mode, he informed Emma:

> I have made a will out in your favour, all of it, then if anything becomes of me. The reason that I have done this is because there was a (lad?) got killed and he had not made a will out and when his wife went for to claim she could not get it until she had sent to his sergeant so it will save a lot of trouble for you.

He added, hopefully: 'Trusting to God nothing happens'. Frederick Whitham was killed on 26 September 1915, the second day of the Battle of Loos. His body was not recovered or identified, and he is commemorated on the Loos Memorial. His letters remain as a testimony to managing separation; juggling the roles of soldier, husband and father; giving and receiving support; and keeping hope alive.

## Leave

Letters were of such importance because the need for love and belonging would rarely, at least for rankers, be fulfilled face-to-face. Captain G.B. Manwaring, writing home in 1917, gave the interesting description of most men as having 'a dual personality, a dream-life and a real one'.[81] He was undoubtedly referring to the 'home world', so distant, and the 'war world'. As we have seen from Frederick Whitham's letters, leave was a much discussed issue. Officers received more than the other ranks. Lieutenant-Colonel Robert Clarke, commanding 1/4th Royal Berkshire, had five periods of leave whilst CO between 23 March 1916 and 25 February 1918, totalling 120 days in all.[82] In contrast, Graham Greenwell had to deal with a letter from a soldier's wife, saying that she had not seen him for 14 months. Greenwell was forced to reply that 'there are many who haven't been home for sixteen and eighteen months!'[83] Indeed, in mid-1917 there were over 100,000 men on the Western Front who had not had home leave for eighteen months, and over 400,000 who had been so deprived for a year.[84] Private Harry Drinkwater was one of the latter. This prolonged absence pushed him to a peculiar place of separateness, for he described reaching a 'stage where home seemed to be a thing I once remembered'.[85]

Captain Robert Manion stated that leave was the 'be-all and end-all of anyone who has been at the front for any great time'.[86] Corporal William Andrews told of a comrade who walked nine miles to Bethune for a leave train, only to be told leave was cancelled: 'He had no words to express his disappointment. He was crushed'.[87] Lord Moran, who described how fatalism could lead to lack of care of one's safety, noted how a sense of self-protection could suddenly return with leave at hand.[88] Manion similarly observed that men about to go on leave would 'take no extra chances either with shells or superstitions'.[89] Private James Racine, anticipating the possibility of leave, was struck by 'the fear of possibly being hit whilst knowing that any day might see me on the way home'.[90] Private Arthur Wrench was told in December 1916 that he had been granted leave three days hence. He similarly developed a 'rotten nervous feeling … almost afraid I will never survive till then'.[91] William Andrews recorded that: 'We had a superstitious dread that we should be killed the night before we left'.[92]

---

81 G.B. Manwaring, *If We Return*, p.17.
82 P.E. Hodgkinson, *British Infantry Battalion Commanders in the First World War*, p.202.
83 Greenwell, op. cit. p.190.
84 C. Messenger, *Call to Arms*, p.441.
85 J. Cooksey & D. Griffiths, *Harry's War*, p.153.
86 R.J. Manion, *A Surgeon in Arms*, p.228.
87 W.L. Andrews, *Haunting Years*, p.81.
88 Lord Moran, *The Anatomy of Courage*, p.60.
89 Manion, op. cit. p.229.
90 J. Racine, 'Memoirs of the Great War', http://www.seaforthhighlanders.ca/museum/?p=540 p.70.
91 A. Wrench, Private Papers, IWM Docs 3834.
92 Andrews, op. cit. pp.81-2.

Understandably, little is written about leave. Soldiers had no need to write letters about it, and recorded very little in their diaries. Captain Douglas Bell simply wrote 'HAPPY DAYS!' in his diary covering a period of leave 7-11 April 1915.[93] Emmanuelle Cronier suggests that leave provided both soldiers and families with a 'horizon of expectation in the short term', something of positive normality to be immediately looked forward to, a prospect much more reassuring than any distant prospects for peace.[94] J.G. Fuller believed that 'for all its disorientations', leave held out the opportunity not only of seeing loved ones and an 'intense interval of pleasure', but also 'release from discipline'.[95] One soldier recorded: 'Every moment was one of joy and each of the 15 days was like a day in heaven'.[96] Cecil Longley, anticipating leave, wanted to 'get free and out of uniform for a day or two to be a gentleman once again!'[97] He contemplated 'six short days of bliss! Hooray!'[98] Geoffrey Husbands, released from hospital after receiving an arm wound on the Somme described 'ten days of civvy delights' with leave speeding by 'all too soon in a whirl of happiness'.[99] Similarly, Henry Russell described: 'Two glorious weeks ... how I revelled in the wonderful comfort of home life'.[100] Lieutenant John Reith found an 'extraordinary sense of safety and security' getting into bed at home, with his mother 'coming to tuck me up as of old'.[101] Second-Lieutenant Llewellyn Griffith took the view that in going on leave he had 'had triumphed over war for ten days'.[102] Conningsby Dawson wrote that his leave had passed 'with most tragic quickness', but added 'they'll be days to remember as long as life lasts'.[103] Leave offered him hope. He wrote of his 'respite' that there had 'been times when my whole past life has seemed a myth and the future an endless prospect of carrying on'. He could now 'distantly hope that the old days will return'.[104]

Leave was undoubtedly a sustaining vision and its reality was deeply enjoyed by most. John Lucy was one of the few rankers who did write about leave in his native Ireland in spring 1915, but he did not share other writers' euphoria. On the Western Front since August 1914, landing at Rosslare: 'I devoured every Irish field from there to Cork'. He was met with 'fervent welcomes', which left him 'dumb and emotionally upset'. He came back to a home from which his dead soldier-brother was now

93 D.H. Bell, *A Soldier's Diary of the Great War*, p.110 (capitals in original).
94 E. Cronier, 'Soldiers on Leave', http://podcasts.ox.ac.uk/series/first-world-war-new-perspectives.
95 J.G. Fuller, *Troop Morale and Popular Culture in the British and Dominion Armies 1914-1918*, p.73.
96 Anonymous, quoted in I.R. Bet-El, *Conscripts*, p.142.
97 Longley, op. cit. p.159.
98 Longley, op. cit. p.162.
99 Husbands, op. cit. p.369.
100 Russell, op. cit. p.246.
101 J. Reith, *Wearing Spurs*, p.132.
102 L.W. Griffith, *Up to Mametz*.
103 C. Dawson, *Carry On*, p.104.
104 Dawson, op. cit. p.109.

absent, and 'spoke with caution of the fighting, and withheld the horrors'. Whilst being home was 'heavenly', his stomach could not cope with rich home cooking, and he slept on the floor, unable to rest in a soft bed. He felt distant from friends, and 'fled them, and sought peace in the country'.[105] On leave again at the end of the year, the experience was sadly 'a nightmare'. He slept badly, dreaming of the dead. His voice 'trembled because my breathing was all wrong'. His family found him 'very strange', and became critical of his behaviour. A doctor was called and Lucy was diagnosed with 'neurasthenia'.[106] With rest, he slowly returned to his normal self.

There was thus an intense dissonance between the home and war worlds for some. The intensity of the war experience had welded a new and powerful identity across the Channel. Lieutenant Bruce Bairnsfather wrote of his first leave in 1915 that: 'I was anxious to get back. Strange but true'. He felt that 'slogging away out in the dismal fields of war was the real thing to do'.[107] Alfred Pollard 'enjoyed every minute' of leave in 1915, but 'was not sorry to be back'. He wanted to be with his unit and 'should have felt a shirker' otherwise.[108] Lieutenant Edward Stoneham felt when on leave that: 'I really belonged at the front' and was 'quite ready to get back'. He clearly felt a sense of isolation: 'My family didn't understand what was happening out there'.[109] His sense of belonging in France was echoed by others. William Fraser, commanding 1/6th Gordon Highlanders, was due leave in December 1917 but the responsibility for the battalion weighed heavily. He wrote home: 'I am looking forward to my leave, but even so, one half wants to stop with the battalion'.[110]

Cronier claims that leave was 'one of the best ways for soldiers to forget what they had to go through in the trenches'.[111] This is a proposition more difficult to sustain. Sent back to England in 1916 because it was discovered that he was underage when he had volunteered in 1914, Private Walter Williams found it 'claustraphobic' to sleep in his room rather than in a tent. He also experienced his mother and sister's 'constant attention irritating'. He found the encouragement to talk about the front in the local pub to be unwelcome 'when all I wanted to do was forget for a while what I had seen'.[112] He was unable to distract himself. Lieutenant Siegfried Sassoon when on leave perversely found that the 'only way to forget about the War was to be on the other side of the Channel'.[113]

For some, leave became more unsatisfactory particularly as the war progressed, and such individuals experienced it as disruptive of coping. Douglas Gillespie wrote after

---

105 Lucy, op. cit. pp.317-8.
106 Lucy, op. cit. pp.349-350.
107 B. Bairnsfather, *Bullets and Billets*, pp.184-5.
108 Pollard, op. cit. p.99.
109 E.W. Stoneham, quoted in Arthur, op. cit. p.200.
110 D. Fraser (ed.), *In Good Company*, p.195.
111 Cronier, op. cit.
112 M. Williams, *With Innocence and Hope*, Kindle edition locations 1977-1984.
113 S. Sassoon, *The Complete Memoirs of George Sherston*, p.270.

'I Will be Glad When I Can See Your Dear Face Again' – Family and Home   71

leave in August 1915: 'While the war lasts I would much rather be out here than at home, except for leave occasionally'.[114] Returning to the front, Raymond Lodge described himself as 'quite in the swing again after the unsettling effect of coming home'.[115] Second-Lieutenant Carlos Blacker managed to push away thoughts about his brother Robin who had been killed at Loos whilst in the trenches. On leave with his parents in Paris, however, 'personal memories would intrude' of when they were children together.[116] Being with loved ones disturbed the coping mechanisms which allowed thoughts to be kept at bay. For Conningsby Dawson, relishing his time with his wife, there was a danger of a different aspect of coping being undermined: 'I felt that I had slipped back to a lower plane; a kind of flabbiness was creeping into my blood – the old selfish fear of life and love of comfort'.[117] On leave in London, G.B. Manwaring felt an absence of purpose, doing familiar but now 'aimless, meaningless things'. Mortality hung heavy on him, wondering 'if I should ever do them again'.[118]

Cronier notes that soldiers often expressed a 'sense of disconnection'. There was often a mis-match of expectations between those at home and the temporarily returned soldier. Gerald Garvin's mother wrote to him in France about a fellow officer who was home on leave yet clearly suffering psychologically: 'What is really wrong with Stuart – can't you tell me?' Garvin replied cautiously: 'His people rouse him and drag him round on visits when he needs hours of sleep'.[119] There was also a discrepancy in conceptions of the war. William Andrews on his second leave in 1917 found himself 'increasingly awkward in society' listening to civilians propound their views on how the war should be won.[120] Second-Lieutenant Guy Chapman experienced this at the front during the Somme offensive, describing how 'I let my mind retreat further and further from thoughts of home. I could find nothing to say in letters'. England became alien in other ways, Chapman experiencing how in London on leave, 'I was as foreign as a Chinese'.[121] John Reith found that: 'London irritated me beyond expression; was this what one was fighting for: loafers, profiteers, the whole vulgar throng in the street?'[122] He experienced Glasgow as 'claustrophobic', redolent with 'war-unawareness', and wanted to return to action.[123] Arriving home and seated in his aunt's drawing room, James Racine found 'the extreme quietness ... uncanny and I felt as if I had been transported into another world'.[124] Lieutenant Harold Mellersh found that this sort of atmosphere at

114 Gillespie, op. cit. p.282.
115 Lodge, op. cit. p.56.
116 J. Blacker (ed.), *Have You Forgotten Yet?*, p.82.
117 Dawson, op. cit. p.112.
118 Manwaring, op. cit. p.134.
119 Pottle & Ledingham, op. cit. p.115.
120 Andrews, op. cit. p.259.
121 G. Chapman, *A Passionate Prodigality*, p.107.
122 Reith, op. cit. p.205.
123 Reith, op. cit. p.208.
124 Racine, op. cit. p.72.

home made him feel that 'I did not any longer fit in'.[125] Second-Lieutenant Bernard Martin found it disturbing that life was proceeding unchanged when he returned on leave. He thought: 'How could they understand the ever-changing quality of the life I'd been clinging on to for the last six months?' Whilst everyone referred to him as a hero, they only enjoyed this as an abstract concept, for 'they were not interested to hear talk about trench life'. His mother was the only person who asked some questions about his physical comfort. He brought back from his second leave seven months later 'a state of depression new to me'.[126] Home and his parents were now changed and he realised the strain upon them. Frederick Voigt, on leave in 1918, found London to be a similar other-worldly place. He had 'the oppressive sensation' that he was 'in a dream', and felt that there was 'only one reality in the whole world – the war'.[127] Determined to force himself to enjoy his leave, he sought distraction. But whilst those about him spoke of commonplace matters, all Voigt could think about was the front. Henry Russell similarly 'marvelled at the placid demeanour of everyone', and having 'lived and hoped for leave', it being over, he was 'without hope'.[128] Sick of war after the death of a fellow officer, Major Arthur Gibbs described his leave as 'fifteen dream days', yet with days of 'long silences' and 'bursts of violent argument'.[129] When Patrick Campbell came home for leave for the first time, his parents wanted him to tell them 'everything that had happened to me'. Unsurprisingly, there were things he could not. He was unable to 'make them understand', and could not reveal that 'I had become a different person'. He found himself at home, yet absent, 'thinking about the others' all the time. Indeed, 'I was *there*', on the Western Front, 'not here in the middle of Oxford'.[130] When he returned 'it was a relief to be only one person again', a soldier, 'no longer a mixture of two quite different people'.[131] For him, the home and war worlds were becoming incompatible. Second-Lieutenant Huntly Gordon noted friends and relatives 'inanely' asking how he was 'getting on' in France. His reply was, 'Fine, thanks, just fine', but he noted: 'What else could one say?' he did not believe that they could 'begin to understand'. The problem was that 'we were now simply in different worlds'.[132] If soldiers found their 'home world' changed, the civilians in it certainly saw changes in those who returned. Mabel Lethbridge, though only a child at the time, had a father and three brothers at the front. She recalled how when they came home on leave: 'I noticed the strange lack of ability to communicate with us … they would make a joke that to us sounded hollow'.[133]

125 H.E.L. Mellersh, *Schoolboy into War*, p.100.
126 Martin, op. cit. p.140.
127 F.A. Voigt, *Combed Out*, p.129.
128 Russell, op. cit. pp.246-7.
129 A.H. Gibbs, *Gun Fodder*, p.207.
130 Campbell, *Cannon's Mouth*, p.97 (author italics).
131 Campbell, *Cannon's Mouth*, p.99.
132 H. Gordon, *The Unreturning Army*, Kindle edition location 1911.
133 M. Lethbridge, quoted in Arthur, op. cit. p.170.

# 'I Will be Glad When I Can See Your Dear Face Again' – Family and Home

The distance from home created particular deprivations. 'Sexual starvation' was certainly an issue for those at the front. Major Reggie Trench wrote home to his wife about the officers in his mess wishing to put exactly this wording down as a reason for special leave, and how: 'This would pass as far as Brigade with endorsements in favour of leave I'm sure'.[134] Emmanuelle Cronier suggests that there were often particular tensions between soldiers and their wives, the men suspecting infidelity because of the many rumours circulating at the front. This worry may have been part of the thrust of Frederick Whitham's last letter home. In fact, infidelity was not a mass phenomenon, 'more the product of the discrepancy between the sexual fantasies of combatants and the difficulty in recreating intimacy'.[135] Occasionally however, the fear was fact. Private Thomas Pole, Sherwood Foresters, returned home from leave in February 1918 to find that he had a baby daughter he could not have fathered. He drowned the baby in a 'corrugated iron dolly tub' in the yard, the child having been held under water by a chair seat. The local newspaper reported:

> So far as can be ascertained the couple had not quarrelled, and nothing had occurred to suggest the least anxiety. Pole is said to have expressed his forgiveness of his wife's conduct, which resulted in the birth of the deceased, and to have actually been nursing the child just before its death.[136]

A recipient of the Distinguished Conduct Medal, Pole was sentenced to penal servitude for life but was released in 1925. Similarly, Lieutenant Douglas Malcolm was tried at the Old Bailey in September 1917 for killing a man he suspected of threatening the honour of his wife. He was acquitted by the jury.[137] Soldiers themselves, of course, were more prone to infidelity, as is glimpsed through the statistics on venereal disease. The Australians and New Zealanders had a rate of 18 per cent; the Canadians 16 per cent. This likely reflects the fact that no antipodeans, and all but a tiny handful of Canadians, ever received home leave. Of the allied nations who could return to their homes, the French suffered a rate of eight per cent, and the BEF five per cent.[138] Private George Coppard described a brothel in Bethune with 'well over a hundred and fifty men waiting for opening time', and when the red lamp was switched on 'a roar went up from the troops accompanied by a forward lunge towards the entrance'. Coppard, however, observed that the stigma of venereal disease was such that few in the front-line 'would have swapped places with a VD man at a base hospital'.[139]

134 Fletcher, op. cit. p.204.
135 Cronier, op. cit.
136 *Nottingham Guardian*, 13 February 1918.
137 *The Times*, 12 September 1917.
138 Hanna, op. cit. p.25.
139 G. Coppard, *With a Machine Gun to Cambrai*, pp.56-7.

74  Glum Heroes

Leave always had to end, and loved ones had to be left. John Reith described parting with his parents as a 'rather harrowing affair'.[140] One soldier described the crowds of family seeing men off at the stations, and that 'it was indeed an effort … to keep from breaking down'. On the journey to the cross-Channel transport 'not a word was spoken'.[141] Siegfried Sassoon similarly noted that officers back from their ten days' leave were 'usually somewhat silent about it'.[142] At the end of his first leave Carlos Blacker noted 'a good show of cheerfulness' on parting. 'Only one of us failed in the requisite stoicism', his grandmother.[143] Patrick Campbell recorded that 'there were two bad moments on every leave'. The first involved 'the saying goodbye at home when it was over'; the second involved 'the moment of return to the battery when you looked to see, or waited to be told, if anyone was not there'.[144] Returning to France after leave Llewellyn Griffith felt more vulnerable as 'it seemed that I had more to lose'.[145] Ranker Aubrey Smith had four leave periods during his four years on the Western Front, and was hence luckier than some. On his fourth leave in March 1918, however, he left 'feeling this was perhaps really the last time I'd see dear old Blighty's shores'.[146]

**Conclusion**

The fulfilment of the need for love and belonging was achieved in ways that appear simple to modern eyes. Letters created a sense of proximity which acted as the focus for sustaining memories of a place away from the battlefield. Linking objects such a photographs created a sense of presence of the absent loved-one. Yet for many soldiers, writing a letter or having a photograph taken may have been quite unfamiliar and novel. Letters became of central importance for most. For those at war, receiving comfort warmed the heart, and giving emotional support and practical advice maintained roles they had been forced to abdicate. It meant that war was not their sole purpose, giving them hope for a 'normal' future.

Leave was a crucial topic in letters, maintaining the constant hope of being reunited, if briefly. J.G. Fuller was of the opinion that the effect of leave and its absence upon the morale of the army 'appears to have been limited and ambiguous'. There were the downsides of the impact on the soldier of seeing the growing hardships for families as the war progressed, and the mismatch of understanding between those at home and those at the front about the nature, conduct and progress of the war. This is best described as dissonance, more accurate than Leed's dramatic concept of universal 'alienation'. There was, however, the upside of soldiers' renewed contacts with the

140  Reith, op. cit. p.132.
141  Anonymous, quoted in Bet-El, op. cit. p.143.
142  Sassoon, op. cit. p.269.
143  Blacker, op. cit. p.82.
144  P.J. Campbell, *The Ebb and Flow of Battle*, p.107.
145  L.W. Griffith, op. cit.
146  Rifleman, op. cit. p.308.

people and things they loved, which was both sustaining it itself and reminded them of 'what they were fighting for'.[147]

Both mechanisms of attempting to maintain the sense of love and belonging were imperfect. Letter writing had its limitations. Leave was infrequent. For many the brief time at home was deeply satisfying. For others it was disruptive of ways of coping. And as the war went on, the dissonance between the home and war worlds grew as the identity of soldier and the front as the new home took a stronger grip. Here men relied closely on the new primary group of mates.

---

[147] Fuller, op. cit. p.73.

# 3

## 'A Warm Fraternity' – Pals, Chums and Mates

The topic of comradeship in the trenches is soaked in romanticism. The war is inevitably seen as a period of lost friendships. Comrades were undeniably important in maintaining the need for belongingness, particularly for men displaced from the familiarity of family. In viewing friendships through the prism of intimate modern relationships, however, we run the risk of distorting the ways in which they were important in achieving this, and ignoring their limitations. In addition, we run the risk of misrepresenting how soldiers reacted to the deaths of comrades.

We associate certain words with comradeship in the First World War, and all have origins long before the 20th century. Their derivations are instructive. The word 'pal', immortalised in the concept of 'pals battalions', originates from 17th century Romany, meaning 'brother' or 'mate'. The word 'mate' itself is from Middle Low German meaning 'comrade' (itself from Spanish meaning 'roommate') deriving from the word 'meat', i.e. it is based on the concept of eating together. The word 'chum' originates from university life in the late 17th century, meaning 'chamber(mate)' or roommate.[1] The words 'mate' and 'chum', in a very real sense, describe relationships of shared practicalities. This is undoubtedly the brand of friendship the Great War soldier enjoyed.

### A History of Friendship

The historian Barbara Caine states: 'No one can underestimate the importance attributed to friendship in contemporary society'.[2] Indeed, as friendships have become increasingly predicated upon the reciprocal intimacy of personal openness, and the means of furthering them have multiplied, our preoccupation with them has soared. Yet friendships of this sort are of comparatively recent origin, and would have been unlikely to have been enjoyed by the majority of Great War combatants.

---

1    Word origins taken from www.oxforddictionaries.com.
2    B. Caine, *Friendship – A History*, p.ix.

The nature of friendship has changed over time, and attempts to describe and classify it have an ancient history. The Greek philosopher Aristotle was the first to develop a taxonomy of friendships nearly 2,500 years ago, in an era where friendships were considered exclusively the province of men. He detailed utility friendships, pleasure friendships, and virtue friendships, the latter where people were friends because of the other person in their own right.[3] In the modern world we would refer to them as 'emotional' friendships. Sarah Cole takes the stance that it is a mistake to see the bulk of the friendships of the early part of the 20th century as 'private, voluntary relation(s), governed by personal sentiment and easy communion'. Friendship instead had 'its own conventions and institutional affinities',[4] the main such institution for most of the male population being the workplace. Aristotle would certainly have seen the relationships of the working-class of the Edwardian period, based on workplace acquaintance, as utility friendships. He would have viewed the relationships between Great War soldiers in the same vein. Both were relationships based on a common project and the mutual benefits derived. Visiting the workingmen's club in peace or the estaminet in war would have represented a secondary pleasure friendship.

The Greek philosophers took a generally austere view of friendship. More modern notions of intimacy were not ruled out in advanced friendships, but they were closely woven into the notion of virtue, and truly virtuous friendships were seen as rare. Consequently, several hundred years later, the Roman philosopher Cicero would show little interest in the '"insubstantial" friendships of common people'.[5] He dismissively saw such relationships as based entirely on self-interest. The lack of a record of the friendships of ordinary individuals in these distant times creates problems for our understanding, as we have only the musings of intellectuals. As ancient Greek virtue became Christian virtue, friendship came to be seen in the context of the relationship between Christ and his disciples, and for some, subordinate to the relationship with God in the 'next world'. During the Renaissance period it has been noted: 'What little we can know about understandings of friendship among the non-literate classes … suggests that they too spoke the language of everyday Christian, if not Ciceronian, friendship'. Aristotle's utility relationships undoubtedly prevailed. The French Academician, Louis de Sacy wrote in 1703, in a way that would not have seemed patronising at the time, that: 'Persons of the Meanest Parts are not wholly incapable of the Ties of Friendship'.[6] Modern research using the diaries of shopkeepers and others of the time identifies three main types of friendship in the ordinary people of this era: that amongst family members; other ties of mutual dependence, mainly exchange of services (utility or instrumental relationships); and patron-client relations.[7] Thus,

3 Aristotle, *Nicomachean Ethics*.
4 S. Cole, *Modernism, Male Friendship, and the First World War*, p.5.
5 C.J. Mews and N. Chiavaroli, 'The Latin West', in Caine, op. cit. p.91.
6 L. de Sacy, *A Discourse of Friendship*, p.23.
7 N. Tadmor, *Family and Friends in 18th Century England*, pp.175-211.

although there was a 'growing sentimentality of friendship from the middle of the eighteenth century',[8] such relationships for the ordinary person remained largely instrumental in nature. It is interesting that for so lengthy a period family members were considered as friends, but this is perhaps not surprising as many family relationships were, of course, utility relationships. It was the modern concept of emotional friendship that had yet to gain ground, and this would take several more centuries. The prime focus of friendship on instrumentality is hardly surprising – adversity breeds reciprocal assistance, and the lives of common folk were ridden with adversity. Maslow's theory helps us understand why intimate friendship was slow to evolve. Ordinary people were struggling with basic physiological and safety needs well into the 20th century, and clearly it was premature to consider the potential benefits of intimacy if one's preoccupations were food and housing. For the well-heeled and well-educated, the possibility of intimacy was greater.

In the 19th century, in the decades before the Great War: 'The term "friend" continued to be used as it had been in the eighteenth century'. It described those with whom one had close ties 'based on shared interests or activities and also those on whom one might depend in difficult circumstances'.[9] Industrialisation and the poverty of associated urbanisation did nothing to lessen the need for assistance in adversity. Yet it would be unwise to travel too far down the road of sentimentalising urban working class solidarity. As has been pointed out in such communities: 'Women talk of friendly, helpful or good neighbours, but they rarely talk simply of friends'.[10] Sociable contacts were public, often relegated to conversations in the street or pub, and privacy was valued. Ross McKibbin in his review of working class culture in the period immediately after the Great War, dismisses the notion of 'popping in' friendship. He goes as far as stating: 'There is much evidence that people were suspicious of their neighbours and large numbers thought them untrustworthy'.[11] Friendship still largely meant family relationships: 'A man might have no "real friend in the world but his wife, to whom he can communicate his private thoughts, and in return receive consolation"'.[12] The exceptions were perhaps relatives, who were often neighbours. Neighbour relationships often remained superficial and were not maintained if people moved. For men, sociability was still 'largely work-based',[13] and most commonly enjoyed in the pub or workingmen's club, where the talk was 'overwhelmingly about work and sport'.[14] Intimate, emotional friendships were therefore, for the majority, largely a project for the future. The Great War soldier's friendships were relationships

---

8 D. Garrioch, 'From Christian Friendship to Secular Sentimentality', in Caine, op. cit. p.91.
9 M. Brodie and B. Caine, 'Class, Sex, and Friendship: The Long Nineteenth Century', in Caine, op. cit. p.91.
10 E. Roberts, *A Woman's Place*, p.188.
11 R. McKibbin, *Classes and Cultures*, p.181.
12 H. Mayhew, *London Labour Vol. I*, quoted in Brodie & Caine op. cit. p.91.
13 McKibbin, op. cit. p.183.
14 McKibbin, op. cit. p.184.

based on proximity and shared activity, much the same social circumstances that the essentially working-class army was used to in its home communities. These, as noted in the Introduction, fostered 'group solidarity and mutuality', in contrast to our modern individualism.[15] Relationships were therefore predicated upon groups sharing a breadth of activities rather than emotional depth with individuals.

## Comradship in the Trenches

Joanna Bourke writes that: 'It is axiomatic in the history of the First World War that servicemen "bonded" together, united by the gender-specific experiences of warfare'.[16] Basil Liddell Hart, combatant turned historian, waxed lyrical describing 'bands of men, who, if their sprit were right, lived in such intimacy that they became part of one another'. In the next line he downgraded his hyperbole, referring to 'that fellowship of the trenches which was such a unique and unforgettable experience for all who shared it', indicating his notion of intimacy by describing a 'sense of interdependence and sympathy'.[17]

Liddell Hart pointed out that war, and hence the context of comradeship, was group-based. The battalion to which an infantryman belonged was supposedly made up of about 1,000 men. Lieutenant Sidney Rogerson, however, reminds us that in the 'cramping effect' of trench life a man was a member of a 'very small community from which, sleeping or waking, he was never separated'.[18] Indeed, human beings appear to be constrained in terms of the number of people they can maintain a stable social relationship with, the limit being around 150, 'Dunbar's Number'.[19] Further, intimate relationships appear to number no more than five, numbers increasing in layers three times bigger than the previous, so the next layer outside the intimate circle would number 15.[20] The platoon section, the closest grouping that a soldier had, conveniently numbered 12 men under an NCO. Private Frederic Manning wrote of the limitations, only knowing a few of the men 'outside his own section by name'.[21] Private George Coppard was slightly more expansive, stating that 'my world never really extended beyond that bounded by company control'.[22] Lance-Corporal 'Roddy' Rodinson of the Sheffield City Battalion, who meticulously noted the comrades he went on walks

---

15  J. Bourne, 'The British Working Man in Arms' in H. Cecil & P.H. Liddle (eds), *Facing Armageddon* p.347.
16  J. Bourke, *Dismembering the Male*, p.126.
17  B.H. Liddell Hart, 'Foreword' to S. Rogerson, *Twelve Days on the Somme*, p.viii (1933 version).
18  Rogerson, op. cit. p.12.
19  R.I.M. Dunbar, 'Neocortex Size as a Constraint on Group Size in Primates', *Journal of Human Evolution*, p.469.
20  http://www.socialsciencespace.com/2013/11/robin-dunbar-on-dunbar-numbers/.
21  F. Manning, *The Middle Parts of Fortune*, Kindle edition location 363.
22  G. Coppard, *With a Machine Gun to Cambrai*, p.5.

or other outings with in his spare time, only refers in the period between enlistment and his wounding at Serre on 1 July 1916 to 11 such individuals in an 18 month period. Only two were consistent companions, one of whom was a pre-war workplace acquaintance at the Sheffield Telegraph.[23]

Lieutenant Charles Carrington described the interdependence of the small group. He wrote how 'a Corporal and six men in a trench were like shipwrecked sailors on a raft, completely committed to their social grouping'. The interdependence had a very functional purpose, as 'everyone's life depended on the reliability of each'.[24] He is describing both the isolated experience reported by Manning and Coppard and the very practical grounds of comradeship. Sergeant Charles Montague similarly chose the metaphor for the section as a 'little boatload of castaways' with whom the soldier was 'marooned on a desert island making shift to keep off the weather and any sudden attack of wild beasts'.[25] Again, the sense of isolation and pragmatic bonding in the face of threat is perfectly conveyed. The smallest organisational element of the army, the section, was therefore accidentally perfectly engineered for comradeship.

### *Physical presence and touch*

It is clear that Liddell Hart's notion of intimacy was different to modern conceptions. Focussing on the warrior-poets and writers has led to preoccupation with the homoeroticism of male soldier relationships. Lieutenant Stuart Cloete described a fellow officer, Louis Martin as 'one of the dozen or so men I have loved'. He was clear that 'there can be love between men without any homosexual tinge' as they become 'brothers without consanguinity'. Love, for Cloete, was 'a matter of mutual trust respect and affection'.[26] Thus Captain Henry Dundas wrote to his parents after the death of his Eton school friend Ralph Gamble: 'I loved Ralph more than anyone in the world except you two'.[27] Santanu Das in contrast quotes Lieutenant Frank Cocker's letter to his girlfriend, Evelyn, of a moment with a fellow officer: 'The dear lad kissed me once, "that's from Evelyn" he said; then he kissed me again and said, "that's from your mother." I returned his tender salute and said, "that's from me"'.[28] This particular image, however, distracts us from the overarching reality that 'Edwardian men would have been ashamed to cry or to kiss'. In the first half of the twentieth century 'even fathers and sons never kissed or embraced as adults. The physical act of greeting was the handshake'. Shaking hands was a proof of virility: 'The firm hearty grip distinguishing from the flabby hand which betrayed the self-abusing masturbator'. Only two other forms of touch were acceptable: 'One was in corporal punishment. The

---

23  J.R. Rodinson, Diary, author's collection.
24  C. Carrington, *Soldier From the Wars Returning*, p.98.
25  C.E. Montague, *Disenchantement*, p.40.
26  S. Cloete, *A Victorian Son*, p.286.
27  Anonymous, *Henry Dundas – Scots Guards*, p.230.
28  S. Das, *Touch and Intimacy in First World War Literature*, p.109.

other was in sport'.[29] Examples of the limitations of pre-war intimacy are to be found in Ernest Shackleton's Imperial Trans-Antarctic Expedition 1914-17. After the loss of their ship, *Endurance*, Shackleton and his crew had a desperate fight to remain alive and achieve rescue, providing an extraordinary tale of practical male bonding in the face of adversity. On one hand, to keep warm 'every man wanted to cuddle against his neighbour'.[30] On the other, when Shackleton and fellow expedition members saw the first signs on South Georgia of the men who would rescue them, 'we paused and shook hands'.[31] Physical intimacy was acceptable if it had a circumscribed, vital purpose. Thus, on Gallipoli in the bitterly cold and wet November of 1915, Major John Gillam described how officers 'huddled together all night endeavouring to get warmth from each other's bodies'.[32] Otherwise, formality ruled.

Charles Carrington wondered, however, whether 'there is a homosexual element in *esprit de corps*?',[33] and Santanu Das goes further in stating what is probably the obvious that: 'A certain amount of homosexual activity went on in the trenches'. Eric Hiscock wrote that he and two companions all had 'homosexual tendencies.' He himself was propositioned twice, and was once the subject of some fondling. Unashamed to be flabby-handed, he disclosed that in the 'days and nights of stress we masturbated', but that the reality was that 'kisses on unshaven faces were rare, and then only at moments of acute danger'.[34] Stuart Cloete shared quarters with a senior officer who 'was homosexual and made a pass at me'. Cloete threated to knife him and the advance was understandably not repeated.[35] There may have been elements of temporary homoerotic desire encouraged by the absence of women and the closeness of men, powered by the need for love and a sense of belonging, yet the very proximity of other disinclined men likely rendered frank homosexual behaviour infrequent. Only 22 officers and 270 other ranks were court-martialled for indecency between 1914 and 1920.[36] Germany was a country more tolerant of homosexual relationships, and Dr Magnus Hirschfeld, physician, sexologist and campaigner for sexual minorities studied homosexuality at the front. In his *Sexual History of the World War* he claimed both a rise in 'pseudo-homosexuality', i.e. heterosexual men engaging in homosexual activity, and an increased tolerance for such liaisons at the front. He identified three forms

29  P.R. Thompson, *The Edwardians: The Remaking of British Society*, p.145.
30  E. Shackleton, *South – The Story of Shackleton's 1914-17 Expedition*, Kindle Edition location 2911.
31  Shackleton, op. cit. location 3163.
32  J.J. Gillam, *Gallipoli Diary*, p.276.
33  Carrington, op. cit. p.167.
34  E. Hiscock, *The Bells of Hell*, p.76.
35  Cloete, op. cit. p.200.
36  Das, op. cit. p.116.

of 'intimate comradeship': the consciously erotic, unconsciously erotic, and bonds between men that remained non-erotic.[37]

Certainly, the conditions of the army created a permanent physical presence, as it did for the Shackleton expedition. For the first time, for the majority, men lived virtually solely in the presence of other men. Physical intimacy was unavoidable. Men slept in haylofts or tents close to each other, they were medically examined, bathed or swam naked, they defecated in each other's presence, they occasionally danced together, and they sometimes held each other as they died. However, they never developed the freedom of touch of the 21st century. Intimacy was a matter of mutual practical activity in the shared and narrow space of trench or billet, and within it, the rules on physical touch were relaxed in certain circumscribed ways – generally group-based and public.

## The nature of comradeship

The extreme conditions of war made a certain amount of emotional expression unavoidable. There is little evidence, however, to suggest that it was shared privately and purposefully between comrades in what nowadays might be referred to as 'emotional processing'. On the contrary, its expression was avoided as much as possible. Second-Lieutenant Patrick Campbell had been under heavy shellfire at Ypres, and as the day came to an end, 'I suddenly felt an extraordinary affection for Vernon', his companion through the ordeal. Campbell 'wanted to have him always at my side'. The shared experience had created this feeling: 'Together we had been down into the valley of the shadow, together we had climbed a little way out of it'. Yet, outside of trivialities, they 'had nothing to say to each other'.[38] The meaning of the experience would remain private.

Relationships at the front should not be idealised – there were bullies and their victims as there have always been in the male-dominated institutions that are armies. Training with the Hussars, Ernest Parker noted 'mutual friendliness', but at the same time described himself as 'the butt of a group of Easterners' and that 'I had to stand up for myself'. The degree of bullying is evident in his aside: 'Although no boxer, I managed to come off fairly satisfactorily when attacked'.[39] Although later he formed friendships, George Coppard was singled out during training by 'a big fellow … for bullying and foul abuse' and 'got no comfort from the other chaps'.[40] Second-Lieutenant Bernard Martin, similarly during his training, was present at the aftermath of a murder. A ranker had put in a very poor performance on the rifle range. That evening he was mocked and 'surprisingly, his friend joined the others against

37  http://encyclopedia.1914-1918-online.net/article/sexuality_sexual_relations_homosexuality.
38  P.J. Campbell, *In The Cannon's Mouth*, p.85.
39  E.W. Parker, *Into Battle*, p.4.
40  Coppard, op. cit. p.8.

him'. The mocked man pointed the rifle at his friend, and saying: 'I'll show you if I'm afraid of the kick', shot him dead.[41] If not downright bullying, there was selfish disregard for others. Captain Gerald Burgoyne referred to men who would throw a tin of biscuits away, if they could do so in the dark without being caught, rather than carry it, 'even though they know it contains all the rations their pals have to live on for the next twenty-four hours'. He concluded such individuals 'don't know the meaning of "pal"'.[42] He similarly described how a fellow officer 'lost all his kit, revolver, glasses, etc. his first night in hospital', with buttons and badges removed from his uniform. Orderlies boasted of their booty. He observed, as did others: 'The nickname for the RAMC is "Rob all my comrades"'.[43] Private Norman Gladden dispelled much of the sentimentality about supportive comradeship on his arrival as a conscript in a draft to 7th Northumberland Fusiliers on the Somme in 1916. He and his fellow draftees 'had difficulty in obtaining our just rations', and found that old hands left working parties to the newcomers feeling they had 'earned exemption'. Gladden and his fellows were 'without shelter' in the trenches as they had not yet learned the ropes, supposed comrades having failed to show due care in inducting the new arrivals.[44] At Ypres the following year, after returning from illness, he discovered a 'group of practised lead-swingers' in his company who were 'proud of their cleverness' and who 'made no secret of their subterfuges'.[45] Similarly, he identified a company bully who both 'disgusted and frightened me'. This individual exerted favouritism through being mess orderly, thus controlling access to satisfying one of the basic needs. Gladden physically stood his ground with this individual and was thereafter 'put on a sort of neutral list', with no further trouble.[46] A somewhat solitary individual, with only one close pal, Gladden however identified an 'inner "chumship" circle' in the Lewis gun section he joined. Although he never became part of this, he was 'always to be *persona grata*' in the section.[47] Officers were not exempt from disharmony. Second-Lieutenant Siegfried Sassoon noted 'occasional squabblings' in his mess 'which occurred when we were on one another's nerves'.[48] Major Charles Dudley-Ward also noted the tendency to 'squabbling over trivialities' amongst company officers, and felt it was better that they met together as a whole battalion officers' mess, rather than in companies.[49]

Despite these exceptions, the sustaining nature of comradeship is the predominant theme in accounts. The Reverend Julian Bickersteth wrote: 'Is there anything to equal

---

41  B. Martin, *Poor Bloody Infantry*, p.31.
42  C. Davison, *The Burgoyne Diaries*, p.56.
43  Davison, op. cit. p.74.
44  N. Gladden, *Ypres 1917*, p.17.
45  Gladden, op. cit. p.37.
46  Gladden, op. cit. p.85.
47  Gladden, op. cit. p.40.
48  S. Sassoon, *The Complete Memoirs of George Sherston*, p.319.
49  C.H. Dudley-Ward, Private Papers, IWM Docs 6374.

the happiness of the "camaraderie" and friendship of the life out here?'[50] Major Harold Bidder, with battalion command under his belt, returned to a post in England, but soon found it unsatisfactory, noting how he missed the 'cordial friendliness' of life at the front.[51] Captain Graham Greenwell, after two months in hospital and recuperating, returned to his unit. He wrote home that it was 'a great joy being among my old friends again', and that he was 'as happy as a schoolboy'.[52] He and his fellow officers were 'quite a happy family'.[53] Newly commissioned Oxford scholar Stephen Hewett had to find his way into a new model of comradeship. Perhaps lacking intellectual stimulation he wrote: 'For friendships, we have the rough-and-ready fellowships of men who are united to one only by the chances of one's work'.[54] Yet he was able to find something sustaining beyond simple utility relationships, experiencing 'a very sincere though only temporary and quite unsentimental fellowship'. As time went on, however, he came to appreciate that 'there is nothing quite like the rough-and-ready, careless humour and bonhomie'.[55] Once in the trenches he was able to echo Greenwell that 'we officers are a happy family'.[56] Throughout the Somme offensive, Second-Lieutenant Edmund Blunden similarly described 'a warm fraternity, a family understanding'.[57] The family metaphor is common. The wounding of one of his comrades caused Private Clifford Lane to feel a 'sense of desolation' which would normally only 'come if you lost a ... member of your family'.[58] Sidney Rogerson described the 'very comforting sense of comradeship' on the march. To him, comradeship in this situation meant 'a sense of close company; the ability to talk to your neighbour, even to sing to him'.[59] In the absence of personal, intimate discussion, sentimental songs were one of the ways in which emotion that could not be personally owned could be aired amongst friends. Rogerson noted men waiting to be relieved in the front line singing 'all the most mournful ditties they knew', including: 'Oh My, I don't want to Die! I want to go Home'.[60] He, too, used the family analogy, writing of 'comrades, brothers, dwelling together in unity', and continued: 'We saw the love passing the love of women of one "pal" for his "half-section"'.[61] In a very real way, pals came to form a new primary group.

During his training as a ranker, Major Arthur Gibbs recalled two incidents which stood out, both to do with comradeship. The first was a sentimental communal sing-song, Gibbs also using the word 'brothers' to describe the group experience. The

50 J. Bickersteth (ed.), *The Bickersteth Diaries*, p.183.
51 Orex, (H.F. Bidder), *Three Chevrons*, p.223.
52 G.H. Greenwell, *An Infant in Arms*, p.185.
53 Greenwell, op. cit. p.242.
54 S. Hewett, *A Scholar's Letters*, pp.3-4.
55 Hewett, op. cit. p.5.
56 Hewett, op. cit. p.41.
57 E. Blunden, *Undertones of War*, p.130.
58 C. Lane quoted in M. Arthur, *Forgotten Voices of the Great War*, p.108.
59 Rogerson, op. cit. p.9.
60 Rogerson, op. cit. p.90.
61 Rogerson, op. cit. p.60.

second was 'the finding of a friend, a kindred spirit in those thousands which accentuated one's solitude'. Their relationship revolved around the 'comfort of speech' and the sharing of 'experiences'.[62] Gibbs and his friend met only twice a week during this period, and outside of these meetings, Gibbs felt 'more completely alone than on a desert island'.[63] Even though he viewed the men he trained directly with as brothers, he did not mean this in an emotional sense as they remained a mass with whom he felt no individual connection. Gibbs was an intelligent man, a writer, and he clearly felt an intellectual isolation. When, after a period of time at the front as a cavalry trooper, he returned to England to train as an artillery officer, the situation was different. In such company, 'it was extraordinary what a bond grew up between us all'. Whilst the relationships between the volunteers of the 'pals battalions' who spent comparatively long periods spent training together in Britain may have been romanticised, comrades were often particularly missed when killed. Private Harry Drinkwater wrote in his diary in May 1916 of these relationships: 'We miss very much those who have "gone west"', and added: 'New fellows arrive, good fellows no doubt, but they do not take the places of those who go down'.[64] Such initial relationships in pals battalions may have been due, as Private Reginald Davis noted, to the fact that 'in each other we had our only link with home, with past associations'.[65]

What lay at the core of comradeship? How was it sustaining? Harry Drinkwater, true to the age, was not overly sentimental towards the death of pals. His particular friend, Jinks, was killed, and he described him in retrospect as a 'partner in business', remaking on the many occasions when 'we could help each other'.[66] He was describing perfectly the practical essence of comradeship. In Walter Ludwig's study, mentioned in the previous chapter, 'social emotions' were spontaneously listed as the third most popular coping strategy when under significant stress, utilised by 27 per cent of soldiers.[67] Comradeship sustained men in a variety of ways. Bernard Martin made the interesting comment that 'the short friendships of trench life encourage tolerance'. The everyday possibility of death made him accepting of a range of personal habits and opinions he would not normally have indulged. He valued 'the satisfaction that comes from total sharing'.[68] Similarly, Private Henry Russell described men discovering 'in each other traits which led to a mutual understanding'.[69] He also viewed sharing as central. When his long-term chum Mark was wounded, he experienced 'shock', for he had 'equally shared with us the discomforts and dangers'.[70] In August 1918,

---

62   A.H. Gibbs, *Gun Fodder*, pp.11-12.
63   Gibbs, op. cit. p.27.
64   J. Cooksey & D. Griffiths (eds), *Harry's War*, p.81.
65   E. Hodder-Williams, *One Young Man*, Kindle edition location 240.
66   Cooksey & Griffiths, op. cit. p.98.
67   W. Ludwig, cited in A. Watson, *Enduring the Great War*, pp.236-7.
68   Martin, op. cit. p.73.
69   H. Russell, *Slaves of the War Lords*, p.138.
70   Russell, op. cit. p.186.

Henry Dundas wrote home after the death of his pal Ralph Gamble: 'Life without him will be almost unbearable'. He believed that those not at war would be unable to realise the 'extent the War binds people together out here'. He and Gamble 'used to do everything we could together'.[71] Dundas is telling us that proximity, sharing and interdependence under the stress of war was a mix that created a particular glue binding relationships. The normal home/work divide had not previously allowed this. Private Walter Williams defined this intensification of normal male relationships in wartime as 'the sharing of hardships and danger together no matter what the personal cost'.[72] This led, Clifford Lane stated, to 'the sort of trust between men that rarely occurs'.[73] An Australian NCO on Gallipoli, Frank Brent echoed this: 'We just trusted each other blind'.[74] George Coppard was of the opinion that 'the daily comradeship of my pals, whether in or out of the line, gave me strength', and he described a 'silent bonding' together of men who knew there was no other way out but to 'see the thing through'.[75] His emphasis on the notion of silence indicates that the bonding was unremarked by those experiencing it. On arrival in France Reginald Davis walked around camp with his comrades. They were similarly silent: 'We did not speak much. Each had his own thoughts, each was subconsciously leaning on the other for support'.[76] Emotional support was not consciously and verbally sought.

Without this fellowship, Sidney Rogers believed that 'we could never have stood the strain'.[77] Comradeship fostered endurance. Captain Francis Buckley wrote that comradeship sustained him 'during the long delays and bitter disappointments'.[78] Like Coppard, Sergeant Douglas Pinkerton described how the fact that others were 'sticking it out' led to an 'unconscious reaction that draws upon unsuspected wells of nervous and physical strength'.[79] Major Richard Foot argued that friendships made war 'endurable', especially 'when good natured fun and humour cement that comradeship'.[80] Indeed, the memoirs of Second-Lieutenant Edwin Vaughan abound with the sort of 'larks' that would satisfy anyone's fantasy of the public schoolboy.[81] To Foot's mind such larks weakened the power of unpleasant memories.[82] Captain G.B. Manwaring wrote home in 1917 that 'war loses half its terrors when shared by two or more of equal rank, for then a little of the awful responsibility is shared'.[83] Comradeship thus had a particular

---

71 Anonymous, *Dundas*, p.231.
72 M. Williams, *With Innocence and Hope*, Kindle edition location 3394.
73 C. Lane, quoted in Arthur, op. cit. p.108.
74 F. Brent, BBC 'The Great War Interviews'.
75 Coppard, op. cit. p.107.
76 Hodder-Williams, op. cit. location 240.
77 Rogerson, op. cit. p.61.
78 F. Buckley, *Q.6.a.*, p.9.
79 R.D. Pinkerton, *Ladies from Hell*, p.52.
80 R.C. Foot, Private Papers, IWM Docs 3354.
81 E.C. Vaughan, *Some Desperate Glory*, p.148.
82 Foot, op. cit.
83 G.B. Manwaring, *If We Return*, p.125.

role in those who bore responsibility of leadership. This only held, however, up to a particular point in the chain of command. One particular element of stress unique to commanding officers of battalions was that they endured a more solitary existence than more junior officers, alone with ultimate responsibility. The companionship which was a bulwark against stress was denied them.[84]

Private Aubrey Smith epitomises both the mutuality and the uplifting nature of comradeship in describing his disbelief at the death of his oldest army comrade, Claud 'Kimbo' Vallentine-Warne at Arras on 7 April 1917: 'Many a jolly evening had we spent with him; many a parcel and billet had we shared'. And it was not simply a matter of sharing: 'His cheery disposition when anything was going wrong and we were suffering from waves of depression had often put our hearts in the right place'.[85] Frederic Manning also noted soldiers being 'unselfish, even gentle; instinctively helping each other' and there being a 'tacit understanding between them'.[86] Helping and sharing, indeed, were a key part of the experience of the utility relationships that made up comradeship. Private William Quinton described 'sharing everything, down to the last cigarette-end, the last army biscuit'.[87] Similarly, Lieutenant Charles Douie wrote that: 'In the new world men having little yet had that little in common, and shared it with a grace and courtesy not often found in a prosperous and civilised community'.[88] Private W. Walker noted of sharing: 'It means a lot, that, in warfare. Friendship strengthens the heart'.[89] When Reginald Davis's closest 'chum' was killed, a man he had known since he was 13, his grieving father wrote: 'We never thought of you separately at all ... as you shared all in common'.[90]

Private George Brame described his friend H., a fellow section-member: 'Our acquaintance soon developed into the richest friendship. We were constantly together until he met his death'.[91] When H. lay mortally wounded: 'Stretching out his hand and placing it into mine, he said: "George, you have been the best pal I've had"'. Brame's words are 'constantly together' – comradeship was in part a matter of perpetual presence. Infantry, firmly grounded, were in a better position to give and receive support than some. Norman Macmillan, an infantryman turned RFC pilot knew this only too well. As infantry: 'One had the comradeship of men all about one, one knew they were there, at a moment, ready to support one'. In the air, matters were different: 'We did not have the feeling of community spirit'.[92]

---

84  P.E. Hodgkinson, *British Infantry Battalion Commanders in the First World War*, p.115.
85  A Rifleman (A. Smith), *Four Years on the Western Front*, p.213.
86  Manning, op. cit. location 214.
87  W.A. Quinton, Private Papers, IWM Docs 6705.
88  C. Douie, *The Weary Road*, p.47.
89  W. Walker, Diary, http://www.firstworldwar.com/diaries/battleofloos.htm.
90  Hodder-Williams, op. cit. location 433.
91  G. Brame, Diary, http://www.firstworldwar.com/diaries/onthebelgiancoast.htm.
92  N. Macmillan, BBC 'The Great War Interviews'.

Leaving comrades was a matter to be avoided if possible. Private John McCauley, lying wounded, wished to stay with his 'little group' because he wanted to 'prove that I was as loyal as they had been to me'.[93] Lieutenant Reginald Dixon, also wounded, hated the idea of being removed to safety 'while one's friends out there were sticking it out … it was shirking to be elsewhere'.[94] Men would refuse promotion to remain with their comrades. Private William Walls did this on several occasions not wishing to leave his chums.[95] When offered a stripe on the Somme in 1916, Private Giles Eyre responded: 'I prefer remaining with my pals'.[96] Corporal William Andrews lost an opportunity for promotion to sergeant, and was not sorry: 'It would have been awkward if I had been a sergeant and my friend Nick had remained a private'.[97] Aubrey Smith had attempted unsuccessfully to see his CO about a commission on his first leave in mid-1915, after his dreadful experiences at Second Ypres. On his second leave in early 1916: 'There was no thought of a commission this time … I had made fast friends and was absolutely attached to the L.R.B.'.[98] This distancing could also happen for officers on promotion. Patrick Campbell noted in 1918 that 'I was on less friendly terms with Frank than I had been before', describing him as having 'gone over to the other side now that he was a captain'.[99] Harry Drinkwater, however, went cheerfully back to England to be commissioned in January 1917 because 'the fellows I knew best had gone'.[100]

Being sent to another unit could prove a difficult experience due to discontinuity in relationships. When Corporal Geoffrey Husbands returned to the Western Front after a period in Britain following wounding, he was sent to another battalion of his regiment. He described 'a certain loneliness and isolation due to the lack of any real pals'.[101] Patrick Campbell, arriving as a new officer on the Western Front in 1917 in an artillery battery immediately noted 'I was lonely and had no friends'.[102] He had gone to a different division than his friend Dick from training – 'not only my greatest friend', but one 'unlike any friend I had ever had before'.[103] He longed for friends in his new situation 'not to feel outside the battery ring'. He realised, however, that in order to be accepted he would have to be in action with his fellows and have shared danger.[104] His loneliness passed. Nine months later he would write of his fellow officers, using an analogy now familiar: 'We were like brothers, sleeping side by side, within touching

93 J. McCauley, Private Papers, IWM Docs 6434.
94 R.G. Dixon, Private Papers, IWM Docs 2001.
95 W. Walls cited in Bourke, op. cit. p.131.
96 G.E.M. Eyre, *Somme Harvest*, p.139.
97 W.L. Andrews, *Haunting Years*, p.76.
98 Rifleman, op. cit. p.114.
99 P.J. Campbell, *The Ebb and Flow of Battle*, p.74.
100 Cooksey & Griffiths, op. cit. p.214.
101 G.R. Husbands, *Joffrey's War*, p.403.
102 Campbell, *Cannon's Mouth*, p.13.
103 Campbell, *Cannon's Mouth*, p.1.
104 Campbell, *Cannon's Mouth*, p.31.

distance, sharing whatever possessions we had'.[105] Indeed, by this time Campbell considered the spirit of comradeship to be 'what mattered most' in any unit.[106]

Some had to compromise to have company. Private Albert Andrews noted that 'it was useless to say I would not drink or I would have no pals and nowhere to go'.[107] Others formed relatively few close relationships. Private Alfred Burrage stated that whilst he 'liked' plenty of his fellows, 'there was none with whom I could quite form that intimacy of mind which is called friendship'.[108] He however indicated that this might be protective, continuing: 'It isn't safe to have a friend'.[109] Private George Littlefair wrote after the death of his pal Joe Coates: 'That was me pal gone and I was too full to speak to anybody after that. I never palled up with anybody else, not after you got that feeling'.[110] Littlefair thus removed the potential for emotional vulnerability. On the Somme in 1916, Second-Lieutenant Guy Chapman described how this vulnerability could suddenly manifest itself. A fellow officer, Turnbull, shot himself through the foot, this immediately following the death of a particular friend. Chapman believed that 'something cracked' in him. 'The loyalty to one man had been too concentrated, and with his end, it died. Into the vacuum rushed the need for escape'.[111]

Private Arthur Lambert described army friendship as 'sudden, strengthening daily, and ending in separation and suffering'.[112] This draws distinctions for us from our own experience of friendships. They are not sudden and strengthen gradually before we can enter intimacy. Nor do we expect them to end in suffering. Edwin Vaughan observed their potential brevity: 'One of the most pathetic features of this war is this continual forming of real friendships which last a week or two, or even months, and are suddenly shattered for ever by death or division'.[113] Frederic Manning used the following simple words: 'That's the worst o' the bloody army; as soon as you get a bit pally with a chap summat 'appens'.[114] Captain Edward Chapman noted the frequency of sudden discontinuity in relationships in a letter home: 'As for one's friends, they change more rapidly than anything'. Some would be killed, and others get sent home to England, and 'you never hear of them again'.[115] The question is raised as to what Vaughan meant by 'real friendships'. Lieutenant John Allen wrote: 'It has been heart-breaking seeing men one had got to like in a day or so killed'.[116] Clearly 'real friendships' as we understand them do not form in this sort of time span. Rifleman Walter Cobb wrote that apart

---

105 Campbell, *Ebb and Flow*, p.7.
106 Campbell, *Ebb and Flow*, p.10.
107 S. Richardson, *Orders are Orders*, p.26.
108 Ex-Private X (A.M. Burrage), *War is War*, p.28.
109 A.M. Burrage, Diary, http://www.firstworldwar.com/diaries/burrage_intro.htm.
110 G. Littlefair, quoted in R. van Emden & S. Humphries, *Veterans*, p.129.
111 G. Chapman, *A Passionate Prodigality*, p.81.
112 A. Lambert, *Over the Top*, p.64.
113 Vaughan, op. cit. p.23.
114 Manning, op. cit. location 2331.
115 E.F. Chapman, Private Papers, IWM Docs 1799.
116 J. Allen quoted in L. Housman, *War Letters of Fallen Englishmen*, p.29.

from having one 'particular chum' he 'had no other real chums – fellow soldiers – yes, but companionship under conditions like ours was not really possible'. He acknowledged the tenuousness in relationships: 'Everything seemed on a day to day basis'.[117] Lieutenant Denis Barnett clarified, describing that 'the love that grows quickly and perhaps *artificially* when men are together up against life and death has a peculiar quality'.[118] Circumstances of high emotional valency and proximity were instrumental in these 'artificial' attachments. It is a well attested research finding that the members of a group under threat will identify with each other more closely.[119] Richard Tobin, an NCO in the Royal Naval Division described this perfectly. Whilst waiting to go over the top: 'The fellow next to you, he was your best friend, you loved him', though 'you perhaps didn't know him the day before'.[120]

Conningsby Dawson made a distinction between the friendships of peacetime and those of war, writing that the war was 'so monstrously impersonal' that in making so few attachments 'the passionately personal affections of the old days shine out like beacon fires'.[121] Frederic Manning drew a distinction between friendship and comradeship, writing: 'I don't suppose I have anyone whom I can call a friend'. He noted that 'I have one or two chums' and 'good comradeship takes the place of friendship'. Manning's point was that friendship was a matter of choice, and: 'Here you can't choose … At one moment a particular man may be nothing at all to you, and the next minute you will go through hell for him'. He was describing the impulse of the moment born of particular circumstances. 'No, it is not friendship. The man doesn't matter so much; it's a kind of impersonal emotion, a kind of enthusiasm'.[122] Private William Henderson also drew a distinction between friendship and comradeship, noting that comradeship was a product of being forced into 'close contact with one another' and that whilst this relationship might 'mean much', with temporariness 'the feeling comes that it is useless to make friends in the army'.[123]

## Conclusion

Many of those who served looked back with nostalgia on comradeship. Reginald Dixon wrote: 'I have known no such comradeship as those old years gave to us'.[124] Charles Douie similarly considered 'how greatly I had been privileged in my friends'.[125] Mark

---

117 W. Cobb, Private Papers, IWM Docs 10857.
118 D.O. Barnett in Housman, op. cit. p.40 (author italics).
119 K. Schmid & O.T. Muldoon, 'Perceived Threat, Social Identification, and Psychological Well-Being : The Effects of Political Conflict Exposure', *Political Psychology*, p.4.
120 R.H. Tobin, BBC 'The Great War Interviews'.
121 C. Dawson, *Living Bayonets*, p.14.
122 Manning, op. cit. location 1395.
123 W.B. Henderson, Private Papers, IWM Docs 4592.
124 Dixon, op. cit.
125 Douie, op. cit. p.218.

Peel notes the crucial adhesive in the bond: 'Perhaps even more so in the trenches than in earlier forms of war-making, soldiering was literally as well as figuratively a place in which male bonds could keep you alive'.[126] In this he echoes S.L.A. Marshall in his research on combat in the American forces in the Second World War: 'When the chips are down a man fights to help the man next to him'.[127] In a sense, therefore, comradeship in war was the ultimate utility relationship.

The distance from home and the absence of wives, children, mothers and siblings who could fulfil more fully the need for love and belonging produced what we might call a 'distilled' version of the male relationships of peacetime. This distillation stemmed from the perpetual presence of others, the proximity and interdependence of ensuring that basic needs were fulfilled, and the intensity of some of the shared specific moments. Comradeship was a particular type of group experience. Yet there was more similarity than there was discontinuity between peace and war-time male relationships. As has been suggested, the comradeships of war were very much a mirror of the male group-based work and allied social activity relationships of peacetime. Relationships were practical, based on helping and sharing. Peel is certainly correct to state that male friendships 'tended to be tied to specific moments and contexts, characterized by the absence of women'.[128] As Harry Drinkwater was noted earlier to sum up – soldiers were 'partners in business'. In the close-knit groups that were sections, this distillation produced a tolerance and mutual understanding, sometimes experienced *almost* as a family, which fostered strength and endurance, and fulfilled the need for belonging, if not love.

Comradeship was profoundly sustaining, yet it was subject to the universal vagaries of male relations. Men did not fit in and were lonely. Some fell foul of bullies. And in the post-war years, its continuation was limited as men returned to the companionship of wives and families. Indeed, Joanna Bourke claims that: 'After the war, the generation of men who had fought were *more* liable to repudiate emotional expression outside the marital bond'.[129] Thus, many rejected the option of membership of veteran associations. At the height of the post-war 'memoir boom' in 1930 the British Legion (which did not keep records of numbers of members) had issued just under 300,000 membership badges.[130] Whilst this may be an underestimate in terms of those who received free membership, it is unlikely that the Legion ever recruited more than ten per cent of veterans. In terms of the pre-war male affection for clubs, this is notable. David Lloyd suggests that these organisations were unlikely to have appealed to working-class servicemen who did not identify with the values of the officer class who ran them.[131] The degree of interest in regimental associations is unclear. The Old

---

126 M. Peel, 'New Worlds of Friendship', in Caine, op. cit. p.306.
127 S.L.A. Marshall, *Men Against Fire*, p.161.
128 Peel, op. cit. p.310.
129 Bourke, op. cit. p.162 (italics in original).
130 http://www.legion-memorabilia.org.uk/badges/numbers.htm.
131 D. Lloyd, *Battlefield Tourism*, p.37.

Comrades Association of 13th Rifle Brigade (which, interestingly, was only established in 1928), Lloyd notes, took only 18 members and their wives on a battlefield pilgrimage in 1929, and 92 on two trips nine years later. The average ranker likely did not have the funds to go.

The low levels of membership of such organisations speak to the limitations of any persisting sense of comradeship. The Director of Training for the Ministry of Pensions noted that veterans wanted 'to be back at their old homes, near their relatives and their wives' relatives'.[132] They valued privacy and comfort. Yet the comradeship of those who had 'been there' was clearly of immense value to some. It is unclear when George Coppard finished his memoir, *With a Machine Gun to Cambrai*, published in 1969, but on the very last pages he wrote:

> Just recently I have discovered that an old 12th Division man lives close to me and my heart leaps when I spot him walking up the road. We never miss a natter, and his eyes shine as we go over the umpteenth episode of our war experiences. We catch vivid memories of the past and are glad that we were young in 1914.[133]

The friendship, comradeship, mateship of the trenches, whatever word we wish to employ, was no mirror of modern friendships. It lacked the introspective expression of personal thoughts and feelings presented for sharing and mutual analysis. This was simply not part of the cultural norm. Sidney Rogerson, after a spell in trenches, sat with his fellow officers where he had sat a week previously. He was conscious that: 'Many lives had been lost, some out of our own immediate circle', but noted that all were 'cheerful', and that there was 'otherwise no difference in our thoughts or conversation. The topic was still the all-absorbing one of what was going to happen next'.[134] The focus was on the future rather than processing the personal shared past. Emotional support, as we now would see it, was obtained through osmosis – it was not actively sought. This does not mean, however, that friendship was not a crucial element of morale. Stephen Hewett hit the mark when he wrote of 'unsentimental fellowship'. Lieutenant Cecil Bowra concluded that comradeship was 'what held soldiers to their work'.[135] It was, of course, not literally the only thing, but it was one of the major elements of the glue that held the structure of trench life together.

---

132 Major Mitchell, cited in E.T. Devine, *Disabled Soldiers and Sailors. Pensions and Training*, p.187.
133 Coppard, op. cit. pp.134-5.
134 Rogerson, op. cit. pp.117-8.
135 C.M. Bowra, *Memories*, p.90.

# 4

## 'Here I am Doing A Man's Work': Stoicism, Manliness And Coping

---

Family and friends were external resources whom soldiers could rely on for support. But what internal resources did the soldiers of 1914-1918 possess? What mental structures, what attitudes and beliefs bolstered them against the stresses of war? What images did they take with them to the battlefield of how they should carry themselves? Did the constraints of the age on how they should express thoughts and emotions about what they experienced protect and sustain?

The most ingrained of these inner resources was the Stoic position. For an age that was scorched by the white heat of technological revolution, the Victorian era was in many respects a remarkably backward-looking period. Much of its art, writing and architecture harked back to the medieval and classical periods. It was therefore unsurprising that for thinkers, classical influences came once again to the fore, the philosophy of Stoicism in particular. As we shall see, a diffusive Stoicism had come to be seamlessly embedded into the vision of coping at all levels of society. 'Being stoical' is a phrase in common use, and like many such phrases with a long history its meaning has become blurred. We therefore need to understand what Stoic thinking originally involved. How had its impact persisted? What was the nature of the influence it came to exert on attitudes in the Victorian era, that in which the vast majority of those who fought in the First World War were born?

### Stoicism

Stoicism originates in the teachings of Greek philosophers, principally Zeno. It takes its name from the porch (stoa) of the Athenian marketplace where he taught. As none of the writings of Zeno's school survive, it is through Roman Stoic philosophers, especially Seneca[1], Epictetus,[2] and the Emperor Marcus Aurelius[3] that we know it best. Without attempting a complete exposition of Stoic philosophy, it put forward the view

---

1  Lucius Annaeus Seneca (4 BCE – 65 CE).
2  c. 55-135 CE.
3  Marcus Aurelius Antoninus Augustus (121-180 CE).

that the most important thing in life was virtue or 'excellence of character'.⁴ Secondly, the Stoics believed the human mind to be wholly rational, and that 'passions' were harmful and a block to happiness.⁵ Epictetus taught that 'our opinions, desires, are within our own power', and that our attitudes and reactions are 'up to us in a way that external events themselves are not'.⁶ The Stoics acknowledged that there were 'first movements', the initial involuntary stirrings of any emotion. Beyond this they took the view that emotions are within our control because they are based on beliefs and the thoughts (incorrect judgements in Stoic terms) that run from them. These, they insisted, were open to examination and change. This indeed may reflect a universal truth. Modern psychology believes much the same about the cognitive origins of emotion in its practice of Cognitive Behaviour Therapy. Stoicism in its most austere form was therefore not about the repression or denial of feelings. It propounded the uprooting of unpleasant emotion – a matter which required discipline. Acceptable good emotions on the other hand included joy or delight, caution or discretion, and wishing what is 'truly good'.⁷

Stoicism has come to be typified by endurance. Epictetus taught that one should attempt to achieve only what one *can* achieve and attempt to change only what one *can* change. The goal of the individual was to 'cultivate greater strength and equanimity' in the face of what truly cannot be changed. Epictetus advised that what cannot be controlled should be treated as a 'matter of indifference'.⁸ In relation to the thrust of this book, he taught that things that we fear, especially suffering and physical harm, should not be looked upon as evils. Such a fear is based upon the 'false opinion that physical harm is a real evil in the way that vice is'.⁹ Harm did not stem from physical injury but from the 'guilt and shame of the betrayal of the self and the group'.¹⁰ But the Stoic was not a martyr – he was simply complying with necessity. Misfortune is not avoidable, and if it cannot be changed then it must be accepted. Seneca, who worked to develop an everyday Stoicism for the bulk of people who could not emulate the sages, encouraged us: 'Do not grow weary, perform your duty'.¹¹ And amongst the foundations of duty to others and oneself were 'self-command and self-reliance'.¹² This emphasis on duty, constancy, and self-reliance, enduring misfortune with the courage and tenacity of indifference, was the model that the soldier took to the Western Front. Private Henry Clapham and his fellows had self-reliance in spades, demonstrating stoic acceptable good emotion: 'We are a cheerful lot on the whole'. Further, they

---

4    Stoicism Today, *Live Like a Stoic for a Week*, p.6.
5    The passions included lust or appetite, fear, delight, and distress.
6    N. Sherman, *Stoic Warriors*, Kindle edition location 123.
7    Stoicism Today, op. cit. p.7.
8    Sherman, op. cit. location 128.
9    Sherman, op. cit. location 226.
10   Sherman, op. cit. location 165.
11   Seneca, *On Benefits* I.2.
12   Sherman, op. cit. location 2414.

attempted to control what they could control: 'If one makes up one's mind to have as good a time as possible, it is extraordinary what a lot of little things one can do to increase personal comfort'. He was absolutely clear that the absence of these characteristics was the road to perdition: 'If a man once starts to be sorry for himself he is finished and done for'.[13] Not to feel sorry for oneself was the basis of being able to treat discomfort and threat as matters of indifference.

## Stoicism through the ages

The merging of Stoicism with other systems of thought, particularly Christianity, has a long history. Modern scholars now see the influences of Stoicism in the writings of Saint Paul,[14] and assert that the notion of 'first movements' was adopted as 'bad thoughts' by Christian thinkers who needed to develop a doctrine on resisting temptation.[15] Similarly, Saint Augustine used the Stoic concept of 'passions' in his iteration of sin. The Stoic principle of happiness through moral virtue sat very happily within Christianity, and its general principles of discipline and duty clearly influenced the Christian monastic tradition. It is hardly surprising that there were crossovers between such systems of thought. Stoicism was very influential in the Christian Roman Empire. Christianity adopted Stoic thinking, and Stoicism adapted to make itself more acceptable to evolving Christian thought.

Original texts circulated widely again in the 15th century,[16] and in the following century Stoic thought played its role in the Reformation. Erasmus, Calvin and Lipsius all made use of Stoic thinking, in what has become known as 'neo-Stoicism'. The principal of constancy and endurance has remained an ideal in philosophical, religious and general literature through the ages. During the Renaissance the French philosopher Montaigne[17] wrote a lecture on the military life in which he made a statement as applicable to the trenches of the First World War as any other observation: 'The game of constancy is played principally to tolerate inconveniences patiently when they have no remedy'.[18] A hundred years later, Bunyan[19] would write from an austere Christian perspective which the themes of Stoicism suited well: 'Who would true valour see, Let him come hither. One here will constant be, Come wind come weather'. In these expressions, Christian Stoicism reached its high point. The 1700s, however, saw a decline in much of its influence.

---

13  H. Clapham, *Mud and Khaki*, p.58.
14  T. Engberg-Pedersen, 'Stoicism in the Apostle Paul', in S.K. Strange & J. Zupko, *Stoicism: Traditions & Transformations*, pp.52-75.
15  R. Sorabji, ' First Movements in Christianity', in Strange & Zopko, op. cit. p.106.
16  J. Stallard, 'Stoicism and its Legacy', Oxford University podcast.
17  Michel de Montaigne (1533-1592).
18  Montaigne, *Essais* I.12, p.45.
19  John Bunyan (1628-1688).

### *The Victorian Stoic revival*

Stoicism never went away. It continued to influence Western thought entwined with Christianity with a fluctuating popularity. By the time the Victorian era arrived, it might have been thought that Stoicism was due a revival. This it got. As Lee Behlman suggests, for the Victorians: 'Stoicism provided a language for defining manhood' in two main modes.[20] Firstly, one mode used historical figures as examples; the other, expressed in poetry beginning with that of Matthew Arnold, involved exhortations to the control of emotion, largely in response to loss.

In the first mode, the figure who was chosen to be reclaimed as an example was the Roman Emperor and Stoic philosopher Marcus Aurelius, who 'was broadly conceived of as a figure who could reconcile Christian "heartliness" with hard morality'.[21] He had the exciting blend for the Victorians of being both warrior and philosopher, and whilst only a quasi-Christian, left a body of writing in his *Meditations* which 'demonstrated the traits of self-sacrifice, bodily rectitude, and moral probity'. No less a luminary than John Stuart Mill in his *On Liberty* (1859) took up Marcus Aurelius as an example, writing how 'he preserved through life not only the most unblemished justice, but what was less to be expected from his Stoical breeding, the tenderest heart'.[22] This was diffusive Stoicism for a modern world.

In the second mode, Matthew Arnold, especially in a range of his earlier elegiac poems, was one of a group of Victorian writers to incorporate Stoic thinking into their work 'to define resistance to pain and to the memory of death'.[23] It is sufficient to note that one of his major works in this vein was entitled 'Resignation' (1843-8).[24] Both Mill's and Arnold's take on Stoicism was opposed by others, but this is not the point. Stoic thought was particularly alive and well in the Victorian era, and its influence on manliness was carried to the trenches of France and Flanders.

### **Victorian Manliness and the 'Stiff Upper Lip'**

Manliness became a preoccupation for the Victorians. James Garvin, the editor of *The Observer*, wrote to his son Gerald after he had been on the Western Front for four months: 'You are now passing through that last test of manhood'.[25] Lieutenant Conningsby Dawson was also conscious of having passed such a test: 'The great uplifting thought is that we have proved ourselves men'.[26] The task of war demanded it. Lieutenant Leslie Yorath declared: 'Here I am doing a man's work',[27] as did Captain

---

20  L. Behlman, 'Faithful Unto Death: The Postures of Victorian Stoicism', p.1.
21  Behlman, op. cit. p.17.
22  J.M. Robson (ed.), *Collected Works of John Stuart Mill*, Vol 13, p.236.
23  Behlman, op. cit. p.2.
24  M. Arnold, *Poetical Works*, p.52.
25  M. Pottle & J.G.G. Ledingham (eds), *We Hope to Get Word Tomorrow*, p.104.
26  C. Dawson, *Carry On*, p.76.
27  Anonymous, *A Soldier of England*, p.110.

Alfred Pollard on patrol in no-man's land, who enjoyed the idea that 'this was man's work indeed'.[28] Each individual's test was personal. It was only after winning the Distinguished Conduct Medal in a bombing attack at Sanctuary Wood that Pollard in his own view truly metamorphosed 'into a man'. He now possessed the knowledge that he could 'successfully lead men in action'.[29] For Seaman Joseph Murray, it was his father shaking his hand for the first time in his life on his joining the Royal Naval Volunteer Reserve in August 1914 that made him feel that 'I had become a man'.[30] Lance-Corporal William Andrews reported his CO at the Battle of Festubert, Harry Walker, speaking to men after their first time under fire: 'Well, lads; you may have been boys yesterday. You're men now – yes, men'.[31] These statements describe two things. Firstly, the notion of some sort of turning point and passage into manhood; and secondly, something about the nature of what made one a 'man', particularly in war, namely a certain way of behaving when faced with certain types of threats.

With the reassertion of Stoic principles of virtue, discipline, constancy and emotional control, a particular code of manliness emerged during the Victorian era within the public school system. Whilst such an education was the province of the upper and middle classes, it was mirrored in the attitudes of the working classes in a less distinct manner, as we shall later see. The code held up an image of imperial manliness (empire being the patriotic symbol recognised across classes), disinterring the concept of the chivalric warrior-defender, channelled through 'sporting manliness and English honour'.[32] The ideal of imperial Christian manliness at the turn of the century was that if one had to die, one should aim:

> To die young, clean, ardent; to die swiftly, in perfect health; to die saving others from death, or worse disgrace – to die scaling heights, to die and to carry with you into the fuller ampler life beyond, untainted hopes and aspirations, unembittered memories, all the freshness and gladness of May.[33]

Marcus Aurelius would have wholeheartedly endorsed this statement.

James Mangan has described the games cult of the Victorian school as a pursuit of 'success, aggression and ruthlessness, yet victory within the rules, courtesy in triumph, and compassion for the defeated'.[34] To place an emphasis on competitive team sports distorts the vision. The pre-eminence of sport at Edward Thring's Uppingham School certainly fostered 'the manly spirit of competition' in team games, yet athletics was equally valued. This gave boys 'experience of victory without pride and defeat without

---

28  A.O. Pollard, *Fire-Eater*, p.53.
29  Pollard, op. cit. p.127.
30  J. Murray, *Gallipoli 1915*, p.14.
31  W.L. Andrews, *Haunting Years*, p.128.
32  S.J. Bannerman, 'Manliness and the English Soldier', p.1.
33  H.A. Vachell, *The Hill*, pp.313-4.
34  J. Mangan, *Athletic Stoicism in The Victorian and Edwardian Public School*, p.135.

depression'.[35] Whilst Stoicism perceived no value in competitive games themselves, Epictetus used athletics as a metaphor for mental training, and Thring's aim in promoting athletics was absolutely within the Stoic tradition. He believed that the following principles, developed in sport, underpinned manliness: 'Never cheat, never funk, never lose temper, never brag'[36] – never give in to vice, in fact.

These values propounded the maxim *mens sana in corpore sano* – 'a healthy mind in a healthy body'. The healthy body was at the centre of the concept of 'muscular Christianity'. This phrase came into vogue in the late 1850s following the publication of the fitness enthusiast Charles Kingsley's Christian novel of social issues, *Two Years Ago*.[37] The creed is best spelt out in Thomas Hughes' statement that a 'man's body is given him to be trained and brought into subjection, and then used for the protection of the weak, (and) the advancement of all righteous causes'.[38] This was a perfect mirror of the Stoic view that whilst the body in itself was a matter of 'indifference', discipline of the body prepared one for discipline in general. Such a body should be used for the pursuit of virtue. It is obvious how the concept became a keystone of the public school emphasis on sport. Inevitably, muscular Christianity became further bound up in the 'at Heaven's command' view of empire-building, assuming a more aggressive edge. Thus, a 1901 review of the contribution of the public schools to English history held up the vision of 'the Englishman going through the world with rifle in one hand and Bible in the other', adding, without a touch of irony, 'if asked what our muscular Christianity has done, we point to the British Empire'.[39]

Towards the end of the century, however, muscular Christianity began to mutate with the rising tide of public school militarism, a tide reflected in the writings of Rudyard Kipling. This enhanced even further the Stoic concept of duty. Volunteer Corps began to develop in the public schools from 1859; and between 1871 and 1887, a third of those leaving Uppingham, Rugby and Harrow went into the army.[40] Captain Rowland Feilding (actually schooled at Haileybury, virtually a services' college) recorded these values of militarism and virtue in action, a fellow officer remarking on the opening day of the Somme offensive whilst casting his eye over German prisoners: 'Though our ambition is to kill as many of these people as we possibly can, when you see them beaten, like that, with that look in their eyes, you can hardly restrain a feeling of pity'. The officer in question concluded: 'I suppose it is the English sporting instinct asserting itself'.[41]

---

35 M. Tozer, 'Manliness: The Evolution of a Victorian Ideal', p.182.
36 Tozer, op. cit. p.184.
37 C. Kingsley, *Two Years Ago*.
38 T. Hughes, *Tom Brown At Oxford*, p.83.
39 J.G. Cotton Minchin, *Our Public Schools: Their Influence on English History; Charter House, Eton, Harrow, Merchant Taylors', Rugby, St. Paul's Westminster, Winchester*, p.113.
40 Calculation based on figures cited by Tozer, op. cit. p.237.
41 R. Feilding, *War Letters to a Wife*, p.51.

'Here I am Doing A Man's Work': Stoicism, Manliness And Coping    99

Allied to militarism, Baden-Powell's *Scouting for Boys* was another vehicle that bore the code of Stoic manliness. It assumed patriotism, stating the supposition that: 'Every boy wants to help his country in some way or other'. It emphasised courage and co-operation, exhorting Scouts to be 'strong and plucky, ready to face danger'. They were to be 'always keen to help' others and prepared for self-sacrifice in risking life in the patriotic cause. In a spirit of self-discipline (to which a whole chapter was devoted) Scouts were to give up 'personal comforts and desires'[42] in the spirit of 'duty before all'.[43] Virtue was promoted as the Code of the Knights, highlighting chivalry and honour, scouts being exhorted never to 'do a dishonourable thing, such as telling a lie or stealing'.[44] A Scout had to be 'clean in thought, word, and deed'.[45] In an attempt to stave off the flabby-handedness of the masturbator, 'if you have any manliness in you', Baden-Powell exhorted, 'you will throw off such temptation'.[46] Lastly, there was a responsibility to keep oneself 'strong and healthy',[47] to promote endurance (to which yet another whole chapter was dedicated) so that the individual could 'go through hardships and strains where another weaker man would fail', in a spirit of cheerfulness.[48]

Manliness was judged by externals, which were taken as an indication of inner qualities. In the service of *mens sana*, Stoic emotional self-regulation was prized, regulation in which the expression of distress and fear played no part. British attitudes to emotional expression, however, have varied over the centuries. In the Georgian era when the influence of Stoic thinking was at a low point, 'nervousness' was accepted as evidence of good breeding. The display of emotion by men was not associated with any suspicion of weakness or effeminacy. Being manly in a less Stoic early Georgian Britain was a different matter in comparison with the Victorian age, although primarily it involved being 'virtuous and wise'. In stark contrast, 'men were quite comfortable looking inwardly and being reflective about their own physical and psychological experiences'.[49] Near the turn of the century the novelist Helen Maria Williams would, however, write:

> An Englishman has ... sensibility to a generous or tender sentiment; but he thinks it would be unmanly to weep; and, though half choked with emotion, he

---

42  R.S.S. Baden-Powell, *Scouting for Boys*, Kindle edition locations 213-238.
43  Baden-Powell, op. cit. location 3990.
44  Baden-Powell, op. cit. location 369.
45  Baden-Powell, op. cit. location 3541.
46  Baden-Powell, op. cit. location 3547.
47  Baden-Powell, op. cit. location 376.
48  Baden-Powell, op. cit. location 3262.
49  A. Haggett, 'Looking Back: Masculinity and mental health – the long view', *The Psychologist*, p.427.

scorns to be overcome, contrives to gain the victory over his feelings, and throws into his countenance as much apathy as he can well wish.[50]

Distorted evolutionary thinking emphasised gendered differences, the Stoic emphasis on rationality being tailored to fit a vision of men as evolved rational and restrained creatures. This increasingly left 'little room for emotional self-expression'.[51] Exemplifying these distinctions, Victorian author Wilkie Collins put the following words in the mouth of one of his characters in his novel, *The Moonstone*. 'I own I broke down … and burst out crying… an hysterical relief … nothing more! Physiology says, and says truly, that some men are born with female constitutions – and I am one of them'.[52] Indeed, the 1870 edition of *The Dictionary of the English Language* included in its definition of manliness: 'not womanish, not childish'.[53]

Private Arthur Lambert described succinctly how these pressures held sway in an emotion-free parting with his wife on leaving for the Western Front in the brief note: 'Emotion is *infra dig* to the English'.[54] Second-Lieutenant Carlos Blacker, amongst his family following the loss of his brother, similarly referred to: 'The Anglo-Saxon's undemonstrative and phlegmatic façade behind which feelings were concealed'.[55] James Garvin wrote in another letter to his son Gerald on the eve of his departure to Flanders in July 1915 of the things 'too dear and deep to be expressed', and that in avoiding referring to them 'you would no more have me weak, than I would have you'.[56] Ged Garvin played his part in this bargain by never referring to fear in his letters home. Three days before his death in front of High Wood on 23 July 1916, he penned these lines in anticipation of that possibility: 'Try not to grieve for me. I hope my death will have been worthy of your trust and I couldn't die for a better cause'.[57] The few lines are a masterpiece of Stoic striving for virtue and acceptance of what cannot be changed.

The phrase 'stiff upper lip', describing mastery of emotion, has become commonplace to typify the Victorian attitude to emotional expression, yet as Thomas Dixon notes, it 'was unknown to British readers as late as the 1870s'. It was introduced to them in a periodical founded by Charles Dickens,[58] and was explained as meaning 'to

---

50 H.M. Williams, 'Letters From France', *The Monthly Review*, pp.95-6.
51 Haggett, op. cit. p.427.
52 W. Collins, *The Moonstone*, p.441.
53 R.G. Latham, *Dictionary of the English Language*, cited in Tozer, op. cit. p.2.
54 A. Lambert, *Over the Top*, p.23 (italics in original). *Infra dignitatem* means 'beneath (one's) dignity'.
55 J. Blacker (ed.), *Have You Forgotten Yet?*, p.222.
56 Pottle & Ledingham, op. cit. p.34.
57 Pottle & Ledingham, op. cit. p.227.
58 *All The Year Round*, published between 1859 and 1895. The relevant article, 'Popular American Phrases', was published in 1871.

remain firm to a purpose, to keep up one's courage'.[59] It was a handy catch phrase to define a way of being that was well-established by that point. Dixon continues:

> The expectation that emotions should be contained rather than expressed was extended to people of all classes and both sexes in various ways during the later Victorian period. Women were praised for suffering in silence, and men were mocked when their feelings were displayed.

Indeed, a Victorian policeman who wept while giving evidence against a former colleague in 1888 became the subject of national mockery in a satirical magazine as 'Robert Emotional'.

This vision of manliness held good for the upper and middle classes. The 'stiff upper lip' combined with rationality, the ability to 'keep your head when all about you are losing theirs', as Kipling expressed in his poem *If*, was the way to 'be a Man, my son'.[60] The vision embraced more or less consciously by the working classes was perhaps more complex. The notion of resilience in devaluing the 'impact of externals'[61] and the virtues of 'hardiness and endurance,'[62] were characteristics not just embedded in the public school experience. They were demonstrated daily in the uncomplaining acceptance of the working class of lives that were hard. As John Burnett notes, 'most of those who experienced such conditions are not, in their writings at least, consciously discontented', there being 'a sense of patient resignation to the facts of life, the feeling that human existence is a struggle and that survival is an end in itself'. The early death of wives or children engendered 'a fatalistic attitude that "God gives and God takes away", and that although one may mourn, one does not inveigh against the Fates'.[63] The upper, middle and lower classes therefore all approached the Great War with a stoic attitude to discomfort and emotional expression based on the notion of restraint implanted on a bedrock of endurance.

The concepts of self-discipline and duty were disseminated in the literature of the time accessed by the working class. That great Victorian moralist Samuel Smiles championed self-improvement. He devoted chapters in his great work *Self Help* to 'Application and Perseverance' and 'Energy and Courage'. He wrote of the Stoic need for 'self-discipline and self-control' and the 'honest and upright performance of individual duty, which is the glory of manly character'.[64] Indeed, he wrote a whole tome

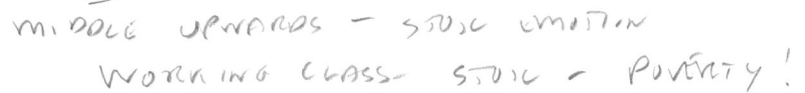

59 https://emotionsblog.history.qmul.ac.uk/2012/10/the-history-of-the-stiff-upper-lip-part-2/
60 R. Kipling, *Rewards and Fairies*, p.181.
61 Sherman, op. cit. location 2042.
62 J.A. Mangan and J. Walvin (eds), *Manlinesss and Morality*, p.1.
63 http://www.victorianweb.org/history/work/burnett6.html from J. Burnett, *Annals of Labour*.
64 S. Smiles, *Self Help*, ix.

entitled *Duty*.[65] Thus a Great War soldier would write: 'Ah, it's a bad thing is war and I don't want to go back but then, it's duty you see'.[66] How many of the poor working classes read Smiles' work given their literacy levels is unclear, but the skilled working classes with aspirations were manifestly willing to absorb his ideas. Drilling down into the working poor, there were certainly many organisations striving to ensure, as Ilana Bet-El describes, that 'middle-class morality' became the 'overriding social force'. This was achieved 'through a vast network of middle-class social workers, reform projects and philanthropic agencies' which smuggled middle class values into working class lives. These created opportunities primarily for male engagement and self-improvement, through clubs for working boys, working men's co-operatives, and religious associations. There were sports societies and social and literary clubs, and for those with the highest aspirations, university extension classes.[67] Whilst the working class boys whom the burgeoning scouting, Boys' Brigade, and other boys' club movements intended to reach no doubt saw themselves as having little in common with the ethos of their public school counterparts, middle-class values were infiltrating their lives. Indeed, it has been estimated that by 1914 over 40 per cent of British adolescents belonged to some form of youth organisation.[68] Hugh Cunningham describes the character-building values of these organisations as: 'Self-help, local initiative, discipline, order, health-giving recreation' and patriotism – a class specific reworking of public school values.[69]

The heroic vision of manliness was not only disseminated in the public schools. The jingoistic *Boy's Own Paper* and similar vehicles for the young championed the notion of the British Empire as the highest achievement of civilization. Robert Roberts notes in *The Classic Slum* that boy's papers such as *Magnet* and *Gem* were widely-read and admired by boys in working-class Salford. A form of the Christian-imperial ethos was absorbed into a 'might is right' philosophy based on a sense of national superiority.[70] Richard Holmes describes a 'working class music-hall patriotism with its noisy affirmation that British was best and foreigners were funny'.[71] Roberts saw support for the notion of empire as strong and unquestioned,[72] and even the very poor joined in national celebrations enthusiastically, enjoying the symbols of their culture. Miner and poet Sergeant Will Streets, who worked down a Derbyshire pit from the age of 14 to 28, wrote that any Englishman 'ought to count it a privilege to die for his country',[73]

---

65   S. Smiles, *Duty*.
66   Unattributed, quoted in D. Winter, *Death's Men*, p.32.
67   I.R. Bet-El, *Conscripts*, pp.187-8.
68   J. Springhall, 'Building Character in the British Boy: The Attempt to Extend Christian Manliness to Working-Class Adolescents, 1880–1914', in Mangan & Walvin, op. cit. p.52.
69   H. Cunningham, *The Volunteer Force*, p.98.
70   R. Roberts, *The Classic Slum*, p.128.
71   R. Holmes, *Tommy*, p.530.
72   Roberts, op. cit. p.145.
73   W. Streets, quoted in A. Fletcher, *Life, Death and Growing up on the Western Front*, p.49.

and did just that with the Sheffield City Battalion at Serre on 1 July 1916. Whilst a 'King and Country' preoccupation was shared by all classes, patriotism for the working class was a complex matter. It was centred particularly on local allegiance[74] – 'for most soldiers their England was a very local and particular place'.[75] Working class men built their own version of the loyal manly ethos in local working men's clubs and football teams. Valerie Burton notes: 'Working-class masculinity seems more robust, at least in so far as it involved a greater degree of collective identification and mutual affirmation'.[76]

As Jessica Meyer however demonstrates, there was not just a heroic notion of manliness. In the patriarchal society there was also, for the middle and working classes, a 'domestic' manly identity. This was 'located much more clearly in relation to women with its emphasis on men's roles as good sons, husbands and fathers, as both protector and provider'. This sort of domestic manliness meant 'being a heterosexual and ruling over a domestic sphere'.[77] In understanding this, the power of men over women and their assignation to certain domestic roles must be appreciated. Industrialization had hastened this vision: 'Masculinity was locked more firmly than ever into a notion of paid, productive work'.[78] For the middle classes there was the luxury of a preoccupation with profession; for the working classes it was driven by immediate availability of jobs. This was a vision of manliness that required no transmission by the public schools or though muscular Christianity, and could be shared equally across class. As John Tosh puts it: 'Manliness had much more to do with one's standing in the sight of men than with one's standing with the Almighty'.[79] It was about being seen to be an appropriately potent economic provider and family man. The two visions of manliness, heroic and domestic, were linked in terms of the war. Men fought to protect their homes and families. Both visions were sustaining, but the war also placed major demands on them in entirely different ways; on heroic manliness by trial, and on domestic manliness by separation.

## Stoicism and Personal Control

Living in an age when stoicism is out of favour, and introspection and emotional expression the norm, it is easy to be dismissive of the emotional self-control of a century ago. There are good reasons to believe, however, that it was powerfully self-protective. Psychologists have long been interested in the extent to which individuals believe that they can control their own destiny. In this they essentially follow the Stoic

---

74  J. Benson, *The Working Class in Britain*, pp.148-150, 160-62.
75  Fletcher, op. cit. p.48.
76  V. Burton, review of M. Roper and J. Tosh, *Manful Assertions*, p.393.
77  J. Bourke, 'Gender Roles in Killing Zones', in. J. Winter (ed.), *The Cambridge History of the First World War*, p.156.
78  J. Tosh, 'Masculinities in an Industrializing Society', *Journal of British Studies*, p.332.
79  Tosh, op. cit. p.335.

viewpoint that wellbeing 'depends upon a sense of control and agency, a sense that even in the most constrained circumstances we are not entirely powerless'.[80] They have drawn distinctions concerning the locus of the sense of control that people experience, namely either internal or external, these distinctions being seen as stable characteristics of the person.[81] 'Internals' tend to attribute the outcome of events to their own control; 'externals' attribute the outcome of events to circumstances outside of their control. The distinction is important in that people who have a high external locus of control respond more poorly to stress, suffer more physical and psychological symptoms, and demonstrate ineffective coping strategies.[82] Matters are, of course, not quite this black and white, thus there are individuals who use a combination of the two strategies, taking responsibility for effective actions when appropriate, and accepting surrender of control to external sources when appropriate. To a certain extent, the Stoic is of this mixed breed. Further, we also know that problem focussed coping, i.e. working out a practical solution to a difficulty, is adaptive when the stressor is seen as controllable; and that emotion-focussed coping, i.e. trying to reduce the negative emotional responses associated with the problem, such as frustration, fear, anxiety or depression, is adaptive when the stressor is seen as uncontrollable. These two modes of coping the Stoic would encourage fully. There are also circumstances, namely situations where the outcome is likely to be unfavourable whatever one does, where avoidance is the most adaptive coping strategy.[83]

The positional warfare of the First World War created prolonged experiences of discomfort and threat which demanded management. The soldier, however, had limited control over these and the associated sense of helplessness was a partly inevitable and often disturbing experience. Jessica Meyer suggests that this experience 'threatened the very root of those Victorian ideals of masculinity, self-help and self-reliance'.[84] This may be an overstatement. The Stoic trick was to be satisfied, if necessary, with the very few things one *could* control, and dismiss the things one could not. There were a myriad of small ways in which soldiers could make life more comfortable or safer for themselves. And if they could not control the direct threat in the final analysis, then at least they could attempt to control their responses to it. This is where the coping techniques of the age proved of value. If soldiers aimed for stoic indifference, suppressing emotion, then they were controlling a different form of threat, that of their coping being undermined. Cheerfulness and humour, reversing some of the

---

80  Sherman, op. cit. location 2066.
81  J.B. Rotter, *Social Learning and Clinical Psychology*.
82  M. Zeidner, & N. Endler, *Handbook of Coping: Theory, Research, Applications*, p.414; A. Roddenberry & K. Renk, 'Locus of Control and Self-Efficacy: Potential Mediators of Stress, Illness, and Utilization of Health Services in College Students', *Child Psychiatry & Human Development*, p.353.
83  Zeidner & Endler, op. cit. p.414.
84  J. Meyer, *Men of War*, p.139.

sense of victimisation, were an essential part of this. These strategies were, for the most part, successfully protective.

## Conclusion

There is perhaps no more evocative image of British Stoicism in the trenches than the description given by Rifleman Aubrey Smith of Lance-Corporal Thomas Pace who had had an arm and leg blown off. 'Limbless, and suffering terribly from loss of blood, he nevertheless smoked a cigarette and waited patiently for a stretcher that we dare not tell him was most unlikely to arrive'.[85] Similarly, Lieutenant Reginald Hargreaves was critically injured at St Eloi in March 1916, and as gangrene set in, lost both foot and hand. Captain Billy Congreve VC wrote: 'He is so maimed ... yet I feel he is the splendid sort of fellow who will bear it well and have a happy enough life'.[86] Stoic constancy would see him through.

Stoicism was the solid core of Victorian manliness. As Robert Sherriff's character Stanhope declares in *Journey's End*, all would 'just go on sticking it because they know ... it's the only decent thing a man can do'.[87] Whether of the officer class or the other ranks, diffusive Stoicism governed the reactions of all. At its heart was the maintenance of virtue and the control of emotion. Courage, self-sacrifice and constancy in the pursuit of duty when faced by threat and suffering, were givens. Virtue involved honour, discipline, and decency. Emotional control was maintained by uncomplaining acceptance. The mix was made heady by patriotism. Intertwined with this was a complementary vision of manliness that had been strengthening during the period – domestic manliness, the male as economic protector and provider, who was now fighting for hearth and home. These attitudes and beliefs were vehicles that facilitated both motivation and the ability to endure. Although contrary to the modern spirit of 'working things through', stoic emotional control and the vision of manliness gave soldiers a model for sustaining themselves in the face of seemingly interminable stress and fuelled their self-esteem.

> Really, it is fortunate this does not exist today as racism & all other evils would still exist.

---

85  A Rifleman, *Four Years on the Western Front*, p.50.
86  B. Congreve, *Armageddon Road*, p.117.
87  R.C. Sherriff, *Journey's End*, Act Two, Scene Two.

5

# 'We Must Go On Trusting In God' – Faith, Fatalism, Intuition and Superstition

The inner resources of those who fought in the Great War were shaped not only by the cultural mainsprings of stoicism and manliness, but also by an eclectic spiritual identity. John Terraine has written that: 'Two elements, above all others, separate the 1914-1918 people from ourselves: patriotism and religion'.[1] In grappling with the metaphysics of trench existence, individuals relied on mix of theological sophistication, simple faith and downright magical thinking.

## Religion

### Christianity in Britain in 1914

Despite Lieutenant Robert Graves' assertion that 'hardly one soldier in a hundred was inspired by religious feeling of even the crudest kind',[2] Britain would have undoubtedly seen itself as a manifestly Christian nation in 1914. The churches themselves were, however, alarmed at what they saw as a rising tide of secularism and a lack of church attendance.[3] The working class, just as they made up the bulk of the population, still made up the bulk of churchgoers. Even if their appearances were sporadic, they still maintained a strong allegiance to the religious ceremonies of baptisms, marriage, and funeral.[4] What therefore was the nature of the Christianity that the soldier took to war in 1914?

1  J. Bickersteth, *The Bickersteth Diaries*, p.ix.
2  R. Graves, *Goodbye to All That*, p.166.
3  In fact, all Protestant church numbers increased prior to the war, although the rate of growth in the Church of England was slower than that for Nonconformists. (K.C. Fielden, 'The Church of England in the First World War', p.17). Those who claimed membership were naturally far more numerous than those who attended or were communicants. The total number of communicants in 1901 was 1,945,000 and by 1906 had grown to 1,988,000 and continued to grow until 1911 to 2,293,000. (A. Halsey, *Trends in British Society Since 1900*, p.424).
4  C.G. Brown, *The Death of Christian Britain*, p.166.

By the time of the Great War, even those within the church were describing the notion of 'diffusive Christianity'. This represented a drift away from theological dogma towards the idea of Christianity as representing 'a code of behaviour, an ethical system and not a religious faith'.[5] Private Stephen Graham affirmed that 'the general army point of view' was that 'Christianity was character and it was conduct'.[6] The nature of the Christianity that the working-class man took to the trenches was something of a patchwork. The evidence examined in this chapter demonstrates that there were upper and middle-class soldiers who carried both a devout faith and a Church of England theology with them to war. The spiritually intense religious revivals that were a feature of the Victorian era, however, swept primarily through the working-class. The last great pre-war revival had its epicentre in non-conformist Wales in 1904-5, but spread to Scotland and England. Estimates of the number of converts in Wales vary from 40,000 to 100,000, with many more across the UK. With the Nonconformist emphasis on salvation through personal experience, the revival had a strongly emotional flavour and was accompanied by ecstatic phenomena such as auditory hallucinations.[7] The effects of this revival, particularly amongst younger converts were not long-lasting,[8] but whatever its nature or longevity, it indicates that in addition to the fervent Catholicism of Irish soldiers, ardent Protestant faith of a variety of denominations was alive and well in working class volunteers and conscripts.

Second-Lieutenant Bernard Martin was Methodist by persuasion, but on being issued with kit en route to France was subject to some delightfully muddled doctrinal advice by an elderly quartermaster sergeant. On stating that he was 'not really C of E', he was advised to 'stick to C of E, Sir. You wouldn't want to be buried by the Pope, I'm sure'. Martin was indifferent to who might inter him, but was told earnestly that 'RCs go to Hell before they get to Heaven – that's official'.[9] The sergeant clearly thought that the denomination of the officiating padre would inflict on Martin an unwelcome and unnecessary long-cut on his route to the hereafter. For many of the working class, religious belief was less clearly demarcated by the distinctions of denomination than it was for Martin's quartermaster. One NCO remarked to a padre during the war: 'To most men religion means nothing, except the notion that there was one above, a sense of duty to live cleanly, and a belief that there would be a reckoning sometime'.[10] In her analysis of religious belief and popular culture in the London Borough of Southwark between the years 1880 and 1939, Sarah Williams concluded that in general, belief should be conceived of as a 'dynamic process which drew on folklore, superstition,

---

5  J. Drewett, 'Diffused Christianity: Asset or Liability?', *Theology*, p.84.
6  S. Graham, *A Private in the Guards*, p.255.
7  C.T. Fryer, 'Psychological Aspects of the Welsh Revival: 1904-5', *Proceedings of the Society for Psychical Research*, p.196.
8  C.R. Williams, 'The Welsh Religious Revival, 1904-5', *British Journal of Sociology*, p.242.
9  B. Martin, *Poor Bloody Infantry*, p.34.
10  A. Wilkinson, *The Church of England and the First World War*, p.149.

formal belief and occasional or conditional conformity to institutions'.[11] Similarly, Andrew Crome describes a 'folk religion', a kind of Christianity based on superstition, including 'a general belief in Jesus, no really strong theological beliefs, maybe a bit of Sunday School teaching, maybe a few old hymns, but no theological basis'.[12] Thus, sitting with a man destined for execution on the Western Front, the Reverend Julian Bickersteth noted: 'To him, hymn singing meant religion'.[13]

The ever-present possibility of death in trench warfare brought the issue of any afterlife sharply into focus. For the ordinary soldier, heaven was often a concept 'removed from doctrinal precepts',[14] or as Crome puts it, soldiers 'might think that they could get to heaven but they might not know exactly how'.[15] Julian Bickersteth despaired, meeting 'man after man to whom religion is simply a name and has never touched either his heart or mind'. He lamented that no one seemed to have 'been brought into contact with any sacramental teaching of any kind'.[16] David Cairns, in his post-war review of religion in the army, reported a study carried out by the Bishop of Kensington estimating that 80 per cent of men from the Midlands had never heard of or understood the meaning of the sacraments.[17] Cairns records one padre as stating dryly: 'The British soldier has certainly got religion. I am not so sure, however, that he has got Christianity'.[18]

### *The churches and war*

If the men going off to war in 1914 needed a mental Christian template providing justification to fight in addition to a patriotic one, then the churches provided ample reason. Article 37 of the 39 articles of the Church of England followed the teachings of St Augustine in allowing a Christian to take up arms in a 'just cause', and indeed the church presented the war as thus. Lieutenant John Reith's father wrote to him on arrival in France in 1914: 'The cause is a righteous one if ever there was a righteous cause. God is and must be on our side'.[19] The Nonconformist denominations, often previously pacifist, by and large offered unconditional support to the war with the exception of the Quakers. So did the English Catholic Church, even if its Irish counterpart was more divided in its views for political reasons.

---

11  J.M. Strange, *Death, Grief and Poverty in Britain 1870-1914*, p.52.
12  A. Crome, '"Mobilise the Nation for a Holy War" – Churches, Chaplains and British Religion in World War I', Manchester University podcast.
13  Bickersteth, op. cit. p.193.
14  Strange, op. cit. p.52.
15  Crome, op. cit.
16  Bickersteth, op. cit. p.78.
17  D. Cairns, *The Army and Religion*. The seven sacraments of the Roman Catholic Church include Baptism, Confirmation, Eucharist, Penance, Anointing of the Sick, Holy Orders, and Matrimony. The Anglican Church recognises only two as ordained by Christ, Baptism and the Eucharist.
18  Cairns, op. cit. p.448 & 156.
19  J. Reith, *Wearing Spurs*, p.54.

The Archbishop of Canterbury, Randall Davidson, stated that Britain could not 'without sacrificing principles of honour and justice, more dear than life itself, have stood aside' from the war.[20] The Archbishop of York, Cosmo Lang, was more martial, stating that 'there could be no peace until this German spirit had been crushed'.[21] Alleged German atrocities, the sinking of the *Lusitania* and the execution of Edith Cavell (the daughter of a clergyman) served to bolster the 'just war' thesis. The Bishop of London, Arthur Winnington-Ingram, went the furthest of the church hierarchy in exhorting the nation to band together:

> In a great crusade ... to kill Germans. To kill them, not for the sake of killing, but to save the world; to kill the good as well as the bad; to kill the young men as well as the old, to kill those who have showed kindness to our wounded as well as those fiends who crucified the Canadian sergeant, who superintended the Armenian massacres, who sank the Lusitania and who turned the machine guns on the civilians of Aerschott and Louvain, and to kill them lest the civilisation of the world should itself be killed.[22]

The private views of some Church of England ministers accorded well with these sentiments. Julian Bickersteth (not yet serving on the Western Front) wrote to his parents in May 1915 using words about the enemy unlikely to be found in the New Testament: 'God cannot allow such scum to exist'.[23]

Whilst the man at the front may have had little interest in the more technical aspects of the position of the established church, its notion of the 'just war' was certainly popular. The Anglican deployment of the atrocities issue to support this was much in tune with the preoccupations of the soldier on active service. Many personal accounts refer to their occurrence, both real and mythical. They were hence clearly lodged in the popular military consciousness, at least early in the war. Second-Lieutenant Carlos Blacker described a fellow officer, Overton-Jones, who believed the allied cause to be 'righteous'. For him it was a 'matter of religious faith that, in the end, we would win'.[24] The disquieting fact, however, was that both sides felt they were fighting a just war. Henry Williamson, observing burials during the 1914 Christmas Truce, watched a German soldier inscribe on a wooden cross 'for fatherland and freedom'. Williamson protested: 'But how can you be fighting for freedom, *you* started the war, *we* are fighting for freedom". The reply came back in disagreement: "But *we* are fighting for freedom". The churches never claimed that God was 'on our side', even if the man in trenches may have interpreted it thus. Williamson similarly watched another German

---

20  *The Times*, 10 February 1915.
21  *The Times*, 12 October 1914.
22  Wilkinson, op. cit. p.217.
23  Bickersteth, op. cit. p.35.
24  J. Blacker (ed.), *Have You Forgotten Yet?*, p.118.

dedicate the grave of an unknown soldier to God. When he again drew attention to this, the German remarked 'God is on our side'. Williamson responded: 'But ... he's on *our* side', adding that this revelation was a 'tremendous shock'.[25] Such cognitive dissonance was inevitable with Christian nations fighting one other, each relying on the the same reasoning. The Prussian belt buckle, declaring 'Gott mit uns', demonstrated this only too well.

Some soldiers, however, would have no truck with religious justification. Sergeant Ben Keeling took the view that 'I have no use for "God" or for the sentiment that we in our holy righteousness are fighting a nation of brutes'.[26] Lieutenant Horace Fletcher wrote to his mother in early 1916, expressing his disgust for the church's support of the conflict: 'Ought we not to be praying that the mind of the Church ... may be led by the Holy Spirit and guided by His power, to stop war henceforward?'[27]

### *God in the trenches*

The extraordinary Bernard William Vann is the epitome of muscular Christianity.[28] He was a teacher and ordained clergyman who won the Victoria Cross. Born in 1887, Vann attended Chichele College and Jesus College, Cambridge, and was a notable sportsman in the muscular mold. He was captain at football, hockey and cricket at Chichele, and on leaving school he played football for Northampton, Burton United and Derby County. In 1906, whilst teaching at Ashby-de-la-Zouche school he qualified for Leicestershire hockey colours. Going up to Cambridge in 1907 he obtained college colours at football and hockey, and represented the university at football on several occasions. He was ordained deacon in 1910, serving as curate of St Barnabas, New Humberstone, until he took up post as chaplain and assistant master at Wellingborough School in 1912. Frustrated by the delay in his application for an army chaplaincy, with his bishop's permission he was commissioned second-lieutenant in the 8th Sherwood Foresters. Estimates of the number of times Vann was wounded vary between seven and 13. He was first buried by a trench mortar in April 1915 in an action in which he won the Military Cross. Hospitalised briefly with 'shellshock', within days of his return he was patrolling no-man's land again. He was shot in the left forearm in a vicious bombing fight during the assault on the Hohenzollern Redoubt in October 1915. Wounded again in June 1916 on the Somme, he was further wounded in September that year leading a highly successful raid on Vimy Ridge in which he won a bar to his MC.

He was promoted lieutenant-colonel of the 1/6th Sherwood Foresters in October 1917. His supreme achievement was in the 46th Division's crossing of the St Quentin

---

25  H. Williamson, BBC 'The Great War Interviews'.
26  F.H. Keeling, *Letters*, p.264.
27  L. Housman, *War Letters of Fallen Englishmen*, p.109.
28  P.E. Hodgkinson, *British Infantry Battalion Commanders in the First World War*, pp.178-180.

Canal on 29 September 1918. Held up by fire he personally led the line forward. Subsequently, attacking the German guns at Lehaucourt, he 'led his men straight for the guns, shot down the German gunners as they fired, and having emptied his revolver, he gave one man a kick which sent him down a dug-out and maimed the last two men who showed fight with his riding crop'.[29] His VC was awarded posthumously as he was killed five days later on 3 October 1918 at Ramicourt. In his obituary, a brother officer described him as 'a fighter, not merely against the enemy in the field, but a fighter against everything and everybody that was not an influence for good to his men'.[30] Beyond this evident diffusive Christianity, Vann carried a small communion altar and cup in his pack – 'He never forgot that he was a priest of God, for it was his greatest joy to be able to do the double duty of commanding his battalion and giving Communion to the sick and wounded'.[31] There was no contradiction for Vann between the communion cup and the revolver, boot or riding crop – he had no doubt the war was a righteous cause.

Lieutenant Bernard Adams railed that if men were Christian there would be no war, but added: 'In the arena there are many who have felt Christ by their side'.[32] Laurence Housman's collection, *War Letters of Fallen Englishmen*, demonstrates a range of use of general religious statements in relation to soldiers' sense of purpose. Captain Theodore Wilson noted simply about looking beyond the everyday experience of the war: 'There is always God'.[33] Others deployed theological ideas to reinforce their reasons for fighting. Private Roger Livingstone expressed the view in a letter to his mother in October 1917: 'The very principles for which Christ gave His life are identically those principles for which Britain is to-day giving her life-blood'.[34] Captain The Honourable Robert Palmer wrote from Mesopotamia in 1915 that he hoped that the war would 'mark a distinct stage towards a more Christian conception of international relations'.[35] Others referred to faith for more personal reasons. Lieutenant Bernard Pitt recorded how he needed to draw on reserves of energy that were beyond those he felt he could normally access: 'Sometimes one has great need of a strength which is not in one's power to use, but is a grace of God'.[36] The day before his death on 1 July 1916, Second-Lieutenant John Engall informed his parents that he had attended communion and was resigned to whatever might come: 'I placed my soul and body in God's keeping, and I am going into battle with His name on my lips, full of confidence and trusting implicitly in Him'. Engall mistakenly had 'a strong

---

29 *London Gazette*, 14 December 1918.
30 W.D. Jamieson, *Men of the High Peak*, p.122.
31 *The Wellingburian*, cited in Cheltenham & Gloucester WFA Newsletter, no.83 September 2013.
32 B. Adams, *Nothing of Importance*, p.302.
33 Housman, op. cit. p.300.
34 Housman, op. cit. p.176.
35 Housman, op. cit. p.203.
36 Housman, op. cit. p.216.

feeling that I shall come through safely'; but nonetheless gave a higher meaning to his possible death: 'Should it be God's holy will to call me away, I am quite prepared to go'.[37] Lieutenant The Honourable Gerald Grenfell used the same basis for reassuring his mother following the death of his brother, the poet Julian: 'He has just passed on … there is no interruption even in the work which God has for him'.[38] Belying Robert Graves, in censoring letters Lieutenant Eric Marchant noted: 'The percentage that showed a realisation of religious truth and faith in God, was tremendously bigger than ever I suspected', such phrases as 'we must go on trusting in God' being present in 'dozens of letters'.[39]

Some soldiers clearly took the view that God was taking a personal and active interest in them. Sergeant W. Daniels knelt and prayed with the padre on the firestep of his trench, regarded with amusement by his fellows. Daniels told his fellows what he had requested of his maker, 'that I hoped he'd save me from death'. Surviving the action reinforced his belief in the utility of this: 'I really think without a doubt that praying to God did save my life'.[40] Private Norman Demuth used to find himself 'sitting and thinking about God quite a lot'. He was clear that He existed as: 'You see one very often felt something behind one'.[41] Captain James Lusk, whose territorial unit of the Scottish Rifles suffered many losses at Festubert in June 1915 wrote home in the aftermath: 'God has helped me wonderfully at every turn of the way, and will still lead on'.[42] Lieutenant Hugh Shields, a medical officer, stated on 25 September 1914 that 'somehow I don't feel that God means me to get killed yet'.[43] He was right in the short term but this protection did not last, dying at Ypres exactly a month later. Some of those with strong faith echoed this sentiment, believing that if God spared them then it was for a special purpose. Reginald Davis, a YMCA devotee before the war described having the feeling that 'God will give me another chance of doing more work'.[44] The Reverend Philip 'Tubby' Clayton, founder of Talbot House, Poperinghe ('Toc H'), indeed introduced a pledge for those in the process of taking holy orders: 'If God decides to bring me through this war, I vow to take it as a hint from Him that I shall help and serve the Church in future throughout the life that He gives back to me'.[45] Lieutenant William St Leger similarly held the belief that God would take an individual after He decreed his earthly mission was complete but added pragmatically

---

37  Housman, op. cit. p.107.
38  Housman, op. cit. p.115.
39  E.L. Marchant, Private Papers, IWM Docs 12054.
40  W. Daniels, quoted in M. Arthur, *Forgotten Voices of the Great War*, p.140.
41  N. Demuth, quoted in Arthur, op. cit. p.165.
42  J. Lusk, *Letters and Memories*, p.84.
43  H.J.H. Shields, quoted in A. Watson, *Enduring the Great War*, p.95.
44  E. Hodder-Williams, *One Young Man*, Kindle edition location 483.
45  P.T.B Clayton, quoted in M. Snape, *God and the British Soldier*, p.29.

on 10 October 1917, 'I wonder when I shall have fulfilled my parts'.⁴⁶ In his case the date was in question was six months later, on 27 April 1918.

*Emergency religion*
Others called on God as and when needed. Soldiers might attempt to reassert faith before going into the front line, especially when action loomed. Stephen Graham, ending his first tour in forward trenches reported one of his fellow soldiers as remarking: 'I'm going to make my peace with God before ever I go up to the line again.'⁴⁷ Captain Douglas Cuddeford noted that it was always noticeable 'how religious many men became when death was looming ahead', but added disparagingly 'in most cases the mood only lasted as long as the danger'. This was, of course, precisely how the bulk of the working class population would have used formal religion prior to the war.

At Mons, Lieutenant Aubrey Herbert noted how many of his men, under their first fire, 'were praying and crossing themselves'.⁴⁸ Scout Joe Cassells wrote: 'I suppose that everyone under shell fire, at one time or another, in some manner, prays', and often did so himself.⁴⁹ Private Cecil Thomas, who prayed daily, realised when subject to a box barrage at Vimy Ridge in May 1916 that: 'Now we are really praying for the first time, in the full realization of our own microscopic smallness and the impossibility of all protection save from above'.⁵⁰ In a shellhole in no-man's land on 1 July 1916, Private George Ashurst watched wounded soldiers being shot and bodies blown into the air, and 'as I gazed on this awful scene and realised my own terrible danger I asked God to help me'.⁵¹ Similarly, lying face-down under fire, Private Ernest Parker later wrote that 'after a time I prayed and fell into a peaceful reverie'.⁵² Such sudden interest in supplication was not limited to rankers. Before the first day of the battle of Arras, Douglas Cuddeford described a young officer of his battalion up all night praying.⁵³

Soldiers naturally resorted to prayer or sought reassurance in the face of certain death. Private George Brame's pal was mortally wounded and asked him to 'pray for me now'. Brame, conscious that he was 'not much used to praying', knelt down and 'offered up a simple prayer'. He interestingly added: 'I was conscious that the prayer was received'.⁵⁴ Julian Bickersteth described a dying officer, one arm blown off, who was less certain than Brame about God's presence on the battlefield. He asked: 'Padre,

46 W.B. St. Leger, Private Papers, IWM Docs 20504.
47 Graham, op. cit. p.199.
48 A. Herbert, *Mons, Anzac and Kut*, p.18.
49 J. Cassells, *The Black Watch*, p.126.
50 C. Thomas, quoted in T. Donovan (ed.), *The Hazy Red Hell*, pp.64-5.
51 G. Ashurst, *My Bit*, p.101.
52 E.W. Parker, *Into Battle*, p.55.
53 D.W.J. Cuddeford, *And All for What?*, p.136.
54 G. Brame, Diary, http://www.firstworldwar.com/diaries/onthebelgiancoast.htm.

is that you? Is there a God?'[55] Lieutenant John Allen on Gallipoli similarly reported a dying soldier asking: 'Shall I go to heaven or hell, sir?' Allen, who probably had little option, answered in the preferred direction, whereupon the soldier replied: 'At any rate, I'll say my prayers'. Seemingly knowing no formal utterance that fitted his predicament, he made up his own: 'Oh God, be good and ease my pain – if only a little'.[56] Escape from death might prompt spiritual re-evaluation. After his wounding in March 1915 at Neuve Chapelle, Private Frederick Whitham wrote to his wife: 'If God spares me to get over this, I mean to be a better lad'.[57]

'Woodbine Willie', the Reverend G.A. Studdert Kennedy, was clear in his contempt for orisons of self-preservation, noting 'that's not prayer, it's "wind" ... selfish prayer is not prayer at all'.[58] One ranker admitted to the following selfish prayer: 'Oh God, for Christ's sake, don't let me be killed or maimed: don't let me lose my arms or legs'.[59] Another, who confessed to having previously not been over-familiar with his supplications reported prior to the Battle of Neuve Chapelle in March 1915 that he prayed every night: 'I believed there is a God because I prayed to him before the battle to keep me safe and He did'.[60] The non-believer Captain Gilbert Carré questioned believer Second-Lieutenant Alan Thomas in 1917: 'You mean it's as well to be on the safe side? Praying might help and anyway it can't do any harm?'[61] He no doubt voiced the attitude of many. Private Alfred Burrage had been brought up as a Roman Catholic, but was no longer practising, yet as he noted, 'I couldn't quite disbelieve', and on the ship crossing the Channel realised that not being in a state of grace: 'If it were all true ... things might be very awkward for me if I happened to die'.[62] Second-Lieutenant Huntly Gordon rejected this kind of activity, writing: 'It is no use praying to be protected from shells or bullets'. Applying logic he questioned why God should save him above others: 'Why should I be spared?' His view was that it was inappropriate to regard God as a 'lucky mascot'.[63] Gordon was, however, happy to use his theological knowledge as a comfort: 'In this strange world the Psalms can be a very present help in time of trouble' especially when they were 'written by a fighter who knew what it was to be scared stiff'.[64] Like 'Woodbine Willie', Lieutenant Burgon 'Bishop' Bickersteth spoke contemptuously of 'religion which suddenly bubbles to the surface' dismissing it as largely valueless.[65] Noting that this was disparagingly referred to as 'funk religion',

---

55 Bickersteth, op. cit. p.140.
56 Housman, op. cit. p.27.
57 F. Whitham, Letters.
58 G.A. Studdert Kennedy, *The Hardest Part*, pp.225-6.
59 Quoted in R. Holmes, *Tommy*, p.524.
60 Quoted in Holmes, op. cit. p.524.
61 A. Thomas, *A Life Apart*, p.87.
62 Ex-Private X (A.M. Burrage), *War is War*, p.13.
63 H. Gordon, *The Unreturning Army*, Kindle edition location 1543.
64 Gordon, op. cit. location 1536.
65 Bickersteth, op. cit. p.169.

'We Must Go On Trusting In God' – Faith, Fatalism, Intuition and Superstition    115

David Cairns had the good grace to refer to it as 'at best a very elementary form of religion', thus capturing perfectly the faith of the majority of working class soldiers.[66] It is impossible to estimate what percentage of men resorted to religion in the face of danger. The only contemporary evidence available on religious thought in the moment of 'greatest danger in order to overcome the fear of death' comes from the German side of the front lines. Walter Ludwig reported that religious thinking was the most frequently used coping mechanism, employed by 45 per cent of soldiers.[67]

For its part, the army regarded religiosity as a 'key indicator of high morale',[68] and believed that it actively enhanced the soldier's fighting abilities.[69] Both the religious insurance policy and sustained faith were reflected in attendance at organised religious observance at the front. Holy Communion having been flagged up in battalion orders, John Reith was disappointed that only 65 of 400 or so men from his unit attended.[70] In contrast, Private Henry Russell described a drum-head service just prior to going into action at Messines in June 1917, and how 'men sang hymns with reverence and prayed with understanding. It reached the heart and soul'.[71] Reginald Davis noted that 'the real Sunday services are voluntary ones' and that the men who attended 'and there are quite a large number' went because they felt 'the need of such a service'.[72] Services provided moments of quiet sanctuary. Captain Geoffrey Dugdale attended Holy Communion at Ypres in 1917. He described how 'I felt at peace; away from the war and all the beastliness it entailed' presuming that 'the others must have felt the same'.[73] Julian Bickersteth observed during the bombardment on the Somme prior to 1 July 1916 that during voluntary services 'the little church was again overflowing'.[74] Maurice Murray, chaplain with the 12th and 13th battalions Sussex Regiment would normally have expected 50 voluntary communicants, but on the eve of the opening of the Third Battle of Ypres found himself with 200, and in need of a larger venue.[75] Neither padres sneered at what Michael Snape has described as 'emergency religion'.[76]

Roman Catholicism inspired a more steady attendance. Lieutenant-Colonel Rowland Feilding, commanding 6th Connaught Rangers, an Irish unit, recorded that it was a case of 'keeping (his men) away' from mass, rather than forcing them to go. The intensity of their religion was 'something quite remarkable, and I had underestimated it', he noted with some surprise.[77] Sergeant John Lucy, Royal Irish Rifles,

66   Cairns, op. cit. pp.7-8.
67   W. Ludwig, cited in Watson, *Enduring*, pp.236-7.
68   Snape, op. cit. p.179.
69   Snape, op. cit. p.186.
70   Reith, op. cit. pp.157-8.
71   H. Russell, *Slaves of the War Lords*, pp.142-3.
72   Hodder-Williams, op. cit. location 511.
73   G. Dugdale, *'Langemarck' and 'Cambrai'*, p.63.
74   Bickersteth, op. cit. p.92.
75   M.W. Murray, Private Papers, IWM Docs 7097.
76   Snape, op. cit. p.45.
77   R. Feilding, *War Letters to a Wife*, p.85.

recorded the fatal wounding of a fellow NCO, Sergeant Kelly, struck in the stomach by a shell splinter. 'Imperturbably he faced this new situation, resigned himself to his fate'; and, propping himself against the wall of the trench: 'Calmly fished out his Rosary beads and began to tell them'.[78] He was actually killed by a German bayonet before the shell splinter had done its work, with the beads still in his hands. Catholic priests were, however, equally as sceptical as their Church of England counterparts. Roman Catholic chaplain Charles Plater thus wrote: 'Speaking roughly, the fervour of the men's Catholicity was at any moment proportioned to the amount of danger that was to be faced'.[79] Second-Lieutenant Guy Chapman, no doubt with some sarcasm, observed that 'the Church of Rome sent a man into action mentally and spiritually cleaned'.[80] John Lucy did not doubt that he had been cleansed. Prior to the Battle of Mons in August 1914, having examined his conscience, he said a 'few prayers to make up for my missed Mass, and for our protection in any coming ordeal'. Like Alfred Burrage, he wanted to die in a state of grace. Satisfied, Lucy viewed his conscience as 'well and healthy'.[81]

Formal religion was, of course, delivered by a person. Conningsby Dawson wrote that there were two types of army chaplains: 'The one who plays the game; the other who issues season tickets to heaven, but is afraid of travelling on them himself'.[82] The Reverend Lauchlan Watt wrote of the padre's role: 'He has to be the comrade of all, friend of the weary, helper of the weak, and light-bringer in the dark hour'.[83] The wise chaplain placed his religious message within a broad range of concerns that soldiers might have. On Gallipoli, the Reverend Oswin Creighton was in no doubt that the work of the padre was mainly pastoral in nature:

> His work comes after the attack, and perhaps most of all when the men come away tired and worn out for a little rest, or when they are spending those continuous days of wearisome strain in the trenches. And not least of all is the fact that he is the best channel of communication between the men and those at home.[84]

Reginald Davis was clear about the importance of pastoral care. At services 'the padre is sure to be there first, and he sits about and has a chat with each man',[85] his sermons covering 'the troubles and difficulties of the day in the most practical manner'.[86] Afterwards he would hold 'get-away-from-the-war chats', about 'home ... books, and

---

78  J.F. Lucy, *There's a Devil in the Drum*, p.250.
79  C.D. Plater, *Catholic Soldiers: By Sixty Chaplains and Many Others*, p.50.
80  G. Chapman, *A Passionate Prodigality*, p.91.
81  Lucy, op. cit. p.108.
82  C. Dawson, *Living Bayonets*, p.109.
83  L. Maclean Watt, *In France and Flanders with the Fighting Men*, p.viii.
84  O. Creighton, *With the Twenty-Ninth Division in Gallipoli*, p.33.
85  Hodder-Williams, op cit. location 518.
86  Hodder-Williams, op cit. location 525.

all general topics'.[87] Stephen Graham, observing padres, noted that whilst rankers 'liked those who talked to them of home', they were 'cold towards them in the matter of religion'. Soldiers were warm to the individual but naturally cold to doctrine they had often never fully understood or valued. Burgon Bickersteth wrote of the padre responsible for his unit that he needed to make the effort to get 'to know the men personally', as otherwise his 'moral cowardice successfully smothers all vestiges of a religion which was never strong'.[88] As Julian Bickersteth, no moral coward, repeatedly demonstrated, some of the most taxing and important work that he did was in casualty clearing stations with the dying. And as we shall also see in Chapter Nine, there was one particular concern in relation to which a padre's offices were particularly welcome – the importance placed on 'decent' burial.

## *Loss of faith?*

It has become axiomatic that the experience of the war led to considerable loss of faith. Lieutenant Peter Layard wrote to his parents that any faith he had in religion had been 'most frightfully shaken by things I've seen'. He added, with more than a touch of naivety: 'It's incredible that if God could make a 17-inch shell not explode (that) he lets them explode'.[89] Padre Innes Logan wrote that 'I am afraid it is true that modern war knocks and smashes any faith he ever had out of many a man'.[90] Stephen Graham used almost identical words in recording the statement of a drunken soldier: 'War, I tell you, knocks all the religion out of a man'.[91] Captain Robert Ross believed that familiarity with death led to religious indifference,[92] and indeed, Private Winston Groom wrote of Third Ypres: 'Where, oh where was God in this earth-covered ossuary, this mud swamp receptacle for the bones of the dead?' He experienced a 'moment of truth' in his experiences there in which his 'belief in a Church which condoned killing faded away'.[93] Second-Lieutenant Arthur West not only became a pacifist during the war, he also lost the faith he once had. Blaming God for 'all the present woe', he continued 'if there is a God at all responsible for governing the earth, I hate and abominate Him'.[94] He was aware this was as a result of emotional changes in him, as 'I seem to have lost in softness and become harder, more ferocious in nature'.[95] The spiritual shift left others aghast. Describing himself as a 'respectable atheist' to fellow officers, they responded with shock: 'You aren't really an atheist, are you?'[96]

87 Hodder-Williams, op cit. location 525-532.
88 Bickersteth, op. cit. 210.
89 Housman, op. cit. p.171.
90 I. Logan, *On the King's Service*, p.53.
91 Graham, op. cit. p.236.
92 R.B. Ross, *The Fifty-First in France*, p.230.
93 W.H.A. Groom, *Poor Bloody Infantry*, p. 122.
94 A.G. West, *Diary of a Dead Officer*, pp.35-6.
95 West, op. cit. p.47.
96 West, op. cit. p.71.

Undoubtedly, some did lose their faith during the war. For others, it was their expression of it that changed. Conningsby Dawson wrote that beforehand, prayer had simply been a habit. Once in the trenches he lost that habit, and 'it seemed best not to interrupt Him with frivolous petitions'.[97] He came to see God in the endurance of his fellow soldiers, and to 'trust God without worrying him'.[98] Bernard Martin was put in Second-Lieutenant Mark Hardy's company on arrival at Ypres. Hardy had been at theological college at Cambridge before the war, but the trenches had changed him. He had lost confidence in church leaders. From pulpits in Britain they could 'know precious little about men'. He had determined not to return to the 'parson factory', but to enter 'social work involving politics based especially on his experience with our men'.[99] Lauchlan Watt described the 'tide of religion' that swept over soldiers 'like a vast contagion of enthusiasm', passing to a position where religion was 'much more a matter of the individual'.[100] Burgon Bickersteth, his own faith unchallenged, echoed this view, believing that the constant presence of death was 'naturally sweeping away *mere conventional faith*'.[101] He observed that there was a 'marvellous increase of personal philanthropy ... the so-called practical religion professed by many in peace time'.[102] If his analysis is correct, he is describing a burgeoning 'diffusive Christianity'.

Others clearly gained a particular faith. Indeed, war saw religious revival rather than loss of faith.[103] Julian Bickersteth described holding a number of confirmation services at the front, and wrote: 'Is not all this very encouraging for the future of the Church after the War?' He added that many a man told him 'that it was only the coming out here which had turned him to God once again'.[104] Not only was there something of a religious renaissance in the trenches, this persisted for a period in the post-war world. Although researchers such as Edward Wickham, in his industrial mission to Sheffield, took the view that the First World War had a very negative effect on the religious life of the nation, Michael Snape and others have claimed 'a complex and multifaceted *revival* of religion in British society' as result of both world

---

97 C. Dawson, *The Glory of the Trenches*, p.138.
98 Dawson, *Glory*, p.141.
99 Martin, op. cit. p.62.
100 Maclean Watt, op. cit. p.167.
101 Bickersteth, op. cit. p.168 (author italics).
102 Bickersteth, op. cit. p.168.
103 Anglican communicants fell by 6 per cent between 1914 and 1917, before rising in 1918, the upward trend being maintained in the immediate post-war years. Adult 'membership' of faith bodies in Britain at the end of the war in 1918 was probably around 8,000,000. This equates to around 29 per cent of the estimated adult civilian population of Britain in 1918, compared with 27 per cent of the whole adult population in 1914. (C. Field, Some Historical Religious Statistics, http://www.brin.ac.uk/news/2012/some-historical-religious-statistics/ )
104 Bickersteth, op. cit. p.152.

wars.[105] The Catholic Church claimed 40,000 conversions on the Western Front,[106] and demonstrated a rise in worshippers during the post-war period.[107] Snape asserts that there was no indication of an overall drift towards atheism as a result of the experiences of those who fought, citing the thriving of the Toc H movement in veterans.[108]

## Fatalism and Intuition

### *Fatalism*

Andrew Crome suggests that soldiers 'embraced a kind of atheism and a functional fatalism'.[109] He uses the word atheism because the fatalism of the First World War soldier was less grounded in a view of God's will than it had been for soldiers fighting in the wars of previous centuries.[110] Fatalism is resignation in the face of some future event, in this case death, which is thought to be inevitable. The Church of England was so concerned at the rise of fatalism that its Society for Promoting Christian Knowledge published a pamphlet on the subject in 1917, describing it as 'incompatible with Christianity', because it denied the power of prayer.[111]

Machine gunner David Polley wrote that 'every soldier becomes more or less of a fatalist'.[112] In the context of the Great War, fatalism was essentially a protective mechanism. Private Hugh Quigley put this clearly: 'Fatalism remains the only means of warding off depression'.[113] It was common from the least educated ranker to the best educated officer, but Lord Moran described it as 'common especially in the ranks'. He gave the example of a runner who was always taking messages 'up unhealthy roads out of his turn', his view being that 'if you're for it, you're for it'.[114] Conningsby Dawson similarly recorded that 'you get to believe that if you're going to be hit you're going to be'.[115] He described how he had come to the point where death seemed 'very inconsiderable',[116] adding that as one could only die once 'the chief concern that matters is how and not when you die'.[117] And by 'how', he of course meant doing one's duty.

Alexander Watson describes a swing from optimistic risk-taking to fatalistic risk-taking. He suggests that troops new to the front were 'especially inclined to assess risk

---

105  Snape, op. cit. p.4 (italics in original).
106  M. Purdy, 'Roman Catholic Army Chaplains During the First World War', p.2.
107  Purdy, op. cit. p.1.
108  Snape, op. cit. p.245.
109  Crome, op. cit.
110  Snape, op. cit. p.28.
111  R.H. Malden, *Fatalism*, p.16.
112  D.J. Polley, *The Mudhook Machine Gunner*, p.20.
113  H. Quigley, *Passchendaele and the Somme*, p.18.
114  Lord Moran, *The Anatomy of Courage*, p.59.
115  C. Dawson, *Carry On*, p.47.
116  Dawson, *Carry On*, p.99.
117  Dawson, *Carry On*, p.127.

inappropriately'.[118] Such new arrivals, he claims, behaved with naïve optimism in the front-line, exposing themselves to danger. This, of course, may have been the result of inadequate preparation rather than innate optimism. Such men were, however, likely in the minority compared with those who were excessively fearful on their first exposure to threat. There was both over and under-appreciation of threat. All learnt to take appropriate care quickly – there was a rebalancing of risk assessment. As Watson correctly states, in order to survive, soldiers 'had to learn to judge risk without being overwhelmed by it'.[119] He claims, however, that as soldiers became more aware of danger, 'they became more fatalistic about the possible consequences of their risk-taking'.[120] He quotes Walter Ludwig who suggested that fatalism was 'often so strong or of such long influence that the will to live is crushed and makes way for a mindless apathy and resignation'.[121] In contradiction to Hugh Quigley's notions of fatalism as protection against depression, Watson believes that fatalism was a negative state of mind that dulled the awareness of need for care.

Fatalism did not equate with pessimism. The evidence reviewed here suggests no necessary link between fatalism and apathy and carelessness with life. Undoubtedly many accepted that death or wounding was inevitable. Second-Lieutenant Charles Carrington, during his worst day at Third Ypres, trapped in a shell-hole under fire, 'calculated ... making imaginary bargains with fate, laying odds' with himself.[122] Douglas Cuddeford noted that those who continued to escape death and survive wounds felt that according to the laws of chance, 'our turn must come sooner or later'.[123] At Ypres in October 1914, Captain Harry Dillon noted that: 'I know I have got to stop my bullet some time', viewing it as 'merely a question of where it hits one, whether it is dead or wounded'.[124] A sense of inevitably hung heavy. Private Harry Drinkwater became resigned to losing old comrades, writing in his diary: 'It seems as if the fates have decreed that they have had a good run and it is time they went'.[125] Private George Wear recorded that as the war dragged on, 'I began to feel like one who had outlived his time'. He had no hope of surviving much longer: 'The odds were heavily against it'.[126]

Soldiers certainly weighed the odds. During the war, 11.8 per cent of British soldiers were killed, and 45 per cent were wounded.[127] Captain Robert Manion was

---

118 A. Watson, 'Self-deception and Survival: Mental Coping Strategies on the Western Front, 1914-18', *Journal of Contemporary History*, p.249.
119 Watson, 'Self-deception', p.251.
120 Watson, 'Self-Deception', p.251.
121 Ludwig, cited in Watson, *Enduring*, p.168.
122 C. Edmonds, *A Subaltern's War*, p.127.
123 Cuddeford, op. cit. p.90.
124 H. Dillon, quoted in P. Hart, *Fire and Movement*, p.289.
125 J. Cooksey & D. Griffiths (eds), *Harry's War*, p.103.
126 G.F. Wear, Diary, http://www.firstworldwar.com/diaries/17-21.htm.
127 N. Ferguson, *The Pity of War*, p.285 & p.299.

of the view that 'the odds are against you', and the longer one spent at the front 'you are almost mathematically certain to lose out in the end', a reality that he believed everyone shared.[128] Lieutenant Leslie Sanders did his maths. He wrote to his mother: 'I estimate my chance of getting wounded at one in four; of getting killed or totally disabled at one in ten'. He added that they were 'pretty heavy averages' and that he would be 'foolish not to be prepared for the worst'. He came to a startling conclusion, shared by others: 'In a sense, therefore, I count myself already dead'.[129] Captain G.B. Manwaring performed a different set of sums. He acknowledged how 'for a hundred days one lives with death around one in a hundred forms, and on the hundred and first one's turn comes. When, and where, these are the questions'.[130] Private Arthur Lambert's calculations were made on an alternative basis. Conscripted in 1916, he spoke of his return on parting with his wife, but with four brothers in the army his 'logical mind could not conceive immunity for all'.[131] Sergeant George Ashurst was another who indulged in fatalistic calculation. He returned to his unit, having twice been wounded and having had periods of convalescence in the UK, with the thought that 'the third time would pay for all'.[132] Returning from leave, Henry Russell 'calculated that I had three chances, and only three' namely getting wounded, taken prisoner, or being killed. Having been on the Western Front for well over a year, he believed the possibility of carrying on safely 'was too remote to contemplate'.[133] He was right in his contemplations, as a month or two later a shoulder wound in the German Spring offensive of 1918 took him out of the conflict. Alfred Burrage reckoned 'on form', which he took to be a 50 per cent casualty rate, 'we have each of us an even money chance'. He was not 'unduly depressed', accepting inevitably that sooner or later he was 'bound to become a casualty'.[134] Some tasks were more risky than others, and altered the odds. When Private Giles Eyre was required to be company runner on the Somme at Pozieres in 1916, his immediate reaction was: 'Chances of survival lowered by fifty per cent at least!'[135] None of these soldiers had, however, lapsed into mindless apathy, even though there was a prevailing certainty of death for some. Lieutenant Kenneth Mealing lived with 'the ever present unforgettable knowledge that, if not today, then tomorrow, if not tomorrow, then some day later, but in any case eventually your turn would come'.[136]

Soldiers learned to recognise the type and direction of incoming shell-fire. They were thus able to compute dangerousness to a degree. One soldier described how experienced

---

128 R.J. Manion, *A Surgeon in Arms*, pp. 11-12.
129 Anonymous, *A Soldier of England*, p.66.
130 G.B. Manwaring, *If We Return*, p.108.
131 A. Lambert, *Over the Top*, p.24.
132 Ashurst, op. cit. p.109.
133 Russell, op. cit. p.247.
134 Burrage, op. cit. p.109.
135 G.E.M. Eyre, *Somme Harvest*, p.223.
136 K.W. Mealing, Private Papers, IWM Docs 5514.

men would be 'watching each shell, predicting where it would fall, & then scuttling'. Survival was thus not entirely dependant on chance, and this common behaviour militates against the notion of wholesale fatalistic risk-taking. Some rationalised danger in a positive vein. Ronald Poulton consoled himself by thinking: 'I suppose in this war one bullet hits in three or four million fired'.[137] In 1921, Lieutenant-Colonel Maxwell McTaggart, who had commanded 1/5th Gordon Highlanders on the Western Front for nearly three years, propounded the idea that men should be encouraged to think in terms of realistic risk appraisal. Thus, noticing that soldiers on night carrying duty were showing signs of particular mental strain, he calculated that the chance of being hit during such duty was 3,000 to 1, and took the view that if they adopted this risk perspective it would 'considerably lessen their apprehension'.[138] Where McTaggart got this estimate from is not entirely clear. A contemporary (German) calculation suggested that it took 329 shells to hit one German soldier, and approximately four times as many to kill him.[139] For others, there was no elaborate calculation. Captain Harry Yoxall wrote to his mother: 'It's wonderful how many shells it takes to kill a man'.[140] Private Harry Drinkwater escaped death on so many occasions, often in situations in which it seemed unreasonable to escape, that such calculations became irrelevant. He came to believe that 'I was ordained to come through the war alive'.[141]

In July 1915 Carlos Blacker showed his brother Robin, also a subaltern, the newspaper report of the death of a friend. With calm fatalism Robin replied: 'Don't worry about this. We are *all* going to be killed. You and I and everybody else'.[142] Robin Blacker indeed died a matter of months later during the Battle of Loos – Carlos survived. In conversation with another officer about their respective attitudes to the war and their reasons for fighting, Second-Lieutenant Denis Garstin realised the certainty this individual 'had of his own death, and the freedom of thought this ... gave him'. Echoing Leslie Sanders, in 'his own mind he was dead already'. In talking to Garstin, given that he believed his fate was out of his hands, the officer in question was taking the only control that he could: 'He wanted to know in whose hands ... he was leaving his men'.[143] Ralph Scott demonstrated how a particular fatalistic vision could suddenly settle on one in response to a particular set of events. He was involved in desperate fighting in August 1918, holding off a German counterattack at the tip of the Merryway Salient, near Kemmel. Surrounded by the dead and dying of his platoon, for the 'whole night I calmly regarded myself as a dead man. It seemed quite natural that I should be, and I can't remember that I had the slightest regret'.

---

137 E.B. Poulton, *The Life of Ronald Poulton*, pp.347-8.
138 M.F. McTaggart, 'Danger Values', *Journal of the Royal United Services Institution*, p.290.
139 Watson, *Enduring*, p.264.
140 H.W. Yoxall, Private Papers, IWM Docs 22290.
141 Cooksey & Griffiths, op. cit. p.149.
142 Blacker, op. cit. p.33 (italics in original).
143 D. Garstin, *The Shilling Soldiers*, p.281.

In fact, he felt 'distinctly happier and more tranquil' than he ever had before.[144] He was not seized by apathy, more by relief. Captain Claude Bartholomew during the Somme offensive similarly gave his opinion to a fellow officer that the war must be over in six months, remarking 'how damnable' this was given his belief that it was 'a moral certainty that, after surviving so many months, you and I will both be dead in a fortnight'.[145] Both, happily, survived. Harry Yoxall found that 'while life becomes more desirable death seems less terrible'.[146] He is telling us that there was a balance to be achieved – accepting the strong possibility of death but wanting to live.

### *The bullet meant for me*
Burgon Bickersteth outlined a typical attitude: 'Well, sir, yer'll be 'it when yer'll be 'it and not afore'.[147] Many a soldier believed that he would die only 'when my number's up', fatalism becoming concrete in this notion of 'the bullet meant for me'. Arriving in Salonika in 1915, Major Arthur Gibbs found himself pondering just this question: '*Did* every bullet have its billet? Was there a bullet for the Colonel ? For *me* ?'[148] After their first unit casualty at Mons, one of John Lucy's comrades remarked: 'Well ... his number was on that shell all right'.[149] Days later, at Le Cateau, Lucy was hit on the buttock by hot shrapnel, and received the same sentiment: 'Your number was not on that'.[150] Private George Coppard, allowing hunger to overcome circumspection, climbed a fruit tree which was then subject to fire. Despite being a 'sitting duck', he avoided injury and concluded that 'none of the bullets were meant for me'.[151] Charles Carrington's servant, Stanley, said to him 'a dozen times' that 'the shell 'aint made yet with my name on it sir'.[152] The sheer bravado and mental avoidance implicit in this remark was made clear to Carrington when Stanley was shot through the eye in front of him at Third Ypres. Private George Brame thought death stealthy, noting that he had often heard it said 'that the shell which was meant for you always went about it quietly'.[153]

Harry Drinkwater, now commissioned and serving at Ypres in 1917, examined the fatalist's thinking in his diary, describing the circular argument as 'very satisfactory'. If one was shot then clearly the inscribed bullet had found its mark, but if one came through a particular action, '"your" shot has not been fired yet'. The man who viewed himself as 'ordained' to survive took a logical standpoint on this occasion. He observed

---

144 R. Scott, *A Soldier's Diary*, pp.87-8.
145 Feilding, op. cit. p.76.
146 Yoxall, op. cit.
147 Bickersteth, op. cit. p.169.
148 A.H. Gibbs, *Gun Fodder*, p.115 (italics in original).
149 Lucy, op. cit. p.119.
150 Lucy, op. cit. p.133.
151 R.L. Mackay, Diary, http://www.firstworldwar.com/diaries/rlm1.htm.
152 Edmonds, op. cit. p.140.
153 Brame, op. cit.

that narrow escapes were simply the rule of the battlefield. Loss of life, he believed, was most often simply the result of 'the fact that a fellow sometimes temporarily loses his head', failing to take normal care, matters in which 'fatalism had no share'. Yet at the same time, he confusingly acknowledged that the notion of 'divine interference' did seem the 'most reasonable construction' to put on one's survival when particular circumstances were examined.[154] Drinkwater clearly demonstrates how there were different shades of magical thinking – a particular individual could be rational on one occasion, yet slip into magical thinking on another. Thus, Lieutenant-Colonel William Fraser mused on the death of a friend: 'It's odd – some shells … are forged to kill … Do they look any different in the furnace, I wonder?'[155]

It is impossible to assess how common fatalism was amongst the British soldier. Private Arthur Wrench may have believed that 'we are all Fatalists here believing in the preordained order of things',[156] but the only contemporary evidence available again comes from Walter Ludwig's study which reported that that 22 per cent of soldiers were prone to fatalism in the face of danger.[157]

### Luck

Avoiding losing one's head increased the chance of survival, and Harry Drinkwater viewed it as the sign of a 'healthy mind', untainted by pessimism.[158] But the reality was that beyond taking judicious care, the remainder of continued survival was down, if not to divine interference, then to simply being in the right place at the right time. Robert Manion described all the narrow escapes from death 'as common as is plum jam in the rations'.[159] Many soldiers had the experience of a nearby shellburst which injured everyone but them, or the bullet that passed through clothing but did not touch flesh. Captain Gerald Burgoyne, feeling a slight blow on his arm, thought he had been hit by a clod of earth. He gave a typical description of the very near-miss:

> A bullet had gone through the outside seam of my left coat sleeve, making two holes about three inches apart, and ripped a hole one and a half inches long in the back of my coat just below the shoulder blade. Three holes in all and in neither case had it cut the lining of the coat. A wonderful escape.[160]

---

154 Cooksey & Griffiths, op. cit. p.259.
155 D. Fraser (ed.), *In Good Company*, p.146.
156 A.E. Wrench, Private Papers, IWM Docs 3834.
157 Ludwig, cited in Watson, 'Self-deception', pp.236-7.
158 Cooksey & Griffiths, op. cit. p.259.
159 Manion, op. cit. p.144.
160 C. Davison, *The Burgoyne Diaries*, p.127.

Private James Racine reflected on his experiences and realised 'the luck of the game'.[161] As he observed, he was an as yet uninjured veteran of the trenches, yet another man's leg was blown off on his first time in the front line having only been there for an hour'.[162] As human beings, we seek reasons for why things happen – we abhor randomness. In the trenches of the Western Front and elsewhere, however, there was often no clear reason why one man should be injured and another should not. R.L. Mackay had a narrow escape from a 5.9 inch shell and avoiding explanation which involved divine intervention, noted: 'No theory ever invented will account for our escape'[163]. The notion of luck thus became important. Rowland Feilding had a newly arrived officer who was dead within half an hour of entering the front line, and noted 'is that not a case of hard luck "chasing" a man, when you consider how long others of us last?'[164] Lieutenant Patrick James Campbell formed the fatalistic belief in 1918 that 'I should probably be killed before the end of the year'. He felt that he had had 'a lot of lucky escapes', but seemed to think that his bank of luck was running low: 'There came a day when one's guardian angel was not looking, his back was turned, and in that moment it happened'.[165] Under shellfire at Ypres in 1917, Second-Lieutenant Hope Floyd reassured himself with the thought that 'I do not see why my luck should desert me'.[166] His intuition was good. By 1916, Lieutenant Stuart Cloete, who had experienced many fellow officers being killed, was tending towards Campbell's view that his luck was running out. He worried that 'you can only count on Mr Luck so far' and felt by this point 'that Mr Death had his eye on me'.[167] Cloete's luck, however, also held – he survived the war to become an author in South Africa. For some, however, luck remained an inadequate concept. Private Tom Dry, an Australian on Gallipoli, had a soldier sit next to him on his right who was promptly shot through the thigh. On his right there had been barely enough room, on the left, plenty; and Dry must have shifted to allow the man to sit down. Musing 'here is where fate comes in', he wrote to his parents that 'had he sat on my left that bullet would have been mine. Some call it luck, but I would like to know what prompted him to sit on my right'.[168]

Alexander Watson draws our attention again to Walter Ludwig's study, where eight per cent of German soldiers 'expressed a firm belief in their own invincibility'.[169] This certainly gives grist to his theory that soldiers survived emotionally though

---

161 J. Racine, 'Memoirs of the Great War', http://www.seaforthhighlanders.ca/museum/?p=540 p.43.
162 Racine, op. cit. p.57.
163 Mackay, op. cit.
164 Feilding, op. cit. p.83.
165 P.J. Campbell, *The Ebb and Flow of Battle*, p.75.
166 H.T. Floyd, *At Ypres With Best-Dunkley*, p.18.
167 S. Cloete, *A Victorian Son*, p.230.
168 Housman, op. cit. p.95.
169 Watson, 'Self-deception', p.256.

'self-deception'. He amplifies a quote from Charles Bird in the *American Journal of Psychology* in July 1917: 'Bird observed that most possessed an "inner conviction that they themselves will not be killed"'.[170] Actually, what Bird says is: 'Towards the death of comrades they are indifferent due *probably* to the inner conviction that they themselves will not be killed'.[171] What Bird is drawing our intention to is not in fact a sense of invincibility, but rather, it seems likely, an assessment of probability. By the law of averages, if the person next to you is killed, then as only a certain percentage will be killed, you yourself have been spared on a random basis. In this context it is interesting that Ludwig's list of coping strategies does not include luck.[172]

Assertion of luck was not primarily 'self-deception', nor was it necessarily unrealistic optimism as Watson suggests,[173] although it could sometimes be just that. It was a way of explaining the inexplicable. Private Stephen Graham indicated that the issue of luck generalised: 'The experience of a soldier's life in escaping death and wounds impresses him with the idea of lucky chance.' Discussing the popular game of Crown and Anchor, he wrote: 'War breeds gambling as a natural and inevitable fruit'. Many soldiers were 'devotees of luck and have their theories of chances'.[174]

### Intuition

Captain Francis Buckley had a friend from his training, Second-Lieutenant Burt, who was killed at Hill 60, Ypres, immediately on arrival. Buckley remarked, 'Poor lad, he was always certain that he would be killed as soon as he got out to France!'[175] Whether this represented intuition or simply anticipatory fear is difficult to judge. Arthur Lambert, on the eve of the Battle of Broodseinde in 1917 described a normally cheerful fellow-soldier moaning 'this ends it'. Lambert recognised him as 'one of those men who knew definitely that their last day had come', a condition which became a 'familiar, unexplainable phenomenon' to him.[176] Intuition was not always about death. Thus, in the days before going into action at Third Ypres, Charles Carrington had 'a growing presentiment that I should be wounded'.[177] Sometimes, intuition was about others. Moving up to attack at Passchendaele in 1917, Alfred Burrage looked into his platoon commander's eyes 'and as he smiled I saw Death looking at me … I knew his number was up'. The officer was killed in the first few minutes of the assault.[178] Mostly, however, intuition was about oneself. In the March retreat in 1918, Burrage's company commander declared that he did not know where they were going or what

---

170 Watson, 'Self-deception', p.256.
171 C. Bird, 'From Home to the Charge', *American Journal of Psychology*, p.336.
172 Ludwig, cited in Watson, *Enduring*, p.237.
173 Watson, 'Self-deception', p.256.
174 Graham, op. cit. p.186.
175 F. Buckley, *Q.6.a*, p.38.
176 Lambert, op. cit. p.55.
177 Edmonds, op. cit. p.106.
178 Burrage, op. cit. p.122.

was going to happen, adding: 'And I shan't be with you at the end of the day'. He, too, was fatally wounded a few minutes later.[179] On the Somme, Captain Charles Clayton's battalion HQ, which he had just left with 'a kind of severe restlessness' was shelled, and on arriving back at the scene he found that a heavy round had struck the shelter which had been made for him. He noted that it had been 'so quiet … and yet "something" would not let me stay there'. He posed himself the question: 'Is there such a thing as intuition, and if so, what is it?'[180] The first part of his question may have been answered positively some months later, when commanding his unit. He wished to place a particular NCO, Lance-Corporal Marr, in charge of the machine guns. The day before they were due to go into the line, Marr disappeared and was found drunk. Apparently, Marr knew 'that he was going to his death'. He was convinced that he was 'doomed', and as he set out, 'declared that he was going to be blown to pieces by a shell'. Immediately on setting out, a shell fell amongst Marr's section. Clayton noted: 'He alone was killed outright and it appears to have happened exactly as he had foretold'.[181] Robert Graves pondered the same issue. In a trench at Cambrin he dropped flat and a second or two later a whizz-bang hit the back of the trench where he estimated his head would have been. He asked: 'How did I know that the shell would be coming my way?'[182] In his case the answer was likely subliminal perception – he automatically registered the noise of the shell and took action, as this was second nature to him.

Frederic Manning described an officer who had survived the Somme but 'had a feeling that he would be killed if he went into the line here'.[183] He was, of course, killed. Second-Lieutenant Arthur Behrend, at the Third Battle of Krithia in June 1916, noted that 'Percy Wolf, who had had a presentiment of his death in action, was the only officer killed'.[184] Sergeant George Ashurst left his unit temporarily for a safer duty just prior to an attack, and was met in farewell by another sergeant who said 'quite solemnly, "I think this is my last trip over the top"'. As Ashurst left, he felt 'rather queer myself to see the carefree Faller looking strangely despondent'. Faller was indeed killed in the attack Ashurst missed.[185] Second-Lieutenant Dormer Treffry marched into action on 15 September 1916 on the Somme and told his sergeant that: 'He was certain he was going to be killed. He knew it and he told me so'. As predicted, he was dismembered by a shell.[186]

Intuition was a self-fulfilling prophecy. The occasions when intuition was correct were much more impressive than when they were wrong. Second-Lieutenant Charles

179 Burrage, op. cit. p.247.
180 C.P. Clayton, *The Hungry One*, p.145.
181 Clayton, op. cit. pp.175-6.
182 Graves, op. cit. p.111.
183 Manning, op. cit. location 1391.
184 A. Behrend, *Make me a Soldier*, p.145.
185 Ashurst, op. cit. p.124.
186 Blacker, op. cit. p.132.

Douie, on the Yser in 1917, noted that he had a 'strange premonition that my days were numbered', a thought which developed into certainty one day when he 'had occasion to acquire a duty which seemed to me ... to confer no chance of survival'.[187] Douie survived to write his memoirs eleven years after the war's end, but did not comment on the false premonition. Diaries and memoirs largely, of course, only identify the occasions when these prophecies of impending death came true. There is little record of unfulfilled visions of imminent doom, false positives seemingly being discounted. R.L. Mackay wrote that before a particular action: 'I did not feel the least bit afraid'. Previously he had gone into action 'feeling that I would come out again'. This time he 'had no such feeling. Felt, almost knew, that I would not come out again.'[188] Mackay survived, and like Douie, did not reflect on why his feeling of inevitable death was wrong.

**Superstition**

Andrew Crome states that 'men would engage in activities that were borderline magical',[189] and Frederic Manning wrote of being continually 'amazed by the superstition and the sentimentality of the ordinary man'.[190] Western Front chaplains Thomas Wentworth and Geoffrey Gordon regarded superstitions as 'idle and sometimes degrading' but crucially held 'side by side with a vague belief in God'.[191] Clearly, their pre-war ministry had not brought them into contact with the reality of this in everyday working-class life. But it was not just the working class who were partial slaves to superstition. Robert Graves, probably not one of Manning's 'ordinary' men, described an officer's unlucky words in stating that a particular trench location was heavy on casualties for rankers, but not officers. 'Touch wood!' went up the cry. Graves noted that 'everybody jumped to touch wood, but it was a French trench and unrevetted. I pulled a pencil out of my pocket; that was wood enough for me'.[192] In exactly the same vein, a fellow officer remarked to Bernard Adams that they had not had an officer casualty for several months. Adams cried 'for heaven's sake, touch wood'.[193]

Fortune-telling assumed a particular prominence during the war, not just amongst relatives but amongst soldiers on leave from the front. Most of the information we have for this comes from police reports, obtained during crack-downs on this practice. Owen Davies, examining these sources, notes that Elizabeth Sixsmith, or 'Madam Betty', reported that she was 'very busy with soldiers', whilst Agnes McDonald, or 'Madame Vox', was arrested in the act of 'examining the palm of a wounded officer

---

187 C. Douie, *The Weary Road*, p.199.
188 Mackay, op. cit.
189 Crome, op. cit.
190 Manning, op. cit. location 3290.
191 T.W. Pym & G. Gordon, *Papers from Picardy*, p.201.
192 Graves, op. cit. p.172.
193 Adams, op. cit. p.163.

through a magnifying glass'. When Marie Charles was visited by the police she was found to be being consulted by no less than a brigadier-general.[194] There were clearly many, even those whose education might have led them to believe otherwise, who were prepared to place their faith in such quacks. It was a reflection of the need to grasp at certainty.

Spiritualism was popular during the Victorian era and achieved a particular pitch during the Great War, after which its popularity plummeted. The Society for Psychical Research was founded in 1882, and the physicist and developer of wireless telegraphy, Sir Oliver Lodge, was its president from 1901-3. After his son was killed in 1915, Lodge was a regular attender of the medium Mrs Osborne Leonard, who purportedly relayed communication from Raymond in another plane of existence which Lodge called 'Summerland'. This was detailed in *Raymond*, published in 1916,[195] which was certainly read by soldiers at the front.[196] There is, however, little evidence of participation in séances on active service. Indeed, given the evidence that soldiers tended to have only brief reactions to the death of their fellows,[197] there is no reason to believe that they would have had reason to conduct attempts to contact them. They may, however, have drawn comfort from 'evidence' of an afterlife, particularly for their relatives. Whilst soldiers often wrote home of having little fear of death, they frequently recorded a fear of the effects that their death might have on loved ones.

Whilst not an indication of spiritualism, individual soldiers had their own supposed experiences of the ghostly. Hereward Carrington's *Psychical Phenomena and the War* is replete with second-hand accounts of prophecies, premonitions and ghostly appearances. Most of his accounts of the appearances of dead soldiers predictably stem from their loved ones safely at home in Britain. There are, however, a handful of first-hand accounts of supernatural phenomena in the trenches. An officer conversing with a weary and pallid soldier on the march later discovered him to have been killed three days earlier. A colonel, dying on a hospital train in Britain, allegedly appeared in his old battalion's trenches in Flanders at the precise moment of his death with a previously amputated arm restored.[198] Robert Graves claimed to have seen the ghost of a private with whom he had been well acquainted in Britain, who had said 'I'll meet you again in France, Sir', passing his billet months after he had been killed.[199] Private Frank Richards described how he and a fellow platoon member, Dann, were attempting to kill a particularly large rat when Dann went very pale and said that the rat had 'made him feel queer'. He claimed that he 'saw something else besides that you didn't see', and that 'when I do go west that rat will be close by'.[200] Months

---

194  O. Davies, *Witchcraft, Magic and Culture, 1736-1951*, pp.267-8.
195  O.J. Lodge, *Raymond or Life and Death*.
196  J. Winter, *Sites of Memory, Sites of Mourning*, p.64.
197  See Chapter Nine.
198  H. Carrington, *Psychical Phenomena and the War*, pp.172-228 & 270-326.
199  Graves, op. cit. pp.191-2.
200  F. Richards, *Old Soldiers Never Die*, p.158.

later, and miles away during the capture of High Wood in September 1916, Richards saw 'the huge black rat we had seen at Hulluch, It was looking straight past me at Dann'. Moments later, Dann was killed by a shellburst, and by his side, 'also dead was the large rat'. Richards seemingly had no doubt that it was the same rat.[201] Given, as Lieutenant George Goddard wrote in a spiritualist journal, 'in a world of Death one would expect to penetrate the veil when it hangs so constantly before one',[202] it is perhaps surprising that there are not more such accounts from the front-line. If, however, one assumes that appearances of the dead to those at home represents an aspect of the psychological reactions that make up bereavement, then it is entirely predictable that there is a dearth of such experiences reported from the front given the curtailed emotional reactions that followed loss of friends in action.

Superstitions were of several different types, both collective and personal. The folk religion of the ordinary soldier facilitated the rise of legends. One of the longer-lasting legends or superstitions of the war was that of 'The Angels of Mons'. The battle on 23 August 1914 was at the time interpreted as a British victory in terms of miraculous escape from a superior force and the myth developed that some form of divine intervention had occurred. This myth was not, however, current in 1914, no soldier ever reporting seeing the angel at the time, and it was undoubtedly an article in the spiritualist *Light* magazine in April 2015, concerning the divine intervention of 'Invisible Allies' in the battle, that sparked the myth. This may well have had its seed in a story published by writer Arthur Machen in September 1914 in the *London Evening News* recycling the Agincourt legend of spirit bowmen led by St George coming to aid of the British army. The parish magazine of All Saints, Clifton, Bristol then published an article reporting that the daughter of a Cannon Marrable was told by two unnamed officers that a troop of angels had appeared between them and approaching German cavalry and stampeded them. Other corroboration from equally discreditable sources appeared. Such a legend fell happily into the belief that God was on the side of the Allies. The 'world of reinvigorated myth' that the war created was a fertile ground for such morale boosting material, and clearly many were willing to take this particular myth at face value.[203] Similarly, by 1915, there were many accounts of a 'White Comrade' ministering to British wounded in no-man's land. British soldiers were predictably vulnerable to legends which suggested supernatural forces working to protect them. Frank Richards wrote of 'the many of us who saw things on the Retirement'.[204] At least here the explanation lay in an altered state of consciousness produced by lack of food, water and exhaustion.

Another superstitious legend was that of the leaning or hanging Virgin, a statue of the Virgin Mary in gold holding the baby Jesus on the Basilica of Notre Dame de

---

201 Richards, op. cit. p.183.
202 G. Goddard quoted in Winter, op. cit. p.69.
203 D. Clarke, 'Rumours of Angels', *Folklore*, p.151.
204 Richards, op. cit. p.183.

Brebières in Albert. Shelled and left hanging, it had been secured by hawsers, but various superstitions grew up that whoever knocked her down would lose or win the war. In the version adhered to by British troops, her fall would mark the end of the war. Private Walter Williams wrote: 'We were a superstitious lot and I for one gave up a silent prayer begging her to fall'.[205] This legend was simply part of a more extensive belief in the possible supernatural properties of religious iconography. In February 1915 Gerald Burgoyne examined the church at Bailleul, noting that 'it is remarkable that the Christ on the outside wall of the church is quite untouched'. He recorded that: 'Similar instances are common' and noted that his men 'wondered at the way the Sacred Image has so very generally escaped damage'. He mused, 'Is it remarkable, I wonder?'[206] Julian Bickersteth described an officer drawing his attention to a solitary crucifix remaining facing the German trenches, stating 'it's a miracle'.[207] The belief in the sparing of such calvaries was common. Private James Moddrel noted 'the curious way in which these shrines escaped destruction', and that whilst in argument with fellow soldiers no conclusion was ever agreed on the reason, 'nobody ever denied on all parts of the battle front the same thing had happened'.[208] The sergeant-major conducting Alan Thomas to his unit through Albert, mused on a graveyard they passed: 'All the other monuments have been blown to hell. But the Madonna isn't touched. It's queer to my way of thinking'.[209]

In addition to the preoccupation with spared calvaries, church buildings, as scared ground, also became a source of superstition. Walter Williams sheltered in a church crypt and a comrade took a crucifix from a coffin. Williams was appalled. Within an hour the grave-robber was dead, a shell splinter in his head. 'Was it pure coincidence or was it God's judgement for his needless act of vandalism?' Williams pondered. 'It certainly strengthened both my faith and fear in God', he recorded.[210] Robert Graves similarly noted a fellow officer taking a piece of stained glass from a church to be admonished by an Irish soldier: 'Shouldn't take that, sir; it will bring you no luck'. Graves noted that it did not – 'Jenkins got killed not long after'.[211]

More common, however, were the minor personal superstitions. Conningsby Dawson wrote home that he would never forget his first corpse, a dead German wearing black boots. Thereafter, he had 'the superstitious feeling' that to wear black boots would bring him bad luck.[212] Corporal Eric Rossiter encountered five dead Canadian soldiers in a shell-hole and something flashed into his mind that he had previously forgotten. He had an uncle who had dabbled in palmistry who had told

---

205 M. Williams, *With Innocence and Hope*, Kindle edition location 652.
206 Davison, op. cit. p.115.
207 Bickersteth, op. cit. p.154.
208 J.F.R. Moddrel, quoted in Snape, op. cit. p.43.
209 Thomas, op. cit. p.49.
210 Williams, op. cit. location 2483.
211 Graves, op. cit. p.100.
212 Dawson, *Carry On*, p.89.

him that he would be killed before he was twenty. 'It never hit me till then'. Rossiter had the unwelcome thought, '"Jesus! I've only got four days to go!"'[213] Private Walter Williamson, left out of action with the battle reserve during Third Ypres, was asked to look after another soldier's treasures. This, he recorded, was looked upon as a 'bad omen' by many in the battalion, but he accepted the task as 'omens did not interest me particularly'.[214] The soldier in question was killed, and Williamson, loosening his resistance to superstition, vowed that he would never do such a thing again. In the trenches on the La Bassée front in 1914, John Lucy recorded that one of his section 'had lately taken to seeing sign and portents'. Awaiting a German attack: 'He called our attention to some queer cloud shapes in the sky and told us we were finished'.[215]

Soldiers also fell prey to protective ritual. Charles Carrington gave examples, when under shell-fire, of the impulse to 'sit in a certain position' or to touch a particular object.[216] Similarly, he would 'hum a little tune' to himself, or drum his fingers on his knee a specific number of times. If he could get through the ritual before the next explosion it gave him 'a sort of curious feeling of safety'. Carrington, confessing to 'a quite irrational desire' to complete the ritual, continued that if you 'complete the charm in time, you are safe'. He added that inevitably the effect was only temporary 'until the next one'.[217] Perhaps more to the point Carrington believed the ritual protected an individual from the 'nervous collapse which may come at any moment'.[218] It provided both a distraction and a temporary sense of control. Alexander Watson, examining German accounts, cites soldiers declaiming words and performing actions to deflect shells, and a man who decided that as it was the thirteenth of the month he would be killed 'unless he could appease the gods by offering a blood sacrifice of thirteen flies'.[219]

Common to many soldiers was the practice of carrying amulets or charms, objects whose main characteristic is the alleged protection of the owner from danger or harm. Their use is recorded from antiquity. Private Frederick Whitham, as we saw, received a lucky horseshoe in the trenches of the Gohelle in February 1915.[220] Fortune-teller Louise Hutchinson informed the police that she would offer to obtain charms and amulets and 'have them blessed before sending them on'.[221] Michael Snape notes that in addition to objects of religious iconography, amulets included 'rabbits' feet, lucky coins, trinkets, sheep's cauls and even pieces of coal and shrapnel, the latter being seized upon in the belief that like repelled like'. Captain Francis Hitchcock was given

---

213 E. Rossiter quoted in L. McDonald, *Somme*, p.308.
214 D. Priddey, *A Tommy at Ypres*, Kindle edition location 3049.
215 Lucy, op. cit. p.222.
216 Edmonds, op. cit. p.126.
217 Edmonds, op. cit. p.126.
218 C. Carrington, BBC 'The Great War Interviews'.
219 Watson, *Enduring*, p.98.
220 F. Whitham, Letters.
221 Davies, op. cit. p.268.

a cross as a 'charm' made out of a 'Belgian copper bullet' by one of his corporals, who said he 'would not be killed' whilst wearing it on the principle that it was 'hard to kill a bad thing'.[222] Guy Chapman described how when a company commander was killed many of his men thereafter carried his photograph 'as a kind of amulet'.[223] The Horniman Museum in London has twelve protective charms carried in the First World War in its collection. These include a horse brass in a lunar shape; an African black bean with a seed shell, threaded with a shoe-lace; a crescent moon with a face, with a wooden bead suspended in arc of the crescent; a stone threaded on a piece of twine; a monkey carved from soapstone; a 1914 shell fragment; a medal; a horseshoe; a heart-shaped medallion made from a German shell with a cross of Lorraine and flower on it; a piece of mother of pearl; and three icons either of the Madonna and child or saints.[224] The Science Museum, London, lists among its collection similar amulets, including a tiny compass embedded in a cowrie shell; a metal hand and the model of a soldier; an inscribed shamrock; and two black cats, one in metal and another made from paper.[225]

Although many of the above would have had a very personal meaning, some tokens were commercially manufactured, including the 'Fumsup Touchwood' charm of a little figure with a brass or silver body, sometimes with moveable limbs, and a wooden head. White heather pendants and lucky number charms were similarly for sale. These items had become popular at the time of the Boer War, when Protestant soldiers came to carry charms as frequently as Irish Catholic soldiers carried rosaries or devotional medals. The day before an attack at Ypres in 1917, Second-Lieutenant Edwin Vaughan, a Roman Catholic educated by the Jesuits, demonstrated an interesting mix of religious and secular charms, ensuring that 'my rosary was sewn into my tunic with the sovereign that Marie had given me for luck, and that my holy medals were firmly attached with my identity discs to my braces'.[226] This practice showed a good deal of faith crossover, as protestant soldiers came to carry catholic symbols. The Protestant Carlos Blacker was sent 'luck-bringing objects or small scrolls' by American Catholic relatives, some of which he carried about to please his mother, and: 'Those I did not use I passed on to Catholics who were grateful for them'.[227] The very Protestant Robert Graves, who had in his lineage a Protestant bishop, was confronted with a dead German at night and 'needed a charm to get myself past this sinister figure. The simplest way, I found, was to cross myself'.[228] The Presbyterian John Reith had a charm that also crossed the boundary between the secular and the religious. He had

---

222 F.C. Hitchcock, *Stand To!*, p.76.
223 Chapman, op. cit. p.50.
224 www.horniman.ac.uk/collections/browse-our-collections/authority/event/identifier/event-36.
225 www.sciencemuseum.org.uk/broughttolife/objects/display.aspx?id=6517.
226 E.C. Vaughan, *Some Desperate Glory*, p.193.
227 Blacker, op. cit. p.213.
228 Graves, op. cit. p.187.

requested a signet ring from his parents which came in the shape of a shield with the family crest engraved inside 'God or Shield-Father-Mother', noting that 'it seemed a protection against danger'.[229]

There were thus several types of amulets/charms. The first were the personal idiosyncratic items. Secondly, there were traditional 'good luck' symbols, some of which were commercially manufactured; and thirdly, there were those involving religious iconography. Normal religious practices and the simple possession of a bible also came to assume mystical, superstitious properties. Andrew Crome infers that emergency religion was partly motivated by frank superstition, and that 'communion was seen as a semi-magical rite'. Partaking in the Eucharist before going over the top, 'some men believed you would be guaranteed a place in heaven' or even be protected from bullets. Chaplain Maurice Ponsonby, searching the bodies of the dead after the Battle of Festubert in 1915, was amazed to find that nearly every man possessed a Bible or a cross. He mused that 'perhaps they carried them as a charm – a sort of magic', conceivably because they felt that 'such things contained the secret of life and death and immortality'. Woodbine Willie was distributing New Testaments at Rouen and described the following response as emblematic of attitudes towards the bible: 'Yes, I'll 'ave one, sir; you never know your luck; it may stop a bullet'. Indeed, Private Arthur Wrench claimed that many men carried a New Testament in their breast pocket to protect their hearts,[230] the existence of bibles with partial thickness bullet holes indicating that this was not an entirely forlorn hope. Woodbine Willie viewed men's attitudes as a mixture of superstition and sentiment. The Good Book had 'inherited respect', but was viewed very much as a 'decent man thinks of his grandmother. It is ancient, and therefore demands respect'.[231] Thus, when the moment of desperation came, as Gerald Brennan noted on 1 July 1916, the wounded who could not be reached had 'crawled into shell holes, wrapped their waterproof sheets round them, taken out their Bibles, and died like that'.[232]

## Conclusion

It is clear that many men went to war with a belief in God. For some this was within a clear theological framework; for others it was within a much more confused folk religion. The expressed positions of the various denominations of British churches gave soldiers a justification for participating in the war if they felt they needed it, and in a more general way there were those who saw their commitment to fighting as taking place within a Christian ethos. It therefore buffered self-esteem. Men like

---

229 Reith, op. cit. p.108.
230 Wrench, op. cit.
231 Kennedy, op. cit. pp.51-3.
232 G. Brennan, quoted in J. Keegan, *The Face of Battle*, p.269.

Bernard Vann could take to the battlefield spared cognitive dissonance between faith and killing.

It is not the role of this chapter to delve into the meaning of faith, and self-evidently, faith is much more than a set of psychological mechanisms. Without entering a debate concerning the existence of God or the degree of a deity's involvement in human affairs, it can no doubt be agreed that religions are, at one level, systems of thought through which people manage understandings about their existence. Religions impart a sense of meaning and purpose. A modern study with the American military, investigating both the concepts of hardiness and religiosity, however, concluded that 'religiosity may not be as directly relevant to dealing effectively with stressful circumstances as is hardiness'.[233] Faith undoubtedly, however, strengthened the endurance of many Great War soldiers. Religion, perhaps unsurprisingly, went through a revival in the trenches. The other matters discussed in this chapter, fatalism and superstition, were variations of the same strengthening process.

Front-line chaplains Thomas Pym and Geoffrey Gordon, who believed that the superstitious man was 'just a fool', wrote that 'a sound theology ... has the great merit of being incompatible with superstition'. But a sound theology was exactly what the great bulk of the ranks lacked. Whilst Pym and Gordon envisaged a God who would not 'punish a man for sitting down thirteen to his dinner or for being the third to light his fag from the same match', the reality was that in the folk religion of so many soldiers trust in the Christian God was only one aspect of the attempt to control the 'vagaries of the lord of chance'.[234] And it was not only the ill-educated who fell prey to superstition.

The importance for human beings of achieving a sense of control has been noted. Faith, an affirmative choice, established for some a sense of positive certainty over a destiny that might otherwise seem bleak. Faith, fatalism and superstition were all part of soldiers' attempts to achieve a limited sense of control over the experience of threat, a process which potentially diminished the sense of helplessness. Thus both taking care and exposing oneself recklessly were an indication of choice, of exerting some control over the randomness of constant threat. One was positive, born of preserving the value of one's life; the other was negative, born perhaps of surrendering to some sort of despair. None the less both were a means of relocating the locus of control inside the soldier.

Fatalism, as we have noted, was a protective mechanism. If one accepted the fact that one was going to die there was the possibility of giving up worrying about it, assuming a different set of thoughts, or narrowing the focus of worry. If investing in religion or using charms in an attempt to influence fate was problem-focussed coping, then fatalism was emotion-focussed coping. Fatalism involved mitigating anxiety

---

233 S.R. Maddi, *Hardiness – Turning Stressful Circumstances into Resilient Growth*, Kindle edition location 769.
234 Pym & Gordon, op. cit. p.202.

about an unknown rather than attempting to influence it. Fortune-telling also fell into this category of coping. Fatalism was an assumption, but having a fortune teller confirm that you would survive or die, as long as you accepted the premise of the transaction, empowered one with knowledge. Knowledge is nearly always better than uncertainty because it reduces the range of stressors, enabling individuals to focus on the particular thing that they need to develop a coping strategy for. Soldiers strove for ways to avoid what psychologists have called 'learned helplessness', the belief that whatever one does the outcome is not altered, a pathway to depression.[235]

Intuition may similarly provide an example of emotion-focussed coping. Stephen Hewett wrote home after his first tour in the trenches: 'I came through all right, as I will do *always* after this well-omened beginning';[236] and a young medical student trapped with Charles Carrington in a shell-hole during Third Ypres would declare that he had a 'very strong presentiment; nothing was going to hit him that day'.[237] Both were temporarily giving themselves positive certainty over their destiny. The intuition of death may have been a similar attempt to grasp at certainty of one's fate when conditions brought one to a state of desperation. It may simply have been more satisfactory to take up the idea that one was going to die at a particular time and in a particular place than having to put up with the uncertainty as to whether one would live or not any more.

Many soldiers wrote that death held no fear for them. Most, no doubt, would have echoed the sentiments of Captain Thomas Kettle, who wrote to his brother on the day before his death on the Somme in September 1916: 'I am calm but desperately anxious to live'.[238] Soldiers could exert little influence over whether they were killed in action or not, but both strong continued faith and emergency religion assisted them by enabling them to reassure themselves that they had done their best to gain God's protection in battle. Superstitions were a folk magic means of achieving this end, the amulet a tangible piece of evidence of the effort, an appeal to luck rather than simply to God to decrease the odds against death. The battlefield legends were not just, as Eric Leed suggested, an attempt to 'quieten and reorder the world',[239] but an attempt to create an image of divine protection and succour. In the event of their demise, soldiers were best positioned in terms of any afterlife by the emergency activity of attending Holy Communion before going into action. In a society with a strong underlying Christian ethos, if they had to die, they would get to heaven if they could. They were attempting to control outcomes in the way they best knew how, and in a belt and braces approach, they were prepared to use any resource to achieve this.

---

235 M.E.P. Seligman, *Helplessness: On Depression, Development, and Death.*
236 S. Hewett, *A Scholar's Letters*, p.46 (author italics).
237 Edmonds, op. cit. p.126.
238 Housman, op. cit. p.168.
239 Winter, op. cit. p.67.

# 6

## 'Depths of Terror Hitherto Undiscovered' – Fear in the Trenches

---

The Great War has been described as consisting of 'months of boredom punctuated by moments of terror'.[1] Fear, or 'funk' (a word first noted in Oxford University slang in the mid 1700's, deriving from Flemish meaning 'disturbance' or 'agitation')[2] was both a public and personal preoccupation in the age of the white feather. Private Alfred Burrage's prime motivation in volunteering was that 'I hated being thought a funk'.[3] The donning of uniform, however, did not remove the personal experience of fear. The almost universal terror generated by being under bombardment presented a challenge in an era when its expression was regarded as breaching the code of manliness.

### Stoicism and Fear

Within the Stoic creed fear was irrational because external danger was not a true evil. For Epictetus its expression led to 'dishonour'.[4] The Victorian linkage of the absence of fear and maintaining personal honour therefore had deep roots. But few could be Stoic sages. Given that the 'first movements' of fear were acknowledged as unavoidable, eliminating fear was a near impossible goal. The more diffusive Stoicism, espoused by Seneca, required distinguishing between 'trivial and tragic losses'.[5] He acknowledged 'the reasonableness of certain kinds of fears', and that there were '"respectable" forms of grieving'.[6] He took the practical view that a genuine fear of death was not a triviality. In certain situations controlling behaviour rather than the internal experience was all that could be achieved. Conversely, whilst advocating rational caution, Seneca deprecated imaginary, anticipatory fear which could derail honourable behaviour.

---

1  The origin of this phrase is uncertain.
2  www.oxforddictionaries.com.
3  Ex-Private X (A.M. Burrage), *War is War*, p.12.
4  N. Sherman, *Stoic Warriors*, Kindle edition location 1637.
5  Sherman, op. cit. location 1668.
6  Sherman, op. cit. location 1688.

Fear is adaptive. From an evolutionary standpoint it is a positive thing – an organism without fear would likely become extinct in a world of predators. The 'first movements' of fear are physical responses. These are driven by the autonomic nervous system and the release of that group of hormones called catecholamines, particularly the one we know as adrenalin. This in turn leads to an increase in heart and breathing rate, the diversion of blood to the muscles to energise them (thus making the face go pale), sweating to cool the active heated body down, and the widening of eyes to take in information. These physical changes all make up the 'fight or flight reaction' (a concept developed by the physiologist Walter Cannon during the war),[7] preparing the body to deal with threat. There is an optimal level of such changes which leads to effective performance – too little and we do not react effectively, too much and we may become incapacitated. Scout Joe Cassells recognised exactly what was happening to his body in the moments before going into action: 'The blood was pounding through my arteries. I felt much as I used to before the start of an important race'.[8]

Fear is only maladaptive when it occurs too strongly, too frequently, or in response to inappropriate things, and disables the person. Yet it is not simply a physical reaction. In addition to the physical 'first movements' it involves subjective experience including fear-related thoughts and fear behaviour. These are the elements the Stoics urged mastery of. Moreover, these components are may vary independently. They are desynchronous, not necessarily all moving in unison. People who describe themselves as frightened may thus be encouraged to approach a feared situation with little or no seeming visible fear – the Stoic ideal. Research shows that repeated performance of courageous behaviour leads to a decrease in both physical reactions and verbal reports of fear. Behaving bravely in a feared situation therefore actually has a positive effect.[9]

**Fear in the Trenches**

The author Henry Williamson, who served on the Western Front, devotes five volumes to the Great War in his 15 volume semi-autobiographical *Chronicle of Ancient Sunlight*. The second is entitled *A Fox under my Cloak*. The fox in question was fear, continually gnawing at one's insides. But it was not just the experience of fear itself, but what to do with it, that mattered. Second-Lieutenant Huntly Gordon thus described Seneca's ideal of getting 'used to living in constant fear without ever showing it', seeing this as the '*real* battle, secret and silent'.[10]

---

7   W.B. Cannon, *Bodily Changes in Pain, Hunger, Fear and Rage*.
8   J. Cassells, *The Black Watch*, p.77.
9   D.W. McNeil et. al., 'Anxiety and Fear,' in V.S. Ramachandaran (ed.), *Encyclopaedia of Human Behaviour*, p.161.
10  H. Gordon, *The Unreturning Army*, Kindle edition location 1266 – italics in original.

### *The first encounter with war*

The initial encounter with war, inevitably different from expectations, was not necessarily marked by fear. Henry Dundas, newly commissioned into the Scots Guards thought going into the line for the first time was 'rather thrilling'.[11] Captain Alfred Pollard (then a private) 'watched, fascinated' as his first shells burst nearby, noting that 'my pulses raced with excitement'.[12] He felt no fear, only a 'tremendous interest and excitement' on his inaugural tour in the trenches.[13] On his first exposure to shellfire in 1917 Lieutenant Teddy Shears wrote in his diary that 'my chief sensation was, I think, excitement'.[14] The adrenalin was flowing for these three soldiers but they did not label this as fear. When Captain Douglas Bell first came under fire in 1914, he similarly did not feel 'a bit nervous; merely interested'. He added that he was pleased, 'because I didn't know how it would affect me'.[15] It was a test for him, although he regarded himself as 'not much cursed with nerves'.[16] Lieutenant-Colonel William Malone wrote with satisfaction in his diary three days after arriving on Gallipoli that 'my nerve is quite good'. He seemed surprised to find it thus. 'I was inclined to think that I was too high strung to stand the racket of real hard war. It is not so'.[17] The role of innate optimism or simple lack of training in the initial absence of fear has already been discussed.[18] Private Bryan Dewes, a territorial with limited training claimed that under shellfire for the first time: 'We didn't realise at first the danger we were in, and stood up and laughed'.[19] The excitement of Henry Dundas may also have been due to the same factor. He viewed himself in retrospect as 'far too incompetent and ignorant myself at the time to appreciate the situation'.[20] He simply did not credit the danger. The reverse was true for Captain Robert Ross. He described how 'our ignorance was phenomenal' when he went into the trenches with his battalion for their first night. With 'nerves strung to the highest pitch' he was not at all fearless. He found that 'fears too fantastic to be real assailed the faint heart'. His men were in a high state of alert and kept expecting to be attacked, mistaking trees and mounds of earth for advancing Germans.[21]

The fearless were likely a minority. Squadron-Leader William Tyrrell, a past regimental medical officer, in his evidence to the War Office Committee of Enquiry into

---

11   Anonymous, *Henry Dundas – Scots Guards*, p.67.
12   A.O. Pollard, *Fire-Eater*, p.36.
13   Pollard, op. cit. p.38.
14   E.H. Shears, *Active Service Diary*, p.26.
15   D.H. Bell, *A Soldier's Diary of the Great War*, p.61.
16   Bell, op. cit. p119.
17   J. Crawford (ed.), *No Better Death*, Kindle edition location 2812.
18   See Chapter Five.
19   B.O. Dewes, quoted in A. Watson, 'Fear in Combat and Combating Fear' p.5 http://www.inter-disciplinary.net/ptb/wvw/wvw1/Watson.pdf.
20   Anon, *Dundas*, op. cit. p.68.
21   R.B. Ross, *The Fifty-First in France*, p.69.

'Shell-Shock' stated: 'All men know fear. Some conceal it better than others. A few bury it out of sight, but it is there all the same'.[22]

Veterans often specifically recalled their first encounters with warfare, even if they were relatively mild in intensity. Major Evelyn Fryer gave lengthy details of his first days in France even though they were 'nothing compared with other things later on which one hardly remembers'.[23] Anticipatory anxiety of initial contact was common. Approaching the front-line for the first time, Second-Lieutenant Edwin Vaughan recorded that his 'teeth began to chatter', and that he had to stop talking, 'for my voice trembled so'.[24] On his initial night-time duty 'a cold fear chilled my spine and set my teeth chattering', and in this state he mistook a hanging greatcoat for an intruder.[25] Private Ernest Parker described how his inauguration to the firing-line generated 'great tension';[26] and Private George Ashurst was 'too windy to sleep'.[27] Second-Lieutenant James Hyndson wrote in his diary the night before the Battle of Mons that, like Ashurst, he was unable to sleep. The thought of his first encounter with the enemy had 'made me far too excited'. He confided, however, that 'I feel very frightened'.[28] When Second-Lieutenant Charles Clayton experienced his first bullet, it seemed to him that 'the wings of death have swept by'. There was 'a sense of consciously pulling myself together'.[29] Behind the front line with a working prior to entering the trenches, Lieutenant Ronald Poulton (a rugby legend capped 17 times for England) proceeded down the road 'in fear and trembling' as it was known that the area was subject to German machine gun fire.[30] Private Geoffrey Husbands, on his first working party, dropped to the ground at the whiz of any bullet, although he soon became aware that 'it was a fond delusion in our minds that we were dodging them'.[31] Private Walter Williams described the moments prior to his initial spell in the trenches and, how looking at his fellow soldiers, he could see 'nervous tension showing in everybody's face'.[32] All 'laughed nervously trying to put on brave faces', Williams in the knowledge that he had had nightmares the night before and had struggled not to vomit his breakfast.[33] Approaching the front line, a sniper's shot rang out. Having dived to the ground, he and his fellows rose and 'a dozen hands furtively felt the back of their trousers for tell-tale signs of moisture'.[34]

22 *Report of the War Office Committee of Enquiry into 'Shell-Shock' (RWOCESS)*, p.31.
23 E.R.M. Fryer, *Reminiscences of a Grenadier*, p.18.
24 E.C. Vaughan, *Some Desperate Glory*, p.22.
25 Vaughan, op. cit. p.31.
26 E.W. Parker, *Into Battle*, p.25.
27 G. Ashurst, *My Bit*, pp.36-7.
28 J.G.W. Hyndson, *From Mons to the First Battle of Ypres*, Kindle edition location 215.
29 C.P. Clayton, *The Hungry One*, p.17.
30 Poulton, op. cit. p.342.
31 G. R. Husbands, *Joffrey's War*, p.182.
32 M. Williams, *With Innocence and Hope*, Kindle edition location 671.
33 Williams, op. cit. location 677.
34 Williams, op. cit. location 756.

Experience led to a more realistic appreciation of danger and management of reactions, especially with the assistance of 'old hands'. Private Henry Williamson on his first experience of the trenches described himself as 'rather nerve-shaken', but being mixed with regulars as models, who imparted knowledge quickly, the feeling of nervousness 'soon left us'.[35] Lieutenant-Colonel George Laurie, commanding 1st Royal Irish Rifles wrote to his wife after three weeks on the Western Front describing acclimatisation with exposure. His nerves had 'grown stronger, as I've had a good baptism of them when going about'.[36]

## Shellfire

The experience of shellfire is totemic of the experience of trench warfare. Private Henry Russell wrote that 'men feared shellfire more than they feared God'.[37] To endure it was a trial of every coping mechanism. Corporal Geoffrey Husbands was clear that 'to "stick it"' through a bombardment was 'perhaps the severest test of a man's nerve on active service'.[38] Lord Moran was in absolute agreement: 'The acid test of a man in the trenches was high explosive; it told each one of us things about ourselves we had not known till then'.[39] He described a man who during shelling looked 'just like a boy who is beginning an illness with shivering attacks' and who described himself as 'just petrified'. Outside of this, 'his mind is quite normal'.[40]

Fear was particularly evident in the initial experience of shellfire. On his first exposure to a heavy shell Private Douglas Pinkerton fell flat on the ground and remained there 'until the sergeant-major delivered a well-directed kick on a fitting portion of my anatomy'.[41] Second-Lieutenant Bernard Martin was progressing alone along the road to Ypres when a shell burst near him. He had not counted on the fact that 'the thing tells you it's coming', which had compounded his fear. 'Terror mounted' as the sound progressed and he flung himself to the ground, 'pressing my body to the earth passionately'. In his shaken state afterwards, he concluded that he was 'a coward', and wondered what had 'gone wrong?'[42] He had expected different behaviour from himself, and his self-image had been up-ended. Private George Coppard described a newly arrived subaltern being shelled on his first day in the line who refused to budge from his dugout, describing how 'the poor devil was paralysed with fear'. He added: 'To my embarrassment, he would burst into tears'.[43] Lieutenant Patrick Campbell arrived at Miraumont in 1917 for his introduction to front line duty and hearing the

---

35  A. Williamson, *Henry Williamson and the First World War*, p.135.
36  G.B. Laurie, *Letters*, p.15.
37  H. Russell, *Slaves of the War Lords*, p.58.
38  Husbands, op. cit. p.285.
39  Lord Moran, *Anatomy of Courage*, p.71.
40  Moran, op. cit. p.45.
41  R.D. Pinkerton, *Ladies from Hell*, p.66.
42  B. Martin, *Poor Bloody Infantry*, p.42.
43  G. Coppard, *With a Machine Gun to Cambrai*, p.116.

sound of artillery, experienced this as 'terrifying, more sinister than anything I had ever imagined'.[44] He was 'stunned' on his first day,[45] but, as the firing became more intermittent the noise 'seemed less evil' and he decided that he might be able 'to learn to endure it'. Like Bernard Martin, he feared failing to cope.[46] Ronald Poulton, subject to his first bombardment wrote in his journal that the shelling was 'very frightening, the report, the nearing whistle and the burst, and then you wonder if you are alive'.[47] Private Frederick Voigt's introduction to shelling was on a working party behind the lines. It was not immediately close, and could have done the group no harm, yet one young soldier was 'stretched out at full length, trembling, and sobbing hysterically and clutching at the grass with hands that opened and closed in mad spasms'. Another man was 'cowering down by one of the trucks, his face buried in his arms'.[48] On the retreat at Noyon in 1914, Captain Cecil Brownlow was subject to a two hour bombardment. The experience was so intense that 'something seemed to snap inside my head, and I thought I was going mad'.[49] Lieutenant Evelyn Broadwood, under shellfire for three hours at Mons in 1914 managed to keep his head clear. He noted that 'my brain seemed extraordinarily cool and collected which I was proud of', but when he looked at his hands he saw them 'moving and twisting in an extraordinary way'.[50] During his first experience of a bombardment Second-Lieutenant Charles Douie 'clung close to the parapet, almost wild with fear'.[51] Similarly, on 1 July 1916, when 1st Lancashire Fusiliers attacked at Beaumont Hamel, George Ashurst described men who 'sat at the bottom of the trench shaking and shouting, not wounded, but unable to bear the noise, the smell and the horrible sights'.[52] Many soldiers were therefore unprepared for the degree of fear and their own reactions.

Major Harold Bidder was in no doubt about the psychological destructiveness of shellfire, describing 'hours of nerve-wracking shelling', like Ashurst surrounded by sights and sounds 'round to break the hardest nerve'.[53] Second-Lieutenant Edmund Blunden found the experience 'mental torture'.[54] Raymond Lodge confessed how he became 'awfully shaky'.[55] Second-Lieutenant Arthur West described how men under shellfire 'cowered and trembled'. He observed the fear behaviour of men in 'funk-holes' in the side of a trench: 'One simply looks at his hands clasped on his knees, dully and lifelessly, shivering a little as a shell draws near'; yet another 'taps the side

---

44 P.J. Campbell, *In the Cannons Mouth*, p.2.
45 Campbell, *Cannon's Mouth*, p.4.
46 Campbell, *Cannon's Mouth*, p.5.
47 Poulton, op. cit. p.345.
48 F.A. Voigt, *Combed Out*, p.44.
49 C. Brownlow, *The Breaking of the Storm*, p.102.
50 E. Broadwood, quoted in P. Hart, *Fire and Movement*, p.113.
51 C. Douie, *The Weary Road*, pp.102-3.
52 Ashurst, op. cit. p.100.
53 Orex (H.F. Bidder), *Three Chevrons*, p. 70.
54 E. Blunden, *Undertones of War*, p.171.
55 O.J. Lodge, *Raymond*, p.21.

of his hole with his finger-nails, rhythmically'.[56] Hugh Quigley wrote of 'trying vainly to keep knees from shaking and teeth from chattering, with a deadly sick feeling in the stomach as bits of shrapnel hit the side of the trench'.[57] On the Somme in 1916, old-hand Private Giles Eyre was shelled in a trench where there were no dug-outs. He crouched, gritting his teeth, with a 'shrinking, trembling' body. In this bombardment he described how 'one felt oneself completely alone' separate from the companions around, his thinking focussed only on 'self-preservation'.[58] Sapper B.R. Richards, alternatively, described how 'reason was completely blasted out of (your mind) ... you had no time to think'.[59] Under a three hour bombardment, Private Harry Drinkwater 'did not for a moment think we should get out of it alive', describing his situation as being 'helpless to protect ourselves'.[60] A fellow soldier 'burst out crying'. Drinkwater stated that it was the only occasion during the war he saw this occur, but that 'in this instance it was not out of place'.[61]

When Major Arthur Gibbs was first exposed to shellfire in Salonika, he wrote that it was like 'what turning on the quarter current in the electric chair must be – most invigorating, but a little jumpy'. His understated response may have been related to the type of gun he was being shelled with – 'they were only pip-squeaks'.[62] Shelling by particular types of heavier guns, whose sound was easily recognisable, would trigger a more intense fear. The noise of an oncoming shell, as Bernard Martin found, was a central part of the experience of fear. He was in good company. Evelyn Fryer noted that howitzer shells could be heard coming 'some seconds before their actual arrival, and this increases their horror enormously'.[63] Lieutenant Malcolm West wrote in contrast of the 'whizz-bang', a shell fired from light artillery that travelled faster than the speed of sound, which would burst 'almost before you know it is coming' so that there was 'no time to feel frightened'. Like Martin and Fryer, he knew that the shells of heavy guns could be 'heard whistling for some time, and one can tell if they are coming in one's direction or not.' He added with the same understatement that graced Arthur Gibbs' account of his reactions: 'These have affected me unpleasantly'.[64] Edwin Vaughan, so fearful on his first exposure to the trenches, soon adapted to shellfire. Under bombardment at Cambrai in May 1917 he decided that 'the best antidote to fear is food', and calmly began to prepare something to eat whilst the shells fell. Yet he knew in this display of sang-froid what he needed to worry about. With the

---

56  A.G. West, *Diary of a Dead Officer*, p.68.
57  H. Quigley, *Passchendaele and the Somme*, p.122.
58  G.E.M. Eyre, *Somme Harvest*, p.205.
59  B.R. Richards, BBC 'I Was There'.
60  J. Cooksey & D. Griffiths (eds), *Harry's War*, p.93.
61  Cooksey & Griffiths, op. cit. p.141.
62  A.H. Gibbs, *Gun Fodder*, p.118-9.
63  Fryer, op. cit. p.22.
64  H.E.E. Howson, *Two Men*, p.238.

burst of a *granatenwerfer* projectile overhead,[65] 'a cold fear gripped me' as he knew there was 'no cover from these'.[66] Second-Lieutenant Llewellyn Griffith described how a series of 5.9 inch shell explosions caused him to plumb 'depths of terror hitherto undiscovered by me'.[67] Ten minutes of shelling by such guns 'drove us into a stupor of fear, and fear brought its terrible thirst'.[68] George Coppard described the 'terror' of the *minenwerfer*, a trench mortar, which 'put fear in the heart of the bravest'. Private Stephen Graham cited the words of one of his fellow soldiers to describe the effect of this particular horror, its shell 'coming at us was like a row of houses rushing through the air'.[69] Duration of shellfire was another issue. Captain Julian Grenfell wrote home about shells: 'After a day of them, one's nerves are really absolutely beat down'.[70] On the other hand, the sudden unexpected arrival of a single shell caused Second-Lieutenant Carlos Blacker to experience 'the most acute spasm of physical fear I experienced during the war – or indeed during my life'.[71] He had been asleep and was hence completely unprepared. Soldiers' responses were also governed by their physical condition. On Gallipoli, Major John Gillam would hear 'the shriek' of a heavy shell coming and, being physically under par with a stomach upset, found the experience of fear was magnified.[72] Sergeant Ben Keeling agreed. Weak from three successive attacks of flu in March 1916 he wrote that shelling 'affects one's nerves a lot more under these circumstances'.[73]

In a dug-out in conversation with fellow officers, Huntly Gordon heard an oncoming shell and thought: 'Keep talking at all costs'. However as the shell neared, they 'gave up the pretence', looking at each other 'with wan smiles'.[74] The very sound that terrified allowed protective decision making of a sort. Second-Lieutenant Charles Carrington described how when he heard a 5.9 inch shell incoming, he realised that had a brief period of grace, and in those 'five or six seconds' an individual could pass through 'quite a number of psychological changes.' As the shell got nearer the sound indicated the possibility of a direct hit or not. Carrington was told that 'you never heard the shell that hit you', but that even if one heard it 'it might be going to fall 20 or 30 yards away' and still represent threat. As the roaring increased there would come the moment when the shell was 'right on top of you, and your nerve would break and you'd throw yourself in the mud and cringe'. Carrington described a 'fifth of a second'

---

65 A spigot mortar type weapon which threw grenades.
66 Vaughan, op. cit. pp.119-120, italics in original.
67 L.W. Griffith, *Up to Mametz*.
68 Griffith, op. cit. The physiological reactions of anxiety cause water to be diverted from the mouth to other parts of the body, the sensation of a dry mouth mimicking thirst.
69 S. Graham, *A Private in the Guards*, p.199.
70 J. Grenfell, quoted in L. Housman, *War Letters of Fallen Englishmen*, p.119.
71 J. Blacker (ed.), *Have You Forgotten Yet?*, p.137.
72 J. Gillam, *Gallipoli Diary*, p.158.
73 F.H. Keeling, *Letters*, p.274.
74 Gordon, op. cit. location 1491.

where the soldier could decide whether the shell was for him or not. If it missed, all would 'get up and roar with laughter'.[75] Edwin Vaughan, in furious action in August 1917 at Ypres, gave a similar description of this hysterical release. Another soldier was leaning against him, shaking with fear, when a dud shell arrived, hit the ground and slid underneath him. The fearful soldier immediately began to laugh, as did Vaughan who realised that this was 'hysterics … a temporary madness'.[76] George Coppard similarly described the process of listening to the sound of a shell and wondering: 'Which way will it go? This way or that?' Like Carrington, he would realise that there were 'a couple of seconds in which to decide which way to run'.[77] Bernard Martin found that *minenwerfer* shelling 'put the wind up me more than anything else'.[78] The two second glimpse of the projectile at the top of its trajectory allowed him to run a few feet in either direction, but he would then lie wondering whether his judgement had been right whilst anticipating the explosion. Second-Lieutenant Alan Thomas would reach a point where he felt that he had a bombardment 'taped', knowing where shells would fall and when they were due.[79] These experiences make clear one way in which men came to manage fear. Although Charles Carrington stated: 'We pretended to get very expert in the sounds of shells',[80] soldiers did learn to identify which sounds indicated which type of shell was coming with some indication of direction. They thus had the opportunity of taking cover, creating some sense of managing their own safety.

Charles Douie, however, wrote that watching the flight of shells 'placed a great strain on the nerves'.[81] Lieutenant-Colonel George Scott-Jackson, a doctor who commanded 1/7th Northumberland Fusiliers for 20 months, viewed the 'concentrated attention' of attempting to avoid trench mortar shells as an exhausting experience. Observing the shell in flight 'you have to watch him and dodge him, and just as you dodge him there is another coming'.[82] Fear of the precise landing point of an incoming shell could unfortunately lead to paralysis. Lieutenant Arthur Dugmore became aware of the 'singing' of a grenade, which he knew was coming straight for him. 'My feet seemed nailed to the ground, and I simply could not move, it was a case of undiluted terror'.[83] Fortunately for Dugmore when the grenade landed three yards behind him it proved to be a dud. Douglas Pinkerton, after the experience of an NCO's foot in his backside, described a 'stoical complacency' that developed 'after the first five or six shells have failed to make you their mark'. He however thought a soldier never really became accustomed to shelling, and it was for this reason that 'many men are captured after

---

75   C. Carrington, BBC 'The Great War Interviews'.
76   Vaughan, op. cit. pp.211-2.
77   Coppard, op. cit. p.38
78   Martin, op. cit. p.103.
79   A. Thomas, *A Life Apart*, p.111.
80   Carrington, op. cit.
81   Douie, op. cit. p.174.
82   RWOCESS, p.46.
83   A.R. Dugmore, *When the Somme Ran Red*, p.130.

a heavy shelling'. They would be unhurt, but the ordeal would have sapped 'their will to fight'.[84]

A shell landing in a crowded area could cause a multiplicity of grotesque injuries and fatalities. Approaching Ypres in 1917, Hugh Quigley's unit was shelled. One explosion caused 60 casualties. Quigley described that 'the scream of despair and agony was dreadful to hear, men shell-shocked out of reason', and that the event 'shook the whole battalion for several days'.[85] Lord Moran described men prepared for death if it 'came swiftly and cleanly'. Obliteration was different: 'That shattering, crude bloody end by a big shell was too much for them'. Such an end was 'something more than death'.[86] Captain Theodore Wilson was 'horribly afraid' under shelling but his fear was not of being hit himself, rather 'of seeing other people torn'.[87] Quigley's experience of a random shell causing mayhem was more or less universal, whether in a front line trench or elsewhere. In the case of his unit, it jeopardised their response to further shellfire. Signs of continued adrenalin-driven overarousal, including post-traumatic hypervigilance which left soldiers scanning all around for threat and the jumpiness of exaggerated startle, gripped them all: 'The sudden roar of a gun made us start guiltily, half-ashamed, and yet unable to control our agitation'.[88] Huntly Gordon never lost his hypervigilance, and even when out of the line found that he could not 'rid myself of the unconscious habit of listening for approaching shells'.[89]

Patrick Campbell, when being advised how to react to a shell that seemed likely to land near, was told to dive into the nearest dugout. 'Nobody minds your dropping in on them in such circumstances', for 'they know it may be their turn to drop in on you next time', he noted.[90] Seeking safety was not showing fear. Second-Lieutenant Douglas Gillespie took the view that his prime responsibility as an officer was to save himself, and wrote home that 'I take every care, and am not afraid of being thought afraid'.[91] Huntly Gordon however thought it 'bad for morale to be dropping into shell-holes too often' to avoid shellfire.[92] Second-Lieutenant Alec Dawson may have simply been attempting to reassure his wife when he wrote: 'Bombardment doesn't affect one's mind much. You don't feel the slightest bit afraid'. He was clearly physically aroused, however, noting he was 'only a lot more alert than usual, and rather keyed up'.[93] Men adapted to shellfire in that the recovery periods became shorter. Second-Lieutenant Bertram Medley would write after two days in the line:

84 Pinkerton, op. cit. p.55.
85 Quigley, op. cit. p.123.
86 Moran, op. cit. p.72.
87 T.P.C. Wilson, quoted in Housman, op. cit. p.295.
88 Quigley, op. cit. p.125.
89 Gordon, op. cit. location 1737.
90 Campbell, *Cannon's Mouth*, p.34.
91 A.D. Gillespie, *Letters from Flanders*, p.33.
92 Gordon, op. cit. location 1233.
93 A.J. Dawson, *A 'Temporary Gentleman' in France*, p.125.

'I feel at peace ... even with the shells pounding outside'.[94] After several months in the trenches, Captain Gerald Burgoyne described how the physical reactions of fear abated, describing 'how very quickly (an hour's quite sufficient) one's nerves recover and one's heart beats normally'.[95] Lieutenant Bruce Bairnsfather, creator of the phlegmatic 'Old Bill', imbued this character with his own adaptation to shellfire: 'I soon got to know these affairs, and learnt to take them calmly'.[96] Second-Lieutenant Graham Greenwell was bowled over by a *minenwerfer* shell and described how 'I felt most frightfully shaken and pretty rotten, but after about half an hour it passed off'.[97] He noted that once he understood where shells were landing, or 'rather that they aren't directed against your particular spot, you cease to take any interest'. He viewed adaptation as the only option, for when 'shells have begun to get on your nerves, it is time to apply for permanent leave'.[98] However, events could always shake this sort of composure, and when three shells arrived suddenly and hit three men beside him, Greenwell described that he was so shaken that his reaction bordered on 'temporary insanity'.[99] Stephen Hewett also described adaptation, writing home that one got over 'purely physical fear' with 'very little practice'.[100] Such adaptation, as Greenwell found, was not necessarily permanent. Ernest Parker was sent to Britain to be trained as an officer. On his return to the front in mid-1917, discovering 'with chagrin that I was much more nervous under shellfire than in 1916', although quite quickly 'this initial shakiness began to wear off'.[101] The long break had deskilled him. Each soldier had their own way of managing the stress induced by shellfire. Giles Eyre described a fellow ranker who amidst explosions would 'feverishly jot down some verses'.[102] Henry Russell, commenting on the role of cigarettes as the 'greatest nerve-restorer', described how at the start of a bombardment the first thing that a soldier did was to 'feel for his "smokes"'.[103] Conningsby Dawson reassured his parents that danger was not appreciated 'until you come to think about it afterwards', distraction being the tool that achieved this as 'you take too much interest in the sport of dodging to be afraid'.[104] Second-Lieutenant Thomas Heald similarly wrote of shellfire: 'It is quite alright if one has something to do'. He would not 'notice it if you have not time to think'.[105] Captain Evelyn Southwell went through a process of rationalisation: 'When you know how

94 B. Medley, quoted in C. Moore-Bick, *Playing the Game*, p.87.
95 C. Davison, *The Burgoyne Diaries*, p.70.
96 B. Bairnsfather, *Bullets and Billets*, p.40. Shelling proved, however to be his nemesis, as after a particularly close burst he was returned to England with 'shell shock'.
97 G.H. Greenwell, *An Infant in Arms*, p.77.
98 Greenwell, op. cit. p.116.
99 Greenwell, op. cit. p.214.
100 S. Hewett, *A Scholar's Letters*, p.39.
101 Parker, op. cit. p.68.
102 Eyre, op. cit. p.43.
103 Russell, op. cit. p.47.
104 C. Dawson, *Carry On*, p.46.
105 T. Heald quoted in A. Woolf, *Subalterns of the Foot*, pp.10-11.

little damage a high explosive shell' might potentially do 'compared with the noise it makes, you don't fear him so much'.[106]

### *The many sources of fear*
Not feeling fear under shelling did not mean that a man was completely without fear. On Gallipoli, John Gillam was talking to a fellow officer who claimed no anxiety in shellfire but that 'when bullets are about his head always feels ten times as big as it really is'. Second-Lieutenant Robert Graves similarly found rifle-fire 'more trying' than shell-fire, because a rifle bullet felt 'purposely aimed'.[107] Not only was there the real potential of doom falling from above, but there was also the threat of fatal inhumation from being blown up from below. Harry Drinkwater was subject to a heavy bombardment at Arras in May 1916, and aware of the continuous mining beneath him, 'thought the mine was probably going up at any moment and they were coming over'.[108] Drinkwater, who had been employed in carrying earth out of the mines and was sensitive to underground sounds, continued that 'every unusual noise' made him think a German mine was about to be exploded.[109] The threat from above came in different forms. Geoffrey Dugdale, after his experiences at Third Ypres in 1917 developed a particular fear of night-time bombing by aircraft when behind the lines at rest. This was a place where one was supposed to be safe, but aircraft removed this security. When a raid was warned, Dugdale would leave his tent and listen for aircraft with 'a sickening feeling at the pit of my stomach'. He described how he 'lay and shivered', hoping no one would find him, 'wondering how I should explain it if they did'. With shame he admitted: 'It was funk, sheer unadulterated funk'.[110]

Arthur Dugmore did not write of fear on his introduction to shelling, but when first exposed to the 'much dreaded gas' found that it 'scared me badly'.[111] Private John Hall described how he was 'more frightened with gas' than he was with shell fire.[112] Captain Edward Simeons wrote that when the gas alert gongs were first sounded he remembered how Henry V knelt down and prayed before the Battle of Agincourt and did the same.[113] If it was silently agreed that visible fear under shellfire was acceptable, then certainly when 2nd Lancashire Fusiliers fled in response to the gas attack of 2 May 1915 at Second Ypres, there was no criticism from George Ashurst. He was suddenly aware of the fleeing front-line jumping over his trench, and 'there was a rush to get out'. An officer tried to calm them, but 'we ran across the open, not knowing

---

106 Howson, op. cit. p.37.
107 R. Graves, *Goodbye to All That*, p.91.
108 Cooksey & Griffiths, op. cit. p.71.
109 Cooksey & Griffiths, op. cit. p.72.
110 G. Dugdale, *'Langemarck' and 'Cambrai'*, pp.86-7.
111 Dugmore, op. cit. p.114.
112 J. Hall, IWM Sound 14599.
113 E.E. Simeons, Private Papers, IWM Docs 2808.

or caring where to'.[114] Arthur Gibbs had become an old hand at shellfire when he was subject to a gas bombardment in Armentières, at which point he decided that 'I had no idea of war'. It was as if his notion of fear had recalibrated in one event. He declared that he had no conception that 'human nature could go through such experiences and emotions and remain sane'.[115] Wearing a gas mask gave rise to a different fear. Captain Robert Manion, after hours under a gas bombardment, had a feeling of impending suffocation, and removed his mask, thinking death by gas to be preferable.[116] Gas indeed had its own psychological effects, both in battle through anticipation and after exposure. Battle weary soldiers often misinterpreted bombardments and assumed they were being assailed by gas when they were not. In the aftermath, Lord Moran noted 'hysteria' and that in mild cases after the physical effects had disappeared there was left 'an emotional disturbance like a mild attack of shell shock'.[117] Colonel A.B. Soltau, consultant physician in France for gas cases found that mustard gas poisoning resulted in the greatest number of psychological reactions, amongst them photophobia, aphonia, persistent cough, and persistent vomiting, which had no physical basis.[118] In some, there was a longer term effect, with psychological symptoms including photophobia, palpitations and laryngitis. Indeed, there was a move in 1918 to define a 'gas neurosis syndrome'. Pension records show that in the post-war years veterans tended to attribute any respiratory symptoms to exposure to gas.[119]

### *Helplessness under shellfire*
William Tyrrell was of the opinion that 'lack of control or the power of control' was crucial in terms of psychological collapse.[120] Lord Moran agreed – the uniqueness of shellfire was that 'it happened to passive men'.[121] Under bombardment on the Somme, Captain Douglas Cuddeford observed that 'the nerve-trying part of it was that we could do nothing'.[122] As Hugh Quigley described of the experience of sustained shelling, options were limited: 'All we could do was to lie motionless on our back and pray'. In the face of this helplessness his reaction 'went beyond fear, beyond consciousness', to the extent of 'a grovelling of the soul itself'.[123] Donald Hankey did not even resort to prayer: 'You can do nothing. You cannot retaliate in any way. You simply have to sit tight and hope for the best'.[124] Giles Eyre was at least able to swear: 'There

---

114 Ashurst, op. cit. p.54.
115 Gibbs, op. cit. p.197.
116 R.J. Manion, *A Surgeon in Arms*, pp. 74-5.
117 Moran, op. cit. p.187.
118 RWOCESS, p.74.
119 E. Jones & N. Greenberg, 'Long-term Psychological Consequences among Chemical Warfare Survivors of World War I and their Current Relevance', *Psychiatric Annals*, p.727.
120 RWOCESS, p.34.
121 Moran, op. cit. p.78.
122 D.W.J. Cuddeford, *And All for What?*, p.58.
123 Quigley, op. cit. p.123.
124 D. Hankey, *A Student in Arms: Second Series*, p.119.

is nothing to hit back at, all a man can do is to grit his teeth, wait in suspense and curse impotently!'[125] Geoffrey Husbands described the test of endurance: 'One can only wait powerless and helpless, praying for a cool head and power to keep a brave front'.[126] Lieutenant Edward Tennant wrote home of the seeming endless nature of helplessness. There was 'nothing to do all the time bit sit waiting for the next, and the next'.[127] The sense of not being able to exert a viable choice experienced by Henry Dundas made him feel that all options were without value: 'You're absolutely helpless, as to go into a dug-out is merely to exchange burial alive for disintegration'.[128] Captain Frederick Chandler felt dehumanised, waiting 'like a dog'.[129] Douglas Pinkerton described this waiting as 'far more wearing than any fighting that I ever afterward experienced'.[130]

The celebrated Doctor William Rivers, of Craiglockhart fame, gave a neat demonstration of how degree of distress correlated with decreasing degree of control in comparing Great War pilots with their observers and those of the balloon section. Pilots, in his experience, demonstrated levels of psychological disturbance 'almost trivial compared with the cases in the army'. Their observers, having 'not the same chance of manipulative activity as the pilot', had more severe symptoms. The most severe cases Rivers encountered were those of men moored in static balloons, sitting ducks absolutely unable to take avoiding action.[131]

On Gallipoli, John Gillam was shelled out of the sea whilst bathing and retired to his bivouac made of packing cases. He confided to his diary: 'I feel safer there, somehow, but why I should I cannot explain'. He claimed that 'all who have been under shell fire will bear me out in the statement that even if one is in a tent one feels more confident ... than if in the bare open'. What he was of course indicating was that the act of taking shelter, however illusory, decreased the sense of passivity and helplessness. Soldiers worked hard to decrease such feelings if they could. Judging from the nature of the sound of a shell where it might fall was not so illusory, and similarly soldiers could avoid certain enfiladed area of trenches, and could be aware of active snipers. It all increased the tenuous sense of control.

### *Aloneness and fear*

Private Arthur Lambert wrote that under shellfire it was 'easy to be brave with companions all around, but a more difficult task when entirely alone'.[132] Patrick Campbell noted under heavy bombardment that it was 'when one was alone that shell fire was

---

125 Eyre, op. cit. p.26.
126 Husbands, op. cit. p.285.
127 P. Glenconner, *Edward Wyndham Tennant: A Memoir*, p.146.
128 Anon, *Dundas*, pp.70-1.
129 F. Chandler, Private Papers, IWM Docs 15460.
130 Pinkerton, op. cit. p.70.
131 RWOCESS, p.57.
132 A. Lambert, *Over the Top*, p.183.

so frightening', but being in the company of others it was merely 'disagreeable'.[133] Charles Carrington similarly described himself as 'always very nervous' when alone under shell-fire.[134] Geoffrey Husbands got lost in a trench system on the Somme under heavy bombardment and being alone found himself feeling 'a very insignificant atom in an ocean of noise', fear being a 'very close companion'.[135] He was worried that his fellows might think that he had simply 'hidden somewhere through cowardice'.[136] Norman Gladden got lost during a relief and 'alone out there in the dead ground between the lines, I was panic stricken'. He kept shouting and at last there was an answer – 'companionship then meant so much'.[137] Patrick Campbell, searching for a cut signal wire in fog on the eve of the German 1918 spring offensive similarly felt 'alone and lost'. Having been primed by rumours of the attack he began to feel afraid. This was not the 'ordinary fear of shells', rather it was 'the fear of the unknown'.[138] Lieutenant Sidney Rogerson wrote that 'worse than all the anticipation of battle', was to be 'alone, and lost and in danger'. His own particular dread was likely shared by others. He feared 'being struck down somewhere where there was no one to find me' and suffering an unknown obliteration 'where I should lie till I rotted back slowly into the mud'.[139] Harold Bidder, on the Somme in 1916, set out alone in partial darkness to check tape prior to an attack. Becoming lost on the way back, he too shared the fear that 'one might drop wounded into a shell-hole and be seen no more'.[140] George Coppard was clear about the comforting presence of others that helped modulate fear, writing: 'In company, the dangers are shared'. Going back to search for a revolver lost coming out of the line, he described how 'when alone, amid darkness and the dead, there is no sharing'. Like Sidney Rogerson, his worst fear was being killed 'without a pal knowing about it'.[141] It was not simply the fear of an unknown death. A wounded man needed help. Major George Davidson, a normally phlegmatic individual, was fired on alone on a walk during the Gallipoli campaign and wondered 'how long you may have to lie, if you get wounded, before anyone comes your way'.[142] Lieutenant Harold Macmillan, wounded and making his way back with a fellow officer, became separated from him: 'Fear, not to say panic seized me'.[143] A sergeant of 22nd Manchester wounded at Fricourt on 1 July 1916 was aware of members of his

133 P.J. Campbell, *The Ebb and Flow of Battle*, p.66.
134 C. Edmonds (C. Carrington), *A Subaltern's War*, p.119.
135 Husbands, op. cit. p.331.
136 Husbands, op. cit. p.332.
137 N. Gladden, *Ypres 1917*, p.144.
138 Campbell, *Ebb and Flow*, p.13.
139 S. Rogerson, *Twelve Days on the Somme*, p.92.
140 Bidder, op. cit. p.206.
141 Coppard, op. cit. p.97.
142 G. Davidson, *With the Incomparable 29th*, pp.178-9.
143 H. Macmillan, *Winds of Change*, p.89.

platoon crawling past and described how: 'It's being cut off from human beings that's as bad as anything when one's wounded'.[144]

Cecil Brownlow, an artillery officer, came under shellfire on his own on the Aisne. He gave a cogent account of why he found being alone in danger to be so debilitating. Like George Coppard, he believed that: 'It is a common experience that in moments of danger a companion is of untold value; if he is braver than you, you imbibe his courage, and feel strengthened'. He described a process of comparing reactions. 'If you are braver than he, you feel a gratifying sense of superiority. If you both are of the same courage value, you mutually support each other'. This had the value of focussing outside oneself on someone else. Being alone could lead to an unhelpful inwards focussing, Brownlow suggested: 'When you are utterly alone you become introspective and imaginative, which is more dangerous than the danger itself'. William Tyrrell was clear that aloneness had to be prevented: 'The C.O. should avoid detailing one man for lonely and dangerous duty – two, not one, should be sent'.[145]

**Managing Fear**

Alfred Burrage noted an interesting phenomenon. He described himself as 'horribly afraid', but that 'I was never terrified as I had been on comparatively trivial occasions unconnected with the war'.[146] It was as if a threshold had recalibrated – continued fear seeming not as bad as everyday life very occasionally punctuated by minor episodes of fear. Colonel John Fuller described a progression of the experience of fear. A soldier would start off being 'healthily afraid', but this would not last long, to be 'replaced by a type of callousness'. This position of adaptation might progress in two unhelpful directions; some soldiers would make very little effort to protect themselves, whilst others might become 'obsessed with fear'.[147] Lieutenant John Reith was very clear that managing fear was an active process, stating that: 'Nor were those who proclaimed their fright by any means the most frightened'. He described how some soldiers 'bluffed themselves frightened and rid themselves of what fright they had'. He therefore seems to be suggesting that some soldiers actively attempted to experience fear in order to desensitize themselves to it. Otherwise it was a process of stage-management, as others 'bluffed themselves not frightened when they really were'. Lastly, some resorted to simple repression, trying 'to suppress their feelings altogether'.[148] Harold Macmillan explained that 'courage is mainly, if not wholly, the result of vanity or pride' and that in action 'proper behaviour, even acts of gallantry, are part of the show',

---

144 Quoted in G. Chapman, *Vain Glory*, p.324.
145 RWOCESS, p.33.
146 Burrage, op. cit. p.68.
147 *RWOCESS*, p.29.
148 J. Reith, *Wearing Spurs*, p.65.

and that 'one moves and behaves almost automatically as a member of a team or an actor on the stage'.[149]

### *Accepting fear in others*
Fear was easily perceived or sensed, and a sliding-scale of the experience of the emotion was understood. Frederic Manning noted that two new arrivals 'seemed a bit windy, that is, restless and impatient, not really in a funk'.[150] These men were simply visibly demonstrating physiological arousal – the adrenalin was flowing. Others came to understand that what did not affect one individual might significantly affect another. Thus, Captain Rowland Feilding was subject to a low whizz-bang burst. The sapper officer he was with collapsed into the bottom of the trench, 'blinded by the shock'. Feilding began uncharitably by thinking 'he was making too much of it' as the shell had burst just as close to himself'.[151] The man's reaction persisted, and Feilding realised that he was genuinely affected. It was also accepted that having been in action before did not necessarily mitigate fear. Waiting to go 'over the top' at Gommecourt on 1 July 1916, Second-Lieutenant Edward Liveing noted the corporal beside him, a veteran of Gallipoli, 'shaking all over, and white as parchment'.[152]

Most soldiers were charitable to their fellows. Memoirs record seeing fear in others that went without comment. Second-Lieutenant David Campbell, under shellfire on Gallipoli, was joined in his dugout by an orderly who 'was shivering with fright and every time a shell burst nearby we felt him shrinking more closely to the back wall'.[153] The man's behaviour went unremarked. Graham Greenwell, at Hébuterne in December 1915, described how 'another fellow last night got the jim-jams', leaning against the side of the trench 'with a white face'.[154] Greenwell ignored this. Patrick Campbell encountered a young signaller who was 'in a pitiable state, literally shaking with fear', despite being in safety. He wanted to say to him: 'Stop being in such a bloody funk', but did not. He remembered a time when he himself 'had been afraid before there was anything to fear'.[155] Artillery officer Hugh Dalton, in Italy in 1918, gave example of a 'strong contrast in psychology' of two drivers. One was 'superbly cheerful', the other, younger man 'was a bunch of visible nerves' and when a shell exploded nearby, fell to the ground convinced he was hit 'and for some time after that he was suffering from shell shock'.[156] Dalton simply described with interest, he did not condemn. Charles Carrington, in front of Ovillers in July 1916, found a young private 'crouched against a chalk-heap almost in tears' saying that he could not go over

---

149 Macmillan, op. cit. pp.89-90.
150 F. Manning, *The Middle Parts of Fortune*, Kindle edition location 2857.
151 R. Feilding, *War Letters to a Wife*, p.26.
152 E.G.D. Liveing, *Attack*, p.62.
153 D. Campbell, *Forward the Rifles*, p.43.
154 Greenwell, op. cit. p.84.
155 Campbell, *Ebb and Flow*, p.55.
156 H. Dalton, *With British Guns in Italy*, p.208.

the top. Other soldiers about him 'looked rather sympathetic than disgusted'.[157] They knew that fear was temporary. Within 24 hours, and after action, the same man was sitting joking, 'his fears forgotten'.[158] On the cusp of action, Private George Brame noted that there were ten in his section, all with different reactions: 'Some taking it as an adventure; one or two were developing nerves – none more so than the lance-corporal who was supposed to be in charge of us'. Indeed, this individual 'was in a bad way; his face was the picture of death'. Brame felt sorry for him, for it was evident that he was 'feeling his responsibility'.[159] Some were able to offer verbal support. Private Geoffrey Husbands found a young soldier on sentry duty in the trenches 'trembling and shaking like a jelly'. He did his 'best to cheer him up', telling him that 'You'll be alright when you're used to it'.[160] Charles Carrington himself suffered a similar moment at Third Ypres under prolonged shellfire, when all mental coping mechanisms failed, and 'I swore and moved nervously and lost control of my features'. A fellow officer noticed, and simply said 'Steady', putting a hand on Carrington's arm.[161] He recovered his composure. Sidney Rogerson on the Somme recognised fear in one of his men, and was keen not to draw attention to it: 'One look at his drawn and ashen face showed me that, tough old hand as he was, he had had a fright'. Rogerson restrained his first impulse 'to curse him' and merely engaged him factually as to what had happened.[162] Help offered was sometimes more tangible. Private Frank Richards, who never wrote about experiencing fear himself, described a man in his platoon as 'one of the most windy men I ever saw in France'. A gunshot was enough to make him 'jump back in the trench shivering with fright', his condition being 'pitiable'. Administration of extra rum, however, made him, 'the bravest man in France', if only for half an hour.[163]

It is clear that both other ranks and officers had a certain sympathy with naked fear, which was based on personal understanding. Second-Lieutenant George Devenish was in the trenches when a shell explosion half-buried three men. He described how 'they came running along to us, in a fearful state of nerves', adding, 'I don't blame them!'[164] Soldiers recognised that any man could be afflicted by fear momentarily, and recover. Edwin Vaughan was approached by one of his corporals who asked if he 'could be relieved as he had lost his nerve'. His response might be seen as harsh – he told him to return to his post to 'set an example' – he asked the man to behave bravely when he did not feel so. This individual was 'shaking with fear', but whilst Vaughan felt 'very sorry for him' he feared 'the rot would spread'. He acted to contain the composure

---

157 Edmonds, op. cit. p.56.
158 Edmonds, op. cit. p.77.
159 G. Brame, Diary, http://www.firstworldwar.com/diaries/onthebelgiancoast.htm.
160 Husbands, op. cit. p.245.
161 Edmonds, op. cit. p.128.
162 Rogerson, op. cit. p.55.
163 F. Richards, *Old Soldiers Never Die*, p.101.
164 G. Devenish, *A Subaltern's Share in the War*, p.50.

of all the others.[165] Charitableness was not universal. Cecil Brownlow described one man who 'turned a pale sea-green and shut his eyes at every explosion'. This individual soon became 'the butt of the others, who kept on cracking jokes at his expense'. One unsympathetic humourist picked up a pebble and threw it at his midriff when he next closed his eyes. The man thought he had been hit and reacted accordingly.[166] Rankers clearly expected their officers to have mastered fear. Geoffrey Husbands, in trenches at La Bassée in early 1916 noted that his company found it 'lamentable' that 'most of their officers were "windy" in the line', and that this 'decreased their respect for them'.[167]

Soldiers could be charitable, but that did not mean that they were always comfortable with seeing fear in others, not least of all for worry that their own fear might be visible, or that fear might be contagious. Frederic Manning claimed that in the moments before battle soldiers would attempt to avoid seeing each other's fear. He described 'men breathing irregularly beside him ... licking their lips, trying to moisten their mouths', swallowing. Some moaned or 'even sobbed a little'.[168] His eyes met one comrade's, and 'both turned away at once from the dread'.[169] Recognising fear in others could conversely be a coping mechanism in its own right – it meant that one was not alone. Ernest Parker, about to go into action on the Somme in 1916, noted a young man from a recent draft, seemingly cocky, 'but now his face was green with fear'. This had a positive effect on Parker for 'in noticing him my spirits rose'.[170]

### Controlling fear

Arthur West mused on what it was he actually feared under shellfire. He considered that it was not death, and that he did not fear the 'infliction of pain or wound'. He could not tie his fear down to 'anything definite', other than the thought that being hit by a shell would produce a situation with which he would not be able to cope, and that 'one's old resolutions of courage' would fail.[171] Second-Lieutenant Guy Chapman, setting off for the Western Front, recorded that not only was he 'very much afraid' he was 'afraid of being afraid, lest I should show it'.[172] Using exactly the same words, Second-Lieutenant Hazel Clements wrote on the eve of the first day on the Somme: 'We are afraid of being afraid'.[173] Captain Wilfred Bion acknowledged that 'fear of fear was ... common to all'. He noted an 'inability to admit it to anyone, as there was

---

165 Vaughan, op. cit. p.41.
166 Brownlow, op. cit. p.103.
167 Husbands, op. cit. p.195.
168 Manning, op. cit. location 3750.
169 Manning, op. cit. location 3750.
170 Parker, op. cit. p.54.
171 West, op. cit. p.68.
172 G. Chapman, *A Passionate Prodigality*, p.8.
173 H.T. Clements, Private Papers, IWM Docs 3413.

no one to admit it to without being guilty of spreading alarm and despondency'.[174] There were two aspects to the stoic mastery of fear. Firstly, stage-managing it so that others did not see; and secondly, mastering it silently for oneself.

Major Frederick Packe, at Ypres in October 1914 wrote that: 'I am glad to say my nerves are very good'. He denied that this was to do with 'pluck', attributing it to a 'somewhat phlegmatic temperament'.[175] He was likely in the minority – for others controlling fear was more of a struggle. Sapper B.R. Richards described the effort of keeping a grip: 'You were in a maze and you felt any time if you relaxed control you'd become haywire'. Indeed, he spoke of how 'it was quite common to see people who had relaxed control get up and run round in circles like sheep' until they 'met shellfire which finally finished them'.[176] German ranker Stefan Westman described a similar breakdown of control during the preliminary Somme bombardment: 'Soldiers in the bunkers became hysterical, they wanted to run out and fights developed to keep them in the comparative safety'.[177] It was not just fear-driven behaviour that had to be kept under control, it was the thoughts that might lead to it. Under bombardment, Norman Gladden 'found it difficult to keep my mind clear of the most frightful thoughts'.[178] Indeed, at particular moments of stress he 'found my reason struggling strenuously against the fearful temptation to run'. Stoic thinking saved him – it was only 'a real sense of duty' that prevented this.[179] Distraction was a potent resource. In action on the Somme, machine-gunner George Coppard described how: 'My stomach rolled in a funk, and I know Clark felt the same'. Activity came to the rescue: 'Keeping the gun going was the surest antidote to our rising fears'.[180] Subaltern 'Vedette', ordered to take charge of one end his regiment's line in action, similarly 'rejoiced at having a definite job which would keep him from thinking about the horrors piling up on every side' of him.[181] Given that anticipation of going into action was often worse than the feared situation itself, the best option was to face it. Norman Gladden was sick with anticipation of going up to the front line to assist stretcher bearers. He realised that 'the only cure for my sad condition ... was the thing I most feared' – he wanted the order to do something to be given rather than 'to squat there waiting for it'.[182] Similarly, Sapper Richards, subjected to a continuous bombardment reported that 'the emotional strain was terrific', relieved only 'when you got the order to advance', activity which, though dangerous, felt like a 'sort of a release from that bondage'.[183]

174 W.R. Bion, *War Memoirs 1917-19*, p.204.
175 F. Packe, Private Papers, IWM Docs 1653.
176 B.R. Richards, BBC 'The Great War Interviews'.
177 S. Westman, BBC 'The Great War Interviews'.
178 Gladden, op. cit. p.96.
179 Gladden, op. cit. p.92.
180 Coppard, op. cit. p.91.
181 'Vedette', *Adventures of an Ensign*, p.260-1.
182 Gladden, op. cit. p.167.
183 Richards, 'I Was There'

Alexander Watson notes: 'Card playing was ubiquitous in shellfire and folk singing provided a welcome distraction for men'.[184] Donald Hankey noted men smoking a pipe with a newspaper in front of them, but that 'as a rule their pipes are out and their reading a pretence'.[185] He described two options; firstly to force 'joke and smile', secondly to 'feign stoical indifference'. Humour was thus another distraction used to dampen fear. As Alfred Burrage noted: 'One could always say light-hearted and stupid things even when one was frightened to death'.[186] Prior to an attack on the Somme, Lieutenant Stuart Cloete wrote how he and his fellows 'joked obscenely to keep up our spirits'.[187] Under shellfire, Ernest Parker 'found that the men appreciated a little cheerfulness' during a bombardment, when 'even the worst jokes were better than none'.[188] George Coppard was precise about the nature of pre-battle humour as well: 'Anything approaching merriment was dead. Rude jokes, yes, but no merriment'.[189] Alfred Burrage managed to laugh publicly at his own fear. His logic was: 'Since we knew each other so well it was better to own fear and make fun of ourselves than try to run a bluff which wouldn't have deceived a blind infant'.[190]

One complication was that fear was not necessarily predictable. Just as one individual might experience fear when another did not, so fear might be felt in one threatening situation but not another. Thus Henry Williamson, waiting to attack in December 1914 described how: 'When I tried to get up, I couldn't, my knees were wobbling'. On listening patrols, however, lying in no-man's land: 'I can honestly say there was no fear at all, it was a picnic'.[191] This unpredictability sometimes rendered fear not easy to control. Second-Lieutenant Arthur Adam recorded that 'my nerves at times still go shaky when there is absolutely no reason'.[192] Stuart Cloete on a wiring party described himself as having 'never been so terrified in my life', but that in battle: 'I had not had time to be frightened'. He continued that 'I slowly learned to control my nervousness'.[193] Captain Rowland Feilding was testament to the power of suppression of fear. 'Once it is over, you shake yourself and recover, and if you are healthily minded you soon have forgotten it'.[194] William Tyrrell was of the opinion, however, that controlling fear was very expensive of emotional energy. 'Under its stimulus a man squanders nervous energy recklessly' in order to 'mask or camouflage that which if revealed will call down ignominy on his head'.[195]

184 A. Watson, 'Self-deception and Survival', *Journal of Contemporary History*, pp.265-6.
185 Hankey, op. cit. p.119.
186 Burrage, op. cit. p.130.
187 S. Cloete, *A Victorian Son*, p.234.
188 Parker, op. cit. p.68.
189 Coppard, op. cit. p.62.
190 Burrage, op. cit. p.88.
191 H. Williamson, BBC 'The Great War Interviews'.
192 A.M. Adam (ed.), *A Record Founded on His Letters*, p.154.
193 Cloete, op. cit. p.214.
194 Feilding, op. cit. p.33.
195 RWOCESS, p.31.

Patrick Campbell was very clear in setting out the cognitive process which allowed him to understand and manage his fear. On his second direct experience of being shelled, he noted that although his heart 'was thumping a little' he had 'a feeling of elation – I had come under fire, and it was all right, I could take it'.[196] He later described the process of thinking by which evidence had modified emotion, noting that he was pleased 'to find that shells could fall quite near and yet cause no casualties'.[197] He learned to correctly judge risk, 'when I ought to feel afraid and when fear was unnecessary'.[198] Campbell was particularly pleased that his fear had not leaked out: 'Captain Cecil had told the others that I never turned a hair, I was as cool as a cucumber, he had said'.[199] He had established a funk-free reputation. Although he came to view shelling as endurable, he never entirely lost his fear of it, especially at night. In a dug-out at Ypres attempting to sleep, he appraised his surroundings, knowing that it could not protect him from a direct hit. He listened to each incoming shell, finding 'the screaming sound' more frightening than the explosion. He described the noise as having 'a fiendish malevolence' and experienced the thought that it seemed to be coming 'straight at me'. The only control he could exert was attempting to identify when the bombardment had ended. After each explosion, he would count, and if he got to 200 'it would probably mean that the enemy battery had finished for the night'.[200] Cecil Brownlow similarly described a cognitive process, a mental argument, where on one hand he acknowledged that he feared being killed or getting a 'ghastly wound'; and on the other, that the danger was only 'a few odd shells', and 'nothing to kick up a fuss about'. He rationally appraised the danger, and reminding himself that he 'had a job to do', he pushed on.[201] Frederic Manning described his own way of rationalising fear: 'When one recognised the symptoms, it became objective, and one seemed to escape partly from it that way'.[202] By naming it, its potency was reduced. Arthur West, on a patrol in no-man's-land, and well aware of the danger, found himself 'more interested than afraid'.[203] He had learned to re-label the bodily arousal that the experience generated as something other than fear.

Although he thought he had adapted, Patrick Campbell had an experience of being paralysed with fear under shell-fire at Ypres. In the aftermath, he 'wanted to think about it'.[204] He needed to mentally process the event. Reflecting, he attributed the extent of his reaction as a build-up to certain things. Firstly, he ascribed his fear to the sheer volume of the dead about him, which made him feel 'sick'. Secondly, he

---

196 Campbell, *Cannon's Mouth*, p.16.
197 Campbell, *Cannon's Mouth*, p.36.
198 Campbell, *Cannon's Mouth*, p.42.
199 Campbell, *Cannon's Mouth*, p.39.
200 Campbell, *Cannon's Mouth*, p.72.
201 Brownlow, op. cit. pp.142-3.
202 Manning, op. cit. location 3745.
203 West, op. cit. p.11.
204 Campbell, *Cannon's Mouth*, p.87.

had seen British soldiers fleeing, expressionless, 'as though they had lost their souls'. Thirdly, the bombardment had started 'suddenly, before I was prepared for it'.[205] Fear of annihilation had overwhelmed him. After analysis, he concluded: 'I need not suffer again in the same way. I had been warned now'. He thought that he would be ready for that kind of fear again. He applied Stoic logic – there was 'no use' in feeling afraid, it was not possible to prevent death, it was 'simply a matter of endurance'.[206] Despite his rationalisation, his learning to cope was never quite complete: 'I was deceiving myself, I never conquered it'.[207] One specific fear at Third Ypres never left him. En route to the front line and exposed to the Houthulst Forest, he always had a feeling of being watched, 'that a German gunner had his gun trained on a certain point on the track and was waiting for me to get there'.[208] On occasions this thought was so strong that he left the safety of the duckboard, to avoid the 'Watching Eyes',[209] and risking drowning, walked across the mud. He returned after the war to face this again with his father, to see whether the spot still had 'the power to inspire terror in me'. His father 'only saw a lot of shattered tree trunks' and Campbell did not tell him 'what else had been there once'.[210]

*Stage-managing fear*
Brevet-Colonel Guy Stubbs, CO 2nd Suffolk, who described himself as 'in an awful funk the whole time', was of the opinion that 'there is an idea among young soldiers especially that there should not be such a thing as fear'. He thought that it would be helpful during training to explain that '99 per cent of the men were afraid of shells'.[211] Conningsby Dawson believed, however, that: 'Physical fear is too deeply rooted to be overcome by any amount of training'. The only realistic strategy that remained in his view was 'to train a man in spiritual pride, so that when he fears, nobody knows it'.[212] Henry Russell noted that there were few individuals who were not 'painfully conscious of the limitations of their pluck', but that the 'hall-mark of quiet courage' was the ability to preserve an attitude of 'apparent calmness'.[213] Second-Lieutenant Edward Brittain wrote to his sister Vera: 'It is hard to be sufficiently brave' but 'one has to keep up appearances at all costs'.[214]

As the code of manliness dictated, shaming oneself was a matter to be avoided. Subject to his first shellburst above him at Mons, Aubrey Herbert fell flat. He noted:

205 Campbell, *Cannon's Mouth*, p.88.
206 Campbell, *Cannon's Mouth*, p.88.
207 Campbell, *Cannon's Mouth*, p.89.
208 Campbell, *Cannon's Mouth*, p.114.
209 Campbell, *Cannon's Mouth*, p.134.
210 Campbell, *Cannon's Mouth*, p.135.
211 RWOCESS, p.47.
212 C. Dawson, *The Glory of the Trenches*, p.101.
213 Russell, op. cit. p.134.
214 A. Bishop & M. Bostridge, *Letters from a Lost Generation*, pp.235-6.

'I was ashamed of myself before I reached the ground',[215] but when he looked around was relieved to find that everybody else had done the same. Lieutenant Arthur West acknowledged that 'my nerves were shaky and I could have cried for fright as each shell drew near' but 'I did not betray any kind of weak feeling'.[216] Manliness demanded a demonstration of personal strength. Walter Williams wrote that 'I was probably more afraid of being a coward and letting everybody down than I was of dying'.[217] Whether all would have rather died than being perceived a coward is a moot point, but undoubtedly the fear of showing fear was often stronger than the fear of whatever the threat actually was. Second-Lieutenant Denis Garstin, arriving in France with his fellow soldiers stated that, untested as yet, 'not one of us for eight months had lived a day free from the dread of our cowardice'.[218] Hugh Quigley similarly wrote that he had always suffered the fear of 'showing myself unworthy, cowardly'.[219] On the beach at Gallipoli awaiting medical evacuation, John Gillam looked at the label attached to him of 'syncopal attacks' (fainting due to lack of oxygen to the brain). He looked enviously at the wounded, thinking that his own condition read 'like another title for "cold feet"'.[220] In the wake of the first day on the Somme, Arthur Dugmore, described his nerves as in a 'very ragged state'. With his brigadier close to the front line, a bullet passed some 30 or 40 feet from him, 'and *I ducked*'. He felt 'most deeply ashamed'. He wished fervently that he had been able to control his reaction, to the extent of wishing at the time that the next bullet would bestow on him the 'order of the R.I.P.'[221] 'Vedette', on first hearing the sound of a shell on arrival near the front was 'concerned mainly with the fear' that his companion should notice that he 'had the wind up'.[222] In the trenches he was 'shamed' by the solid behaviour of his platoon into adopting the 'prescribed air of indifference'.[223] Edward Tennant at Loos in 1915 was relieved to write home that under bombardment: 'I don't think I showed I was any more frightened than anyone else'.[224] Douglas Gillespie reported the words of Captain Claude Wreford-Brown, killed in May 1915, spoken quietly in response to the braying of martial achievement of others on a train to a railhead in Flanders: 'Personally, if I get through this war alive without feeling I have disgraced myself publicly, I shall be jolly well pleased'.[225]

215 A. Herbert, *Mons, Anzac and Kut*, p.18.
216 West, op. cit. pp.67-8.
217 Williams, op. cit. location 685.
218 D. Garstin, *The Shilling Soldiers*, p.11.
219 Quigley, op. cit. p.166.
220 Gillam, op. cit. p.159.
221 Dugmore, op. cit. p.250 (italics in original).
222 'Vedette', op. cit. p.35.
223 'Vedette', op. cit. p.75.
224 Glenconner, op. cit. p.147.
225 Gillespie, op. cit. p.184.

When the appearance of manliness was crucial, the Stoic mechanisms of making threat a matter of indifference were put to the test. Conningsby Dawson described 'the habit of courage which grows out of the knowledge that you let your pals down by showing cowardice'.[226] Henry Dundas wrote home that 'personal courage' was a matter of the 'power of concealing terror'. The challenge lay in 'how much fear there is to conceal'.[227] Lieutenant Cyril Rawlins wrote that 'I must be a bit of a coward', wanting to run or hide under shellfire, 'but one must stride along as nonchalantly as if out for a moonlight stroll at home'.[228] On his arrival in the trenches, Geoffrey Dugdale was told by a sergeant: 'We all get the wind up, Sir, but we try not to let the troops know'.[229] Lieutenant Charles Stiebel wrote to his wife from Mesopotamia with the hope that 'I may be – not fearless – but showing no fear'.[230] Similarly, Theodore Wilson wrote to his mother about being under fire: 'Thank God I didn't show any funk. That's all a man dare ask, I think'.[231] This way of behaving held as good for the private as it did for the officer. On his first time in the trenches, Walter Williams was 'shaking with fear'.[232] An old hand advised him: 'You'll never get used to it but in time you'll learn to cope', adding 'I was just as scared as you, I've just learned not to show it'.[233] It was a matter of acting a part. George Devenish arrived near the front and heard his first 5.9 inch shell. Nearby were two signallers 'looking on as if prepared to be amused, so I pretended I didn't notice it'.[234] Similarly, David Campbell arrived on Gallipoli and was under shellfire for the first time immediately. He saw men going about their business 'as if nothing were happening'. He and his men tried to emulate them: 'We pretended we were just as indifferent as they appeared to be'. It being the first occasion, 'it did not quite come off'.[235] Second-Lieutenant Max Plowman on the Somme in 1916 described the task under shellfire being 'to pretend that nothing unpleasant is happening'.[236] This game might sometimes be acknowledged. John Gillam, in the final stages of the Gallipoli campaign was talking to an Australian officer when a shell passed close overhead. Gillam disclosed that: 'I wanted to duck, but as you didn't, I didn't', the Australian replying 'Same here, son'.[237] Bernard Martin described the matter perfectly, himself and his fellows as actors on a stage: 'We screened our nerves by acting an entirely imaginary character – the fearless man'. But this was a role that

226 Dawson, *Glory of the Trenches*, p.33.
227 Anon. *Dundas*, p.72-3.
228 C.S. Rawlins, Private Papers, IWM Docs 7314.
229 Dugdale, op. cit. p.33.
230 C. Stiebel, quoted in Housman, op. cit. p.267.
231 T.P.C. Wilson quoted in Housman, op. cit. p.295.
232 Williams, op. cit. location 917.
233 Williams, op. cit. location 937.
234 Devenish, op. cit. p.15.
235 D. Campbell, *Forward the Rifles*, pp.41-2.
236 Mark VII (M. Plowman), *A Subaltern on the Somme*, p.50.
237 Gillam, op. cit. p.269.

162  Glum Heroes

could be sustained by many for only so long – 'I'd known brave men gradually lose their nerves till they couldn't play this tragedy any longer'.[238]

### *Verbalising fear*

The era in which the soldiers of the Great War grew up did not prize introspection, as we have seen. Talking was not amongst their coping mechanisms. Walter Shewry could not verbalise his experiences even to his brother: 'We just could not communicate'. He could not bring himself to 'tell him of my great misery and suffering nor my fear and horror'.[239] Norman Gladden described his company under shellfire as suffering 'a sort of communal terror' during which 'I saw men crying', but it was not an experience that was discussed.[240] However, despite the horror of demonstrating funk, there were soldiers who verbalised fear. Patrick Campbell described a newcomer who had not been under shellfire who confessed to feeling afraid and said that 'he wasn't going to do anything more than he had to or put his nose outside a dug-out if he could help it', remarking 'I'm not one of your heroes'.[241] He described another officer at Ypres pressing on to help the wounded, but returning as he confessed he 'hadn't the guts to go on'.[242] At Ypres in 1915, Charles Clayton encountered a captain alone on the firestep, describing his face as 'like chalk' with 'a haunted look'. Clayton proffered help to receive the response: 'No … my nerve's gone … I'm done and it's only nerves'.[243] Second-Lieutenant Geoffrey Thurlow wrote to Edward Brittain, another subaltern, in September 1916 disclosing that: 'I was always more or less windy but now I'm far worse than I was'.[244] John Lucy, a commissioned sergeant, was under shellfire with two other officers. They perceived him as 'cool', walking calmly away from the site of landing shells, and disclosed that: 'As you were a sergeant, we had to kind of hold ourselves in'. Lucy disclosed to them that he had been 'in a frightful dither' himself, and 'we had another drink on our mutual confession of "wind-up"'.[245] To speak of fear, permission had to be given for the topic to be opened up.

## Conclusion

There was a tacit acknowledgment that fear was universal in certain circumstances, especially under shellfire and before going into action. There was a tolerance of fear, as long as control was reasserted. However, there was also a realisation that the excessively fearful were a liability. Geoffrey Husbands on the Somme in a tense stand-to

---

238 Martin, op. cit. pp.140-1.
239 W. J. Shewry, Private Papers, IWM Docs 508.
240 Gladden, op. cit. p.178.
241 Campbell, *Ebb and Flow*, p.29.
242 Campbell, *Ebb and Flow* p.81.
243 Clayton, op. cit. p.76.
244 Bishop & Bostridge, op. cit. pp.271-2.
245 J.F. Lucy, *There's a Devil in the Drum*, pp.363-4.

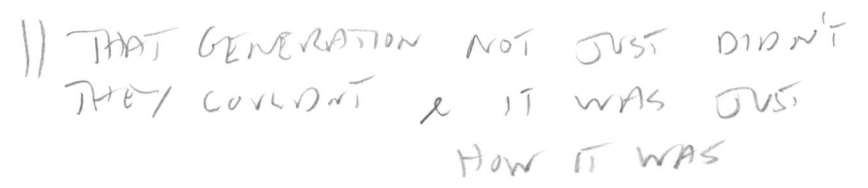

situation 'sensed nerves affecting the new draft men', the fear being that they 'might turn panicky, and get out of control'.[246] Giles Eyre wrote of a fellow ranker who was evacuated: 'And about time, too! That man had been a danger to himself and others for quite a long time!'[247] Captain Francis Hitchcock, involved in a trench raid on The Triangle, Loos, in January 1917, noted the importance of training – 'when a man knows his job he has confidence in himself'. A man who did not was 'liable to get "windy" and cause alarm' amongst his comrades.[248]

A sense of control is of central importance to human beings. Fear as an emotional end-product is directly connected to the ability to establish control over the threat or its potential outcome. Helplessness was damaging to coping. Soldiers under shellfire would do as much as they could to predict where shells would fall. This may or may not have been realistic, but it is known that that belief in the ability to establish control is sufficient to moderate human fear, even if it is illusory.[249] If they could not control the threat then they could attempt to control their reaction to it. Distraction through some sort of activity helped.

There were degrees of fear. Geoffrey Husbands noted that 'windiness' was not the same as 'sheer cowardice', and observed that he did not meet a man who 'would assert that he was never afraid in France'. He probably spoke for most soldiers when he wrote that 'it was the man who could be frightened and yet not show it, or at best could keep cheerful under the strain, whom we admired'.[250] Soldiers clearly expected themselves to try to master fear in everyday trench duties – Stoic endurance and manliness placed a premium on it. Adaptation to fear was achieved by many, if never totally. There would always be the potential for a situation whose mastery was beyond current resources. This partly was down to experience which allowed rationalisation – threat came to be seen in proportion. Reducing a threat to a realistic size through accurate appraisal reduced the power of negative thoughts to cause fear. This was nearly always done in private. Fear was rarely verbalised – the code of manliness demanded that it be so. But in many situations soldiers simply became adept at stage-managing it, practising the precepts of Seneca. If, as psychological research suggests, repeatedly behaving courageously diminishes the subjective experience of fear, then such principles of behavioural discipline played a large part in increasing a sense of control and making fear manageable.

246 Husbands, op. cit. p.356.
247 Eyre, op. cit. p.44.
248 F.C. Hitchcock, *Stand To!*, p.232.
249 Rachman, op. cit. pp.14-15.
250 Husbands, op. cit. p.195.

# 7

## 'It Isn't Natural To Be Brave' – Courage and Cowardice

In the modern age military courage is typified by the wounded or disabled soldier. This individual has paid a price for doing their duty, and their bravery in the face of adversity will not be confined to war, but will continue for the rest of their life. The popularity of the British military charity, 'Help for Heroes', is testimony to this. This is not, however, a new definition of courage. Rather, it is a shift in emphasis within the changing complex of characteristics that over time have made up the concept of the hero, which has always contained the notion of self-sacrifice. This chapter seeks to understand both how courage was understood and how models of bravery acted as sustaining factors in the trenches of the First World War.

### A History of Courage

Lieutenant Conningsby Dawson reflected on his experience of the trenches that 'it isn't natural to be brave'.[1] The Stoic philosopher Seneca put his finger on the spot: 'And what is bravery? It is the impregnable fortress for our mortal weakness'.[2] Courage, the choice and willingness to confront a challenging situation, was therefore in his view a means of coping with the threat of weakness – a behavioural antidote to fear. Heroism, being the one who steps forward, was an important concept in the Victorian era. The classics that the officer corps would have studied at school presented the vision of the flawed semi-divine individual of Greek mythology tempered by the Stoic Roman man of action. This individual's 'prime virtues were first and foremost an indifference to circumstances and a sense of civic duty in his actions'.[3] The polymath Patrick Shaw-Stewart, classicist, financier and poet, was killed by a shell fragment hitting him in the mouth on Welsh Ridge, Cambrai, on 30 December 1917 whist commanding Hood Battalion, Royal Naval Division. Perhaps anticipating his fate on Gallipoli in 1915, he appealed to such a classical hero looking from Imbros

---

1   C. Dawson, *The Glory of the Trenches*, p.119.
2   Seneca, quoted in N. Sherman, *Stoic Warriors*, Kindle edition location 1640.
3   M.C. Smith, *Awarded for Valour*, p.7.

towards Troy in the lines: 'Was it so hard, Achilles / So very hard to die?'[4] Second-Lieutenant Douglas Gillespie similarly wrote home that after the death of his brother he found himself constantly thinking of men who had been killed in battle: 'Hector and Achilles and all the heroes of long ago'.[5] Victorian literature revelled in these themes. The ideal of Christian virtue and chivalry was cultivated through imagery of the Round Table knight, which was widespread and highly popular.[6] Indeed, the reporting of air-battles of the Great War between named pilots is steeped in this ideal of the 'knights of the air'. Novels such as those of George Henty and H. Rider Haggard provided both a military and empire setting for these deeds of courage. Unsurprisingly, early Great War recruiting posters emphasised the chivalric notion of defending home, hearth, women and children. But the military and the empire were not just images of literature. In the Victorian era the deeds of 'great men' were held up as exemplary lives. In this cult of the hero, the pantheon contained almost exclusively Christian warriors acting as heroes of national defence, such as Nelson; or heroes of empire, such as General Charles Gordon.[7] Gordon's death at Khartoum in 1885 at the hands of Islamic extremists is a good example. It presents an image both of the characteristics of the British officer as physical courage, patriotism, devotion to duty and self-sacrifice; and of the Christian evangelist attempting to hold back a supposed heathen onslaught. This was the very epitome of manliness.

As the 19th century progressed, just as the notion of domestic manliness grew alongside that of heroic manliness, so both the notions of who could demonstrate such courage and the very concept of courage itself broadened beyond the military hero. As John Price has noted, in the Victorian spirit of improvement examples of everyday heroism were increasingly held up to the working class 'as didactic examples of model behaviour'.[8] These examples were particularly relevant, the achievements of stellar individuals such as Gordon being outside the reach of the ordinary individual. The transition is seen in the progressive establishment of awards for valour. The Crimean War led to the institution of the Victoria Cross being established in 1856, allowing the heroism of the other ranks to be recognised. Similarly, 21 years later the remit of the Albert Medal was extended to all acts of lifesaving bravery,[9] and a raft of publications on everyday bravery followed from the 1880s onwards. Heroism thus became more egalitarian. By the opening of the Great War, the concept of heroism had broadened from the cult of the military hero, turning somewhat away from the

4   http://archives.balliol.ox.ac.uk/Past%20members/PHStewart.asp.
5   A.D. Gillespie, *Letters from Flanders*, p.133.
6   William Morris's 'The Defence of Guinevere' is such an example.
7   J.M. Mackenzie, *Popular Militarism and the Military*, p.113.
8   J. Price, *Everday Heroism*, p.7.
9   The Albert Medal for Lifesaving (since replaced by the George Cross), was originally established for acts of lifesaving at sea. In 1877 a version was established for acts of lifesaving on land, following the rescue of five trapped miners in the Tynewydd Colliery disaster.

ideal of the individual who deliberately put themselves in the way of danger, to include the individual who became an unexpected and unprepared hero.[10] Second-Lieutenant Siegfried Sassoon brought in a wounded man from no-man's land when part of the evacuating party during his first trench raid. He prided himself on 'having pulled off something rather heroic', but on reflection concluded that it was only the 'sort of thing which people often did during a fire or a railway accident'.[11]

The traditional view of heroism was still powerful, however. The deaths of Robert Falcon Scott and two of his fellow explorers on the march back from the South Pole on the ill-fated Terra Nova Expedition (1910-12) exemplified this traditional notion just prior to the war's outbreak. Universally within Great Britain, Edward Madigan suggests, the dead explorers were seen as 'exemplars of courage because they had endured suffering and deprivation in pursuit of a noble objective'. Suffering and death, as per Gordon, were key to the image. Thus, 'crucially, when fate offered them death instead of glory they faced it with dignity and a sense of willing self-sacrifice'.[12] Madigan argues that this remained the prevalent view of courage on the home front for much of the war. He quotes from a November 1914 article in Horatio Bottomley's tub-thumping jingoistic periodical *John Bull*: 'Tommy faces death with a calmness, and even a merriment, which astonish friend and foe alike. Being an Anglo-Saxon he regards it as the merest matter of course to risk life and limb whenever his country is threatened'.[13] This arrant nonsense was only tempered slightly in a quote from the *War Illustrated* of July 1916, allegedly describing the mood in the British trenches just prior to the catastrophe of the first day on the Somme: 'The hour before the advance on July 1st found British soldiers in high spirits, laughing, joking, confident in a "ready to do or die" humour'.[14] Conningsby Dawson was aware of the gaping disparity between the illusion of courage created by journalism and the reality of courage in the front line when he wrote home: 'There's far more heroism in the attitude of men out here than in the footlight attitude that journalists paint for the public'.[15]

### Courage and cowardice – a view from the trenches

Charles McMoran Wilson, later Lord Moran, and famous for being Winston Churchill's physician during the Second World War, served as a captain with the Royal Army Medical Corps on the Western Front with 1st Royal Fusiliers. He took it upon himself to later write a treatise on fear, cowardice and courage based on his experiences. He gives a good picture of the views of the educated person of the time

---

10  Price, op cit. p.10.
11  S. Sassoon, *The Complete Memoirs of George Sherston*, p.307.
12  E. Madigan, '"Sticking to a Hateful Task"': Resilience, Humour, and British Understandings of Combatant Courage, 1914–1918', *War in History*, p.79.
13  'The True Tommy: A Study of the Boy in Khaki', *John Bull*, 21 November 1914, quoted in Madigan op. cit. pp.82-3.
14  *War Illustrated*, 22 July 1916, quoted in Madigan op. cit. p.83.
15  Dawson, *Carry On*, p.75.

on the subject – views whose judgmental nature grate on modern sensibilities. Moran summarised 'four degrees of courage', namely: 'Men who did not feel fear; men who felt fear but did not show it; men who felt fear and showed it but did their job; men who felt fear, showed it and shirked.'[16] He himself undoubtedly possessed courage, and his view doubting that there was any person who did not actually feel fear was likely very personal. His Military Cross citation describes how 'hearing that an officer had been wounded, he passed through 100 yards of the enemy's artillery barrage, dressed his wounds, and finally got him into safety'.[17]

Moran was writing a quarter of a century after the end of the conflict. Captain R.J. Manion, RAMC, writing during the war, gave a view of courage very much in tune with the preoccupations of the era. He took the positive view that individuals are generally brave when the situation required it – 'war makes brave men of most of us'.[18] Courage for him had slight echoes of *John Bull*, being based on soldiers' 'pride in themselves, their loyalty to their native land, their love of their comrades, and their hatred for the enemy'.[19] He observed that there were certain moments of danger when all men 'really feel afraid'. He claimed that 999 out of 1,000 men would conquer the impulse to fly in the face of this, and the one remaining individual would 'thereafter be branded "coward"'.[20] Whilst his calculations have no real basis in fact, the words used remind us that this was an era preoccupied not only with courage, but also with cowardice. Private Norman Gladden, his company recalled during an attack at Ypres in 1917, fled back, stepping over his mortally wounded best friend, whom he did not even recognise. He later regarded his behaviour with 'disbelief', seeing his reaction as 'one of inferiority that ought to be controlled'.[21] Cowardice was moral inferiority.

Cowardice has become a far less popular concept than it used to be, and its meaning has shifted as the concept of duty has faded. We now delineate the 'cowardly terrorist', the individual who does not 'fight clean'. Unlike the notion of courage, which has a body of scientific literature refining it, cowardice has received no such attention. It is uncertain who set out the definition:

> Cowardice is a trait wherein fear and excess self-concern override doing or saying what is right, good and of help to others or oneself in a time of need – it is the opposite of courage. As a label, "cowardice" indicates a failure of character in the face of a challenge.[22]

---

16  Lord Moran, *The Anatomy of Courage*, p.22.
17  *London Gazette*, 26 September 1916.
18  R.J. Manion, *A Surgeon in Arms*, p.159.
19  Manion, op. cit. p.161.
20  Manion, op. cit. p.162.
21  N. Gladden, *Ypres 1917*, p.167.
22  http://en.wikipedia.org/wiki/Cowardice

As we saw in the last chapter, fear, particularly under shellfire, was almost universal. The experience of fear did not equate to cowardice, however. Cowardice was specific behaviour driven by fear, e.g. running away. If the hero is the individual who steps forward, the coward is the one who steps backwards. Yet the anonymous definition complicates matters by also identifying cowardice as a matter of character. Professor G. Roussy, neurologist to the French army, stuck to a behavioural definition whilst giving evidence to the War Office Committee of Enquiry into Shell-Shock in 1922. He suggested that: 'Any man who can control himself is a courageous man, but the man who runs away, or who does certain other actions not esteemed worthy, is defined as a coward'.[23] Put simply, behaviourally, a coward is someone who fails to perform their duty because of fear. Whilst duty is a concept that has a much lower profile in the modern era, diffusive Stoicism made it powerful at the time of the Great War. Private Harry Drinkwater, writing of the death of Lance-Corporal Sidney Page, 'never knew him to flinch from what he considered to be his duty'. He linked the man's sense of duty and his 'pluck'. Following these 'sound principles' indicated in Drinkwater's eyes that he was 'of that stuff of which, perhaps, the best type of men are made'.[24] Conningsby Dawson wrote from the trenches expressing his belief in the approving eye of higher authorities on such individuals as Page: 'God ... can't be too hard on men who did their duty'.[25]

The white feather has for centuries been a symbol of cowardice. It is a strong indication that a revulsion for any form of presumed cowardice was rife in 1914 when at the instigation of Admiral Charles Fitzgerald women began to hand out white feathers to men not in uniform. The intended creation of shame is the burden that the coward is supposed to carry. Private Alfred Burrage wrote that 'most of us were cowards – I was certainly one', but stated that there 'are as many degrees of cowardice as there are shades of a primary colour'. He and his fellows 'laughed at' their cowardice and 'owned to it'. He reserved condemnation for 'the really repulsive coward', the 'horrible worms' who were actively 'scheming to get out' rather than simply 'wanting'.[26] He wrote contemptuously: 'The funks were nearly always bullies and the bullies always funks'.[27] Like Lord Moran and Harry Drinkwater, Burrage returned to the idea of character flaw. He takes our understanding further, however, by highlighting that he believed such a flaw encompassed a failure in a sense of duty towards comrades at all levels. This again reminds us of the dangers of a romanticised view of comradeship in the First World War.

23 *Report of the War Office Committee of Enquiry into 'Shell-Shock'* (RWOCESS), p.21.
24 J. Cooksey & D. Griffiths (eds), *Harry's War*, p.165.
25 Dawson, *Carry On*, p.76.
26 Ex-Private X (A.M. Burrage), *War is War*, pp.96-8.
27 Burrage, op. cit. p.116.

Moran acknowledged that 'any man may be brought down to the coward's level'[28] through 'some intense emotional shock',[29] although he believed this to be infrequent. He believed that cowards, soldiers who gave up the 'effort to control fear',[30] were 'plainly worthless fellows'. They were individuals without 'moral sense',[31] who came from 'bad stock'.[32] So, for Moran, courage was largely a matter of good breeding, a view which was the product of his era. His unselfconscious use of the word 'worthless' seems unnecessarily judgmental in the modern world where we seek explanations, explanations that Moran's age would likely have seen as excuses. But Moran was far from alone. Lieutenant Arthur Martin, RAMC, also took the view that breeding was the issue. He thought the genetic heritage of neurasthenic officers made them 'more emotional and imaginative', but he took care not to use the word coward – they were 'no less courageous'.[33] Lieutenant John Reith wrote with sympathy: 'Matter of nerves or temperament or both; no question of being brave or not brave. Some men are lucky, others unlucky, in their make-up. To what extent are we responsible for it?'[34]

Chaplain Maurice Ponsonby was clear about the reality from which the character flaw argument distracted attention. He wrote from the field that he supposed that courage was such an admired virtue because 'everyone has a knowledge that he is himself a coward at heart, and dreads that some day his will-power may fail and he will show it'.[35] The crucial matter was, therefore, what it was that sustained will-power. The conclusion of a study of American Civil War soldiers no doubt holds equally good for most First World War combatants: 'They desperately wanted to avoid the shame of being known as a coward – and that is what gave them courage'.[36] The most effective inhibitor of cowardly behaviour was, of course, fellow soldiers. Everyday courage was therefore self-motivated behaviour guarding against falling below the expectation of group norms – this in essence was much what Alfred Burrage was getting at. His coward/bully had no sense of positive, mutually supportive group norms. Whatever his views on character, Moran understood that self-control was central to courage. R.J. Manion shared this view. Both the brave individual and the coward could experience the same sensation of fear. The coward would allow the emotion to 'conquer him', whilst the brave individual 'grits his teeth and carries on'.[37] Captain G.B. Manwaring took the interesting slant on the matter of teeth-gritting that: 'In warfare only cowards

---

28 Moran, op. cit. p.37.
29 Moran, op. cit. p.38.
30 Moran, op. cit. p.39.
31 Moran, op. cit. p.35.
32 Moran, op. cit. p.39.
33 A.A. Martin, *A Surgeon in Khaki*, pp.211-2.
34 J. Reith, *Wearing Spurs*, p.65.
35 M. Ponsonby, *Visions & Vignettes of War*, p.28.
36 J.M. McPherson, *For Cause and Comrades*, p.77.
37 Manion, op. cit. p.73.

are the really brave men, for they have to force themselves to do things that brave men do instinctively'.[38] Supportive group norms stiffened self-control.

Manion viewed shell shock as 'legitimate nervousness'. Those who demonstrated this were 'not cases of cowardice', although to a 'superficial observer they might appear so'.[39] Lieutenant-Colonel Rowland Feilding agreed, also taking a different tack to Moran, stating that 'I disapprove in almost every case' of a soldier having been shot for 'so-called cowardice'. He viewed the behaviour which earned such a description as uncontrollable 'nervous collapse'. He acknowledged the reality that 'the best of men have their ups and downs in war'. He sympathetically perceived that those 'capable of the bravest actions' may 'break down under certain conditions of strain', especially when they had 'been kept too long in the battle line'.[40] Similarly, Henry Croft, who had progressed from regimental officer to brigade commander believed that men with 'nerves shattered and trembling like children', unable to go into action again, had been 'put to a greater test than mortal man is meant to bear'.[41] But many did not demonstrate sympathy. After the Battle of Neuve Chapelle in March 1915, Lance-Corporal William Andrews described a 'youngster' who was a 'pathetic sight, his face swollen with crying', his face 'childish and frightened'. He repeated: 'Don't take me back to they shells'. Andrews took him to the medical officer instead, whose only supportive comment was: 'You're a white man, you know'.[42]

For Moran, being a coward was part of the poorly developed morality that stemmed from deficient breeding. For Alfred Burrage it stemmed from a character deficient in true comradeship. For Rowland Feilding, it was longstanding stress and strain. For Second-Lieutenant Max Plowman, desertion was the act of a 'distraught man', who 'determines that the last act of his life shall at least be one of his own volition'.[43] Of the 346 men executed during the war, only 18 were convicted of cowardice,[44] for which offence there were 551 convictions of officers and men in total.[45] In terms of the executions, most were for refusing a direct order, although as Corns and Hughes-Wilson note, 'some of the men executed for cowardice appear to have been suffering from battle fatigue', particularly during the Somme offensive.[46] The charge of cowardice was always, of course, a subjective judgement. The 3,904 convictions for self-inflicted wound were just as much avoidance of duty, although as Major George Davidson noted when dealing with a man who had shot his foot off: 'I have never before seen a man shoot off more than a finger or toe, carrying off a foot shows that the man has

---

38  G.B. Manwaring, *If We Return*, p.96.
39  Manion, op. cit. p.164.
40  R. Feilding, *War Letters to a Wife*, p.208.
41  H.P. Croft, *Twenty Two Months under Fire*, p.240.
42  W.L. Andrews, *Haunting Years*, pp.67-9.
43  Mark VII (M. Plowman), *A Subaltern on the Somme*, p.12.
44  *Statistics of the Military Effort of the British Empire in the Great War*, p.648.
45  *Statistics*, p.669.
46  C. Corns and J. Hughes-Wilson, *Blindfold and Alone*, p.177.

plenty of pluck of a sort'.[47] There were also 38,630 convictions for desertion, although this no doubt had a range of motivations. It is perhaps surprising that the figures, given the number and unselected nature of those who served, were not higher. One can only conclude that 'cowardice' was not a major problem, and that the men who truly 'felt fear, showed it and shirked', were not numerous.

Moran saw courage as Stoic 'will power'. It was a 'cold choice' in favour of 'fixed resolve not to quit' – it was honour and duty. In his world good breeding allowed for this higher moral sense. He was not, however, completely black-and-white in his thinking. He was well aware of one of the components of fear which was so troublesome – cognitions, those 'doubts and hesitations' which 'occupy and mock the minds of men'. He described a process of military expectation of appropriate behaviour driving repression of such thoughts. An individual was expected to 'suppress unhealthy sentiments' and thus sit on 'the safety valve'.[48] Moran is often credited with inventing the analogy of courage as a bank account, whose assets might be spent. In fact, this concept appears to originate with Squadron Leader William Tyrrell of the Royal Air Force Medical Service in his evidence to the War Office Committee of Enquiry into "Shell-Shock". Tyrrell compared 'a man's store of nervous energy to a capital and current account at a bank'. He conjectured that in 'minor crises', the 'expenditure is usually out of his current account', and consequently is not missed. Moran similarly described how 'the call on the bank might be only the daily drain of the trenches'.[49] In times of life's 'great crises', Tyrrell claimed that the current account 'draws upon the capital account for reinforcement'. A 'run on the bank' would constitute a series of such crises 'without intervals for replacing energy' which would drain the capital account dry.[50] Continuing Tyrrell's thesis that energy could be replaced, Moran noted that the account could be boosted by a deposit due to something positive such as success or the experience of good leadership.[51] Whilst there is no evidence that there is such a thing as a bank of courage it is clear both that prolonged stress – the 'daily drain' – could indeed erode a soldier's will to endure, and a particular crisis could destroy it.

The famous case of Sub-Lieutenant Edwin Dyett crystalizes some of these issues. Described as the 'well-educated son of a merchant navy captain',[52] he volunteered for the Royal Navy but was commissioned into the Royal Naval Division to fight as infantry. On his own admission, his 'nerves' were not 'strong'. He had approached his commanding officer for transfer to a sea-going post because of this. In the Georgian era, as we have seen, such a state of affairs would have been seen as evidence of good breeding – in the age into which Dyett was born, it was not. Sent from reserve to the front line during the Battle of the Ancre in November 1916 as a replacement, Dyett

47  G. Davidson, *The Incomparable Twenty-Ninth*, p.198.
48  Another concept Moran borrowed, this time from Dr Henry Head, (RWOCESS, p.68).
49  Moran, op. cit. p.71.
50  RWOCESS, p.30.
51  Moran, op. cit. p.71.
52  Corns & Hughes-Wilson, op. cit. p.261.

deserted and hid for nearly two days. He had set off with another officer, who left him and then 'rambled about and lost touch with everybody'. Being alone on the battlefield, as we saw in the previous chapter, was a particular source of fear for some. In his letters published in *John Bull* after his execution, he described his nerves that day as 'completely strung up ... completely gone and my head was singing'. A wounded officer who encountered him described him as 'white and scared'.[53] But by the standards of the day, the only ones against which he can be judged in terms of his fate, Dyett failed in his duty as an officer. He did not go to the front line to join his fellow officers and men, and even failed to get help for the wounded he met – he thus failed the group norm of mutually supportive comradeship. As Corns and Hughes-Wilson note: 'It is absolutely clear that Dyett was not shell-shocked or suffering from battle fatigue'.[54] In Moran's terms, Dyett had given up the effort to control fear and he was a coward. Sadly, the fault lines that ran though his make-up made it impossible for him to exert control. That he should not have been an infantry officer is undoubted, but he lived in an era when there were next to no processes, other than the tragic failure that occurred, for weeding him out.

Exactly how many men suffering from shell shock were executed is impossible to determine. One such case is that of Lance-Corporal William Moon. Moon had been continuously off sick and in hospital twice over a five month period in 1916 after 'a shell burst close to him and blew part of a comrade's head and brains into his face'. In a period of four months' absence his colonel wrote to his family stating 'your son had twice suffered from shell shock during the campaign'. Despite being described as one of his 'best soldiers', Moon, whose absence had been lengthy in comparison with Dyett's, was shot.[55] Perhaps Moon's original condition would have been viewed by Moran as a case of 'intense emotional shock', a crisis of which had drained his account of courage completely. His behaviour in terms of evading custody for four months would undoubtedly have earned him Moran's epithet 'shirker'. We can now see Dyett as a vulnerable individual, and Moon as a victim of combat stress. That many at the time might have viewed them as cowards is not a matter for disgust. This was how such behaviours were then viewed. The 2006 pardon extended to those executed for cowardice or desertion is, in effect, a pardon to a bygone age for a failure of understanding.

### Courage – character or cultivated?

We have been considering courage as if it were a single entity, but in terms of modern psychological concepts, psychologist Frank Farley divides heroes into three types. First are the soldiers, policemen, firemen, and rescue workers; 'professional heroes' who face grave risks but do so as part of their daily job. The second sort of hero

---

53 Corns & Hughes-Wilson, op. cit. pp.269-273.
54 Corns & Hughes-Wilson, op. cit. p.275.
55 TNA WO 71/520, quoted in Corns & Hughes-Wilson, op. cit. pp.319-321.

(who was familiar by the turn of century) is the 'situational hero'; the ordinary, accidental hero who 'is the man of the hour, because he and only he can do what must be done'.[56] Farley calls the third type of hero the 'sustainer', 'the breadwinner for an extended family or the indispensable man of a corporation'. These roles reach the level of heroism 'only when the struggle involved becomes intense and the efficacy required titanic'. This was the vision of heroism to which the Great War gave birth – the Stoic endurance hero who stuck to his duty under exceptional duress. Indeed, recruitment posters as the war went into 1915 passed from chivalric visions to images of the military uniform and the ordinary man as soldier.

But what makes a man courageous? Clearly, in the Victorian/Edwardian era, courage was seen as a matter of character. Moran concluded: 'A man of character in peace becomes a man of courage in war'.[57] Conningsby Dawson did not necessarily agree, writing amusingly from the trenches: 'The most unendurable people act like heroes in the face of death'.[58] Moran also gave a nod to certain environmental factors in courage, namely discipline, the 'support of numbers', and good leadership.[59] Modern research suggests that there are indeed personal characteristics that influence courage, but that environmental factors play an equally powerful part. Such factors may positively influence the personal characteristics, which are not immutable traits. The bravest soldiers prove firstly to be those with a high level of self-confidence. Those with a sense of self-efficacy, possessing a strong belief in their ability to reach a goal, experience the lowest levels of fear in battle.[60] Secondly, there is the matter of competence. Having a belief in one's skill, acquired through training, also reduces fear. Thirdly, there are situational issues. As Lord Moran would have agreed, these include the presence of courageous models and the experience of group cohesiveness. It is easier to be brave when there are courageous actors around one, and one feels close to fellows who share the danger.[61] Courage is thus less a matter of being of brave character, and more a matter of the interaction of a sense of efficacy and skill with situational demands. Perseverance courage is an important idea as it draws our attention to the distinction between courageous acts and courageous actors. Psychological research within the military on courage in the face of dangerous situations now shows that 'the successful practice of courageous behaviour leads to a decrease in subjective fear and finally to a state of fearlessness'.[62] Repeatedly being a courageous actor makes one more courageous.

56 http://www.artofmanliness.com/2011/02/14/the-art-of-manliness-podcast-34-the-attributes-of-a-hero-with-dr-frank-farley/.
57 Moran, op. cit. p.154.
58 C. Dawson, *Living Bayonets*, p.16.
59 Moran, op. cit. p.16.
60 D. Cox, R. Hallam, K. O'Connor, and S. Rachman, 'An Experimental Analysis of Fearlessness and Courage', *British Journal of Psychology*, p.107.
61 S.J. Rachman, *Fear and Courage*, p.298.
62 Rachman, op. cit. p.317.

## Courage in the Trenches

### *'Over the top'*

Courageous behaviour was sometimes simply borne on physiological arousal – it was adrenalin-driven. In action at Ypres in 1917, Private Hugh Quigley noted enthusiastically 'how excited one becomes in the midst of great danger'. This shut out fear-related thoughts: 'I forgot absolutely that shells were meant to kill'.[63] An aircraft strafed him and his comrades with machine gun fire, and Quigley, his adrenalin sending him into euphoria, 'never enjoyed anything so much in my life'.[64] Private W. Walker also described the same effects going over the top at the Battle of Loos. His first step was behavioural: 'We braced ourselves and leapt on to the open field'. Once under fire, adrenalin took over. 'The darkness of cowardice that had so clouded my mind and filled me with self-despair had fled. I marvelled at my carelessness'.[65] Captain Alfred Pollard stated that he 'thoroughly enjoyed going into action'. Reflecting on this after the war he came to the conclusion that his motivation was a 'keen desire to win'.[66] He won the Victoria Cross on 29 April 1917 at Gavrelle, repelling an enemy counterattack. The citation refers to 'force of will, dash and splendid example, coupled with an utter contempt of danger'.[67] Both his own view and his behaviour confirm that he possessed the necessary self-efficacy – he not only desired to win, he believed he could. In his account of this action written 13 years later, Pollard described an initial fear, in response to which: 'There is nothing so soothing to the nerves as to be doing something'. Like Walker, the behavioural first step was all that was needed. In charging the enemy, adrenalin took over: 'I felt a thrill only comparable to running through the opposition at Rugger to score a try'.[68]

Many soldiers thus did not experience fear in action. Sergeant Douglas Pinkerton recorded a conversation with another soldier at Givenchy. 'I don't mind the fighting a bit; it is before and after the fighting that hurts', the man said.[69] Action itself was thus a different matter to anticipation or reflection. The anxiety generated by anticipation had the potential to undermine the ability to be courageous by hampering the first step. William Tyrrell acknowledged that the height of battle was a 'fruitful period' in the generation of shell shock, but also listed 'the hour before going over the top'.[70] Lieutenant Shallett Raggett described how: 'The mental stress before an attack, the strain of waiting and wondering what will happen is far more trying

---

63 H. Quigley, *Passchendaele and the Somme*, p.148.
64 Quigley, op. cit. p.151.
65 W. Walker, Diary, http://www.firstworldwar.com/diaries/battleofloos.htm.
66 A.O. Pollard, *Fire-Eater*, p.200.
67 *London Gazette*, 8 June 1917.
68 Pollard, op. cit. pp.219-220.
69 R.D. Pinkerton, *Ladies from Hell*, p.93.
70 RWOCESS, p.34.

than the actual attack'.[71] Donald Hankey identified negative thinking as the problematic process. A soldier was more liable to fear in the period before an attack because at such a time 'he still has leisure to think'.[72] Before the capture of the Messines Ridge in June 1917, Norman Gladden described the anticipation of battle. 'Time hung heavily on our hands', and there was little talking. Soldiers had retreated inside themselves, dwelling.[73] Scout Joe Cassells drew a distinction between an action in mobile warfare that began suddenly and one in positional warfare that was anticipated. 'It is one thing to go at them with steel and rifle, but quite another to sit around and wait for the short blast of the whistle which sends you out to kill or to be killed'.[74] During the early Somme fighting in 1916, Second-Lieutenant Charles Carrington described himself before action as in 'an elevated state of mind'. A victim of his own thoughts, he was subject to bouts of 'naked fear', his brain 'took sides and disputed with itself', whilst his body was 'numb and void' and 'an emptiness almost like a physical pain tormented my bowels'.[75] Second-Lieutenant Edward Liveing experienced various reactions in the hour prior to going 'over the top' at Gommecourt on 1 July 1916. Firstly, he experienced an 'excessive desire for the time to come', a time when the bombardment would stop. Secondly, there were 'moments of intense fear'. Thirdly, another victim of negative thoughts, he reflected on his mortality. He thought he only had twenty minutes left of life in 'comparative safety', and found himself musing: 'What was the difference between twenty minutes and twenty years?'[76] In taking the first step forward into action, the soldier was demonstrating Moran's 'cold choice' of courage in favour of 'fixed resolve not to quit'.

Going over the top transmuted arousal into useful and focussed action. Captain Richard Haigh believed that 'the first time that a man goes into an attack, he as a rule enjoys it'.[77] In action, Alec Dawson described 'the splendid feeling of the charge itself' a feeling he delightfully described as 'champagney', and 'by long odds the finest feeling I ever had in my life'.[78] Advancing in action, Patrick Campbell found that 'now that we had started, I was no longer aware of anxiety, only of excitement'.[79] Captain Geoffrey Dugdale at Third Ypres in 1917 described himself as 'wildly excited'.[80] Second-Lieutenant Huntly Gordon, an artillery officer, found himself with rifle in hand in March 1918 beating off a German attack, killing at least one of the attackers.

71  S.H. Raggett, Private Papers, IWM Docs 1027.
72  D. Hankey, *A Student in Arms – Second Series*, pp.116-8.
73  Gladden, op. cit. p.58.
74  J. Cassells, *The Black Watch*, pp.163-4.
75  C. Edmonds (C. Carrington), *A Subaltern's War*, p.33.
76  E.G.D. Liveing, *Attack*, pp.60-1.
77  R. Haigh, *Life in a Tank*, p.2.
78  A.J. Dawson, *A Temporary Gentleman in France*, p.246.
79  P.J. Campbell, *In The Cannon's Mouth*, p.76.
80  G. Dugdale, *'Langemarck' and 'Cambrai'*, p.72.

He described 'a thrilling mad, desperate moment'.[81] In contrast, Evelyn Southwell felt merely 'pleasurably excited' when shooting attacking Germans.[82] Private Walter Williams, working as a stretcher bearer, was suddenly enveloped in the thick of fighting and found himself 'caught up in the excitement ... screaming encouragement' and bayoneting one of the enemy.[83] Siegfried Sassoon, in his famous mad dash to clear a German trench of a sniper in front of Mametz Wood in July 1916 described himself as 'idiotically elated', putting a finger on his right ear and emitting hunting cries when he had achieved his task.[84]

A sergeant of the 22nd Manchester Regiment advancing at Fricourt on 1 July 1916 wrote: 'I hadn't gone ten yards before I felt a load fall from me'. He had been frightened of being frightened, that his legs would refuse to move. 'Now I knew it was all right. I shouldn't be frightened and I shouldn't lose my head'. Moving forward, he felt 'quite happy and self-possessed'. He was undoubtedly displaying courageous behaviour, walking into machine gun fire, yet he concluded that 'it wasn't courage', as he was suddenly taken by the quite unrealistic idea that he was safe and would not be hurt.[85] Donald Hankey described men in action as proceeding in an 'absolutely abnormal condition'. He noted that 'their emotions seem to be numbed'. Noise and sights which would 'ordinarily produce intense pity, horror or dread, have no effect on them at all'.[86] Shallett Raggett experienced the cognitive change: 'In an attack one forgets everything in the excitement ... one has no time to think'.[87] Richard Haigh wrote of watching German machine gunners shoot down their own men who were surrendering at Cambrai in 1917 and rather than be horrified 'one simply doesn't have time to pay any attention to it all'.[88] Geoffrey Husbands, going into action on the Somme in late 1916 found himself proceeding in an altered state which was 'impersonal ... one seems to watch one's actions from outside, a spectator without emotion'.[89] In battle Lieutenant Harold Macmillan described being overtaken by: 'A kind of daze that makes one impervious to emotion'.[90] Douglas Pinkerton could claim that in advancing 'there was no fear'. In the midst of the noise of battle 'one becomes only a shrivelled nonentity, incapable of conscious thought'.[91] Scout Joe Cassells reminisced: 'I can but faintly recall the actual close fighting'. He was clear however that: 'I was not thinking of what might happen to me'.[92] Once

81  H. Gordon, *The Unreturning Army*, Kindle edition location 2514.
82  H.E.E. Howson, *Two Men*, p.36.
83  M. Williams, *With Innocence and Hope*, Kindle edition locations 2338-2357.
84  Sassoon, op. cit. p.344.
85  Quoted in G. Chapman, *Vain Glory*, p.320.
86  Hankey, op. cit. pp.116-8.
87  Raggett, op. cit.
88  Haigh, op. cit. p.81.
89  G. Husbands, *Joffrey's War*, p.359.
90  H. Macmillan, *Winds of Change*, p.76.
91  Pinkerton, op. cit. p.65.
92  Cassells, op. cit. p.77.

advancing, Edward Liveing proceeded 'in a dream, but I had all my wits about me'.[93] Second-Lieutenant Alan Thomas explained that he simply 'forgot to feel afraid' advancing at the head of his company at Arras in 1917: 'There was so much to think about, so much to distract my attention'.[94] The essence of the state of altered experience is caught by a private in the Royal Welsh Fusiliers attacking Mametz Wood in July 1916, who described a 'state of not-thinking, not-feeling, not-seeing'.[95] In these adrenalin-driven moments, soldiers' attention was focussed on moving forward. Extraneous sensations were filtered out. Alexander Aitken concluded that: 'Only safety, or the shock of a wound will destroy such auto-hypnosis. At the same time, all normal emotion is numbed utterly'.[96]

Conningsby Dawson may have thought that it 'isn't natural to be brave'. To go over the top was a two-step process. The first step was the decision to make the first step despite the anticipation. The process of launching oneself into danger was assisted by two things in an army composed of civilians. Firstly, it was driven by a strong sense of duty. Secondly, soldiers were not simply acting as individuals but as part of a group. In the second step, moving forward under fire, soldiers were not in a natural state. In that adrenalin-driven condition of focussed numbness, devoid of fear, they could display behaviours that were undoubtedly courageous which they might otherwise have thought themselves incapable of.

### *Irreflective courage or the courageous actor?*

Frederic Manning believed that there could be a 'pleasure in daring'.[97] He wrote of men carried forward in action 'on a wave of emotional excitement', yet afterwards relapsing into 'sore and angry nerves sharpening their temper', and being 'morose and sullen'.[98] So far he is describing adrenalin-driven courage. He also, however, described the act of a man 'risking himself for another' as a 'spontaneous and irreflective action, like the kind of start forward you make instinctively when you see a child playing in the street turn and run suddenly under a car'.[99] Conningsby Dawson advised his parents that 'unconscious heroism' was 'the virtue most to be desired'.[100]

Although he did not know it, Manning chose a poor example. We now know that the male hormone testosterone, which in the face of competition can drive men to be anti-social, also enables men to be fiercely protective.[101] This is likely to

---

93 Liveing, op. cit. pp.66-7.
94 A. Thomas, *A Life Apart*, p.119.
95 Quoted in J. Ellis, *Eye Deep in Hell*, p.102.
96 A. Aitken quoted in Ellis, op. cit. p.101.
97 Manning, op. cit. location 387.
98 Manning, op. cit. location 686.
99 Manning, op. cit. location 1405.
100 Dawson, *Carry On*, p.45.
101 M.A.S. Boksem, et. al., 'Testosterone Inhibits Trust But Promotes Reciprocity', *Psychological Science*, p.2306.

be even more the case in respect of protectiveness towards children – good sense in terms of evolution. Some acts of protective courage are therefore reflexive in terms of our biology. Whether *all* acts of risking life for another are 'irreflective', without conscious thought, is doubtful. Rowland Feilding was walking through a yard with a fellow officer and heard an explosion behind him. He turned to find the battalion bombing officer, Lieutenant Grey de Leche Leach, lying in a pool of blood with both hands blown off. Leach had lost a pin from a bomb, and to protect his men, told them to lie down whilst he ran outside with it. Feilding estimated 'he then had less than four seconds in which to decide what to do', and guessed that seeing the two officers in the yard where had intended to get rid of the bomb, concluded 'that his one chance of throwing it safely away was gone'. Leach therefore 'turned his back to us, faced the wall, and hugging the bomb in his hands, allowed it to explode between his body and the wall'. If Feilding is correct, Leach went through a detailed thinking process in a matter of seconds. He concluded that 'it is impossible to speak much of such courage and self-sacrifice'.[102] Leach, a model of the virtue of the self-sacrifice celebrated in Victorian heroism, was awarded the gold Albert Medal posthumously.

Leach's behaviour leaves us with a conceptual problem. If his courage was not irreflective, what guided his thinking process? Max Plowman described the courage of his fellow subaltern, Hardy. He viewed this as demonstrating the 'merits of the public-school system'. 'If there's danger about', he wrote, 'Hardy at once considers it his duty to be there, and he is reckless to a fault'. He was not a calm man, 'easily sacred out of his wits', but his education, Plowman believed, taught him to behave this way – such an individual 'appraises the danger and then goes calmly into it'.[103] Plowman is thus describing is the making of a decision to behave bravely. Soldiers became courageous actors.

Lieutenant Patrick Campbell actively wanted to win the Military Cross, and noted how 'sometimes as I was falling asleep I had imagined myself doing some brave action'.[104] Campbell was a man who reflected very actively on fear. To provide himself with necessary reassurance, he rehearsed brave behaviour in his head. Lord Moran wrote of 'the shadow of fear' which drove men into reckless behaviour through which a 'sensitive soul hoped to school himself or test his self-control'.[105] Lieutenant Stuart Cloete claimed: 'One thing I noticed repeatedly was that those men who were fearless at first cracked suddenly, and were never any good again'.[106] Second-Lieutenant Charles Carrington described the secret of some of the brave as being 'lack of perspicacity'. These officers were suggesting that there were men who pushed themselves

---

102 Feilding, op. cit. p.64.
103 Mark VII, op. cit. p.100.
104 P.J. Campbell, *The Ebb and Flow of Battle*, p.23.
105 Moran, op. cit. p.46.
106 S. Cloete, *A Victorian Son*, p.214.

into brave acts without balanced judgement, and that sooner or later events, either wounding, death, or inner collapse would catch the unwise courageous actor out. Courage balanced by caution made a soldier and those around him safer. Captain Rowland Feilding, a notably phlegmatic man, was sent to an entrenching battalion after recuperation following an injury. He wanted 'a more dangerous job' but was told that he was 'too chancy' and 'too brave'. He wrote to his wife that 'I have tried to act as I have thought you would like me to act'.[107] His performance was thus at least partly directed by a particular aspect of duty, by how he felt those he loved expected him to act. Others judged that he had overplayed his part – unsafely, too.

On his first exposure to shellfire in Salonika in 1915, Major Arthur Hamilton Gibbs watched two French soldiers walk through the bombardment he was sheltering from 'without turning a hair or attempting to quicken or duck', with a 'sangfroid that left me gasping'.[108] Either they had calculated something about the bombardment that Gibbs had not, or they were simply brave actors. Gibbs, in any case, had clearly not yet developed the appropriate repertoire. Second-Lieutenant Huntly Gordon was conscious that he had to rehearse the role of courage, noting: 'I think you need to practice taking occasional risks or you become too trench-minded'.[109] Supporting SOS calls from infantry battalions, he and his battery commander 'strolled about in the open', Gordon using a prop for his role as 'I smoked my new pipe and tried to appear unconcerned'.[110]

Lieutenant-Colonel Jack Sherwood-Kelly vowed to win the Victoria Cross on joining up in 1914, and did so in attack on 20 November 1917 at Cambrai, in astonishing sustained feats of courage:

> (He) personally led the leading company of his battalion across the canal and, after crossing, reconnoitred under heavy rifle and machine gun fire the high ground held by the enemy. The left flank of his battalion advancing to the assault of this objective was held up by a thick belt of wire, whereupon he crossed to that flank, and with a Lewis gun team, forced his way under heavy fire through obstacles, got the gun into position on the far side, and covered the advance of his battalion through the wire, thereby enabling them to capture the position. Later, he personally led a charge against some pits from which a heavy fire was being directed on his men, captured the pits, together with five machine guns and forty six prisoners, and killed a large number of the enemy.[111]

---

107  Feilding, op. cit. p.49.
108  A.H. Gibbs, *Gun Fodder*, p.119.
109  Gordon, op. cit. location 2180.
110  Gordon, op. cit. location 2485.
111  *London Gazette*, 11 January 1918, p.722.

Another courageous actor, Sherwood-Kelly was undoubtedly one of the small group of fearless 'overconfident performers' that psychologists have identified (7.5 per cent of military personnel) who have much less physical responsiveness in fearful situations, and who perceive such situations as much less dangerous than they actually are.[112] Thus at Third Ypres in 1917, R.L. Mackay, an officer of 11th Argyll & Sutherland Highlanders described his commanding officer Lieutenant-Colonel Horace Duncan as 'a perfect marvel' who showed a total indifference towards danger, a disdain akin to 'the disregard of a religious maniac for death'.[113]

Some acts of protective courage are biologically reflexive. Others are based on very swift courageous reflection. Some are the acts of a small group of 'overconfident performers'. For the most part, however, soldiers became everyday courageous actors. Being such on the battlefield required several things. Firstly, as in going 'over the top' into fire, there had to come the decision to act bravely. This, as previously set out, was a group act of perceived duty. Secondly, to be a courageous actor and survive, one had to have both the judgement as to when one's performance began and ended, and an appropriate repertoire. Both the code of manliness with its models of courage and experience of the trenches provided excellent stage directions. And the more an individual perfected their part, the braver they became.

### *Modelling and inspiring courage*

Soldiers wrote often of the courage of comrades. Harry Drinkwater watched a ration party toiling uphill through shellfire. He noted that they could have dumped the rations and sought shelter, but they did not. 'Twenty minutes is a long time to face such an ordeal of one's own free will – it was cold courage, and well done'.[114] Captain Gerald Burgoyne noted that a fellow officer was 'a very cool man, a most trustworthy soldier'.[115] He evidently equated courage with reliability when it counted most. Second-Lieutenant Charles Douie said of his friend, Robin Cornish: 'Eager always for battle, he was magnificent in attack; in the most trying periods of trench warfare, under continuous shell fire and in every circumstance of hardship, he remained undaunted, resolute, and unfailingly cheerful'.[116] Cornish evidently, like Pollard, possessed the key element of self-efficacy. There was thus not only the image of manly heroism as a beacon to follow. The courage of fellows was not only admired, it was manifestly an inspiration, providing examples of how to act.

The army knew well the power of example. Giving evidence to the War Office Committee of Enquiry on 'Shell-Shock', Lieutenant-Colonel James Burnett, who commanded 1st Gordon Highlanders for a year, observed that in a pre-war Regular

---

112 T.M. McMillan & S.J. Rachman, 'Fearlessness and Courage in Paratroop Veterans of the Falklands War', *British Journal of Psychology*, p.275.
113 R.L. Mackay, Diary, http://www.firstworldwar.com/diaries/rlm1.htm.
114 Cooksey & Griffiths, op. cit. p.131.
115 C. Davison, *The Burgoyne Diaries*, p.25.
116 C. Douie, *The Weary Road*, pp.145-6.

unit, 'so long as the officer himself did not go back with a nervous breakdown, very few of the men would'.[117] Henry Croft believed that the greatest strength of the British officer was that he was trained 'not to get excited and to take things quietly', and that it was this 'silent strength' that gave confidence to the ranks.[118] Private Geoffrey Husbands agreed. He did not expect his officers to be 'heroes of the melodramatic variety', but felt that he had 'a right to expect' officers to set an example of 'cool-headedness and equanimity'.[119] Private Henry Russell described the display of coolness by officers giving men the 'faith in leadership that is essential'.[120] Captain Allan Hanbury-Sparrow was very conscious of this. Summoning the courage to look over the parapet he had to take himself in hand: 'For very shame's sake, pull yourself together man ... set them an example'.[121] Officers therefore had a particular impetus to courageous acting. There was a keen balance between example and safe behaviour. Geoffrey Dugdale on his first tour in the trenches was advised by his sergeant against recklessness: 'Don't try to be too brave. Only do what you are told; be cautious'.[122] An artillery officer wrote: 'True courage is prudent and limits itself strictly to what is necessary'. He believed it should never 'bluster' unless men wavered and had to be 'carried along by the force of example'.[123] By 1918, when command was taught to infantry battalion commanders at Senior Officer School, Aldershot, courage was deemed the first essential of leadership.[124] Indeed, of the 703 awards of the Distinguished Service Order made to infantry battalion commanders during 1918, 'example' is the most frequently recorded category.[125] Thus, on 10 April 1917 during the attack on Feuchy, Arras, R.L Mackay, noted that apart from Intelligence Officer: 'I bet there was not another officer in the Brigade nearer the Boche than old Colonel MacNeil'. He did not presume that MacNeil was without fear: 'He didn't like shells, I'm sure', but he had the facility for courageous acting: 'He could play with them all the same'. Nor was bravery solely demonstrated in the face of bullets or shells – Huntly Gordon's severely wounded CO Major Sumpter had 'a serene quality which gives confidence and strength to all the rest of us'.[126]

Modelling was thus both powerful and successful. Patrick Campbell, in the 1918 spring retreat, was alone one morning and saw a senior officer approaching. 'Without fear himself' this man 'expected others to be equally unafraid'.

117 RWOCESS, p.46.
118 Croft, op. cit. pp.35-6.
119 Husbands, op. cit. p.195.
120 H. Russell, *Slaves of the War Lords*, p.59.
121 A.A.H. Hanbury-Sparrow, *The Land-Locked Lake*, p.19.
122 Dugdale, op. cit. p.34.
123 H. Carrington, *Psychical Phenomena at the War*, p.77.
124 P.E. Hodgkinson, *British Infantry Battalion Commanders in The First World War*, p.128.
125 Hodgkinson, op. cit. p.153.
126 Gordon, op. cit. location 1402.

Campbell had unfortunately been feeling afraid ever since he had woken up that day. Ordered to go with him, 'an extraordinary thing happened. As I walked beside him I no longer felt afraid'.[127] Alfred Pollard depicted the well-respected Lieutenant-Colonel Ernest Boyle, 1/1st Honourable Artillery Company, as a man who 'never knew fear and who inspired all with whom he came into contact with his own enthusiasm'.[128] How much of example was deliberate modelling is not clear. Captain Francis Hitchcock observed Lieutenant-Colonel Alfred Murphy clearly deliberately modelling endurance. Soaked through and going into action: 'The C.O. was in great form. He always showed his 100 per cent soldiering qualities under discomfiture, and would appear to revel in it, which I well knew was not the case'.[129] Second-Lieutenant Alan Thomas viewed Lieutenant-Colonel Bob Dawson, 6th Royal West Kent, as a man of immense courage. Thomas, however, once found Dawson clinging to the side of a trench, where he acknowledged his fear of the shelling but stated: 'I don't show the fear I feel'. Dawson clearly well understood the importance of modelling coping. Lieutenant Harold Macmillan similarly described walking about at Loos under fire 'trying to look as self-possessed as possible under a heavy fire'.[130] He was aware that when in action and 'responsible for men under one's command', leadership demanded that one demonstrate 'proper behaviour, even acts of gallantry'.[131]

Inspiring courage was not, however, the sole province of officers. Private George Coppard described the number one in his machine gun team, Lance-Corporal William Hankin, as a 'brave cool customer', adding 'his cold grey eyes did more than anything else to help me control my fears'.[132] When he fainted due to exhaustion, 'it shook me'. Coppard feared that he might 'lose some of the superb control he always showed, no matter how hard the conditions'.[133] Conningsby Dawson, pondering the risks he took, did not appear to be clear about how much he was deliberately imitating 'other people's coolness'. He seemed to worry that if he was, then he might have no genuine courage, and was concerned as to whether he would 'fear life again when the war is ended'.[134]

## Changing Concepts of Courage and Heroism

Jessica Meyer refers to the emergence of 'citizen heroes' during the war. Whilst this is truism – a largely citizen army would inevitably breed citizen heroes – the truth is

---

127 Campbell, *Cannon's Mouth*, pp.41-2.
128 Pollard, op. cit. p.178.
129 F.C. Hitchcock, *Stand To*, p.161.
130 Macmillan, op. cit. p.76.
131 Macmillan, op. cit. p. 89.
132 G. Coppard, *With a Machine Gun to Cambrai*, pp.36-7.
133 Coppard, op. cit. p.96.
134 Dawson, *Carry On*, p.88.

more complex. The concept of 'citizen heroes' and their acts of spontaneous courage, as we have seen, was already well established in the late Victorian era. It is not really *who* was seen as courageous that altered, it was *what* was viewed as courage that changed.

The institutional view of bravery is to a certain extent portrayed in the reasons for the award of the Victoria Cross. Melvin Smith's research shows that during its first fifty years, 52 per cent of awards were for aggressive 'war-winning' acts, and 54 per cent for 'humanitarian' acts.[135] In 1914, when no VCs had been awarded for ten years, 'the Victorian heroic ideal survived', with 56 per cent of medals going to war-winning actions, although the figure for humanitarian acts dropped to 30 per cent.[136] The position began to shift in 1916, and in the second half of the year, covering the period of the battle of the Somme, the figure for war-winning acts rose to 64 per cent, awards for humanitarian behaviour dropping to 19 per cent of the total.[137] The army was in the process of redefining heroism. It seemingly 'no longer wanted men who would rush to the aid of the fallen'. Rather, it required 'killers first and foremost'.[138] In 1917 this trend continued, the figures being 84 and 13 per cent respectively, and in 1918, 90 and 6 per cent.[139] The two awards of the VC to Captain Noel Chevasse, Olympic 400 metre athlete and regimental medical officer, in 1916 and 1917 for rescuing and treating the wounded under fire, mortally wounded himself on the second occasion, are therefore extraordinary.

The institutional and the popular views of heroism began both to change and to diverge. The pure Victorian vision of heroism passed away in both accounts. For the institution of the army, courage became 'lean and merciless'.[140] Whilst the press attempted to maintain an absurd vision of romantic heroism, the bulk of the population would no doubt, as the war progressed, have increasingly concurred with the words of Winston Churchill that the heroes of the war lay 'out in the cratered fields, mangled, stifled, scarred; and there are too many of them for exceptional honours. It is mass suffering, mass sacrifice'.[141] The popular concept of heroism shifted during the war from a vision of individual dash to one of endurance and perseverance. The balance changed from the heroic to the Stoic. A letter in the *Church Times* in August 1917 indicates this change:

> To read as I did the other day ... of the soldier hero waiting 'with eager heart and starry eyes' to go over the top is as sickening as it is silly. Soldiers hate it. They recognise it for the hysterical tosh it is. It's stupid, false, dishonouring, and

---

135  Smith, op. cit. p.96.
136  Smith, op. cit. pp.118-9.
137  Smith, op. cit. p.144.
138  Smith, op. cit. p.151.
139  Smith, op. cit. pp.157-161.
140  Smith, op. cit. p.185.
141  W.S. Churchill, *Thoughts and Adventures*, p.200.

wicked …. No, the splendour and wonder of our men in France and Belgium … lies not so much in the dash and glory of it all, but in their grimly doing their duty; sticking to a hateful task amid conditions that every right-minded man must hate and loathe with fierce intensity.[142]

Soldiers themselves increasingly valued Stoic endurance courage. Rowland Feilding described a fellow officer who was severely wounded and lay for hours in a trench awaiting his turn to be taken to a Casualty Clearing Station, 'never once by word or gesture betraying the pain he must have been enduring'.[143] Similarly, Lieutenant-Colonel William Malone on Walker's Ridge, Gallipoli described his wounded men as all 'very brave. No cries or even groans'. Many greeted him 'cheerfully … many smiled'.[144] Private Giles Eyre described similar courage on the Somme in 1916. Moving up to the front line, shrapnel caught their party. One young soldier lay with his whole side ripped open. 'True to his type he is silent, only his heaving chest and staring eyes denote the torment he is suffering'.[145] Those who returned after serious wounds were regarded as having particular reserves of endurance. Huntly Gordon described his battery commander, Major Sumpter, as having a scar two foot long, remarking that it needed 'great guts to come back for more after that lot'.[146] Similarly, Major George Ardagh, the popular second-in-command of 13th Royal Fusiliers, had his femur smashed by a shell in November 1916, yet he returned to France six months later, Guy Chapman recording the quartermaster's comment: 'What a tiger, eh?'[147] Endurance courage, of course, also manifested itself in facing the appalling physical conditions on the battlefields, particularly during the terrible winters of 1914-15 and 1916-17, and the mud of both the latter stages of the Somme campaign and Third Ypres. As Conningsby Dawson stated: 'The courage to endure remains one's sole possession'.[148] The British working man brought his traditional ways of coping with daily life, hardiness and endurance, to the battlefield. The behaviour was far from new, but in a different setting it was now increasingly relabelled as courage. This so-called typically 'British' type of courage, dressed in cheerfulness, was epitomised by the cartoon character 'Old Bill', redolent with 'endurance, resourcefulness, black humour, and comradeship'.[149]

On 1 July 1916, 1st Hampshire assaulted the Hawthorn Ridge on the Somme. Casualties in officers were 100 per cent. Lieutenant-Colonel the Honourable Lawrence

---

142 *Church Times*, 17 August 1917.
143 Feilding, op. cit. p.73.
144 J. Crawford, *No Better Death*, Kindle edition location 2769.
145 G.E.M. Eyre, *Somme Harvest*, p.119.
146 Gordon, op. cit. location 1402.
147 G. Chapman, *A Passionate Prodigality*, p.131.
148 Dawson, *Glory*, p.21.
149 J. Meyer, 'Citizen Heroes', https://www.futurelearn.com/courses/ww1-heroism/steps/15161/progress.

Charles Walter Palk, going forward in white gloves and carrying only a stick, was hit. 'Whilst lying mortally wounded in a shell-hole, he turned to another man lying near him and said "If you know of a better 'ole, go to it."'[150] The son of Baron Haldon was thus happy to use the words of 'Old Bill' and be identified with this image of courage. In the post-war world the writings of the soldier wordsmiths such as Wilfred Owen, Henri Barbusse, and Erich Maria Remarque mocked the old vision of courage.[151] The value of endurance courage, which psychologist Frank Farley would personify as the 'sustainer' decades later, held good instead.

## Conclusion

Jessica Meyer suggests that 'cowardice remained ill-defined' in memoirs because the 'belief that experiencing fear denoted cowardice could not be maintained under circumstances in which all men felt fear'. One hundred years on it is still not easy to define. A man would generally not be judged a coward by his fellows on the basis of an episode of loss of control. Indeed, Meyer suggests that courage came to be defined not simply by self-control, but 'by the ability to regain self-control even after it had been lost'.[152] The evidence to support this claim specifically is thin on the ground, but self-control, within the Stoic ideal, certainly remained a central plank of the concept of courage.

The psychic researcher, Hereward Carrington, provided thoughtful comments on courage in 1920. He described its complex nature, being 'compounded of various elements which make up a complex whole that appears under different aspects'. Firstly, he noted 'accidental courage' which he thought 'comparatively easy to practise' (an easy comment, perhaps, for one who did not serve). Within this, we can perhaps include adrenalin-driven courage and any acts of reflexive courage. Secondly, Carrington described 'continuous' courage, which he found more difficult to analyse, although he took the view that in some cases 'habit makes it almost unconscious'. In this, he was undoubtedly describing courageous actors and endurance courage. He chose to record the words of a French officer from November 1914: 'Our idea of courage has changed. It has not lessened, but it has become more modest, more reserved, more humble', and less 'brilliant and aristocratic'.[153]

The courage of Stoic endurance, carried from everyday life, enabled the soldier both to cope with and restrain fear that would undermine courageous behaviour. The heroic concept of courage, the courage of brave acts, was still admired, but the spotlight of admiration was now shone on ordinary men doing their duty under extraordinary

---

150 H.C. Rees, Private Papers, IWM Docs 7166.
151 Wilfred Owen in his 1917 poem 'Dulce et Decorum est'; Henri Barbusse in his novel *Under Fire*; and Erich Maria Remarque in his novel *All Quiet on the Western Front*.
152 J. Meyer, *Men of War*, p.142.
153 Carrington, op. cit. p.77.

conditions. From the vision of the individual hero, courage now had to accommodate the notion of group endurance. Soldiers modelled courageous endurance for each other. Shallett Raggett wrote of the consolation of 'the knowledge of knowing that in after years one cannot be accused of having failed in the hour of need'.[154] Courage was found in not failing each other.

154 Raggett, op. cit.

# 8

## 'Literally We Are Living Among the Dead'

---

The Great War is enshrined in our imaginations in terms of loss of life. Death became part of the soldier's familiar landscape in the form of ever-present human remains. The matters of wounding and death are intertwined, and soldiers often found the former more immediately distressing. Thus Sergeant Douglas Pinkerton wrote home that 'they say that the first wounded man you see remains with you throughout your life, and to this day I remember mine with an awful vividness'.[1] The Great War was above all else an artillery war, and the effects of high explosive on the human frame, fatal or not, could be grotesque.

### Wounding

Captain Douglas Cuddeford described the death of two gunners and the wounding of others by a shell at Arras in 1917. The young artillery subaltern with them staggered into their dugout and 'threw himself on a bunk, his face white as a sheet', vomiting violently. Cuddeford, an old hand, concluded that 'probably it was his first experience of that sort of thing'.[2] Second-Lieutenant Charles Douie's first experience of the suddenness of death and wounding by a shell is recorded in vivid terms: 'I am not likely to forget that cry in the night, the blinding flash, and the nauseating smell ... of blood and explosive which pervaded the whole trench'.[3] He thus reminds us that the experience was an assault on all the senses. Unless it was a head shot that opened the cranium and spilled brain, most would have agreed with Private Frederic Manning's view that: 'It is infinitely more horrible and revolting to see a man shattered and eviscerated, than to see him shot'.[4] Indeed, Sergeant John Lucy described as 'almost the ghastliest sight I saw' the experience of a soldier with his stomach ripped open by shrapnel gazing 'with fascinated eyes at large coils of his own guts, which he held in

---

1    R.D. Pinkerton, *Ladies from Hell*, p.68.
2    D.W.J. Cuddeford, *And All for What?*, p.155.
3    C. Douie, *The Weary Road*, pp.105-6.
4    F. Manning, *The Middle Parts of Fortune*, Kindle version location 200.

both hands'.[5] Second-Lieutenant Carlos Blacker described the fatal injury of his friend Dormer Treffry by a shell on the Somme. Treffry lost a leg, and his bowels protruded from his abdomen. In the aftermath Blacker kept having nightmares and could not 'banish the persistent images'. After a week, Treffry still appeared in Blacker's dreams, but with 'happier backgrounds'. After a month the dreams had become 'disconnected' and repeated themselves less.[6] Soldiers therefore recovered from this violent imagery. They also learnt to distance themselves. Captain Gerald Burgoyne had one of his men shot through the head – 'a horrible mess' – taking six hours to die. He commented however that: 'One gets ... selfish, and I think the dominant feeling is one of relief that it is not one's self'.[7]

Michael Roper criticises military historians for concentrating on the idea that the deaths of and injuries to others simply brought men face-to-face with their own mortality. Whilst acknowledging that this is of course correct, he also believes that primitive feelings of insecurity were stirred by such events – it was the *manner* of death and wounding that made it so disturbing.[8] Indeed, sudden, violent death is recognised today to be more problematic to deal with than death, say, by illness.[9] The spilling entrails of the gut wound described by Lucy above was probably not only the most horrible but also the most feared of all wounds. Anthony Eden noted that 'we all agreed that the stomach was the one to be feared'.[10] For Roper, the manner of death was symbolic. He believes that fear such as Eden's was in fact of mentally spilling out, of falling apart psychologically just as bodies were dismembered. Roper alleges, following the theories of psychoanalyst Melanie Klein, that the experiences of the trenches had the potential to reduce the individual to the 'most primitive and profound anxiety of the baby'.[11] Evidence to support Roper's contentions is sparse. It is interesting, however, that the notion of 'psychological containment' was developed by Captain Wilfred Bion, tank commander and later psychotherapist. He described the effect of cumulative strain at the battle of Amiens in August 1918 which made him feel 'just like a small child' who 'wants to be put to bed by its mother', noting how he 'lay down on a bank by the side of the road 'just as if I was lying peacefully in someone's arms'.[12]

Richard Holmes also believed that serious injuries were more distressing than dead bodies. Captain Robert Ross encountered a hospital train in France in May 1915 and noted: 'The silent endurance on the faces of the sufferers made a greater impression

---

5   J.F. Lucy, *There's a Devil in the Drum*, p.280.
6   J. Blacker (ed.), *Have You Forgotten Yet?*, p.131.
7   C. Davison (ed.), *The Burgoyne Diaries*, p.163.
8   M. Roper, *The Secret Battle*, p.248.
9   P.E. Hodgkinson & M. Stewart, *Coping With Catastrophe*, p.31.
10  A. Eden, *Another World*, p.111.
11  Roper, op. cit. p.260.
12  W. Bion, *War Memoirs*, p.122.

on my mind than the sight of the dead lying in swathes'.[13] Holmes's view was that witnessing disablement/mutilation changes the nature of fear.[14] It certainly broadens its base from a fear of death and sudden oblivion to include both a fear of surviving changed and knowing too much, or a fear of being obliterated so that there was no evidence one had ever existed. The dead needed nothing in their own right, but every account of wounding focusses on the helplessness of those around. Second-Lieutenant Bernard Martin declared himself unperturbed by death. What troubled him 'more than words can tell', were the wounded about whose plight he could do nothing: 'I had no idea how to cope'.[15] Often, the wounded suffered out of reach of help. Seaman Joseph Murray on Gallipoli noted that it was 'heart-rending' to leave a man to die of his wounds in no-man's land, from whence they could not be recovered.[16] Private George Coppard described how: 'One could hardly bear thinking about the agony of the badly wounded who lay unattended'.[17] Major Harold Bidder had a similar dread: 'What one dared not think about was the wounded lying between the lines'.[18] Gerald Burgoyne noted that 'it was too awful', in the aftermath of an attack, to watch the wounded in between the lines of trenches moving and calling for help and 'be able to do nothing'.[19] A dead man made no sound, but the cries of the wounded could be intolerable. Second-Lieutenant James Hyndson, on the Aisne in September 1914, found it 'heartrending to hear the poor fellows cry out for help and not be able to do anything'.[20] On the Apex, Rhododendron Ridge, Gallipoli, in August 1915, Private Benjamin Smart was tortured by the cries of the wounded which 'nearly drove us mad'.[21] Similarly, Second-Lieutenant Patrick Campbell, trapped by shellfire at Ypres in 1917, had to listen to the sounds of wounded men. 'I learnt to distinguish the different crying voices. Sometimes one stopped, and did not start again'. It was a relief to him when this happened, as 'the pain of the crying was unendurable'.[22]

To be asked for help by a wounded man and to be unable to provide it was paticularly difficult. In late 1918, Lieutenant-Colonel Charles Clayton, a man normally not expressive of his feelings, found a field full of the wounded. 'The ghastly pale faces and beseeching looks of some of them is pitiful', he wrote.[23] Private Edward Glendenning of the Sherwood Foresters, pulling back from 46th Division's catastrophic assault on the Hohenzollern Redoubt at Loos on 13 October 1915 experienced much the same.

13  R.B. Ross, *The Fifty-First in France*, p.24.
14  R. Holmes, *Firing Line*, pp.181-2.
15  B. Martin, *Poor Bloody Infantry*, p.72.
16  J. Murray, *Gallipoli 1915*, p.84.
17  G. Coppard, *With a Machine Gun To Cambrai*, p.81.
18  Orex (H.F. Bidder), *Three Chevrons*, p.76.
19  Davison, op. cit. p.152.
20  J.G.W. Hyndson, *From Mons to the First Battle of Ypres*, Kindle version location 610.
21  B. Smart quoted in J. Crawford, *No Better Death*, Kindle edition location 5565.
22  P.J. Campbell, *In the Cannon's Mouth*, p.80.
23  C.P. Clayton, *The Hungry One*, p.228.

He passed men 'crying out and begging for water ... they plucked at our legs as we went by'. One grabbed him by both legs and Glendenning was about to give him water when he was forced to move on. 'In the years that have passed that man's pleadings have haunted me', he remarked.[24] Following the cry of 'Stretcher bearers!' the wounded were, however, often able to be removed – the dead most frequently were not.

**The Dead**

On his arrival in trenches opposite High Wood on the Somme in 1916, Second-Lieutenant Max Plowman tripped over a lump on the floor of a foul smelling trench. It was a corpse. 'Literally we are living among the dead', he wrote.[25] There is virtually no personal account of the Great War that does not describe the omnipresence of the dead, sometimes in great detail. In the twenty-first century, contact with human remains which are gruesome due to damage or decay is viewed as a potential cause of psychological trauma. For the modern soldier it is documented that exposure to human remains on the battlefield is indeed traumatic.

There are three studies which lead to this conclusion. Firstly, a review of American military personnel identifying and repatriating the remains of soldiers killed in the First Gulf War of 1991 showed a significant increase in physical symptoms of stress, the extent of symptoms corresponding with degree of exposure.[26] Higher levels of intrusive thoughts and images and indications of mental avoidance were found in soldiers handling human remains.[27] These are symptoms of Post-Traumatic Stress Disorder (PTSD). Secondly, a further study of American troops on graves registration duty in the same conflict revealed half with sufficient symptomatology to warrant a diagnosis of PTSD. This was strongly associated with depressive and substance abuse disorders.[28] Thirty-five per cent of these affected soldiers specifically referred to the stress of exposure to body parts, including 'identifying with bodies and personalizing the trauma'.[29] 'Identifying' with the dead means, in this instance, seeing oneself in the dead person's place, e.g. with relatives grieving. It is this process of thinking which gives trauma its specific meaning, and which may particularly undermine subsequent coping. Thirdly, a study of British troops similarly engaged in the Army War Graves

---

24   E.W. Glendenning, quoted in M. Arthur, *Forgotten Voices of the Great War*, pp.101-2.
25   Mark VII (M. Plowman), *A Subaltern on the Somme*, pp.45-6.
26   J.E. McCarrol et. al., 'Somatic Symptoms in Gulf War Mortuary Workers', *Psychosomatic Medicine*, p.29.
27   J.E. McCarrol et. al., 'Symptoms of PTSD Following Recovery of War Dead', *American Journal of Psychiatry*, p.939.
28   P.B. Sutker et. al., 'Psychological Symptoms and Psychiatric Diagnoses in Operation Desert Storm Troops Serving Graves Registration Duty', *Journal of Traumatic Stress*, p.159.
29   Sutker, op. cit. p.168.

Service in this war found that, despite preparation and training, after nine months half of those involved had evidence of psychological disturbance suggestive of PTSD.[30]

Historians have noted the reactions of the Great War soldier to the confrontation with human remains and death. Richard Holmes tended to play this down, suggesting that the brutality of the Western Front held similarities with the worst of working class life. Soldiers had 'simply exchanged one harsh and violent environment for another'.[31] This argument assumes that the hardships of ordinary working class life were of the same order as those of the trenches, and it is not convincing. In terms of the confrontation specifically with death, the word 'inured' is often used, e.g. 'as men became inured to wounds, so they also did to the sight of corpses'.[32] Another term frequently used is 'hardened', e.g. 'men quickly hardened to death'.[33] David Cannadine described what he believed was 'numbness combined with callousness', two rather different concepts.[34] Malcolm Brown uses a different word which is less pejorative, in writing that: 'The very scale of the slaughter seems to have produced its own anaesthesia'.[35] Tim Travers is undoubtedly more correct in describing 'adaptation ... through desensitisation and numbing',[36] whilst Peter Liddle presents an alternative to the 'norm of brutality' argument, suggesting that acceptance of death was an unavoidable 'acceptance of reality'. He agrees with Travers that 'accommodation' to an unavoidable situation is a more accurate analysis than simple hardening, which 'implies an insensitive coarsened brutality'.[37] As we shall see, soldiers did not necessarily became either anaesthetised, numb, callous or inured. They adapted creatively, an adaptation which was fluid rather than permanent.

**Victorian and Edwardian Attitudes to the Dead**

In the later Victorian and Edwardian eras people were becoming *less* used to death. The death rate fell from 18.1 per 1,000 per year in 1880 to 14.8 in 1908.[38] More children survived into adulthood and life expectancy increased from an average of 40 years in 1850 to 52 for men and 55 for women by 1911-12.[39] This was due to an improved standard of living, reforms in public health which reduced disease, and better nutrition. Working class men who set out for the Western Front had a greater expectation

---

30  M.P. Deahl et. al., 'Psychological Sequelae Following the Gulf War', *British Journal of Psychiatry*, p.60.
31  R. Holmes, *Acts of War*, p.133.
32  A. Simpson, *Hot Blood and Cold Steel*, p.105.
33  R. van Emden & S. Humphries (eds), *Veterans*, p.123.
34  D. Cannadine, 'War and Death, Grief and Mourning in Modern Britain', in J. Whaley, *Mirrors of Mortality*, p.187.
35  M. Brown, *Tommy Goes to War*, p.204.
36  T. Travers, *Gallipoli 1915*, p.178.
37  P.H. Liddle, *Men of Gallipoli*, p.225.
38  B.R. Mitchell & P. Deane, *Abstract of British Historical Statistics*, pp.36-7.
39  R. Mitchison, *British Population Change since 1860*, pp.39-57.

of life than ever before. The differential longevity between men and women, however, was largely due to the increased risk from death by accidents and violence amongst men. The coal-mining industry held the greatest number of occupational fatalities, and mining communities were familiar with a varying scale of tragedy. Britain's worst mining disaster occurred at the Senghenydd Colliery near Caerphilly on 14 October 1913, when 439 were killed. When considering the scale of the tragedy that befell, say, the town of Accrington on 1 July 1916, when 235 were killed and 350 wounded from the ranks of the Accrington Pals (11th East Lancashire), it might be thought that British working communities could be considered somewhat used to mass death. Simple numbers such as these are, however, deceptive. Such major catastrophes were the exception rather than the rule, and it was the scale of the steadily creeping attrition that made the mounting community tragedy of the First World War so different to the incidence of occupational death of the pre-war years.

The First World War occurred at a time of changing attitudes towards death. Pat Jalland suggests that amongst the middle and upper-classes in the late Victorian and Edwardian eras: 'There were signs of a growing uneasiness about dying, combined with greater emotional inhibition and a loss of the familiarity and assurance about death'. There was a much stronger attitude that death was 'shocking', and that witnessing a death was 'something to be avoided'.[40] This belief came to be much more strongly held as the twentieth century progressed. Even if the Victorian notion of the Christian 'Good Death' was losing power, sudden, violent deaths, which the Great War was to provide in such terrible abundance, were looked upon with dismay in relation to the lack of preparation of the departing soul.

In contrast, the working-classes still had a greater familiarity with death, largely because the cramped arrangement of many working-class homes 'necessitated sharing living space with the sick, the dying and the dead'.[41] Death was talked about in a forthright manner, and 'sharing domestic space with a cadaver was a necessity that left little room for squeamishness or fear'.[42] The very closest encounters with the dead were the province of women, however. The laying out of the dead, washing the body and plugging orifices, was almost exclusively carried out by female family members. Viewing a corpse was universal in working class communities. Thus, 'everybody used to go and look at dead people',[43] as 'it was the thing everyone did in those days'.[44] Adults thought it was good for children to be involved. Private G. Fortune, burying the deceased at a hospital behind the lines wrote:

---

40 P. Jalland, *Death in the Victorian Family*, p.54.
41 J.M. Strange, *Death, Grief and Poverty in Britain*, p.30.
42 Strange, op. cit. p.69.
43 Quoted in Strange, op. cit. p.80.
44 Quoted in Strange, op. cit. p.83.

I was 17 and already acquainted with death. My father brought us up like that. He would let us see our grandparents after death. Our teacher at school let us go to see our priest, Father Broder, when he died, and those who wanted to, kissed him. We nearly all kissed him, for we loved him.[45]

Fortune is here describing confronting death in a sanitised way. Even in civilian life during this period, 'corpses that bore the marks of a horrific and violent death' were, however, 'less likely to be displayed'.[46] Thus, whilst the working-classes were still much more familiar with death than the middle and upper-classes, they shared their discomfort with sudden violent death to a certain extent. The claim that the loss of a family member happened to those 'so bound up with the material problems of life that at worst it seemed no more than an intensification of the misery of existence' is both unfair and inaccurate.[47] It implies an insensitivity to death on the part of the working classes, and leads directly to the idea that the working-man in arms became inured to death on the battlefield through lack of finer feelings.

**Human Remains on the Great War Battlefields**

The Great War soldier was never able to escape the dead. In his civilian life there was a process that led to a dead body leaving the world of the living, but on the battlefield soldiers' corpses were often simply abandoned. The presence of the dead became enshrined in the names given to the landscape. Private Herbert Butt noted on the Somme that there was 'a place along the Sunken Road called Death Valley on account of the dead lying around there'.[48] Rather than leave them exposed, the dead were sometimes lightly covered with earth. John Masefield described the Leipzig Salient on the Somme thus: 'Old wet rags of uniform were everywhere, & bones & legs & feet & heads were sticking out of the ground'.[49] Sometimes corpses were simply built into a trench wall, a practice that Second-Lieutenant Huntly Gordon thought of as 'going rather far in human degradation'.[50] Private Patrick Macgill was party to such inhumations: 'Our boys, engaged in building a new parapet, were heaping the sandbags on dead men'.[51] Charles Douie similarly noted on the Somme at the inappropriately named Hope Post, Munich Trench how 'as each man died he was added to the breastwork by his surviving comrades'.[52] As a company commander, Rowland Feilding simi-

---

45   G. Fortune, Private Papers, IWM Docs 12967.
46   Strange, op. cit. p.86.
47   D. Vincent, 'Love and Death and the Nineteenth-Century Working Class', *Social History*, p.233.
48   H.R. Butt, Private Papers, IWM Docs 6771.
49   P. Vansittart (ed.), *John Masefield's Letters*, p.206.
50   H. Gordon, *The Unreturning Army*, Kindle edition location 1674.
51   P. MacGill, *Great Push*, p.86.
52   Douie, op. cit. p.178.

larly described to his wife, the parapets of his trench were 'dovetailed with ... (dead bodies) ... and everywhere arms, legs and heads protrude'.[53]

As Feilding implied, bodies often re-emerged, for which there were three main reasons. The first was digging. Captain John Glubb noted: 'We have been digging out a lot of these trenches again, and are constantly coming upon corpses'. These remains were 'pretty well decomposed, but a pickaxe brings up chips of bone and rags of clothing. The rest is putrid grey matter'.[54] Lieutenant Sidney Rogerson on the Somme in 1916 described how men vomited over the task of digging new trenches, for 'bodies were unearthed at every yard'. 'Most pitiful' was the unearthing of a dug-out 'where sat huddled three Scottish officers, their faces mercifully shrouded by the grey of the gas-masks they had donned when death came upon them'.[55] The second reason for reappearance was shellfire. Private Bertie Sporton noted how a shell landed nearby and 'lifted a buried man out of his grave'.[56] Similarly, after a heavy bombardment on the Somme, Private Giles Eyre described how 'fearsome bits of human remains that had lain buried had been churned up anew and flung all about the place'.[57] Lastly, bodies were washed out by rain. Trooper W. Clarke observed: 'When the rains came ... you'd see a boot and puttees sticking out, or an arm or hand, sometimes faces'.[58] Captain Lionel Crouch similarly noted: 'The rain is disclosing all sorts of interesting souvenirs behind my trenches'. With wry, if macabre humour, finding 'two fine skulls' he 'carried one on the end of my stick and planted him at the head of a communication trench'.[59]

### *What aspects of the dead were disturbing?*[60]

On his first tour of duty in the trenches at Cuinchy and Givenchy in late 1915, Second-Lieutenant Bernard Adams suffered two casualties, and wrote 'I think the novelty and interest of these first casualties made them easy to bear. I was so busy noticing details'.[61] Arriving on the battlefields, Second-Lieutenant Edwin Vaughan met the dead: 'Lying flat on their backs, with marble faces rigid and calm'. This was his first sight of dead men and he was surprised that it did not upset him. Upset or not, it clearly made a greater impression than he reckoned, because he continued: 'The

---

53 R. Feilding, *War Letters to a Wife*, p.31.
54 J. Glubb, *Into Battle*, p.48.
55 S. Rogerson, *Twelve Days on the Somme*, p.5.
56 B.V. Sporton, Private Papers, IWM Docs 11731.
57 G.E.M. Eyre, *Somme Harvest*, p.205.
58 W. Clarke, Private Papers, IWM Docs 1377.
59 L.W. Crouch, *Letters from the Front*, p.52.
60 The data analysis in this chapter is based on 444 descriptive references to the encounter with corpses on the battlefield extracted from the published accounts, unpublished manuscripts, (and accounts quoted in secondary sources) of 263 officers and other ranks. (P. Hodgkinson, 'Human Remains on the Great War Battlefield – Coping with Death in the Trenches').
61 B. Adams, *Nothing of Importance*, p.36.

one with the black face has stayed with me ... stamped on my brain'.[62] Private Alfred Burrage's first such encounter was with a single dead German, and he noted it was the first dead body he had seen other than his father's. 'Physically and spiritually sick', he wondered how he 'was going to face the Real Thing when it came'.[63] Burrage was squeamish about the sight of blood, but in the aftermath of a shell strike, putting body parts in sandbags, he found that he 'derived an odd sort of comfort at finding that I could endure it'.[64] He had adapted.

The disturbing features of battlefield corpses can be largely categorised according to the senses of smell, vision and touch.

### (i) Smell

Recently arrived in the front line, Private Ernest Parker became 'conscious of a sickening smell' that he would soon come to recognise as 'familiar evidence of the unburied or disinterred dead'.[65] This was unavoidable everywhere on the battlefield. At Loos, George Coppard described the 'sickly odour of death ... it was repulsive'.[66] On the Somme, Giles Eyre wrote how 'an indescribable smell of corruption rises up; the air is thick with it',[67] and how smell would strike 'as with a physical blow, overpowering, suffocating'.[68] In Second-Lieutenant Graham Greenwell's view, the 'awful stench is much worse than the shelling'.[69] Douglas Cuddeford arrived in a shellhole during the battle of Arras where there were three dead Germans. He found the smell so appalling that he ran to another as he would 'rather be cleanly shot than asphyxiated'.[70] Alfred Griffin wrote: 'There's nothing like a dead body's smell. It's a putrid, decaying smell ... you can't describe unless you've smelt rotten meat'. It was unavoidable as 'You've got the smell right under your nose all the time'.[71]

There are a large number of references to smell in personal accounts. Such smells were often of a nature to induce physical revulsion. Private Alfred Griffin described how smell 'makes you stop breathing',[72] and Gunner Frank Bloor vomited as it 'makes you heave your heart up'.[73] Second-Lieutenant Arthur Young stated: 'The smell turned us sick'.[74] Smell tainted everything. A French soldier recorded: 'We all had on us the stench of dead bodies. The bread we ate, the stagnant water we drank, everything we

---

62  E.C. Vaughan, *Some Desperate Glory*, p.32.
63  Ex-Private X (A.M. Burrage), *War is War*, p.46.
64  Burrage, op. cit. p.67.
65  E.W. Parker, *Into Battle*, p.27.
66  Coppard, op. cit. p.31.
67  Eyre, op. cit. p.127.
68  Eyre, op. cit. p.198.
69  G.H. Greenwell, *An Infant in Arms*, p.153.
70  Cuddeford, op. cit. p.177.
71  Griffin, op. cit.
72  A. Griffin, IWM Sound 9101.
73  F. Bloor, Private Papers, IWM Docs 7819.
74  A. Young cited in Housman, op. cit. p.310.

touched had a rotten smell'.[75] Smell was the cause of a truce at the ANZAC positions on Gallipoli on 24 May 1915. Five days earlier a Turkish attack had been repulsed with heavy loss of life, and as Charles Bean, the Australian official historian noted: 'The conditions threatened to become intolerable for the troops' of both sides.[76]

Smell was variably described (in descending order of frequency of word use) as: 'awful', 'appalling', 'horrible', 'sickening', 'filthy', 'nauseating', 'foul', 'ghastly', 'terrible', 'revolting', 'fearful', 'annihilating', 'vile', 'unbearable', 'intolerable', 'overpowering', 'wicked', and 'cruel'. There was a difference between the smell of the newly dead and the decayed. Private Frederick Bolwell, at First Ypres in 1915, spent a day in a trench with recently killed men. The stench was 'sickening', and, clearly familiar with it in civilian life, the smell was of 'warm blood as from a slaughterhouse'.[77] The most frequently used qualitative description of the longer dead used was 'sickly', but also 'sweetish', 'sour,' 'acrid', and 'oily'. Interestingly, Private C. Miles reckoned that 'you could always tell whether it was a dead Jerry or a dead Tommy'. Although he did not describe the difference, for him 'the Germans smelt different in death'.[78] Inventive soldiers employed a range of techniques to reduce the impact of smell. The official remedy was chloride of lime, applied by both British and German armies. Second-Lieutenant Cecil Longley found the remedy worse than the affliction, writing about the 'appalling smell of chlorate of lime – supposed to deodorise'. The two smells 'dodge one another along every trench, neither overcoming the other', the effect being one of 'gripping you in the midriff with a horrible continuous nausea'.[79] On Gallipoli, Major John Gillam noted in his diary: 'I know of no more sickly smell than chloride of lime with the smell of a dead body blended in'.[80] Others became inventive. Private Herbert Cooper, troubled by German corpses recounted how: 'I wore the mouth and nose piece of my gas mask all the time'.[81] Raymond Lodge, a pioneer officer working at Hooge, wrote that 'the men in such places work with their respirators on' yet were still 'often actually sick'.[82] On Gallipoli during the ANZAC burial truce, Aubrey Herbert recorded that: 'A Turkish Red Crescent man came and gave me some antiseptic wool with scent on it, and this they renewed frequently'.[83] Graham Greenwell rubbed an unknown substance 'frozacalone' under his nose.[84] Corporal Charles Smith smeared foot powder on his face.[85] Similarly troubled, Brigadier-General James Jack

---

75  J. Ellis, *Eye Deep in Hell*, p.59.
76  C.E.W. Bean, *The Official History of Australia in the War, Vol II*, p.164.
77  F.A. Bolwell, *With a Reservist in France*, p.103.
78  C. Miles quoted in L. McDonald, *They Called it Passchendaele*, p.187.
79  C.W. Longley, *Battery Flashes*, p.133.
80  J.J. Gillam, *Gallipoli Diary*, p.152.
81  H.H. Cooper, Private Papers, IWM Docs 10892.
82  O.J. Lodge, *Raymond*, p.65.
83  A. Herbert *Mons, Anzac and Kut*, p.115.
84  Greenwell, op. cit. p.155.
85  C.I. Smith quoted in P. Hart, *The Somme*, p.313.

used a 'smelling salts bottle given years ago by an old aunt without any thought of this purpose'.[86] In 1917 at Third Ypres, Huntly Gordon described concrete shelters which were half full of stagnant water where he and his fellows had to crouch down on planks supported at water level over a heap of corpses underneath. The smell was so bad that they all had to 'smoke continuously to keep it down'.[87] Captain Henry Ogle used the same tactic – pleading that he never had a strong stomach he 'smoked Digger Mixture in a corn cob until my mouth felt like pickled leather'.[88] Private Harry Drinkwater, in a shellhole on the Somme in 1916, put his hand through a dead German's chest. Although he became covered in maggots, it was the smell he could not deal with, 'so I lit my pipe and blew the smoke into my haversack'.[89] The smells of dead animals were equally nauseating. Private George Ashurst described the 'almost unbearable' stench of a dead cow in no-man's land. The solution was for two men to crawl out a night with a can of petrol, an officer setting off the cremation with 'star lights'.[90]

It is clear that smell was problematic to accommodate. Indeed, it is much more difficult to cognitively transform a smell than a visual image, hence creating an adaptive mechanism is problematic. Only one combatant, the redoubtable Gurkha Lieutenant-Colonel William Villiers-Stuart could claim of the smell of corpses mixed with chloride of lime: 'One got used to it – not to mind it – and in the end to almost miss it'.[91] More typical was the reaction of Lieutenant Reginald Dixon who stated that he 'never grew accustomed to the all-pervading smell of decayed and decaying flesh'.[92] Major Albert Mure described on Gallipoli how one could get 'used to anything in war' except the 'acrid pungent odour of the unburied dead, which gets into your very mouth, down your tortured throat, and seems even to taint and taste your food'. It was for him the worst thing he had to face on active service.[93] The power of smell as imagery was noted by Reverend Julian Bickersteth: 'One talks of not being able to get scenes and sounds out of one's mind. The same is true of smells'.[94] Even the exceptionally hardy Brigadier-General Adrian Carton de Wiart recorded that his 'worst memory was the stench of putrefying bodies', a memory that lingered: 'I could smell them still'.[95]

---

86  J. Terraine (ed.), *General Jack's Diary*, p.164.
87  Gordon, op. cit, location 1674.
88  H. Ogle, *The Fateful Battle Line*, pp.103-4.
89  J. Cooksey & D. Griffiths (eds), *Harry's War*, p.147.
90  G. Ashurst, *My Bit*, p.40.
91  R.M. Maxwell (ed.), *Villiers-Stuart Goes to War*, p.57.
92  R.G. Dixon, Private Papers, IWM Docs 2001.
93  A.H. Mure, *With the Incomparable 29th*, p.162.
94  J. Bickersteth (ed.), *The Bickersteth Diaries*, p.59.
95  A. Carton de Wiart, *Happy Odyssey*, p.91.

198  Glum Heroes

**(ii) Vision**
Reginald Dixon provides an example of how the dead assaulted vision: 'Their rotten faces stared blindly at us from coverlets of mud; their decaying buttocks heaved themselves obscenely from the filth ... skulls grinned at us'.[96] George Coppard, in describing a pile of mixed British and German corpses agreed that it was not possible to ignore such sights: 'I found it hard to keep my eyes away from them. No matter where I looked I could not avoid them'.[97] Comments which give detailed impressions of the visual appearance of corpses largely fall into four categories, individuals remarking negatively on dismemberment, colour, posture and changed shape.

*(a) Dismemberment*
Dismemberment was often more disturbing than a whole body. Second-Lieutenant Guy Chapman stated that although 'I could look on bodies unmoved, I could not abide bare fresh bones'.[98] At Mametz Wood in 1916, Second-Lieutenant Llewellyn Griffith wrote that 'there were worse sights than corpses. Limbs and mutilated trunks, here and there a detached head'.[99] Giles Eyre described stretcher-bearers on the Somme 'gathering arms, legs and blobs of flesh from amongst the debris shoving them into sandbags anyhow'. He was revolted, viewing the scene with 'sickened feelings and bulging eyes'.[100] At the Butte de Warlencourt, John Masefield noted with horror that 'there were a lot of enemy dead, torn in two & across & generally bedevilled, poor men, & a lot of rats, who probably live upon them, as they were rather gnawed'.[101] At Mouquet Fram he recorded that 'corpses, rats ... legs, boots, skulls ... parts of rotting bodies & festering heads lie scattered about'.[102] He concluded: 'Although I'm pretty callous now I can hardly keep from crying when I see these dead'.[103]

Akin to dismemberment as Masefield implied was the destruction of bodies through insect infestation and animal attack. In the heat of the Somme 1916 summer Captain Francis Hitchcock described corpses 'sitting up straight, their mouths wide open, and full of horrible black flies'.[104] Rats similarly make frequent appearance in accounts of trench life, consuming human flesh. Hitchcock described the corpses of French soldiers left to decompose in the sun providing 'a feast for the rats'. These creatures were 'a colossal size, almost as big as dogs'.[105] Such tales are often viewed as apocryphal yet, at least in terms of size, contemporary photographs suggest they are

---

96  Dixon, op. cit.
97  Coppard, op. cit. p.39.
98  G. Chapman, *A Passionate Prodigality*, p.169.
99  L.W. Griffith, *Up to Mametz*.
100 Eyre, op. cit. p. 228.
101 Vansittart, op. cit. p.221.
102 Vansittart, op. cit. p.263.
103 Vansittart, op. cit. p.240.
104 F.C. Hitchcock, *Stand To*, p.166.
105 Hitchcock, op. cit. p.197.

not. Relatively accustomed to rats, Edwin Vaughan and comrades 'found a huge cat squatting on the chest of a dead German, eating his face'. Suddenly fastidious, he 'sent two men to chase it away'.[106]

*(b) Colour*
Soldiers perceived many colours in the appearance of the dead and recorded them in detail. Medical Officer Captain Charles McKerrow described a dead German's face as being of a *'piebald* hue'.[107] Second-Lieutenant Richard Gale recalled of a dead German: 'His face was a *ghastly grey colour,* like marble in which there was a *tinge of blue*'.[108] Corporal C. Lane encountered a trench full of dead Germans, noting that 'they were all different colours, from *pallid grey to green and black*'.[109] Lieutenant Stuart Cloete recorded that 'the sun swelled up the dead with gas and often turned them blue, almost *navy blue*'.[110] At High Wood, Max Plowman observed a corpse on a stretcher. 'It bears the body of a boy: the face *quite black*'.[111] Surrounded by dead French soldiers, Ernst Junger described 'flesh like mouldering fish gleamed *greenishly*' with 'a few strands of hair on the *bluish-black* skull', and how 'white cartilage gleamed out of *reddish-black* flesh'.[112] On Gallipoli, Compton McKenzie misplaced his foot: 'Looking down I saw squelching up from the ground on either side of my boot like a rotten mango the deliquescent *green and black* flesh of a Turk's head'.[113] Guy Chapman detailed how the dead were variously *'yellow or grey or blue* with the blood dried *black* on their skin and clothes'.[114] It is clear from the quality of the descriptions that such sights lived in memory.

*(c) Posture*
Accounts often refer to the strange postures of the dead. Second-Lieutenant Robert Graves was surprised 'at some of the attitudes in which the dead stiffened'.[115] At Hill 60 Second-Lieutenant Arthur Greg described how 'I didn't like the carpet of Bavarian bodies; their limbs were so horrible arranged'.[116] On Gallipoli a soldier recorded 'bodies sprawling around in all manner of horribly grotesque postures. To me the scene was the personification of stark, naked horror'.[117] Private Hugh Quigley, at Ypres in 1917, described that 'the remembrance of one attitude will always haunt me', a dead

---

106 Vaughan, op. cit. p.94.
107 C. McKerrow, Private Papers, IWM Docs 2386 (author italics).
108 R.N. Gale, quoted in R. Holmes, *Acts of War*, p.177 (author italics).
109 C. Lane quoted in Arthur, op. cit. p.161-2 (author italics).
110 S. Cloete, *A Victorian Son*, p.236 (author italics).
111 Mark VII, op. cit. p.45 (author italics).
112 E. Junger, *Storm of Steel*, pp.25-6 (author italics).
113 C. McKenzie, *Gallipoli Memories*, p.79 (author italics).
114 Chapman, op. cit. p.252 (author italics).
115 R. Graves, *Goodbye to All That*, p.143.
116 A. Greg quoted in N. Cave, *Hill 60*, p.65.
117 R.R. James, *Gallipoli*, p.233.

German doubled up with his knees under his chin and his 'hand clutching hair above a face of the ghastliest terror'.[118] Again on Gallipoli in the Kereves Dere, a French officer wrote of the dead lying in 'confused heaps' and that some of the 'attitudes were extraordinary. Some were in postures of attack, others of defence'. He concluded: 'It was awful. It might have been a drunken orgy'.[119] Stuart Cloete observed that bodies 'dried up like mummies and were frozen in their death positions'. He was particularly struck by 'a man bandaging himself who has been killed by a shell fragment as he unrolled the bandage'.[120] Private Aubrey Smith noted corpses 'in all kinds of attitudes, lying with their faces downwards, huddled in funk-holes, flung backwards with hands raised as if to avert a blow'.[121] Private Frank Richards similarly described a man 'on his knees in a boxing attitude' whilst another had died 'with his right hand pointing straight in front of him'. At Arras in 1917 he encountered a corpse 'down on one knee with his rifle at his shoulder as if he was about to fire'.[122]

Soldiers wanted to understand how the dead had come to be in a certain position. Thus, Private T. Jennings pondered on three dead German soldiers 'kneeling in a pool of blood'. Their faces 'from the forehead to the chin were missing' but Jennings was more preoccupied with the question 'why were they kneeling?'. He pondered: 'Had they been at prayer?'[123] Similarly, on the Somme, George Coppard described British dead on the German barbed wire hanging in 'grotesque postures'. Some looked 'as though they were praying'.[124] It is interesting that posture was often given a religious dimension. At the Battle of Loos, Private W. Walker noted: 'A giant Scotsman stretched out in the posture of crucifixion' and as with Coppard and Jennings, 'a young fair lad of the Lincolnshires, kneeling as if in prayer'.[125] Private John Lawton also described: 'A sergeant quite dead and who, apparently, died in the attitude of prayer', thinking him a 'splendid example for the men who passed that spot continually'.[126] It is almost as if these observers hoped that such soldiers left their earthly life in contact with their God.

*(d) Changed shape*
Decay changed the shape of the human body in disturbing ways. On the Somme, Giles Eyre described exposing 'the dead *bloated* face and upper portion of a Boche'.[127] Gunner Bloor noted bodies '*four times their normal size* owing to the intense heat.

---

118 H. Quigley, *Passchendaele and the Somme*, p.124.
119 James, op. cit. p.155.
120 Cloete, op. cit. p.236.
121 A. Smith, *Four Years on the Western Front*, p.382.
122 F. Richards, *Old Soldiers Never Die*, p.129.
123 T.A. Jennings, Private Papers, IWM Docs 6596.
124 Coppard, op cit. p.83.
125 W. Walker, Diary, http://www.firstworldwar.com/diaries/battleofloos.htm.
126 J.T. Lawton, Private Papers, IWM Docs 2787.
127 Eyre, op. cit. p.205 (author italics).

Awful sights'.[128] Similarly, at Hooge, Francis Hitchcock saw dead men with faces '*swollen* from the three days' exposure to the August sun, and quite unrecognisable'.[129] Joe Murray on Gallipoli wrote how 'within a matter of hours corpses that are exposed to the sun *swell to an incredible size*'.[130] As Ernst Junger discovered, these changes meant that the dead could be noisy. Behind him he 'heard a stifled, unpleasant sound' which came from a 'bloated disintegrating corpse'.[131] Similarly, he was dismayed by 'a quiet hissing and burbling sound'. Moving closer he encountered two bodies which the heat 'had awakened to a ghostly type of life'.[132] Ralph Scott recorded in his diary turning over what he thought to be a dead German, whereupon 'he grunted fiercely like a man awakening from a heavy sleep'. Scott went for his revolver, but then realised the truth, that the sound was the 'gases of decomposition being forced through his mouth when I turned him over'.[133]

### (iii) Touch

Corpses could be briefly touched with equanimity if there was a purpose, such as throwing them over the parados for disposal. On Gallipoli, the Reverend Oswin Creighton who had buried many dead and had sat with men as they died, found himself in a field of corpses at Gurkha Bluff, and having no such purpose wrote in his diary that whilst 'I can stand most things now', he 'could not touch them'.[134] Bernard Martin had a number of men from his platoon buried by shellfire in a Russian sap. He entered it with another officer in case any were left alive, but when he encountered the first corpse he could not touch it. He found himself 'the victim of an obsession',[135] a 'foolish fear of touching a harmless dead man, an empty body. And I was ashamed'.[136] Inadvertent contact, particularly that which was sudden and close, could elicit a worse reaction. Edwin Vaughan had a particularly unpleasant close contact: 'My hand sunk into the open skull and I recoiled in horror'.[137] On his first patrol in no-man's land Second-Lieutenant Alec Dawson similarly placed his hand in the 'upturned face of a far-gone corpse'. He had to contain his reaction of disgust in case the patrol was spotted.[138] Many references involve having to tread on corpses. Patrick Campbell described how there were so many dead, 'sometimes two or three on top of one another', that 'you had to look where you were going not to tread on them'.[139] Private C. Miles spoke

---

128  Bloor, op. cit. (author italics).
129  Hitchcock, op. cit. p.64 (author italics).
130  J. Murray, *Gallipoli as I Saw It*, p.75 (author italics).
131  Junger, op. cit. p.96.
132  Junger, op. cit. p.152.
133  R. Scott, *A Soldier's Diary*, p.120.
134  O. Creighton, *With the Twenty-Ninth Division in Gallipoli*, p.151.
135  Martin, op. cit. p.100.
136  Martin, op. cit. p.102.
137  Vaughan, op. cit. p.191.
138  A.J. Dawson, *A 'Temporary Gentleman' in France*, p.102.
139  Campbell, op. cit. p.64.

of how when the ground 'yielded under your feet you know that it was a body you were treading on'. For him, this was 'terrifying'. To add to his alarm, 'you'd tread on one on the stomach, perhaps, and it would grunt all the air out of its body. It made your hair stand on end'.[140]

### *Adapting to the dead*
Given what we now know to be disturbing in terms of the dead on the battlefield, Signaller Ron Buckell posed the question: 'Why in war does a trip over decayed bodies in every position and showing fearful expressions of pain on their black faces not affect one?'[141] The very things that were so unpleasant to many did not affect him at that moment. Private Stephen Graham noted the seeming contradiction in soldiers developing an 'extraordinary callousness' towards the dead yet at the same time being 'more intensely alive than before to the horror of dying themselves'.[142] Second-Lieutenant Siegfried Sassoon contrasted his own adapted reactions to those of a newly arrived subaltern walking amongst the dead and 'trying to behave as if it were all quite ordinary'. Sassoon reflected that he himself 'had grown accustomed to such sights', but was able to realize the impact they made on a 'fresh mind'.[143] Second-Lieutenant Robert Mackay was sympathetic to the newly-arrived encountering the dead: 'A man hardened to it does not mind so much, but it must be terrible for a new fellow'.[144] Patrick Campbell, new to the Western Front, sat in silence whilst other officers discussed the dead, reflecting: 'I had not seen the dead yet, I dreaded seeing them'.[145]

Soldiers like Sassoon and Mackay were aware of adaptation to the presence of human remains taking place. Another officer described that adaptation was simply a necessity: 'One must learn to be callous – or else break down', callousness being the 'only safe course'.[146] Gerald Burgoyne, referring to corpses, also used the same word, callous, but added: 'I'll never get used to it, it so disgusts me'.[147] Whenever he came across a corpse, he would have it buried. Corporal C. Clark agreed, being able to recover the bodies of mates lying within sight, 'you got callous pretty quick'. He was also clear that this stemmed from necessity: 'You couldn't be anything else. It was no use feeling anything else'.[148] Second-Lieutenant Billie Nevill disagreed with the use of this word. His men encountered a dead German whilst digging, and he wrote home of it being 'gruesome', adding however that 'I've been cured of squeamishness

---

140 Quoted in L. Macdonald, *They Called it Passchendaele*, p. 187.
141 E.R. Buckell, NAM 2002-09-9.
142 S. Graham, *A Private in the Guards*, p.239.
143 S. Sassoon, quoted in J.C. Dunn, *The War the Infantry Knew*, p.313.
144 R.L. Mackay, Diary, http://www.firstworldwar.com/diaries/rlm1.htm.
145 Campbell, op. cit. p.64.
146 'An Amateur Officer', *After Victory*, p.68 & p.30.
147 Davison, op. cit. p.117.
148 C. Clark quoted in M. Shadbolt, *Voices of Gallipoli*, p.45.

by now' but 'not to callousness of course'.[149] He was indicating that he had reached a point some way between revulsion and indifference – he had achieved control over his reactions. Captain Charles McKerrow clarified: 'When the dead lie all around you ... death becomes a very unimportant incident'. He agreed that 'it is not callousness', but 'just too much knowledge'.[150] Lieutenant Cecil Bowra, serving with the Royal Artillery, wrote of his comrades that 'on the surface they had developed what seemed to be callous indifference to death'. If someone was killed they might 'say "he's had it" or "that's another gonner"' but this was 'their defence against feelings which they might otherwise not have been able to master'.[151]

After a couple of weeks Robert Ross found that 'the ghastly sights and sounds had no terrors', with men 'preparing their meals beside the heaps of unburied bodies as if nothing in the world had happened'.[152] One of Patrick MacGill's fellow rankers stated that after exposure to so much, 'nothing disturbs me now'. As with some others he added: 'I never saw a dead person till I came here'.[153] On Gallipoli Private F.E. McKenzie wrote 'one saw a head and shoulders, then a few feet away, an arm then a leg'. Such sights being now common he could 'look at them without a shudder'.[154] Again, it was not callousness, but a matter of control. Sidney Rogerson on the Somme in 1916 noted a soldier describing a German corpse with the head separated from the body 'with no hint of either horror or disgust'.[155] Gunner Aubrey Wade, at the Steenbeek, Ypres, 'stepped gingerly' through a mass of the dead, noting his lack of reaction: 'I was not at all squeamish, the sight of dead men having long lost its terror for me'.[156] Frederic Manning described a corpse and looking 'indifferently at this piece of wreckage'.[157] Ernst Junger recorded that a dead body warranted 'no more than a passing thought' and that he and his fellows looked on one 'as we would a stone or a tree'.[158] Herbert Butt stated: 'We don't take any more notice of a dead person now than we do a rat'.[159] Both had stripped corpses of human significance. Charles Douie would write by 1917 of a dead man lying outside his headquarters dug out: 'He excited no more attention than if he had been asleep'.[160] The Reverend Eric Green, a Roman Catholic chaplain on Gallipoli, described passing corpses with a 'businesslike indifference'.[161] His words impart a sense of purposeful control.

149 R.E. Harris (ed.), *Billie – The Nevill Letters*, p.108.
150 C. McKerrow, Private Papers, IWM Docs 2386.
151 C.M. Bowra, *Memories*, pp.89-90.
152 Ross, op. cit. p.95.
153 P. MacGill, *Great Push*, p.140.
154 F.E. Mckenzie, quoted in Travers, op. cit. p.178.
155 Rogerson, op. cit. p.75.
156 A. Wade, *The War of the Guns*, p.55.
157 Manning, op. cit. location 72.
158 E. Junger, quoted in Holmes, *Acts of War*, p.180.
159 Butt, op. cit.
160 Douie, op. cit. p.200.
161 E. Green quoted in L. Macdonald, *Voices and Images of the Great War*, p.73.

Huntly Gordon implied that mental suppression was at the root of control for him, the task being to 'clamp down on the emotions'. He described how within a month he had come to recognise that 'one can't afford to think about it'. Not only had he learned to suppress emotion, he had redefined what a dead person meant: 'A smashed body is not a ghastly tragedy to fly from, but (a) mere shell, no longer human'.[162] Lieutenant-Colonel Ralph Hamilton also noted this sort of reframing: 'One can no longer look on them as dead human beings'.[163] Reginald Davis at Hill 60 had to lift dead bodies out of the trench and put them on the top of the parapets to keep passage clear. He similarly achieved a redefinition and his logic was brutal: 'You realise that fifty dead bodies are not equal to one living'.[164] Davis made an interesting distinction: 'Time and repeated experiences of this kind toughen if they do not harden a man'.[165] Lieutenant Montague Cleeve defined what was important: 'Eventually one just got over it and thought nothing of it'. In contrast to the dead: 'We were alive and that's what mattered. And being alive, we jolly well had to get on with it'.[166]

Huntly Gordon may have adapted within a month, but there was no clear timescale of adaptation. Frank Richards gave the same estimate to newly joined soldiers who 'turned a bit queer' at the sight of several hundred dead British soldiers. He informed them that 'if they were alive in *a month's time* they would take no more notice of a dead man than they would of a dead crow'.[167] When Private Walter Williams marched towards Thiepval for the opening day of the Somme offensive, his column encountered dead and rotting horses. Several men vomited. His sergeant retorted 'After *a couple of weeks* at the front ... you'll be cutting steaks off the likes of these beauties and thinking it a luxury'.[168] However, the process could clearly take place within a much shorter span. Thus, Private L. Thompson, arriving at Gallipoli, entered a marquee on the beach at Helles to find it was a mortuary: 'I'd never seen a dead man before and here I was looking at two or three hundred of them'. Describing this as 'our first fear' he perhaps naively noted: 'Nobody had mentioned this. I was very shocked'. Within a matter of days, however, this soldier could write wryly of human remains: 'We pushed them into the sides of the trench but bits of them kept getting uncovered and sticking out, like people in a badly made bed'.[169]

## *Mechanisms of adaptation*

Seven mechanisms of adaptation emerge from the references to the dead, although two were infrequently used.

---

162 Gordon, op. cit. location 1226.
163 R.G. Hamilton, *The War Diary of the Master of Belhaven*, p.251.
164 E. Hodder-Williams, *One Young Man*, Kindle edition location 335.
165 Hodder-Williams, op. cit. location 349.
166 M. Cleeve quoted in Arthur, op. cit. p.161.
167 Richards, op. cit. p.226 (italics author).
168 Williams, op. cit. location 740 (italics author).
169 L. Thompson quoted in J. Carey (ed.), *The Faber Book of Reportage* pp.451-2.

(i) DEHUMANISATION

The most common form of adaptation was the treatment of a corpse as an object. An anonymous body in the front line was stripped of its human significance and pragmatically transformed into something of use. On Gallipoli Joe Murray wrote of corpses: 'They served the requirements of the living.'[170] At Ypres, a gentle example is given by Gunner Austin Heraty who described how:

> In front of our guns ran a little gully ... There was one body that lay exposed right in front of my gun and the rains had washed the skeleton's bones like ivory ... his ribs formed a kind of trap which filtered the brushwood that flowed down the gully and left a clear space in the middle of clean rain water into which I used to dip my 'enamel mug' for a clean drop of water for a shave.[171]

Typically, a body was used to build up a trench wall, used as cover, or as an implement. Thirty-nine per cent of such references involved using dead bodies as some form of protection; 27 per cent as a seat or step; 12 per cent as a hook or lever; and 9 per cent as a landmark. Also on Gallipoli, Major George Davidson nonchalantly wrote home of 'a Turk on the top of whose grave I lunched with Pirie up in the firing line last Sunday'.[172] On the Somme Herbert Butt described using 'the dead bodies of Fritz to step on in the trenches to get out of the mud'.[173] Francis Hitchcock, in a water-filled trench at St Eloi, manoeuvred 'by hanging on to the foot of a Boche corpse' which was protruding from the parapet, and thus 'one managed to get to the post without getting drowned'.[174] He also described his brigadier objecting to a German leg protruding from the parapet and telling him to have it buried. Hitchcock 'overheard Finnegan remarking to the next man: "And what the bloody hell will I hang me equipment on now?"'[175] Rudolph Binding, on the other side of the front lines noted the legs of a British soldiers sticking out from the parapet and how 'a soldier hangs his rifle on them'.[176] Joe Murray recorded how his fellows would keep a packet of cigarettes between the toes of a skeleton known as 'Tootsie'.[177] Captain Arthur Dickson described how he learned the landmarks to guide himself about: 'Left by the coil of wire, right by the French legs', the legs in question protruding from the trench wall.[178]

Other uses may seem disrespectful to modern eyes used to the idea of the dead amidst the beauty of the Commonwealth War Graves Commission cemeteries. Thus,

---

170 Murray, *Gallipoli 1915*, p.88.
171 A.J. Heraty, Private Papers, IWM Docs 4609.
172 G. Davidson, *With the Incomparable 29th*, p.86.
173 Butt, op. cit.
174 Hitchcock, op. cit. p.118.
175 Hitchcock, op. cit. p.77.
176 R. Binding, quoted in Holmes, *Acts of War*, p.180.
177 J. Murray, *Gallipoli 1915*, p.126.
178 A.A. Dickson, Diaries, http://www.firstworldwar.com/diaries/varietiesoftrenchlife.htm.

a French doctor watching wiring at Kum Kale noted that as they had no poles, 'we make use of the hundreds of dead bodies lying in front of us'.[179] More dramatically, C.S. Alexander at Ypres noted that 'I have seen human bodies used as temporary railway sleepers and fascines for moving guns over'.[180] Such examples serve as an interesting counterpoint to the sentimentality that surrounded the Lincolnshire Point du Jour burials.

(ii) INTELLECTUALISATION

The next most frequently used mechanism was intellectualisation, often expressed in the form of a questing fascination. Rowland Feilding described how advancing over fought-over ground, his whole company would 'turn and look each time we passed a dead body'.[181] Frederic Manning noted glancing 'with a furtive curiosity' at corpses.[182] Soldiers undertook corpse-viewing trips. Stephen Graham described that there was 'fascination' in inspecting a multitude of bodies 'seeking and looking with great intensity in the heart'.[183] John Masefield described how his servant discovered a pile of enemy dead outside Delville Wood and 'went out for a stroll to see this sight'.[184] Edwin Vaughan divulged that he 'thoroughly enjoyed' wandering around with fellow officers looking at German corpses.[185] Whether a sense of triumphalism motivated this is not clear. Second-Lieutenant Edmund Blunden failed to understand this curiosity, especially in terms of what the dead implied: 'Why should these mortalities lure those who ought to be trying to forget mortality, ever threatening them?'[186]

Lieutenant Richard Kelly went sightseeing as a sort of emotional test, going to look at corpses and 'see what I felt'. He came upon a group of skeletal Germans, their bodies held together by sinews, seated in intact uniforms, finding them 'not a bit horrible'. Indeed, he found it a 'most weird and extraordinary picture and I was absolutely fascinated'.[187] Charles Carrington did the same, and used the same words. He had, somewhat unusually, never seen a corpse despite having been on the Western Front for six months and deliberately went to inspect dead Germans: 'I felt neither afraid nor unhappy but fascinated'. Clearly he was able to redefine what he was looking at: 'These things were less like men than the friendly earth to which they were returning'. He returned to his billet 'satisfied; I had seen a corpse'.[188] Huntly Gordon had similarly never seen a dead body before, and on his first visit to the front

---

179 James, op. cit. p.135.
180 C.S. Alexander, quoted in C. Pugsley, *On the Fringe of Hell*, p.251.
181 Feilding, op. cit. p.29.
182 Manning, op. cit. location 204.
183 S. Graham, quoted in D. Winter, *Death's Men*, p.207.
184 Vansittart, op. cit. p.206.
185 Vaughan, op. cit. p.89.
186 E. Blunden, *Undertones of War*, p.37.
187 R.T. Kelly quoted in Arthur, op. cit. p.90.
188 Edmonds, op. cit. p.49.

line found a soldier he assumed to be asleep until two bluebottles crawled from his nostrils. He recorded: 'I could hardly take my eyes off him'. Questions 'crowded into' his mind: 'How had he died?'[189] Similarly, Captain Robert Palmer who was detailed for burial duty in Mesopotamia noted that he also had never seen a dead person before and 'rather dreaded the effect on my queasy stomach'. He actually found that the task held no horror, but was like a 'sad and impersonal dream', with the corpses like 'waxen models'.[190] He, like Carrington, had achieved a reframing.

Emotional distance was achieved by treating corpses as if they were intellectual riddles to be solved. What had killed them? How had they come to die in that position? An officer at Gallipoli described how his men seemed to be 'obsessed with the novelty of corpses lying around the beaches'. They would drop whatever they were doing, wander over to the bodies, stare 'uncomprehendingly' at them, and note 'in a surprised tone of voice, "Say, mate, that un's gone west!"'[191] Gerald Burgoyne wrote of one dead man 'sitting up in a most lifelike attitude in the act of bandaging a wounded comrade. Both men were dead'. He speculated 'I suppose occasionally a bullet strikes some vital spot which destroys life and does not relax the muscles'.[192] Similarly, Second-Lieutenant Alfred Pollard described one such object of his interest, a 'solitary head' sitting alone in a shell crater. 'For some reason it fascinated me. It looked so droll and yet so pathetic. To whom had it belonged? Was he friend or foe?'[193]

Lieutenant-Colonel William Malone was present at the 24 May 1915 ANZAC burial truce on Gallipoli. He encountered 'a curious tangle', a Turkish soldier lying face down across a private from his own unit in an unusual position with another Turkish body across his legs. Malone wrote: 'I tried to reconstruct the scene', and even drew a diagram in his diary.[194] At Ypres, Walter Williams saw a woman and her child lying by a French soldier. He 'wondered if they had died together or had they only been united after death'.[195] Guy Chapman described his CO as 'actively interested in all phenomena'. He was 'as interested in a dead as in a living man', wanting to know 'just why the corpse lay in that position', and like Pollard would 'speculate on the caprice which left a head and a leg with no body to join them'. Chapman could not participate with the same enthusiasm, and 'after a morning in which the Colonel tried vainly to interest me in a complete jaw without skull or cervicle, and with the teeth still flecked with blood, I excused myself from further operations'.[196]

189  Gordon, op. cit. location 801-6.
190  R. Palmer, *Letters from Mesopotamia*, pp.117-8.
191  Anon, quoted in James, op. cit. p.138.
192  Davison, op. cit. p.37.
193  A.O. Pollard quoted in Simpson op. cit. p.105.
194  Crawford, op. cit. location 3493.
195  Williams, op. cit. location 2149.
196  Chapman, op. cit. p.169.

## (iii) Ascribing living characteristics

Some soldiers distanced themselves from the reality of death by couching their descriptions in words that ascribed living characteristics to the deceased. On exhuming a corpse whilst digging, Edwin Vaughan referred to it as 'a guest'. He 'apologised and patted the earth back'.[197] Private Thompson described how in trench wall burials: 'Hands ... would escape from the sand, pointing, begging – even waving!'[198] John Lucy noted at Sanctuary Wood that a dead sentry leaned back in a standing position against a tree, 'keeping watch'.[199] At Trones Wood Frank Richards encountered a dead German hung up on the branch of a tree, who 'seemed to be carefully watching over the hut'.[200] Patrick Campbell, who was progressing over well fought-over ground at Ypres, tried to avoiding looking at the dead, but when he did, noted that 'they might almost have been sleeping'. He added: 'I was grateful to them for looking alive'.[201]

## (iv) Humour

The role of humour in coping with stress has already been discussed, Lord Moran observing that 'rough gibes and the touch of ridicule' were necessary to rob death of 'its disturbing influence'.[202] Second-Lieutenant Harold Macmillan occupied a trench at Vermelles, cut through a church graveyard. He naturally thought that this might have some effect on morale, 'but quite the opposite'. Perhaps because they were not exposed to the corpses of British soldiers 'there was much joking'. Witty remarks included: 'That's where you'll be tomorrow, mate!', or 'Lor, it's all got ready for us!'.[203] In the Ypres Salient in December 1914, Captain Billy Congreve was introduced to Dead Boot Ditch where a German's foot protruded from the trench wall. Congreve noted: 'Everyone is quite friendly with the gruesome boot'.[204] Stephen Graham described two sergeants lifting the helmet pushed down over the eyes on a German corpse. This action 'pulled up the flesh with it, and the upper lip rose from over the ivory teeth with a ghastly grin'. One offered witty reprimand: 'Take that smile off your face!'[205] Graham viewed this as an illustration of war robbing the soldier of sensitivity, yet it stands as a perfect example of Moran's notion of robbing death of its power to disturb.

There was a frequent cross-over between humour and attributing living characteristics. Aubrey Wade noted how at the entrance to his dugout was the top of a human skull. The French officer he was relieving told him it was so white and shiny because their officers had got 'quite fond of it'. They 'called it Francois and used to

---

197 Vaughan, op. cit. p.34.
198 L. Thompson quoted in Carey, op. cit. pp.451-2.
199 Lucy, op. cit. p.250.
200 Richards, op. cit. p.210.
201 Campbell, op. cit. p.114.
202 Lord Moran, *The Anatomy of Courage*, p.144.
203 H. Macmillan, *Winds of Change*, p.73.
204 B. Congreve, *Armageddon Road*, p.94.
205 Graham, op. cit. p.248.

stroke it as they went in and out of the dugout'.²⁰⁶ Captain James Dunn noted that the weather had exposed an arm on which there was a wrist-watch. Some whimsical passing soldier wound the watch, 'it went, it was a repeater; passers-by would give the winding a turn'.²⁰⁷ In another example, Frank Richards described how on the visit of a corps staff officer a dead German was positioned by some wits on the fire-step 'fixing a lighted candle in one of his hands and a small pocket Bible in the other'. As the officer approached, they 'fixed a lighted cigarette in his mouth. The Staff officer didn't stay long in that part of the trench'.²⁰⁸

Some were perfectly happy to touch the dead in jest. Corporal Lane described having to tread on one a corpse which was partly buried. Every time they did so, 'his tongue would come out, which raised great amusement amongst our people'.²⁰⁹ Robert Graves described a corpse lying on the fire-step, its arm stretched right across the trench. His ex-comrades would joke as they pushed it out of the way to get by: 'Out of the light, you old bastard! Do you own this bloody trench?' They would also shake hands, saying: 'Put it there, Billy Boy'.²¹⁰ Humour defused any disgust. Harold Macmillan passed a dead German on the Somme with his arm extended in 'a gesture of greeting'. His orderly 'shook him warmly by the hand as we went by'.²¹¹ On Gallipoli, Private Thompson passed hands extending from trench walls, there being one he and his comrades all shook in passing, 'saying "Good Morning", in a posh voice'.²¹² A Canadian gunner at Vimy Ridge described a trench wall with 'an emergent head', his comrades stroking its 'flaxen tresses'.²¹³ Similarly, Chaplain W.E. Drury described being shown the remains of 20 or 30 dead Germans in a tunnel. His guide stopped 'to comb the hair of one of the corpses'. Drury described this as 'ghoulish' and 'an ugly development of that indifference ... in face of death' which was a 'necessary and not unhealthy safeguard of sanity'. Robert Graves also concluded that some things were beyond humour: 'One can disregard a dead man. But even a miner can't make a joke that sounds like a joke over a man who takes three hours to die, after the top part of his head has been taken off'.²¹⁴

(v) Avoidance

Although most of these ways of coping can be broadly termed avoidance, there was also straightforward avoidance. Excessive thought could be disabling to the soldier on active service. 'Out of sight out of mind is the rule of the soldier on active service',

---

206 F.P. Roe, *Accidental Soldier*, p.22.
207 Dunn, op. cit. p.187.
208 Richards, op. cit. p.169.
209 C. Lane, quoted in Arthur, op. cit. pp.161-2.
210 Graves, op. cit. p.104.
211 Macmillan, op cit. p.86.
212 L. Thompson quoted in Carey, op. cit. pp.451-2.
213 Quoted in Cave, op. cit. p.77.
214 Graves, op. cit. p.107.

wrote Lieutenant Henry Butters, adding with a note of caution: 'The few who fail to follow it naturally go home with a weak heart'.[215] Hugh Quigley, at Ypres in 1917, describing two dead soldiers bayoneted together, similarly wrote 'if one dwelt on such horrors' for any length of time, 'nervous cowardice would ensue, and the result would be disaster'.[216]

Avoidance could be behavioural, not simply mental. Douglas Cuddeford went forward on the first day of the Battle of Arras with new conscripts. Passing their first corpse they 'sheered round' it 'with white faces and sidelong glances, as if it was something to be avoided'.[217] At Neuve Chapelle Private John McCauley recorded how his companions 'looked neither to left or right, and seemed not to see the corpses lying around', commenting insightfully 'perhaps they preferred not to see'.[218] Francis Hitchcock described Caterpillar Valley as 'a valley of the dead', and that 'no one stayed in it any longer than necessary'.[219] Second-Lieutenant Arthur West and his men dealt with a dead German pulling him 'away out of sight, though not out of smell, into a shell hole'.[220] F.W. Watts encountered a headless corpse in a dug-out one evening and 'it gave me such a shock that I did not look again'.[221] Prior to going into battle at Ypres Edwin Vaughan described how a suddenly espied corpse frightened him. He returned to the scene and 'took with me an old oilsheet with which to cover that distressing body' because 'I was frightened of his unnerving me when I passed him for the last time at zero hour'.[222] Ernst Junger described the same technique, encountering 'severed limbs and bodies, some of which had had coats or tarpaulins thrown over them, to save us the sight of the disfigured faces'.[223] George Coppard similarly wrote of how in response to trench wall burials: 'We would curtain off protruding parts with a sandbag, pinned to the side of the trench with cartridges'.[224] Walter Williams did the same, coving body parts 'with a bit of sacking or camouflage netting held up with cartridge cases', and should a decaying limb be 'too offensive, it would be unceremoniously hacked off with a bayonet'.[225]

Undoubtedly there was oscillation between both behavioural and mental avoidance of the dead and confronting bodies. The degree of mental avoidance is, by definition, unknowable. Deliberate verbal avoidance was evident. In the aftermath of the first day on the Somme, searching for the wounded, Lieutenant Arthur Dugmore wrote:

---

215  H.A. Butters, quoted in Housman, op. cit. p.54.
216  Quigley, op. cit. p.132.
217  Cuddeford, op. cit. p.138.
218  J. McCauley, Private Papers, IWM Docs 6434.
219  Hitchcock, op. cit p.161.
220  A.G. West, *The Diary of a Dead Officer*, p.65.
221  F.W. Watts, Diary, http://www.firstworldwar.com/diaries/nightcounterattack.htm.
222  Vaughan, op. cit. pp.218-221.
223  Junger, op. cit. p.98.
224  Coppard, op. cit. p.46.
225  Williams, op. cit. location 990.

'Some of the sights were too ghastly to be spoken of'.[226] We have already noted how letters home could carry vivid descriptions of the dead. Julian Bickersteth, however, demonstrated deliberate avoidance in a letter to his mother, battlefield sights being 'too appalling for words. I should never wish to give you a description of it'.[227] William Malone, at Helles in May 1915, wrote in his diary that the bodies of Turks two weeks dead 'are a really horrible sight, I do not care to write the details'.[228] Sergeant Roland Mountfield demonstrated the modulation of avoidance revealingly: 'For 500 yards (the trench) is paved with English dead. In places you must walk on them, for they lie in heaps. I won't describe that trench *until I have forgotten it a little*'.[229]

(vi) DISTRACTION

One way of distracting oneself from the significance of human death was to focus on some other aspect of the destruction. Edwin Vaughan wrote: 'The outstanding characteristic of this area was, of course, death'. This was brought home to him, however, 'not so much by the numerous corpses, as by the stranded and battered tanks'.[230] Robert Graves declared himself 'shocked by the dead horses and mules; human corpses were all very well, but it seemed wrong for animals to be dragged into the war like this'.[231] Private Thompson hinted at the displacement involved, writing that it was 'commonplace' for men, 'inured to the passing of their human friends', to express 'grief' at the death of horses.[232] The tasks of the present, however, provided the best distraction. Patrick MacGill, acting as a stretcher bearer wrote of the dead that: 'We had one job to do and that job took up our whole attention until it was completed'.[233] Huntly Gordon experienced collecting the bits of men from his platoon in blankets and sandbags. Exhaustion came to his aid in avoiding thinking about what had happened: 'With lack of sleep, we work in a daze, which helps to shut out yesterday's horror from our minds'.[234]

(vii) RELIGION

We have looked closely at the role of faith, but there are few references which specifically indicate use of religion as a coping mechanism in dealing with the dead, outside of the process of burial. Captain Theodore Wilson, however, was of the opinion that 'you can't face death … there's no facing it. It's everywhere'. He continued that:

---

226 A.R. Dugmore, *When the Somme Ran Red*, p.236.
227 Bickersteth, op. cit. p.132.
228 Crawford, op. cit. location 3061.
229 R.D.Mountfield, quoted in Hart, op. cit. p.250 (italics author).
230 Vaughan, op. cit. p.207.
231 Graves, op. cit. p.106.
232 R. Thompson quoted in R. Holmes, *Tommy*, p.240.
233 MacGill, op. cit. p.131.
234 Gordon, op. cit. location 1385.

'Without the sense of God taking up the souls out of those poor torn bodies – even though they've died cursing Him – I think one would go mad'.[235]

## *Disruption of coping*
Seven causes of disruption of coping appear in soldiers' writings. The first was quantitative, simply 'too much' death. The remaining six involved specific factors.

(i) 'Too much' death
A single death might be bearable, mass death was sometimes a scenario that pushed coping to the limit. Giles Eyre described exposure to a particular scene of multiple death and dismemberment on the Somme thus: 'Inured as I am to sites of death and blood, I feel like retching as I gaze around'.[236] Corporal Clifford Lane recorded in similar circumstances at Thiepval how 'we'd seen plenty of dead people before, but we'd never seen anything like this'.[237] On Gallipoli Lieutenant-Colonel Cecil Allanson experienced the same sense of being exposed to something beyond his ability to cope, writing: 'The nullahs on the journey back were too horrible, full of dead and dying … the smell of death now some two days old'. He 'left that battlefield a changed man'.[238]

(ii) Impingement of mortality
A soldier could suddenly find himself drawn into preoccupation with the possibility of his own death by contact with corpses. Thus, Private Norman Gladden encountered his first corpse on the Somme and 'only a great effort saved my limbs from giving way beneath me'. In his head 'a voice seemed to whisper with unchallengeable logic, "Why shouldn't you be the next?"'[239] Passing a cemetery could have a similar effect, as Herbert Cooper noted: 'One could not help gloomy thoughts flitting through the mind'.[240] Interpreter Paul Maze hurried his men past a yard piled high with wooden crosses: 'Some smiled, others passed a joke, some wouldn't look. But I knew that they all saw and understood'.[241]

(iii) Appreciation of humanity
There were mixed views on taking things from the dead. At Fromelles in 1914, Frank Richards noted: 'If a dead man's clothes or boots were in good condition we never hesitated to take them off him'.[242] He did not construe this as looting. Francis Hitchcock, however, clearly described looting by the men of 3rd Rifle Brigade when dealing with

---

235 T.P.C. Wilson, quoted in Housman, op. cit. p.296.
236 Eyre, op. cit. p.228.
237 C. Lane quoted in Arthur, op. cit. pp.161-2.
238 C. Allanson quoted in James, op. cit. p.297.
239 N. Gladden, quoted in Winter, op. cit. p.133.
240 Cooper, op. cit.
241 P. Maze, *A Frenchman in Khaki*, p.123.
242 Richards, op. cit. p.42.

German bodies: 'The little Cockneys were revelling in their task, searching the corpses for souvenirs, and then rolling them into the vast depths of the crater'.[243] In neither case did the body seem to assume a human identity. There was likely more equanimity in rifling German rather than British corpses, and Sidney Rogerson, on the Somme, was quite accepting of one of the other ranks going out and looting the German dead in No Man's Land, as long as he searched every British corpse and brought back the paybooks, 'after which what he did with the Germans was no concern of mine'.[244]

The humanity of an anonymous corpse could, however, suddenly impinge on a soldier. It is likely that the distaste expressed for looting by many soldiers was caused by a sudden awareness of the transformation of the corpse from object to human being. The encounter with photographs of family in particular could bring a looter face to face with a corpse's humanity. George Coppard described 'ghoulish curiosity' in searching German bodies for souvenirs. Looking through the contents of pocket wallets, however, he 'felt a certain sympathy when scanning photographs of relatives'.[245] At Lesboeufs in 1916 Max Plowman described of unburied bodies, 'How unreal they look!' However unreal, he could not but 'reflect how each one had his own life'.[246] This reaction could be triggered particularly by the face of a corpse. Major C. Wade noted: 'What was unendurable were the bodies with upturned faces'.[247] Similarly, Siegfried Sassoon watched Canadian soldiers carrying the dead slung on a pole. He commented: 'What splendid commonsense! ... But I wish they'd put a sandbag over the face'.[248] Faces were indeed often covered. Stephen Graham, sent to recover the body of an officer, located a group of corpses and had to take 'the coverings off their faces' to identify his man.[249] Undoubtedly they had been placed there for purposes of avoidance.

(iv) SUDDEN EXPOSURE

Sudden exposure to a corpse when not expecting such a sight could lead to negative reactions in otherwise adapted men. Thus the robust Francis Hitchcock was shocked at Loos by 'a very gruesome sight'. Entering the wrong building 'in front of me in the dim light I saw the dead body of an officer of the Sappers stretched on a table awaiting burial'.[250] Such a sight on the battlefield would not have unnerved him – it was encountering it in a place that might normally be safe from such sights that was disturbing. John McCauley had a very similar experience. Pulling a sheet aside he

---

243 Hitchcock, op. cit. p.73.
244 Rogerson, op. cit. p.51.
245 Coppard, op. cit. p.89.
246 Mark VII, op. cit. p.147.
247 C. Wade, quoted in Macdonald, op. cit. p.187.
248 S. Sassoon, quoted in I. and A. Taylor, *Those who Marched Away*, p.265.
249 Graham, op. cit. p.231.
250 Hitchcock, op. cit. p.206.

emitted 'a cry of horror ... there lay a dead German'.[251] Gerald Burgoyne described how: 'Clearing out a drain we came on what looked like a bit of the brain and face of a man, I didn't stay to investigate it – I fled'.[252] Hugh Quigley found a corpse whilst walking at dawn after a sleepless night. The experience made more impression on him than most, and his reasoning was that the time of day was one when 'the body and mind are more open to impression, more easily affected by the unforeseen'.[253]

### (v) Knowing the victim

Finding a corpse known to one was generally particularly upsetting. Aubrey Smith described how 'a horrible sight met my eyes', two dead bodies which had been placed over the back of his trench being 'men I had been speaking to but yesterday'.[254] Guy Chapman similarly described how 'the sight of the rigid bodies of men I had known quivering with vitality', bodies now 'blue and wan, woefully arrayed, made me shudder and stirred in me a hatred of existence'.[255] The normally unflappable General James Jack noted, looking out over the dead of the Rifle Brigade lying close up to the enemy's parapet, saw 'one who had helped me at Harfleur'. He wondered whether he would 'ever become accustomed to these sights?'[256] His comment is a testimony to the truth that developing coping was not a once and for ever process.

### (vi) Something peculiar or unusual

Many of the negative references in the visual and tactile mode refer to encountering something unusual. Gunner Leonard Ounsworth described such an experience suddenly disturbing coping: 'Rollins just had to step back, and then this leg that was up in a tree became dislodged and fell on his head. He vomited on the spot'. Ounsworth, an otherwise adapted soldier, continued: 'Good Lord, it was terrible'.[257]

### (vii) Leave and time away from the battlefield

The notion that coping was battlefield specific and might have to be reworked after a spell of leave is suggested by a note in Bertie Sporton's diary: 'I passed five of our men lying dead on the firestep. Cpl. Maclean was one. Not nice after coming off from leave'.[258] Returning after a year's absence, Walter Williams encountered a collection of corpses of French civilians, and noted: 'A veteran despite my tender years, what I saw was enough to turn my stomach into jelly'.[259] In early 1918 he similarly had

---

251 McCauley, op. cit.
252 Davison, op. cit. p.85.
253 Quigley, op. cit. p.157.
254 Smith, op. cit. p. 51.
255 Chapman, op. cit. p.83.
256 Terraine, op. cit. p.113-4.
257 L.J. Ounsworth, IWM Sound 332.
258 Sporton, op. cit.
259 Williams, op. cit. location 2155.

several months of agricultural leave. Returning in March 1918 to Vimy Ridge he was struck by the sights of death about him, 'sights of war that I had known before and *must learn to accept again*'.[260] In a similar vein Major Edward Cadogan served on Gallipoli and adapted to the omnipresence of death. He then served in Egypt and as a staff officer during the Palestine campaign. Arriving on the Tabsor battlefield, he found that 'the Turkish trenches presented a horrible spectacle'. He committed to his diary a lengthy paragraph about human remains. He particularly described the sight of a group killed by shell and remaining in a sitting position as 'appalling'. It is clear from the detail provided that the sights made a considerable impact on Cadogan: 'The sun had distorted them into the most gruesome and grotesque figures'. The black hands of the corpses were 'like small balloons, their faces, swollen to amazing proportions, were twisted into the most terrible grimaces'.[261] In his time away from battle his mental defences against such experiences had weakened.

*The failure of coping mechanisms*
That there are so many negative references to the encounter with human remains indicates that coping fluctuated. Adaptation might break down temporarily but would be reconstituted to offer continued effective protection. For a few, however, the ability to cope with death failed completely. Documented instances of this are, however, relatively sparse. Lieutenant-Colonel Frank Maxwell described in a letter home how: 'I have two officers both shaken and now useless from mere sights and I suppose there are plenty of men the same'.[262] William Rivers detailed six cases studies in his seminal 1918 paper from his Craiglockhart cohort.[263] Two of these involved symptomatology connected with exposure to human remains. In one case, an officer who had gone out to seek a fellow officer had found him dismembered. 'From that time he had been haunted at night by the vision of his dead and mutilated friend'. The nightmares consisted either of the dismembered body, or of the body with limbs and features 'eaten away by leprosy'. In the second case, an officer had been flung by a shell to land with his face in the abdomen of a rotting corpse. He was suffering nightmares in which these events were repeated. C.S. Meyers, another shellshock specialist, gave the words of a subaltern he was examining: 'To tell you honestly it was not *that* (the shell) that made me fall; it was the horrible sight of the arm (blown off by the shell from a neighbouring soldier) flying in front of me'.[264]

260  Williams, op. cit. location 3126 (italics author).
261  E. Cadogan, *Under Fire in the Dardanelles*, p.147.
262  F. Maxwell, quoted in Hart, op. cit. p.190.
263  W.H.R. Rivers, 'An Address on the Repression of War Experience', *Lancet*, p.173. Craiglockhart was a hydropathic hospital in Edinburgh taken over as a military hospital for officers 1916-1919. William Rivers was a doctor with an interest in psychoanalysis who worked as an RAMC Captain there.
264  C.S Meyers, quoted in Hart, op. cit. p.479.

But there was a difference between breaking down as a result of exposure to death, and retaining memories in different degrees of vividness. Corporal Arthur Razell described the sight of 'men decapitated, empty brain cavities, entrails where they'd been disembowelled' adding that 'that day at Ovillers is absolutely engraved on my brain. I've thought about it all my life'.[265] Llewellyn Griffith noted: 'So tenacious in these matters is memory that I can never encounter the smell of cut green timber without resurrecting the vision of the tree that flaunted a human limb'.[266] These men had vivid memories, but were not disabled by them.

Group morale issues caused by human remains are recorded. Thus, the May 1917 War Diary of 2/12th London Regiment noted: '20 (OR wounded) + 2 shell shock + 1 officer shell shock 23rd – 24th ... The conditions in the trenches were very bad. A very large number of unburied dead were scattered in and near the trenches'.[267] The unit clearly associated the presence of remains with the stress on its personnel. In more marked fashion, the Royal Naval Division War Diary from July 1915 on Gallipoli noted:

> (A) state of involuntary sickness took place at Helles on 13 July when trenches captured by the Royal Naval Division were full of rotting corpses hence 'vomiting and sickness very bad.' The next night, 14/15 July, orders could not be carried out because the captured trenches were basically uninhabitable and the men could not carry on.[268]

The extent of these sorts of references in war diaries is not known. These examples indicate that officers at battalion and divisional level were aware of the effects of human remains on morale, but in both these cases it is most likely that there were a set of conditions degrading morale in these locations, and that this degradation was temporary, morale improving as the units moved out of line. Thus, a medical officer, Lieutenant G.N. Kirkwood, diagnosed collective shell shock on the Somme in the 11th Border Regiment after 1 July 1916:

> The battalion lost all its officers and more than half of its men; later rest days were spent at Contray sorting the belongings of deceased comrades. Afterwards they spent their time carrying up rations under heavy and incessant shellfire, digging out the dead in the trenches and carrying them down the line. They lived in an atmosphere of decomposing bodies, were exposed in open trenches to shelling and went without sleep for long periods.[269]

265 A. Razell, IWM Sound 11952.
266 Griffith, op. cit.
267 WO 95/3009 quoted in P. Leese, *Shell Shock*, p.111.
268 WO 95/4290 quoted in Travers, op. cit. p.181.
269 G.N. Kirkwood quoted in Leese, op. cit. p.28.

Kirkwood is describing an accumulation of stressors – exhaustion, threat, and clearing the dead. However, others were clear that the dead were a significant stressor. Many individuals from top to bottom of the army realised that that the burial of the dead was a morale issue. The Reverend Ernest Crosse wrote: 'Burials on active service had very great practical importance ... nothing is more depressing to the living to see unburied dead about them'. He noted that in some areas such as Beaumont Hamel in the winter of 1916 'the ground was covered with unburied dead and it became a matter of real military importance that the work of burial should be conducted'.[270]

Lieutenant-Colonel Norman Fraser-Tytler bore him out: 'The 'Body Snatcher' or 'Cold Meat Specialist' (Corps Burial Officer) ... was most useful in removing our pet aversions, which otherwise might have remained unburied for months'.[271] Charles Clayton, on encountering a dead Royal Engineer officer was told: 'We mustn't have this facing the youngsters all day, get a couple of the old hands and bury him straight away'.[272] The morale issue of viewing the effects of a failed attack in front of the line is indicated by Frank Richards: 'All along this front from Cambrin to Hulloch and as far as the eye could see, our dead were still lying out in front of us'. Richards and his comrades understood full well that 'any attack that was made by us would involve huge casualties'.[273] After 1 July 1916 on the Somme Captain H.F. Dawes described manpower problems leading to a delay in transfer of bodies to graves, continuing 'the result was a large stack of corpses which was extremely bad for morale'.[274] Giles Eyre, in his account of the Somme in 1916 suggests that there was resentment that equipment was collected from corpses whilst the dead themselves went unburied.[275] Brigadier-General Fabian Ware of the Directorate of Graves Registration & Enquiries was also aware of the effects of the 'pet aversions' and wrote on 29 June 1917: 'We are on the verge over here of serious trouble about the number of bodies lying out still unburied on the Somme battlefields. The soldiers returning wounded or in leave to England are complaining bitterly about it'.[276]

*Clearing the dead*
If morale was to be preserved then the dead had to cleared, and fellow soldiers were the only ones who could do it. Rowland Feilding, at Cuinchy in May 1915 noted that dealing with the dead became unavoidable as the temperatures increased. 'At nights such of them as can be reached are fetched in and buried, or in some cases are covered with chloride of lime ... It is a sickening job'.[277] He noted natural reluctance,

---

270 E.C. Crosse, Private Papers, IWM Docs 4772.
271 N. Fraser-Tytler quoted in Simpson, op. cit. pp.107-8.
272 Clayton, op. cit. p.24.
273 Richards, op. cit. p.156.
274 H.F. Dawes, quoted in M. Middlebrook, *The First Day on the Somme*, p.249.
275 Eyre, op. cit. p.106.
276 F. Ware, CWGC SDC 60/1.
277 Feilding, op. cit. p.4.

continuing that he 'soon found out that a night burying party would always shirk its job'.[278] 'Vedette', with the Guards on the Somme in 1916, recorded his unit recovering and burying some 200 bodies, noting: 'The burial parties had the worst time: you wanted strong nerves to stomach the sights'.[279] Second-Lieutenant Evelyn Fryer was tasked on the Somme in 1916 with burying 200 dead and wrote, in doing so betraying his coping mechanism: 'It was a nasty fatigue, and I won't dwell more on it'.[280]

To clear a field after many months was a grim task. Second-Lieutenant W.N. Collins, burial officer of the 51st Highland Division, described the clearing of Beaumont Hamel in November 1916 of the remains of the Newfoundlanders from 1 July:

> The flesh had gone mainly from the face but the hair had still grown, the beard to some extent. They looked very ragged ... and the rats were running out of their chests. The rats were getting out of the rain, of course, because the cloth over the rib cage made quite a nice nest and when you touched a body the rats just poured out of the front ... And when the flesh goes from under a puttee, there is just the bone and if you stand on it, it just squashes.[281]

Sidney Rogerson on the Somme noted clearing whilst in the line as 'a dirty and dangerous task'. Two companies had been sent out on consecutive nights and had 'accomplished little, since the men on them had been too sick to dig'.[282] A selection of references to clearing includes the following: 'It was a terrible job ... deeply depressing for the men';[283] '(The) most ghastly job I ever had';[284] 'always a gruesome task, disliked by all, and frequently made the hardiest sick, but it just had to be done';[285] 'God, how sick I felt';[286] 'I don't know how many we buried. I'll never forget that sight';[287] 'the most dreadful experience even I have had ... I retched and have been sleepless since ... No words can describe the ghastliness';[288] 'Some of (the men) ... were feeling sick and groggy ... I've thought about it all my life'.[289] Preserving morale therefore perversely ran the risk of damaging morale.

On the Somme, Stuart Cloete described dealing with the dead who came to pieces as they were touched: 'As you lifted a body by its arms and legs they detached themselves

---

278 Feilding, op. cit. p.29.
279 'Vedette', *Adventures of an Ensign*, p.107-8.
280 E.R.M Fryer, *Reminiscences of a Grenadier*, p.117.
281 W.N. Collins quoted in van Emden & Humphries op. cit. pp.130-1.
282 Rogerson, op. cit. p.30.
283 P. King quoted in McDonald, *Passchendaele*, p.210.
284 Sporton, op. cit.
285 T. Brookbank, Private Papers, IWM Docs 8178.
286 R. Gwinnell, Private Papers, IWM Docs 11601.
287 J. Hoyles quoted in L. McDonald, *Somme*, p.113.
288 J. McKenzie quoted in Liddle, op. cit. p.159.
289 E.B. Lord, Private Papers, IWM Docs 6559.

from the torso'. He did not however regard this as the worst thing. 'Each body was covered inches deep with a black fur of flies which flew up into your face, into your mouth, eyes and nostrils as you approached. The bodies crawled with maggots'. He was clear that 'this was a job for all ranks. No one could expect the men to handle these bodies unless the officers did their share'. They worked together 'with sandbags on our hands, stopping every now and then to puke'.[290] John McCauley, recovering from wounds, was attached to a clearing unit between August and November 1918. He described his work:

> Often have I picked up the remains of a fine brave man on a shovel. Just a little heap of bones and maggots to be carried to the common burial place. Numerous bodies were found lying submerged in the water in shell holes and mine craters; bodies that seemed quite whole, but which became like huge masses of white, slimy chalk when we handled them. I shuddered as my hands, covered in soft flesh and slime, moved about in search of the disc, and I have had to pull bodies to pieces in order that they should not be buried unknown. It was very painful to have to bury the unknown.[291]

Yet McCauley learned to cope: 'For the first week or two I could scarcely endure the experiences we met with, but I gradually became hardened'.

W.N. Collins described how amongst his men, tragically: 'Quite a number ... were related to the ones who were dead, brothers, cousins, and they of course were very upset, very, very upset'.[292] He found himself comforting these men with 'a stroke on the head or a pat on the back or some gesture like that, without words'. Collins clearly ruminated on his own mortality: 'For a young fellow like myself, 19, all I had to look forward to at the time was a similar fate. It still has an effect on me now, you never forget it'. He was speaking over 80 years after the event. Julian Bickersteth described typical post-traumatic symptomatology in the men carrying out clearing: 'It tries the nerves and causes a curious kind of irritability which was quite infectious'. All the party were 'cross and out of temper, and it was quite easy to find oneself heatedly arguing some trivial point for no apparent reason'.[293]

The 1/19th London Regiment was used to the clear the battlefield after the successful assault on High Wood on 15 September 1916. The war diary states on 19 September: 'Burial party of 1 officer & 15 ORs supplied for HIGH WOOD'.[294] On the following day (and again on 22 September) it is recorded 'large burial parties for

---

290 Cloete, op. cit. p.237.
291 McCauley, op. cit.
292 W.N. Collins, quoted in van Emden & Humphries, op. cit. pp.130-1.
293 Bickersteth, op. cit. p.274.
294 TNA PRO WO/95/2738, War Diary, 1/19th Battalion London Regiment.

HIGH WOOD'. In contrast to this bald statement of the facts, the reality of the task is conveyed by Reverend David Railton, the 47th Division's chaplain:

> Many men who have stood it all, cannot stand this clearing of the battlefield ... no words can tell you all I feel, nor can words tell you of the horrors of clearing a battlefield. This Battalion was left to do that, and several men went off with shell-shock ... caused not just by the explosion of a shell nearby, but by the sights and smell and horror of the battlefield in general. I felt dreadful, and had to do my best to keep the men up to the task.[295]

Private A. Surfleet, however, joined John McCauley in agreeing that adaptation occurred: 'I'm still amazed at the casual way we piled those bodies, like so many huge logs, without any horror at such a gruesome task; which seems to show we must be getting hardened'.[296]

## Conclusion

The wounded represented a particular challenge to their fellows, but the reality was that either the evidence of their suffering was removed to receive medical assistance, or they died. The dead remained a permanent problem for the living. When Major Wade stated that 'bodies with upturned faces' were 'unendurable',[297] he was confronting the reality that the face is the epitome of one's identity as a human being. In seeing them he was reminded of his common humanity with the dead. As Lieutenant Alexander De Lisle wrote: 'When I close my eyes, I can see one sight in particular'. This involved a pair of shattered legs cut off just below the hips, sticking out of the ground. He kept thinking that 'I myself might be like that any minute – not a pleasant thought'.[298] Similarly, when Rowland Feilding saw his men looking at corpses as they passed, he thought 'perhaps they were thinking that they might soon be looking like that themselves'.[299] Every time one looked at a corpse, there was the potential reminder of one's own mortality.

In being thrust into constant contact with the dead on the battlefield soldiers were only partly assisted in their coping by a greater degree of being accustomed to the presence of the dead, living as they did at a time when death was becoming less familiar. They had no option but to endure this presence, and in their stoical acceptance, soldiers used many inventive mechanisms to distance themselves from the dead, all based on avoidance. They did not become inured or callous, nor did they necessarily

---

295 D. Railton, Private Papers, IWM Docs 4760.
296 A. Surfleet, quoted in Brown, op. cit. p.205.
297 C. Wade quoted in McDonald, *Passchendaele*, p.187.
298 A.C.N.M.P. De Lisle quoted in E. Hancock, *Bazentin Ridge*, p.77.
299 Feilding, op. cit. p.29.

achieve total adaptation. An ability to cope in one situation might be matched by an inability in another – the capacity to protect oneself waxed and waned. In reaching the level of adaptation that they did achieve, they did what they could to prevent 'identifying with bodies and personalizing the trauma', the fate that befell their military successors, the First Gulf War body handlers.

# 9

# 'A Momentary Pang of Regret' – Loss and Burial

Soldiers did not simply have to deal with the anonymous dead. Mates were regularly killed as, sometimes, were serving relatives. How, therefore, did they react to and deal with the deaths of those they were close to in terms of the constraints of both the battlefield and the age?

## Grief in the Victorian/Edwardian World

### *The Stoic attitude to grief*
The Stoic standpoint, as we know, was that one should dismiss concern about things that were outside one's control. The death of a loved one was such a thing. Any pain associated would be a matter of 'indifference', and should be eliminated. The goal of the Stoic sage seems a harsh doctrine in the modern world. Seneca, struggling with a more diffusive Stoicism, believed that we should adopt the attitude towards the dead that 'I have lost them as if I still have them'.[1] This expresses what we might see as the goal of grieving in an astonishingly concise and modern way – to adjust to the idea that we still have a representation of the dead person inside ourselves. He acknowledged the reality of grief, and he even acknowledged the legitimacy of tears if only within the rules of decorum. His emphasis was always on restraint, modifying the outward show of grief.

### *Mourning*
Two concepts need to be taken into consideration; the expression of grief in the Victorian and Edwardian period, and mourning and the use of ritual. The two are separate but obviously connected. Grief is a set of emotions, mourning is a set of behaviours.

Recorded history and archaeology demonstrates that funeral rites have been important throughout human existence. The landscape of Britain is testimony to the

---

1  Seneca, quoted in N. Sherman, *Stoic Warriors*, Kindle edition location 2134.

importance of burial over the centuries, as is the ribbon of military cemeteries snaking across north-east France and Flanders. It is a truism that the Victorian era saw the apogee of burial and mourning rituals.[2] The 1852 Metropolitan Burial Act led to the development of public cemeteries in which the monuments of the wealthy and the middle-class stand dramatic testament to the importance of burial in remembrance. Cremation had been slow to gain popularity after the Cremation Act of 1902 and at the time of the outbreak of the Great War burial remained the prominent means of dealing with the dead. The act of burial itself was the climax and primary focus of the immediate aftermath of death, and from the psychological point of view, leave-taking. Mourning rituals represented an extended act of remembrance. The high period of upper and middle-class Victorian mourning is considered to be roughly 1850-1890. Women wore black ('full mourning') which might change after a period to grey ('half mourning'). A widow would wear such attire for two years and not normally entertain during the first year. Six months was the duration prescribed for this dress after the demise of a sibling. Men wore mourning suits, whilst those in the military wore a black armband. Towards the end of the century the Victorian panoply of mourning props had, however, become less prominent, and the funeral itself had become simpler by the 1870s.[3] David Cannadine has suggested that Victorian mourning customs did not 'help' the bereaved to 'come to terms with their loss', and actually even 'robbed them of the will to recover'.[4] This is a mistaken view. Firstly, there is no evidence except occasional anecdote for his claim that ritual led to chronic grief. Secondly, he is in error if he believes that ritual was established to help the bereaved recover. It was rather a means of channelling emotion acceptably in an era when Stoic restraint was the norm.

The working classes did not have the money to sustain the mourning props, a private grave and monument, or, sometimes, even the cost of burial. In 1883 James Greenwood described a pauper burial in a suburban London cemetery.[5] There was no pomp, and precious little ceremony, but even so, relatives were transported with the coffins for their brief minutes of service by the communal grave. It demonstrates that ritual, leave-taking and remembrance were important for the poor as they were for the rich. Thomas Wright observed at the end of the century that 'the poor are not careless or neglectful of their dead'.[6] This was not a harsh and violent environment breeding insensitivity in the face of death, and economic circumstances did not constrain grief. Wright described the areas where the poor were buried in the great urban cemeteries of London thus:

2  P. Jalland, *Death in the Victorian Family*.
3  Jalland, op. cit. p.202.
4  D. Cannadine, 'War and Death, Grief and Mourning in Modern Britain', in J. Whaley (ed.), *Mirrors of Mortality*, pp.190-1.
5  J. Greenwood, 'Buried by the Parish' in *Mysteries of Modern London*, www.victorianlondon.org.
6  T. Wright, 'Mitey' in *The Pinch of Poverty*, www.victorianlondon.org.

The close-lying coffin-shaped mounds of earth which mark the sites of the graves have many of them flowers or evergreen shrubs planted upon them; some have been more or less successfully turfed; while others have been set out with initials or emblems traced in pebbles or shells. Simple memorials certainly, but the work of loving hands and tributes of loving hearts.

### *Grief*

Ralph Houlbrooke sets out the rules for the expression of grief in upper-class English families in the sixteenth and seventeenth centuries. In true Stoic tradition: 'Excessive grief was generally deprecated'. Giving in to the expression of feelings 'showed a lack of faith, reason, self-control, even a perverse wilfulness'. It was recognised, however, that the expression of emotion had its place: 'Not to feel grief at all, however, was unnatural'.[7] The Romanticism of the later 18th century, as the Stoic influence waned, led to something of a cult of melancholy, which in turn led to the elysian garden cemetery movement of the Victorian era.

With the Victorian Stoic revival, as Pat Jalland states: 'Courageous control of sorrow at a funeral could be particular cause for congratulation'.[8] Men particularly, adhering to the code of manliness, were expected to keep any demonstration of grief private, and women assumed the responsibility for its expression. 'Grief came to be seen as particularly associated with women's frail, emotional nature'.[9] Women had always been viewed, in the words of the 16th century physiologist Joubert, as 'weaker and moister';[10] and in the new manliness of the 19th century, not only grief, but emotional work in general became a woman's burden. Even in the early 20th century, crying was still a woman's monopoly.

Crying is a ubiquitous human behaviour. Its causes are manifold – pleasure, frustration, rage, sadness or grief. In the modern era, expression of tears is commonplace. In times when Stoic influence was less strong, tears were regarded as pleasurable, often associated with religious experience. In the Victorian era, however, tearlessness became the *sine qua non* of male stoic resistance to emotion.[11] Captain Geoffrey Dugdale, serving on the staff at Cambrai in 1917, was given a dressing down by his brigadier and 'burst into tears and wept for half an hour without stopping'. (He attributed this to 'strain', and it is interesting that his outburst 'alarmed the General to such an extent that he did not know what to do with me').[12] Crying is a Stoic 'first movement', and Seneca was driven to acknowledge that tears in immediate response to the death of a loved one were acceptable, whereas voluntary tears, tears of indulgence, were morally objectionable. He would have viewed Dugdale's outburst with distaste.

---

7   R. Houlbrooke, *Death, Religion and the Family*, p.221.
8   Jalland, op. cit. p.222.
9   T. Walter, *On Bereavement*, p.134.
10  L. Joubert, quoted in T. Lutz, *Crying – The Natural & Cultural History of Tears*, p.179.
11  Lutz, op. cit. pp.31-66.
12  G. Dugdale, *'Langemarck' and 'Cambrai'*, pp.112-3.

Captain Douglas Cuddeford on the Somme in 1916 noted men in the aftermath of action who 'had lost their wits and were shedding tears like children'. The words he uses are interesting, suggesting that he saw such expressed emotion as a combination of mental disturbance and childishness. It made him uncomfortable: 'It is painful to see full grown men lose their nerve to that degree'.[13]

Allies during the Great War, but enemies at the time of writing, novelist Helen Maria Williams drew a difference between the French and English national characters in terms of tearfulness in the late 1790s. Observing behaviour at the theatre she noted: 'You will see Frenchmen bathed in tears at a tragedy. An Englishman ... thinks it would be unmanly to weep; and ... contrives to gain the victory over his feelings.'[14] This, as we have seen, remained part of the national psyche – 'Edwardian men would have been ashamed to cry'.[15] Yet by the time of the First World War, however there had clearly been a convergence in national attitudes. André Loez's[16] study of the 'tears in the trenches' of French soldiers cites work which indicates that in the decades before the Great War, the code of masculinity in France also came to associate timidity and expression of feeling with dishonour.[17]

A French infantry lieutenant, André Pézard, wrote during the conflict of having 'the strength not to cry'.[18] Loez suggests this was governed by two things. Firstly, patriotism and the (Stoic) importance of action and effort over emotion. Secondly, and familiar from the discussion about the British concept of manliness, the wartime ethos of heroism and masculinity. In a view that would have been supported by Lord Moran in his belief of the importance of 'breeding', the serving psychiatrist, Maurice Dide, wrote in 1918: 'The inhibition of grief is usually the prerogative of officers, of men with high moral standards, in whom emotion triggers instincts already related with superior tendencies'.[19] That the emphasis on not demonstrating emotion became increasingly medicalised is demonstrated by the work *Le Courage* published in 1918 by French doctors Louis Hout and Paul Voivenel who asserted that tears were not only a 'sign of weakness' but also a symptom of 'nervous discharge' typical of 'unadapted soldiers'.[20]

The French had thus moved to a position in which they had a view of crying even more negative than the British. The shedding of tears was a demonstration of weakness or worse except in situations where a formal 'patriotic ritual turns them into a

---

13 D.W.J. Cuddeford, *And All for What?*, p.49.
14 H.M. Williams, 'Letters From France', *Monthly Review*, pp.95-6.
15 P.R. Thompson, *The Edwardians: The Remaking of British Society*, p.145.
16 A. Loez, 'Tears in the Trenches: A History of Emotions and the Experience of War', in J. MacLeod *Uncovered Fields: Perspectives in First World War Studies*, pp.211-226.
17 R.A. Nye, *Masculinity and Male Codes of Honour in Modern France*, p.227.
18 A. Pézard quoted in Loez, op.cit. pp.216-7.
19 M. Dide, quoted in Loez, op. cit. p.219.
20 L. Hout & P. Voivenel, *Le Courage*, pp.335-344.

sign of sacred emotion'.[21] Such rituals were largely religious in nature and glorified sacrifice. In this way tears about death were rendered acceptable and even motivating, as for the French the notion of sacrifice was a keystone of heroism. The British clearly shared to a certain extent the view that patriotic tears were acceptable. Lieutenant-Colonel William Malone, a British-born New Zealand officer, was present in Egypt at a ceremony where General Godley 'called for 3 cheers for the King'. Malone recorded: 'My eyes got quite moist with emotion. God Bless the King'.[22]

## Loss in the Trenches

The soldier who set out to fight on the Western Front was thus constrained by the Stoic tradition of what was viewed as acceptable to express in response to death, but carried with him a belief, whatever his social origin, in the importance of proper burial. These attitudes had now to contend with mass, violent death on the battlefield.

### *Death of a pal*
When his brother was killed, Private Walter Williams, who was still in training in the UK, described his sergeant as obviously upset at the death of a friend, but that 'in true military fashion he refused to show it'. Williams determined that he would learn to adopt the same behaviour: 'Stiff upper lip old lad, old soldiers don't blub at the death of a mate. Drink to his memory when you get the chance but get on with the job at all costs!'[23] Seneca would have been proud.

Lieutenant Bernard Adams learnt of the death of a fellow officer. 'Here was something new. I had seen death often; *it* was nothing new. But it was the first time it had taken one of us'.[24] Adams is thus telling us that it was the matter of *where* death intruded that was the issue. It was not necessarily a matter of close personal relationship – he was not intimate with the officer in question – but death had now impacted upon *his* group. Lieutenant Burgon Bickersteth, fighting on the Somme in 1916, saw two bombing parties obliterated by shelling, but reported that this affected him 'extraordinary little', and that it was only the death of 'someone near and dear to one' that could disturb him.[25] It was Lieutenant Sidney Rogerson's opinion that 'men do not easily or soon throw off the shock of seeing all that could be found of four of their comrades come down for burial in one ground sheet'.[26] He described soldiers as 'indifferent to death en masse', but that the loss of particular comrades was 'always painful', However often it happened, it could never be 'looked upon with indifference'.[27] Cyclist

---

21  Loez, op. cit. p.211.
22  J. Crawford, *No Better Death*, Kindle edition location 1868.
23  M. Williams, *With Innocence and Hope*, Kindle edition location 418.
24  B. Adams, *Nothing of Importance*, p.174 (italics in original).
25  J. Bickersteth (ed.), *The Bickersteth Diaries*, p.130.
26  S. Rogerson, *Twelve days on the Somme*, p.7.
27  Rogerson, op. cit. p.207.

J. Smith confirmed this particular piercing of the soldier's emotional carapace in simple words when burying his pal Ernie Gay: 'You got very callous ... but when it was your own pal – you couldn't feel callous then'.[28] On Gallipoli, Major John Gillam heard of the deaths of more and more friends. He noted that this upset him far more than personal danger, as it sparked the 'nightmare question' whenever talking to people he knew well: 'I wonder if I shall see you alive again'.[29] He contemplated ruefully weeks later: 'One makes friends – such fine friends – and one is always suddenly losing them', a loss which left 'such gaps as sometimes make one wish that one could follow them'. But he noted the customary defence: 'It is against the tradition of the service to be morbid about it'.[30]

News of the deaths of friends was sometimes received at a distance. Private Norman Gladden, who had already sustained the loss of his closest army chum, received the news of the death of a childhood friend, Eddie Collins. Shock was his predominant reaction – 'I who had seen so much death could not believe it'.[31] Second-Lieutenant Douglas Gillespie learnt the news of the death of his greatest friend from Winchester and Oxford, Isaac Bayley Balfour on Gallipoli. He wrote home: 'I can think of nothing but Bay Balfour'.[32] Plunged into gloom, he clearly began to dwell on the deaths of not only Balfour, but his brother Tom. Like Gillam, he began to feel that 'if it wasn't for all of you at home, I should be quite content to follow them'.[33] Eight days later, however, he had managed to put this sort of thinking behind him and was writing: 'I have enjoyed these last two days'.[34] Captain Evelyn Southwell wrote to his mother after learning that his great friend Lieutenant Malcolm White was posted as missing on 1 July 1916, demonstrating that this was the death that hurt him. Accusing himself of 'terrible selfishness', he observed he had 'faced the casualty list daily without a tremor for two years now', but now, 'when I am hard hit myself, I cry out! Mum, he was *such* a dear'.[35] Writing to a friend a few days later he described how he dealt with his grief, noting 'a curious method by which one pushes aside some feelings that get in the way', indicating that he was used to doing this 'with an almost physical sense of effort which becomes half-mechanical'.[36] Writing to another friend, he set out that he saw two alternatives; 'Carry on', or 'The Man is dead: Carry on'. He could carry on whilst attempting to ignore the death, or carry on whilst acknowledging it. Six weeks later the choice became irrelevant as he himself was shot by a sniper.

28 J. Smith quoted in L. Macdonald, *Passchendaele*, p.161.
29 J.J. Gillam, *Gallipoli Diary*, p.68.
30 Gillam, op. cit. p.122.
31 N. Gladden, *Ypres 1917*, p.110.
32 A.D. Gillespie, *Letters from Flanders*, p.235.
33 Gillespie, op. cit. p.238.
34 Gillespie, op. cit. p.241.
35 H.E.E. Howson, *Two Men*, p.264 (italics in original).
36 Howson, op. cit. p.268.

The news of a mate's death appears to have been more upsetting if received on leave, supporting the observation that men's defensive reactions relaxed at home. Second-Lieutenant Robert Graves wrote of the death of Captain Edmund Dadd: 'News like this in England was far more upsetting than in France'.[37] Second-Lieutenant Guy Chapman, on leave at home, denounced the news of the deaths of two friends as 'a lie, a lie'.[38] Often however, the death of a friend happened in front of one. Private George Coppard experienced the death of his pal, Bill Bailey, shot in the head by a sniper. He felt this death 'acutely, as it was the first time a pal had been struck down beside me'. Demonstrating how he had avoided thinking of threat, he continued: 'It was a shock to realise that death could come from nowhere without actual fighting'.[39] Coppard implied that specific group tasks increased bonding and enhanced loss. In a 'small unit' like a machine gun team, 'it was a deep and personal loss when a comrade was killed'.[40] Similarly, Private Reginald Davis's best chum was killed on a digging fatigue by a sniper, a bullet blowing away his left lower jaw and part of his neck. Davis realised at once that matters were hopeless: 'I could not believe it at all – it did not seem possible that George with whom I had spent every hour, every day in close companionship for so many months past, was dying'. He stayed with him, kneeling with his arm round his shoulder, until he died. Of his own later reactions, Davis noted with typical Edwardian reticence: 'I certainly was not my natural self'.[41] Private Giles Eyre was less reticent. His pal Rodwell was mortally wounded, shot in the face, in the process of saving Eyre from a German bayonet on the Bazentin Ridge in July 1916 and died in front of him and fellow ranker O'Donnell. Eyre's comrade was 'mute, filled with the sense of loss, and we two, who had learned to look on death unmoved, bowed down and wept'.[42] They spent the rest of the day 'brooding', whereupon Eyre in Stoic mood advised O'Donnell: 'Shake up, old boy, no use pining'.[43] Eyre had to repeat this exhortation to O'Donnell, who was still talking about Rodwell, and it is clear that he did so simply wishing to shut down his own thought processes. This proved difficult when O'Donnell was killed a matter of days later by shellfire. Eyre described, on the moment of his death: 'It was unbelievable. I remained there stunned and stupefied'. The sole survivor now of his section, for the rest of the day he remained in silence, 'communing with my thoughts and thinking of my lost pals'. As before, he began to try and detach himself from such thoughts, and the following day he found himself simply 'rather apathetic and downcast'.[44]

---

37  R. Graves, *Goodbye to All That*, p.199. Edmund Hilton Dadd was killed on 3 September 1916 aged 25 and is commemorated on the Thiepval Memorial.
38  G. Chapman, *A Passionate Prodigality*, p.206.
39  G. Coppard, *With a Machine Gun to Cambrai*, p.26.
40  Coppard, op. cit. p.118.
41  E. Hodder-Williams, *One Young Man*, Kindle edition locations 412-425.
42  G.E.M. Eyre, *Somme Harvest*, p.161.
43  Eyre, op. cit. p.162.
44  Eyre, op. cit. pp.211-2.

The words used give insight into the specific nature of the reaction.[45] Private Richard Gwinnell at Salonika, hearing of the death of a particular mate described himself as '*downcast*'.[46] Robert Graves described himself as '*empty* and *lost*'.[47] Private Stephen Graham described 'a *sadness* and a *coldness*'.[48] Lance-Corporal William Andrews wrote after the death of his best friend: 'I was sick at heart with *loneliness*'.[49] Sapper Edward Wettern referred to '*feeling rotten*', and added 'stayed in dugout and slept all day. Kept off grub'.[50] Second-Lieutenant Llewellyn Griffith at Mametz Wood in 1916 describes this general reaction: '*Sadness* fell upon us all'.[51] Second-Lieutenant Carlos Blacker wrote of the death of his brother, 'I felt *empty* and *irritable*'.[52] Raymond Lodge, after the loss of a number of comrades in a short period wrote home, 'we have all been rather *sad* lately', but added 'I am getting over it now'.[53] Private Frederic Manning described a soldier tearful at the death of a pal, who stated: 'I'm damned *sorry* about him'.[54] Second-Lieutenant Arthur West, left out of an attack learnt of three fellow officers killed and two badly wounded, noting: 'I never felt more utterly *sick and miserable* than to-day'.[55] Lieutenant Denis Barnett sums this up in describing the 'love of trench comrades' for each other as 'artificial' and that 'death that cuts it off does not touch the emotions at all … *regret* is what you feel'.[56] The words chosen thus often indicate sadness rather than grief or trauma. Private Bertie Sporton, however, described the news of death of mates as 'hellish',[57] and Lieutenant-Colonel Ralph Hamilton was one who chose to use the word grief. When his fellow officer Arthur Bath was wounded in his presence and later died he confided to his diary: 'It is a terrible grief to me, as he did everything for me, and had been with me night and day for two years'.[58]

Another emotion was anger. This was expressed in a variety of ways, from General James Jack's brief anger expressed in flicking a soldier's pipe out of his mouth in anger on discovering the death of his intelligence officer;[59] to Siegfried Sassoon's cold anger on reckless patrols after the death of both his brother and friend 'Tommy' Thomas. 'I

---

45 Italics used in the following quotes are those of the author.
46 R. Gwinnell, Private Papers, IWM Docs 11601.
47 Graves, op. cit. p.174.
48 S. Graham, *Private in the Guards*, p.239.
49 W.L. Andrews, *Haunting Years*, p.151.
50 E. Wettern, quoted in P.H. Liddle, *Men of Gallipoli*, pp.255-6.
51 L.W. Griffith, *Up to Mametz*.
52 J. Blacker (ed.), *Have You Forgotten Yet?*, p.52.
53 O.J. Lodge, *Raymond*, p.48.
54 F. Manning, *The Middle Parts of Fortune*, Kindle edition location 277.
55 A.G West, *The Diary of a Dead Officer*, p.74.
56 D. O. Barnett, quoted in L. Housman, *War Letters of Fallen Englishmen*, p.40.
57 B.V. Sporton, Private Papers, IWM Docs 11731.
58 R.G.A. Hamilton, *The War Diary of The Master of Belhaven*, p.365. Arthur William Bath died on 7 August 1917 and is buried in Bard Cottage Cemetery near Ypres.
59 J. Terraine, *General Jack's Diary*, p.209.

went up to the trenches with the intention of trying to kill someone', he confessed.[60] Sergeant John Lucy, whose brother had been killed on the Aisne, 'completely lost control' when he met the last remaining survivor of his brother's section, 'going for him bald-headed', telling him in as many words that he should be dead, too.[61]

Soldiers sometimes described a reaction of shock, as we have seen. There was firstly the shock that a man known to have been wounded had died. Second-Lieutenant Evelyn Fryer described how a fellow subaltern, Reginald Corkran, was wounded cutting grass in no-man's land. His later death came as a 'great shock', as it was assumed that the wound was not serious.[62] Secondly, there was the shock of the news of the sudden death of pal. Private John McCauley wrote, for example, 'my best friend ... dead. The news stunned me'.[63] Captain Robert Ross described the reaction on the death of a brother officer in his diary: 'We are a little stupefied by the news'.[64] When death was omnipresent, and fatalism the order of the day, shock indicates that a sense of invulnerability could also be present. As Richard Holmes remarks, 'chief amongst (the) palliative techniques is denial'. The soldier could become convinced that 'nothing will harm him'.[65] Lord Moran similarly wrote: 'War is the business of youth, and no young man thinks he can ever die'.[66] On his way to the front for the first time, Major Arthur Gibbs noted on seeing a pile of weapons recovered from the dead: 'The idea of my being killed was absurd, fantastic'.[67] Whilst training, Walter Williams sat drinking with his friends, planning for the future 'for none of us ever doubted our own immortality'.[68] When he received the news of his brother's death, it thus seemed 'impossible to comprehend' for he had 'always seemed so confident, and one of life's survivors'.[69] John McCauley was one of very few who wrote about the sudden descent into a sense of vulnerability: 'Today, Death snatches the life of my chum. Tomorrow, who? Me?'

Deaths caused by 'friendly fire' must have accounted for a significant proportion of First World War deaths. For Guy Chapman, deaths in the trenches because of enemy shellfire were commonplace – he described them as having 'an inevitable quality'. But the death of one man and the injury of eight others from a British trench mortar projectile blown off course by wind, caused a strong reaction in an otherwise well-adapted man. Chapman saw it as 'a sinister and malignant stroke, an outrage'.[70] Reaction to a

---

60   S. Sassoon, *The Complete Memoirs of George Sherston*, pp.274-5.
61   J.F. Lucy, *There's a Devil in the Drum*, pp.206-7.
62   E.R.M. Fryer, *Reminiscences of a Grenadier*, p.44. Reginald S. Corkran died on 11 June 1915 and is buried at St Margarets, Chipstead.
63   J. McCauley, Private Papers, IWM Docs 6434.
64   R.B. Ross, *The Fifty-First in France*, p.156.
65   R. Holmes, *Acts of War*, p.223.
66   Lord Moran, *The Anatomy of Courage*, p.143.
67   A.H. Gibbs, *Gun Fodder*, p.57.
68   Williams, op. cit. location 540.
69   Williams, op. cit. location 418.
70   G. Chapman, *Passionate Prodigality*, p.64.

friend's death was also affected by the general shape that one was in, physically and mentally. In the German spring offensive of 1918, Arthur Gibbs suffered the death of a junior officer, whom he referred to as 'The Babe'. Gibbs was exhausted and under tremendous strain, barely sleeping and living in a hole in the ground covered by a tarpaulin. He described himself as 'done in completely'. The Babe's death had been a 'frightful shock', the young officer being hit beside him. Gibbs carried him away personally, spouting blood: 'I wanted to get away and hide'. He was not afraid of death, but 'of going on in that living hell'.[71] He was trembling, jumpy and could not concentrate. On the Somme in 1916, Francis Buckley described how he was 'utterly worn out', not only physically exhausted, but emotionally 'with the depression naturally caused by losing so many friends and comrades in a manner apparently so fruitless'.[72] The mounting toll of death was thus a strain in its own right, especially when it was seen as achieving nothing. In Flanders in 1915, Douglas Gillespie surveyed the heavy casualty lists and wrote home that one 'begins to look at them to see who's left alive, rather than who's dead'.[73] Lieutenant O'Hara of the Dublin Fusiliers after landing at Gallipoli found himself the only remaining officer standing. He told a padre that what he felt most was the 'loneliness of it all'. All his brother officers were gone. He had no one to talk to.[74]

On the Aisne in 1914 John Lucy described how one fellow soldier 'morbidly occupied himself by passing in the names of the dead' but noted that he himself 'did not want to hear them'.[75] Silence about death was generally the rule. Bernard Adams noted that after a fatality, 'silence ... reigned for a few hours'.[76] Frederic Manning described soldiers talking of dead comrades 'with anxious, low voices ... unsteady and inclined to break', with 'control gradually returning'.[77] In a post-battle roll call, he perceived men 'anxious to restrain their feelings'.[78] Richard Haigh, a tank officer, watched one the British machines during the Hundred Days advance being consumed by fire. Once it became clear whose tank it was: 'None of us talked much about it'.[79] When there was discussion of the dead it seems to have been very controlled. Sidney Rogerson on the Somme in 1916 described meeting comrades when: 'Since we had last met two of our friends had gone west'. The immediacy of the deaths being gone, 'except for a passing reference – "rotten luck" – their names were not mentioned'. Rogerson and his comrades were simply 'glad to be out, to be alive, and to be together

---

71  Gibbs, op. cit. p.292.
72  F. Buckley, *Q.6.a.* p.98.
73  Gillespie, op. cit. p.140.
74  O. Creighton, *With the Twenty-Ninth Division in Gallipoli*, p.74.
75  Lucy, op. cit. p.173.
76  Adams, op. cit. p.36.
77  Manning, op. cit. location 234.
78  Manning, op. cit. location 377.
79  R. Haigh, *Life in a Tank*, p.86.

again'.[80] There was no morbid analysis of the meaning of their losses – the present was all. Guy Chapman described the same, muted, passing reference to the dead: 'We talked *a little* of vanished friends, of dead men'.[81] Euphemisms prevailed. Lieutenant Conningsby Dawson noted the use of the phrase 'Gone West', adding that 'we rarely say that a man is dead'.[82] In contrast Lieutenant John Allen noted: 'Yesterday we had a quiet day after we left the fire trench. The men talked about wounds and dead men all day'.[83] Bertie Sporton casts further light on this sort of conversation, describing how he was repeatedly asked about the deaths of two comrades. He could only reply that he heard a 'roar and blinding flash and they were both knocked away from in front of me'.[84] It seems likely that what was talked about was factual and designed to put a process of mental questioning at rest, rather than being an emotion-based discussion of loss. As Richard Haigh wrote: 'One's only feeling is the purely primitive one of relief, that it is another and not one's self'.[85]

Giles Eyre, who had wept on the death of his pal Rodwell, later lost two more members of his section. On this occasion the losses simply *'weighed on'* him.[86] He wrote how men whom he liked and had been 'in close intimate touch' with would be killed, and that he would simply feel 'sorry for them', experiencing a sense of loss for only a 'fleeting instant', whereupon 'one plunges back into the activities of the moment'.[87] Reactions to loss could pass swiftly. Second-Lieutenant Edmund Blunden wrote that the death of a comrade failed to 'have its full painfulness in the thick of things'.[88] Trooper W. Clarke stated that feelings of loss 'only came to the fore when it was a special mate' who had been killed but that such reactions 'would quickly go away'.[89] The Reverend Julian Bickersteth wrote of the deaths of officers in his division that 'we feel a momentary pang of regret and then turn our attention to other things'. He was clear that to avoid dwelling on loss was self-protective: 'We dare not let our minds meditate upon these sorrows, or we simply could not carry on'.[90] There was plenty of distraction to assist this. When his great friend Gilbert Carré was killed at Cambrai in November 1917, his company commander Alan Thomas noted that 'fortunately I had no time to think'.[91] Private Alfred Burrage also described how men defended themselves, becoming 'grossly selfish', thinking 'only of our own bellies and our own skins'. He, like Bickersteth, viewed it as a simple matter of necessity: 'It has

---

80   Rogerson, op. cit. p.99.
81   Chapman, *Passionate Prodigality*, p.81 (author italics).
82   C. Dawson, *Carry On*, p.79.
83   J. Allen, quoted in Housman, op. cit. p.29.
84   Sporton, op. cit.
85   Haigh, op. cit. p.136.
86   Eyre, op. cit. p.194 (author italics).
87   Eyre, op. cit. p.195.
88   E. Blunden, *Undertones of War*, p.156.
89   W. Clarke, Private Papers, IWM Docs 1377.
90   Bickersteth, op. cit. p.247.
91   A. Thomas, *A Life Apart*, p.136.

to be that way. Our hearts would break if we ... let our minds dwell on their agonies and their deaths'. For Burrage this defence meant a self-imposed isolation: 'It isn't safe to have a friend. Any moment he may become a mess of human wreckage with a twisted rifle in his hand, and then you've got to look for a new one'.[92] Lieutenant-Colonel J.W. Barnett wrote of the 'very sad' death of a fellow officer, but added: 'One forgets at once'.[93]

Sadness was necessarily temporary. Private Walter Green indicates a timescale of a 'day or two'. Private William Shanahan described the deaths of mates as 'soon forgotten',[94] and Private Nicholson remarked: 'I didn't cry ... If you cried once you'd never stop'. As the war went on he unashamedly remarked that 'you could forget the death of a very fine friend in five minutes'.[95] The mechanism that achieved this was clearly distraction by focussing on purpose. One anonymous soldier wrote of a 'fleeting instant' of 'poignant loss'. After this instant had passed: 'One plunges back into the activities of the present; new people take their place and life goes on'. This was 'no matter of callousness. The exigencies of war demand all one's energies'.[96] This soldier could be describing how in a pre-war industrial workplace, a fellow-worker would leave and his place immediately be taken by another. As Arthur Gibbs noted after the death of an officer who had taken his place temporarily in charge of his artillery battery, 'a new face took his place at the mess table, the routine was exactly the same'.[97] Gibbs was not being callous, indeed, he been profoundly upset by what he saw as the injustice of the man's death, but, as Walter Green wrote simply: 'You got over upset by getting back to the job'.[98]

John McCauley 'feigned calmness and indifference as far as it was possible' after the death of two pals. He was motivated by a particular dread: 'The one thing which we all feared more than death was that we might betray our fears to each other'.[99] Second-Lieutenant Huntly Gordon also described a muted response to news of the death of an acquaintance, a soldier simply responding: '"Bad luck!" with no more concern than you would show for a batsman who is out for a duck'. He had cultivated 'a real poker face' because that he perceived that 'here the very highest virtue is to be hard-boiled'. He attributed this partly to 'pride', but feared that emotion might be contagious.[100] In the face of the death of a relative it was difficult to keep this poise. Edmund Blunden described the dismemberment of a lance-corporal by a shell whereupon his brother

92  A.M. Burrage, Diary, http://www.firstworldwar.com/diaries/burrage_intro.htm.
93  J.W. Barnett, Private Papers, IWM Docs 666.
94  W.D. Shanahan, Private Papers, IWM Docs 6312.
95  Nicholson quoted in M. Shadbolt, *Voices of Gallipoli*, p.90.
96  Anon quoted in D. Winter, *Death's Men*, p.208.
97  Gibbs, op. cit. p.206.
98  W. Green quoted in R. van Emden & S. Humphries, *Veterans*, p.128.
99  McCauley, op. cit.
100 H. Gordon, *The Unreturning Army*, Kindle edition location 1534.

came upon the scene. He was sent to company headquarters 'in a kind of catalepsy'.[101] John Lucy described himself as 'beside myself with grief at the loss of my brave young brother'.[102] He, like others, however, was well able to keep fighting after the death of a close relation. Llewellyn Griffith described a moment of denial at Mametz Wood when told that his brother had been killed by a shell whilst bearing a message that he himself had written, in the following dialogue: '"My God ... he's lying out there now, Taylor!" "No, old man ... he's gone". "Yes ... yes, he's gone".' But Griffith was immediately drawn back to the present: 'Within the unclouded portion of my being a host of small things took their place on the stage, drawing their share of attention'.[103] Second-Lieutenant Bernard Martin's brother had been killed six months before he himself arrived in France. Walking up the road to Ypres he was suddenly confronted with the very graveyard at Vlamertinghe. Yet Martin turned away from the rows of crosses. He was ashamed – he could not face his brother.[104] New to the Western Front, his adaptation to death had yet to crystallise.

### *Loss and tears*

Lance-Corporal A. Laird wrote to Brigadier-General Frank Maxwell's widow: 'Madam, I cried till my heart was liking to burst'.[105] Similarly, when Lieutenant James Marsland was killed, Francis Hitchcock noted that Horrigan, his servant, 'wept for days'.[106] This was the 'grief' of the deferential led for the paternal leader. That the relationship was two-way is demonstrated by Sergeant-Major Sullivan at Neuve Chapelle: 'His eyes were red and swollen ... he was ... seen to weep more than once for his lost men'.[107] Laird, Horrigan and Sullivan broke any taboo on 'tears in the trenches'. They were not alone. An Australian private described the death of Captain H.H. Moffat: 'When B Company heard that he had gone ... they wept unashamedly, too. I have seen hardened soldiers with tears in their eyes when they spoke of Captain Moffat, MC'.[108] Padre Innes Logan wrote that 'I have seen senior N.C.O.'s crying like children because their young officer was dead'.[109] Private R. Lawrence found his comrade Puckrin 'with tears running down his face'. He 'didn't need a second look' to know that Puckrin's pal Roscoe was dead.[110] When Private Alfred Burrage was told that his only close friend, Dave, a stretcher-bearer had been killed at Passchendaele, he 'began

---

101 Blunden, op. cit. p.46.
102 Lucy, op. cit. p.207.
103 Griffith, op. cit.
104 B. Martin, *Poor Bloody Infantry*, p.46.
105 A. Laird, quoted in G. Chapman, *Vain Glory*, p.468.
106 Hitchcock, op. cit. p.89. James Francis Marsland died on 15 August 1915, aged 39, and is buried in Lijssenthoek Military Cemetery.
107 Lucy, op. cit. p.240.
108 Anon, quoted in Holmes, op. cit. p.245. Hayward Hugh Moffat died on 21 September 1918 and is buried in La Chapelette Cemetery, Peronne.
109 I. Logan, *On The King's Service*, p.99.
110 R. Lawrence quoted in L. Macdonald, *Voices and Images of the Great War*, p.239.

to cry like a baby'.[111] Several days later, Dave proved to be very much alive. Burrage found himself cross with him. Having 'wasted a lot of emotion' on him he had 'got used to the idea of his being dead'.[112]

Walter Green described how such tears were generally as private and as brief as possible. Describing men as 'touchy for a day or two' when a mate was killed, he noted that 'it was nothing to see a man in a quiet part of the trench having a little weep'. If a man did not cry, 'then often his voice broke down and he would not want to talk to anybody else', and he would 'perhaps take a quiet five minutes to pull himself together'.[113] Such reactions were clearly short-lived. Natural though they seem to us, Great War soldiers often reacted badly to tears. Reginald Davis described how intensely crying affected him when he wrote: 'To see and hear a man sob is terrible, almost as terrible as some of the wounds I have seen'.[114] As we have noted, however, tears do not only reflect grief. In action on Gallipoli, the dead did not move William Malone, but the wounded did. Writing home to his wife about the bravery of his injured men he described how 'I sometimes … get tears in my eyes'. Otherwise, he stated: 'I am really very callous and hard'.[115]

## Burial

### *Searching*

The death of a friend or relative might trigger a search, sometimes extensive and often fruitless. Second-Lieutenant Billie Nevill described a soldier shot dead on a night patrol in no-man's-land. His officer brother arrived and despite it having been forbidden that an officer should go out he 'hopped out & searched till he found his brother' whereupon he 'picked him up alone and carried him in, & then absolutely collapsed'.[116] After the decimation of 10th Durham Light Infantry on the Somme, Private Ernest Parker similarly 'discovered the Colonel and Adjutant, who had been searching for the body of the Adjutant's brother'.[117] Captain Billy Congreve spent time in the same way looking the body of his uncle, Major Arthur King, killed on 15 March 1915 at St Eloi. He first went out on 21 April, but was 'disappointed'.[118] He went out again on 1 May, and eventually found him on the 4th. King was 'simply riddled with bullets and … very far gone'. Searching for the explanation he knew he would have to provide, Congreve came to the view that 'he must have walked into a machine-gun at least. I can't account for the number of holes any other way'. He could

---

111 Ex-Private X (A.M. Burrage), *War is War*, p.147.
112 Ex-Private X, op. cit. p.158.
113 W. Green quoted in van Emden & Humphries, op. cit. p.128.
114 Hodder-Williams, op. cit. location 342.
115 Crawford, op. cit. location 3555.
116 R.E. Harris, *Billie – The Nevill Letters: 1914-1916*, p.99.
117 E.W. Parker, *Into Battle*, p.58.
118 Congreve, op. cit. p.125.

not bring the body in but 'sent all he had on him, which wasn't much, to Dorothy. The glasses were too smashed and the torch too gruesome'.[119] King's corpse was never recovered.[120] The drive to have knowledge about a death is strong. Captain Llewellyn Griffith on the Somme in July 1916 described a padre who had heard the previous evening that his son had been killed near Fricourt the day before, and who set off at once to try to find his grave. After hours of fruitless searching he 'couldn't find any one who knew where it was, nor could he find the padre who buried him. He walked till he could walk no more'.[121] Conningsby Dawson had a similar experience describing how 'a Major turned up who had travelled fifty miles by motor lorries and any conveyance he could pick up on the road'. He sought 'a glimpse of our front-line trench where his son was buried'. Dawson took him to a safe place where he could see over the ground where the son had died, whereupon he 'forgot all about me and began speaking to his son in childish love-words'.[122]

Sidney Rogerson was asked permission by 'Mac', one of his fellow officers on the Somme: 'To go out and hunt among the dead lying around Dewdrop Trench for the body of his brother', reported missing three weeks earlier. He had learnt that some of the bodies belonged to units of his brother's division. Rogerson refused as 'it was unthinkable that he would ever find his brother', and if he did the body would 'probably be so mangled or decomposed that the discovery would only leave a dreadful blot on his memory'.[123] Given that Mac would have been perfectly familiar with decomposed human remains, Rogerson was indicating that his brother's remains might specifically breech his adaptation. Searching was not confined to relatives. Lieutenant H.G.R. Williams returned to Gommecourt whilst on a signalling course in 1917 to end a different process of questioning. Scouring the battlefield he found a haversack and book belonging to his comrade Lance-Corporal Deane, concluding: 'Our supposition that he had been blown to bits must have been correct'.[124] Similarly, Lieutenant Edgar Lord returned to Thiepval to locate his friend Ivan Doncaster. Having identified him by 'hair, shirt, breeches and lastly by his identity tag', he 'reverently laid him to rest'.[125] As we have seen, individuals will do a great deal to relieve a sense of helplessness – Lord was determined to do the last thing he could for his friend.

Discovering a loved one's grave was naturally important. Finding himself near his brother's burial place, Douglas Gillespie wrote home for more exact details of the location. He however wrote in a rather bleak moment: 'I don't think it matters very

---

119 Congreve, op. cit. pp.133-4. Dorothy King was Arthur King's wife.
120 Arthur Montague King is commemorated on the Menin Gate.
121 Griffith, op. cit.
122 Dawson, op. cit. p.79.
123 Rogerson, op. cit. p.48.
124 H.G.R Williams, quoted in K.W. Mitchinson, *Gentlemen and Officers*, p.163.
125 E.B. Lord, Private Papers, IWM Docs 6559. Second-Lieutenant Robert Ivan Doncaster died on 1 July 1916 and is buried in Lonsdale Cemetery, Authuille.

much though where and how anyone is buried'.¹²⁶ His parents no doubt had a different view, especially when Douglas himself was killed as well in September 1917 at La Bassée.¹²⁷ Perhaps the most moving and instructive account of searching is given by Julian Bickersteth, one of three brothers on active service. His brother Morris was killed at Serre on 1 July 1916. Within days he had travelled to his brother's battalion and obtained an account from a survivor of his brother's last moments. In response to his enquiries, five months later he received a letter from an officer indicating that Morris's body had certainly been recovered as a handkerchief marked 'Bickersteth' had been found on a corpse. Nine months later Julian was again at Serre placing a cross 'within yards of where Morris must have been when he was struck',¹²⁸ and reading the Burial Service. In July 1917 he was in discussion with a corps chaplain who had buried the Serre fallen, and wrote to his mother convinced 'that our dear one's body now lies somewhere in this consecrated cemetery set 100 yards from where he fell'.¹²⁹ In July 1919 the whole family was able to lay flowers by Julian's cross, which was still standing. The process of searching had come, over the years, to a certainty about where the body lay.

*Use of ritual*

As we have seen, the use of ritual was a central part of Victorian mourning practice. Although George Coppard wrote fatalistically of the soldier buried by a falling shell: 'What was the good of digging him out? In one stroke he was dead and buried',¹³⁰ men would make effort to bury dead comrades. Captain James Dunn described how Second-Lieutenant George Heastey, 'the last of the likeable gallant trio of youngsters who joined from Sandhurst in June' was killed and at night 'his platoon carried him back two miles for burial'.¹³¹ Although Stephen Graham described burying the dead as 'such a tedious job', and when carried out as a fatigue being 'done in the most rough-and-ready way',¹³² most soldiers felt an imperative to bury comrades. Near Fricourt, James Dunn recorded how his unit found itself among the dead of the Welsh Division. 'Friends were recognised, and buried in haste lest we had to move on'.¹³³ On the March 1918 retreat, Major Denys Reitz encountered a party of soldiers carrying their dead officer to the rear, one of them commenting 'that they

---

126 Gillespie, op. cit. p.253.
127 Private Douglas Melville Gillespie died on 26 September 1917, aged 34, and is commemorated on the Tyne Cot Memorial.
128 Bickersteth, op. cit. p.169.
129 Bickersteth, op. cit. p.201. Queens' Cemetery, Puisieux.
130 G. Coppard, op. cit. p.38.
131 J.C. Dunn, *The War the Infantry Knew*, p.237. Heastey had sadly not lasted long, being killed within two months on 20 July 1916. He is buried in Dantzig Alley Cemetery, Mametz.
132 Graham, *Private in the Guards*, p.247.
133 Dunn, op. cit. p.225.

weren't going to allow no bloody Boche to bury the skipper'.[134] Dissenting comments were few, although Julian Bickersteth did record that when a soldier died, his body might 'receive scant attention', exhortations to burial being met with the protest: 'Oh surely you wouldn't have us neglect the living for the dead?'.[135] Generally, whilst an unknown body could be stuffed in the parapet, a mate could not, at the moment of death, be treated like an object. On the Somme Giles Eyre put this simply in his comment to his comrades when one of their number was killed: 'We can't leave him to be trampled and heaved about like an old sack. Come on … let's try to cover him up'.[136] Reginald Davis's friend having been killed, he immediately 'made application to the sergeant-major that I might help bury my chum'.[137] When George Coppard's friend Edwin was killed he had to be buried in a great hurry due to shelling, and with no padre: '"Goodbye old pal" were the only words said'. But his mates had seen to it that he was buried. Sidney Rogerson, on losing one of his fellow officers wrote: 'Him we buried before daylight as reverently as we could in the circumstances' even if this meant digging a grave between bursts of machine-gun fire and then only in the parados of the trench.[138] It was likely that everyone hoped to be buried by a pal, as the fear of dying alone indicated.

The burial of mates was generally described in terms of sadness rather than any traumatic reaction; for example: 'sorry task;'[139] 'what a sad sight;'[140] 'melancholy duty.'[141] Only Richard Gwinnell described burying mates as 'a nightmare to me'. [142] Billy Congreve brought in several bodies in front of St Eloi in April 1915 and buried them behind the front line trench. He wrote: 'One gets very callous I find'. There followed a 'poor sort of funeral, no service, nothing; just an old great coat over the face and a few odd curses by some man at another's clumsiness'.[143] Callous though he might have considered himself, he brought the bodies in and buried them. When Arthur Gibbs buried the officer killed in his place, a football match was taking place outside the cemetery. Gibbs recorded that the players didn't stop their game. 'Why should they? They were too used to funerals – and it might be their turn in a day or two'.[144] Soldiers *were*, however, concerned about the manner of their mates' funerals. They describe

---

134 D. Reitz quoted in Holmes, op. cit. p.20.
135 Bickersteth, op. cit, p.270.
136 Eyre, op. cit. p.162.
137 Hodder-Williams, location 418.
138 Rogerson, op. cit. p.44.
139 E. Junger, *Storm of Steel*, p.84.
140 E. Williams , quoted in D. Jones, *Bullets and Bandsmen*, p.47.
141 RSM Boreham, quoted in J.C. Dunn, *The War the Infantry Knew*, p.80.
142 Gwinnell, op. cit.
143 Congreve, op. cit. p.125.
144 Gibbs, op. cit. p.206.

them variously as being carried out with 'solemnity';[145] 'reverently';[146] with 'decency';[147] and 'properly'.[148] By this, they almost certainly meant the use of appropriate ritual. The extent and content of this might vary, as we have already seen, depending on the circumstances. When Giles Eyre knelt by his dying pal Rodwell, the mortally wounded man's last words were, according to Eyre, 'try to bury me – decently'. Eyre and his comrade O'Donnell, still under fire, carried him to a shell hole, scooped earth and debris over him and wrote his name on a bandage wound round a rifle which they stuck in the mound.[149] Sergeant Douglas Pinkerton and fellow soldiers buried a friend. No padre being available, they 'stood about with bowed heads for a little while', this being the 'only tribute that poor Nichols had'.[150] Captain Gerald Burgoyne was struck by finding the body of a soldier who had just reported to him, and 'I buried him at dusk, and said the Lord's Prayer over him'. Burgoyne could not read any specific burial prayers as he could not show any light, being still under fire.[151] Limited though his action, Burgoyne had deliberately used religious ritual.

The fighting at Gallipoli posed particular problems for recovering comrades' bodies. John Gillam described how men would volunteer to go out and rope up a body, which would then be hauled in. Sometimes there were trench burials, but Gallipoli was likely the only place that cremation was resorted to. 'They will soak the body in petrol ... then fire into the body, the white-hot bullets soon setting the petrol on fire, and the bodies in this dry climate quickly get cremated'.[152] Similarly, when there were deaths on hospital ships returning to Egypt, there was a need for burial at sea. Gillam described how the ship would stop, 'a great hush falling over the vessel as the body was shot over the side'.[153]

Burials were not always hasty affairs. Francis Hitchcock described how:

> At 2.00pm I left the front line to attend Lynch's funeral. From the mortuary a party of about 50 officers and other ranks followed the bier, which was bourne on a wheeled stretcher, Father Moloney marching in front, in his surplice. With one of his N.C.O.'s I helped to lift Lynch's body into the grave ... Lynch was buried like all at the Front, his body being sewn up in a brown army blanket ... I returned with a heavy heart.[154]

---

145 S. Graham, *The Challenge of the Dead*, pp.47-8.
146 Rogerson, op. cit. p.284.
147 H. Muller quoted in A.F. Wedd, *German Students' War Letters*, quoted in N. Hanson, *The Unknown Soldier*, p.14.
148 J.B. MacKenzie, Private Papers, IWM Docs 926.
149 Eyre, op. cit. pp.161-2.
150 R.D. Pinkerton, *Ladies from Hell*, p.128.
151 C. Davison (ed.), *The Burgoyne Diaries*, p.14.
152 Gillam, op. cit. p.152.
153 Gillam, op. cit. p.164.
154 Hitchcock, op. cit. p.225.

Burial by a padre was by definition accompanied by Christian ritual. The Reverend J. Bell described such burials behind the lines as being accompanied by buglers sounding the Last Post. The Reverend David Railton added a sentimental touch to his very first front-line burial. 'We buried the brave lad's remains just behind the trench. While they were preparing, I collected a few little blue flowers'. The burial service was shortened: 'No Last Post! ... No officers were there and just the four men joined in the prayer'. He 'dropped the flowers on to him and went back along the trench'.[155]

Gerald Burgoyne, who had, as we have seen, officiated on his own in a humble way, was present when a medical officer of the Wiltshire Regiment was killed, and 'to my relief I met an RC Padre'[156] who carried out the burial. Volume of bodies might make such ritual brief, as might being under shellfire. A padre burying 25 men in five graves wrote: 'Five times I repeated a *very abbreviated* form of the burial service'. Even using existing shell-holes, 'the task took us exactly 2½ hours'.[157] Second-Lieutenant Edwin Vaughan in torrid action at Third Ypres described how: 'The shells continued to pour but we gave poor Breezy a burial in a shell-hole and the padre read a hurried prayer'.[158] This is notable not just for its use of ritual but the fact that the burial of a mate was carried out during an offensive action *and* the padre was with the attacking troops. But often time was limited. Reginald Davis, burying his chum, recorded that 'a chaplain was passing, and we had a service of a minute or two'.[159] Walter Williams described a 'harassed padre' going 'through the motions' of an improvised burial service before 'hurrying on to the next, having no time or inclination to discover if the occupant was Gentile or Jew, Atheist or Agnostic'.[160]

However, if a padre was not present, officers, in the fashion of Burgoyne, would still employ Christian ritual. Captain L. Evans wrote: 'As no padre appeared handy, and I had a Prayer Book in my pocket, I read portions from the Burial Service' as the common grave was being filled in.[161] Lieutenant Harold Knee at Tower Hamlets on 28 October 1917 gave an evocative description:

> Before we heaped the cold dank earth over the bodies I was able to read part of the Burial Service over them. It was a strange scene. One of the blokes had a Book of Common Prayer and it seemed scarcely decent to cover these poor 'bleeding pieces of earth' with filthy mud without giving them some sort of Christian burial – my father had been a lay preacher in his youth and I, too, had been a regular chapel-goer ... at least we, their comrades, could show some

---

155  D. Railton, Private Papers, IWM Docs 4760.
156  Davison, op. cit. p.129.
157  'E.A.F.' quoted in A. Simpson, *Hot Blood and Cold Steel*, (author italics).
158  E.C. Vaughan, *Some Desperate Glory*, p.197.
159  Hodder-Williams, op. cit. location 418.
160  Williams, op. cit. location 3521.
161  Dunn, op. cit. p.514.

measure of love and respect ... My helpers gathered round as I stood by the burial fosse and reverently played the parson.[162]

Second-Lieutenant Charles Carrington, however, described a different scene: 'Before we left we buried our dead men in a shell-hole in front of the trench'. As was required, they left markers: 'We made rough wooden crosses to mark the graves', but on this occasion 'no one seemed inclined to say a prayer'. Carrington could have provided the orisons but was 'much too shy to suggest it', the burial being carried out by the friends of the dead men.[163]

There are few descriptions of emotion expressed at such burials. Lieutenant-Colonel Rowland Feilding described the night-time burial of a private which was attended by his brother: 'The friends lowered the body, wrapped in a blanket', whilst to the accompaniment of artillery fire 'the poor brother sobbed on his knees by the grave side'.[164] Billy Congreve was at the death bed of his friend Captain Maurice Godolphin-Osborne. At his funeral Congreve, typical of most, kept his emotion in check. He noted how it 'made little or no impression on me, which is either because I have lately learned to understand or else forgotten how to'. His father, General Sir Walter Congreve had the following proud perception: 'Billy was splendid and quite collected'.[165] Graveside acting was likely the norm. Leslie Buswell, attending a mass burial noted: 'I stood there by those dead men and tried to look as if it were a natural thing to do'.[166]

### *Maintenance and return to comrades' graves*
Soldiers would generally raise a cross on a mate's grave if they could. In May 1915, Captain James Lusk's battalion of the Scottish Rifles lost its first officer, Captain Allan Lawrie. Lusk described one of his men making a wooden plate to go on the cross, on which he attempted to carve an inscription. Lusk spent days over the task, planed the plaque smooth, then took a rubbing to send to Lawrie's father.[167] John Masefield described a rather different 'rough wooden cross, made of packing case tied together & pencilled "To an Unknown British Soldier"'. He noted how someone had put imitation violets on the grave.[168] Such graves were maintained by comrades where possible. At Bois Grenier, Captain Dunn noted that this was inspired by senior officers: 'As

---

162 H.J. Knee, Private Papers, IWM Docs 6972.
163 C. Edmonds (C. Carrington), *A Subaltern's War*, p.84.
164 R. Feilding, *War Letters to a Wife*, p.10.
165 Congreve, op. cit. p.104.
166 L. Buswell, *With the American Ambulance Field Service in France*, http://www.lib.byu.edu/~rdh/wwi/memoir/Buswell/AAFS1.htm.
167 J. Lusk, *Letters and Memories*, p.59. Allan James Lawrie died on 16 May 1915, aged 27, and is buried in Rue-du-Bois Military Cemetery, Fleurbaix.
168 P. Vansittart, *John Masefield's Letters From The Front*, p.215.

long as O. de L.[169] was in command a party was sent from time to time to tend the Battalion graves there', and his replacement Colonel Crawshay had them 'tidied up before the Battalion left Bethune in 1916.'[170] Medical officer David Rorie described the fruits of these labours in a cemetery thus: 'Some (graves) were surrounded with railings of wood or iron; many had wreaths – one very pretty one was of artificial violets'.[171] Lieutenant Ronald Poulton noted that the Seaforth Highlanders in his brigade were 'very careful of their graves'. The area was 'beautifully turfed over, and planted with primroses and surrounded with a rough palisade of wood'.[172] Only Frank Richards refers to wilfully disturbing graves during winter on the Somme: 'Firewood was … scarce … We took the wooden crosses from lonely graves'. Pragmatism in this case outweighed sentimentality: 'They were no good to the dead but they provided warmth for the living'.[173]

Soldiers would return to comrades' graves. Lieutenant Robert Mackay wrote in his diary during September 1917 on the Scarpe: 'Visited Alan Whyte's grave and got some improvement going'. Within days he had got a cross made.[174] Private T. McDonald returned to the grave of his brother in 1918 noting that: 'My brother's best pals had got a wooden cross and painted on his name, rank etc. and "one of the best". They also loved him'.[175] 'Vedette', a Second-Lieutenant of the Guards, was en route to the front line for the first time and detoured on a 'pious pilgrimage' to the grave of a friend who had died a year before, purchasing plants to be placed there.[176] Similarly, R.H. Bryan, attached to the Red Cross, located the grave of a friend and described how he was able to place some flowers on it and 'keep it in order whilst I was in that district'.[177] John McCauley wrote that, in keeping with pauper burials in London cemeteries, he and his comrades 'would collect small stones and pebbles and work out some epitaph above the grave'.[178] In exactly the same way Douglas Pinkerton and pals went to find one of their officers' graves at Lille. They each gathered a handful of pebbles. 'With them we outlined the approximate boundaries of Mr. Findley's grave, not knowing then whether he rested directly underneath or two or three layers down'.[179] The crucifix-burning Frank Richards described one such visit at Bois Grenier village where the unit had been three years previously. He had a job to locate comrades' graves. Nature

169   Lieutenant-Colonel Oliver de Lancey Williams.
170   Dunn, op. cit. p.126.
171   D. Rorie, quoted in N. Cave, *Vimy Ridge* p.193.
172   E.B. Poulton, *The Life of Ronald Poulton*, p.347.
173   Richards, op. cit. p.217.
174   R.L. Mackay Diary, http://www.firstworldwar.com/diaries/rlm1.htm. Second-Lieutenant Alan Hill Whyte died on 9 April 1917, and is buried in Cabaret Rouge Cemetery, Souchez.
175   T. McDonald quoted in M. Brown, *Tommy Goes to War*, p.206.
176   'Vedette', *Adventures of an Ensign*, pp.30-1.
177   R.H. Bryan, Private Papers, IWM Docs 13953.
178   McCauley, op. cit.
179   Pinkerton, op. cit. p.110.

had taken its course and 'the grass and nettles and poppies very nearly hid the wooden crosses'. As with other such visits: 'We made them a bit respectable before we left.'[180] Walter Green returned to the burial place of a comrade clearly seeking information to put at rest rumination as to whether decency had prevailed. 'Two pieces of wood had been nailed together to form a cross' and the dead man's identification disc had been attached to it. Green was 'satisfied he was temporarily buried'. He had wanted to see the grave because 'I was there and I was involved'.[181] Lastly, Seaman Joe Murray on Gallipoli described another such trip, this time a different psychological purpose being spelt out: 'Most of my pals are buried in the places I visited yesterday; I wanted to say 'Goodbye' to them while I could'. A robust individual, Murray stated that: 'Time and time again I saw and conversed with the dead. I saw their wives, mothers and sweethearts. All the time I wondered why I was still alive'.[182]

## Conclusion

In contrast with the experience of enduring the presence of corpses, where novel methods of coping had to be invented, the Great War soldier had a good template for handling death in terms of the expression of emotion. Stoic non-expression of all but the first reactions of grief was the norm, and this model of restraint was transferred to the battlefield. Further, the era's heavy reliance on ritual, however brief and inadequate in the new circumstances, allowed the soldier who could ensure and perhaps participate in a burial to pull a curtain across the experience of the loss of a pal. Soldiers had effective tools to protect themselves against damage to their coping through loss.

But one thing becomes evident from the use of the particular words used to describe reactions to death. Although pals assumed, as we have seen, a greater personal weight than they might in civilian life due to the absence of family, the expression of loss was muted. 'Sadness' is the word often used. This may reflect the different nature of such friendships from those of the modern world, discussed earlier. There was generally little of the emotional closeness of modern friendships, whose loss calls forth intense emotions of grief. It was often as if a man at the next workbench or machine in a civilian workplace had left for another job. And in a sense, the workplace analogy is entirely apposite. The Great War soldier was therefore doubly protected by both the norms for expression of loss and the nature of the relationships lost.

---

180  Richards, op. cit. p.274.
181  W. Green quoted in van Emden & Humphries, op. cit. p.128.
182  J. Murray, *Gallipoli 1915*, p.167.

# Conclusion

This book began with the assertion that our view of the soldier of the Great War has become permeated with sentimentalism. A century on from the First World War, the quest to connect with those who fought is overshadowed by an image of their presumed experience of suffering, death, futility and trauma. In counterbalance, it was proposed that the ways in which these individuals sustained themselves through the years of trench warfare needed to be identified. The material for this would be contained in the record of their thinking, could only be understood by a close understanding of contemporary beliefs and attitudes, and would reveal whether these guided coping positively.

As we have seen, those who fought the First World War lived, in many ways, in a different world. The Edwardian period was one of extreme discrepancy between rich and poor. For the upper-classes, privilege still held sway. For the working poor and those facing grinding poverty, industrial drudgery and lack of aspiration was the norm. Yet despite this, there were shared values across the social spectrum. Patriotism involving national and local foci, coupled with a diffusive Christianity of varying degrees of theological sophistication, were common to all. These beliefs were sustaining on the battlefield in giving purpose to fighting and reassurance in the face of death. For men across the social divide, both heroic and domestic concepts of manliness provided inspiration in facing fear and sustaining motivation. The era's vision of the courageous individual contributed a behavioural model which offered an antidote to the psychologically corrosive presence of 'funk'. Contemporary attitudes to death and the ritual surrounding it afforded some structure for coping with the hecatombs of trench warfare. And for every individual, Stoic attitudes were built into either the public school ethos or the daily working grind. Hardship was to be endured and emotion was a matter to be contained and not expressed. Acceptance and perseverance were the bedrock of both personal coping and social order. These ways of viewing the world are largely alien to us now, and unless they are grasped rather than regarded as the aberrations of an unenlightened past, the experience of the Great War soldier cannot be fully understood.

Soldiers were not the inevitable and universal victims of trauma. The values and attitudes identified ensured that they were the possessors of resources which enabled most to survive despite occasions of horror and terror, often in conditions that we would now view as insufferable. The predicament of trench warfare included episodes of extraordinary discomfort – deprivation, extremes of temperature and saturation. Exposure to threat was constant in the front line. Coupled with physical hardship this had an abrasive effect that could wear coping skills thin to the point of fracture. Stoic endurance allowed soldiers to be content with physical and safety needs being met on a 'just enough' basis via the rotational system in and out of the line. The need for a sense of love and belonging was filled in a similar 'just enough' way through the limited contact with loved ones that was possible, and the adoption of mates as a proxy primary group. Yet as we have seen, the tendency to view First World War mateship through spectacles tinted with romanticism needs to be resisted. Comradeship was a group experience born of utility. It was largely free of modern introspection and emotional sharing. Such friendships were supportive, but in ways different to 21st century relationships. Lastly, the beliefs of the age allowed those who fought some fulfilment of higher needs, enabling a sense of self-esteem in their performance as soldiers and belief in the importance of what they achieved.

Those who went to fight were not misguidedly 'clinging to an increasingly irrelevant moral code'.[1] It would be inappropriate to deride anyone for being a child of their *zeitgeist*. Yet in today's world we dismiss the code of manliness as macho nonsense. Stoicism now seems archaic, endurance no longer being necessary in a comfortable, materialistic Western world so full of opportunity. We are no longer satisfied with 'just enough'. The necessity to control and avoid the expression of emotion is seen as an aberration, reflecting a lack of understanding about human coping. Exposure of the behaviour of governments erodes any warming sense of possession of the moral high ground. Jingoism is dead. Religion, despite the evidence of revival often amongst the young, is seen by many as an irrelevance. Worse, it is seen as harmful, furthering extremism.

These now unfashionable preoccupations were, however, undoubtedly protective in the context of the Great War. They allowed soldiers to think and behave in particular ways, forming a mental container which reduced the likelihood that unhelpful thoughts and emotions would leak out and undermine coping and performance of duty. Alex Watson, in his thorough work on morale in the First World War, suggests that psychological survival was based on 'self-deception'.[2] The choice of phrase is perhaps unfortunate – distraction is not self-deception. Soldiers utilised strategies that were positive in the light of the situation. Most were directed at reducing a sense of helplessness and establishing some sense of control in an environment where precious little was possible. Strategies were often avoidant rather than self-deceptive, and much coping on the battlefield was in this vein. Current research, as we have noted, finds that in situations where the outcome is likely to be unfavourable whatever one does, avoidance is the most adaptive coping strategy.

1  S. Grogan, *Shell Shocked Britain*, Kindle edition location 144.
2  A. Watson, 'Self-deception and Survival', *Journal of Contemporary History*, p.247.

Alex Watson observes that 'most men clearly overcame battle stress extremely successfully'.[3] Some, however, were clearly broken psychologically. The coping skills that by and large worked so well could not protect everyone all the time from either their own vulnerability or the cruelty of particular experiences. The image of the ultimate failure of coping, the shell-shocked soldier, has become totemic in our vision of the Great War combatant. The extent of shell-shock remains a keen debate. From about five and a half million British soldiers who served, the much-criticised official figures presented in *Diseases of The War* describe 28,533 shell-shock battle casualties to the end of 1917. A maximum 80,000 cases of 'nervous disorder' was finally arrived at.[4] Peter Leese suggests that it is currently estimated from studies of the French and German armies that a more reliable overall figure for cases of psychological disorder is around 200,000 – even with this revision, Watson's point seems well made.[5] Predictably, however, in our modern world increasingly preoccupied with the concept of trauma, such estimates have been amplified. Jay Winter, pushing the boundary of Second World War combat stress estimates,[6] plucks from the air a figure of 20 per cent of all Great War casualties being psychiatric in nature, suggesting 'a band of probability' with its lower end at 4 per cent of all casualties and at its upper end at 40 per cent, concluding: 'A mid-point could be the best approximation we can offer.[7] Based on Leese's review, however, the figure is in fact just under nine per cent of all casualties. If this is correct, the fact is that there were relatively few psychiatric casualties, rather than so many. The coping skills of the time clearly proved effective.

In a recent book on shell shock, Suzie Grogan writes that it was important 'to acknowledge that not everybody exhibited the classic signs of emotional distress linked to war trauma'. She noted that many soldiers returned from war 'exhausted, drained, but essentially in one piece physically and mentally'. She went on to optimistically state that many ex-soldiers 'went on to live happy and fulfilling lives'.[8] This view is undoubtedly correct. Yet, embarking upon the sea of confusion whipped up by the present day expectation of traumatisation rather than resilience, she then uncritically quoted psychiatrist Peter Heinl: 'Unless proof has been provided to the contrary, I regard anyone who has survived … war as having been traumatised in some way or

---

3 Watson, op. cit. p.248.
4 W.G. MacPherson et. al. (eds), *Diseases of The War: Volume Two*, p.9. The number of pensions awarded for shell shock and neurasthenia peaked in 1921 at 65,000. (W. Johnson & R.G. Rows, 'Neurasthenia and the War Neuroses', in MacPherson, op. cit. pp.7 & 56).
5 P. Leese, *Shell Shock*, p.10.
6 The War Office retrospectively estimated that between 5 and 30 per cent of all sick and wounded during the Second World War were psychiatric casualties, this figure largely depending on the type of warfare fought. (E. Jones & S. Wessely, 'Psychiatric Battle Casualties', *British Journal of Psychiatry*, p.243).
7 J. Winter, 'Shell Shock', in J. Winter (ed.), *The Cambridge History of the First World War, Volume Three*, p.332.
8 Grogan, op. cit. location 110.

other'.[9] This statement robs those who experienced the Great War of the dignity of having applied their coping skills and survived psychologically intact. The presumption of inevitable traumatisation is a conceit based on 21st century preoccupations. The desire to acknowledge the ordeal of the First World War soldier is not appropriately fulfilled treating shell shock as a synonym for suffering.

It would be easy for our desire to recognise this suffering to allow us slip into a place where we view Great War veterans as inevitably perpetual victims of their experiences. A good example of the distortion induced by using present-day expectations to anticipate reactions of a century ago is the retrospective use of the symptom-set of Post-Traumatic Stress Disorder (PTSD) to frame veterans' reactions. Re-experience phenomena, including flashbacks (involuntary, vivid images of the traumatic event which occur in the waking state) and nightmares are a hallmark of the diagnosis. Modernity expects the Great War soldier's peace to have been riven by flashbacks and nightmares. It is interesting, therefore, that in a study of war pension files, only half a per cent of 567 First World War veterans reported flashbacks.[10] Indeed, at the time, Professor Graham Brown reported that in the Salonika force, only five per cent of men under fire had nightmares.[11] There seems good reason to believe that the expression of trauma is different not only between cultures, but at comparatively close points in time within the same culture. In respect of re-experiencing, it has thus been suggested that the prevalence of moving visual imagery in the form of film in modern life has encouraged people to have more visual representations of everything, including trauma. As moving imagery became more a part of everyday life, memories became more visual.[12]

Are we in danger in this discussion of minimising the Great War soldier's reactions to warfare? Is it possible that endurance and emotional repression protected soldiers from certain manifestations of traumatic stress, only for it to emerge in other ways? It indeed appears that somatic symptoms (symptoms of stress experienced physically), were more common in soldiers of the First World War than in those of more recent conflicts. This emerges most clearly in the condition known as Disordered Action of the Heart. DAH, or 'effort syndrome', involved fatigue, breathlessness and chest pain. In most cases, no heart disease could be found.[13] It must not, however, be assumed that DAH was purely psychological in nature. Retrospective research found between 21 and 80 per cent of cases associated with the presence of some infectious disease.

---

9  P. Heinl, *Splintered Innocence*, p.77.
10 E. Jones et. al., 'Flashbacks and Post-Traumatic Stress Disorder: The Genesis of a 20th-Century Diagnosis', *British Journal of Psychiatry*, p. 160. They are rarely referred to in personal accounts, either. (P.E. Hodgkinson, 'Human Remains on the Great War Battlefields').
11 Report of the War Office Committee of Enquiry into "Shell-Shock" (RWOCESS), p.53.
12 E. Shorter, 'Paralysis – The Rise and Fall of a Hysterical Symptom', *Journal of Social History*, p.549.
13 E. Jones and S. Wessely, *Shell Shock to PTSD*, pp.43-4.

There was clearly a link between 'infective triggers' and psychological stress.[14] Return to duty rates were good – in 1915 there were 4,485 cases of DAH, 95.4 per cent of which so returned. In the post-war period it comprised 5 percent of pension cases. Neurasthenia, shell shock, anxiety neurosis and nervous debility accounted for 4.2 per cent.[15] Notwithstanding the government meanness expressed in the verdicts of the pension authorities, the figures are quite low.

The reality was, of course, that at points when coping wore so thin that it was no longer effective, psychological symptoms emerged. Such episodes were, however, often temporary. The majority of soldiers affected returned to duty. Removal to a base hospital, especially in Britain, produced a poor return rate. Of a series of cases of nervous disorder from November 1916 to May 1917, sent to a neurological centre in France, however, 65 percent so returned.[16] A Casualty Clearing Station operating in December 1916 produced almost identical figures – sixty-six per cent of 200 returned to 'the firing line' after seven days.[17] Charles Myers had established four special shell-shock centres close to the front-line by the end of that year, and the return to duty rate rose from 50 per cent to 90 per cent.[18] During Third Ypres in 1917 Gordon Holmes claimed that overall 80 per cent returned to duty within two to three weeks.[19] There is no doubt some truth in his assertion that many men who were sent down from the front line were 'merely shaken up', and that these individuals 'slept for 24 hours and after a few night's good rest' were largely recovered.[20] Whilst there is evidence that the army inflated the return rate from hospitals, these particular figures are consistent with more recent experience.[21] What we do not know is how many men across all the studies returned to combat roles. A current estimate of rate of return to duty after psychological treatment is that 'most servicemen can be returned to duty, although fewer than half go back to combat units'.[22]

It is important neither to overestimate nor underestimate the prevalence of psychological casualties. To overestimate reflects an undervaluing of soldiers' coping mechanisms. To underestimate would be to downplay the destructive nature of the war

---

14  Jones and Wessely, *Shell Shock to PTSD*, pp.43-4.
15  E. Jones et. al., 'War Pensions (1900-1945)', *British Journal of Psychiatry*, pp.376-7.
16  MacPherson, op. cit. p.2.
17  T.W. Salmon, *The Care and Treatment of Mental Diseases and War Neuroses ('Shell Shock') in the British Army*, p.36.
18  C.S. Myers, *Shell Shock in France 1914-18*.
19  G. Holmes, cited in Jones & Wessely, 'Psychiatric Battle Casualties', p.243.
20  RWOCESS, p.39.
21  Jones & Wessely, 'Psychiatric Battle Casualties', p.247.
22  Jones & Wessely, 'Psychiatric Battle Casualties', p.247. Once having had such a reaction, a soldier was more vulnerable to a second episode. Of a series admitted to hospital during the months of November and December 1917 just over 20 per cent had previously been hospitalised for shell shock/neurasthenia (MacPherson, op. cit. p.5); and in a study of psychiatric hospital admissions in the Salonika theatre, between 42 and 59 per cent similarly had a previous history of shell shock (Macpherson, op. cit. p.5).

on the human psyche. Peter Leese suggests that there were 'neurotic ex-servicemen' who though affected during the war recovered quickly in its aftermath. This is what would be expected from a positive view of soldier's coping mechanisms. It contradicts the presumption of necessary long-tasting traumatisation. Yet, there were similarly those who did not recover. With a narrow focus on the war, it would be easy to assume that it was necessarily the sole factor in breakdown. The men who went to fight had previous personal characteristics to be taken into account, and for some, these included a vulnerability to breakdown. In a study of hospitalisation in Salonika, 49 per cent of psychiatric casualties had a history of pre-war 'neurosis'.[23] The fact that the more vulnerable had an increased risk of breaking down in the face of war is in itself nothing surprising. It appears a cruel thing to send vulnerable individuals to war, but it is simply a sad reflection of the absence of appropriate selection. As Peter Barham has noted, many of those who remained in psychiatric hospitals for the rest of their lives after the war were those with previous histories of mental illness.[24]

Let us take a less well-known aspect of failure to survive the peace, the prevalence of suicide amongst veterans. Jonathan Scotland's review of two Canadian newspapers in the year following the war shows the press clearly choosing to report disproportionate numbers of soldier suicides as against civilian acts of self-destruction.[25] Some of these men were, as one might expect, badly physically injured, and some were described as shell-shocked. Others fell victim to despondency generated by the struggle of the depression years. This reminds us that the peace held its separate stresses. John Weaver's research on New Zealand First World War veterans suggests that the suicide rate for returned men ranged from two to four times as high as that of civilian men in the same age group.[26] In Australian veterans, David Noonan has traced 550 suicides, mainly during 1919-1920.[27] The number seems large, and in fact represents about a year's worth of male suicides during this period. Given that the vast bulk of Australian troops returned home during 1919, it is interesting that the number of men killing themselves in Australia was in fact slightly lower in 1920 than it was in 1915, and only 20 per cent more than in 1910. Suicide in veterans was a clear risk, yet it is important not to overstate it. It is similarly important not to attribute it solely to war experiences when there were other factors. Thus, the peak in suicide in Australia occurred in 1930 associated with the economic depression.[28]

---

23 Macpherson, op. cit. p.5.
24 P. Barham, *Forgotten Lunatics of the Great War*.
25 J. Scotland, 'Soldier Suicide after the Great War: A First Look', http://activehistory.ca/2014/03/soldier-suicide-after-the-great-war-a-first-look/.
26 J.C. Weaver, *Sadly Troubled History*, p.189.
27 http://www.theage.com.au/comment/why-the-numbers-of-our-wwi-dead-are-wrong-20140428-zr0v5.html. See also D.C. Noonan, *Those We Forget*.
28 1n 1910 there were 410 male suicides in Australia, in 1915 there were 537, in 1920 there were 516, with 791 in 1930. (Australian Bureau of Statistics, *Suicide in Australia*).

The negative effect of the war on general health is a given. Noonan has estimated that three per cent of Australian veterans who saw active service in the Great War would die a premature death due to war-related causes in the post war years.[29] In a war where virtually half of those who served were wounded, this is sadly not surprising. A study of soldiers leaving New Zealand in 1914 to fight and who survived, shows that in comparison to a non-combat 1918 cohort, veterans lived for 1.7 years less.[30] This difference is not that great given the circumstances. The effects of wounds, illness and suicide all played a part in this difference, and the effect did not last beyond 1930. This is interesting, as it suggests that there was a limited period in which the war's physical and psychological effects played their part in life-expectancy. The war of course left many individuals disabled. As Joanna Bourke summarises, for instance, over 41,000 men had limbs amputated during the war and 272,000 suffered limb injuries that did not require amputation.[31] The psychological consequences of such disability are beyond the scope of present enquiry. Yet, as Bourke reflects, those affected joined a wider community of disabled men, women and children. Thus, in 1919, there were 8.6 'crippled' children per every 1,000 in Britain.[32] During the 1920s there were over 200,000 industrial injuries of varying severity a year, 40,000 in the coal industry alone.[33] On one hand, therefore, the disabled of the Great War were a very significant group, whilst on the other, they need to be placed in the wider context of the prevalence of disability in post-war society.

Looking exclusively at veterans' experience of the war, we run the risk of losing touch with the context that surrounded them in the post-war world. The discussion of disability above indicates that the problems of veterans, though numerous, were not unique. In the case of suicide, this indeed was a feature of veterans' failure to cope in the post-war period. Yet the Australian figures show suicide rates at the height of the Great Depression to be much higher than in the main risk period for veterans of 1919-20. Let us therefore attempt to tease out the part that veteran status played in the post-war employment crisis. The 1920s represented a period of unusually high unemployment in Britain, but in 1932 the number out of work reached 3.4 million, one in six of the workforce. Estimates based on national insurance and unemployment payments suggest that up to May 1920, seventy per cent of the unemployed were ex-servicemen.[34] This figure should be viewed in the light of the fact that in 1919, over

---

29 http://www.theage.com.au/comment/why-the-numbers-of-our-wwi-dead-are-wrong-20140428-zr0v5.html. See also D.C. Noonan, op. cit.
30 N. Wilson et. al., 'Mortality of First World War Military Personnel: Comparison of Two Military Cohorts', *British Medical Journal*, p.7168.
31 J. Bourke, *Dismembering the Male*, pp.33-37.
32 Board of Education, *Annual Report of the Chief Medical Officer of the Board of Education, 1919* pp.102-3, cited in Bourke, op. cit.
33 http://www.swansea.ac.uk/media-centre/latest-news/disabilityinthesouthwalescoalfieldexhibitionrevealsanextraordinaryhiddenhistory.php.
34 J. Winter & J.L. Robert, *Capital Cities at War – Vol. 1*, p.208.

four million men had been demobilized. In the eight months following the armistice, the army alone had returned 112,101 officers and 2,816,964 enlisted men to civilian life.[35] Whilst the veteran unemployment problem steadily improved during the next decade, in April 1936 there were still 410,689 unemployed ex-servicemen,[36] representing 22 per cent of the total of 1,895,100 people out of work that month.

What were the factors influencing veteran unemployment? Firstly, there were obviously war-specific effects related to disability. In more lightly or uninjured ex-soldiers, however, the largely unrecognised psychological effects created by the bodily changes of post-traumatic physiological arousal (irritability, poor sleep, hypervigilance, poor concentration, and exaggerated startle) may have created a general difficulty. Thus in US veterans, unlikely to differ from their British counterparts, the 'general restlessness' of the returned soldiers and sailors 'made it difficult for many of them to settle down to the humdrum life of their former jobs'.[37] Further, such individuals may have had specific attitudinal issues. Many ex-servicemen 'felt that they were qualified for better positions than they had held before entering the service'.[38] On the other hand, seeming negative employer attitudes towards ex-soldiers may not have been related to their veteran status at all, but to other features, such as their age.[39] Nearly one and half million people came into the workforce for the first time between 1932 and 1938. As these young workers arrived, the prospects of older individuals, amongst whom were veterans, were bound to suffer.[40] Employers in new, expanding sectors preferred to take on young workers who did not 'bring to their new employment entrenched attitudes'. Similarly, employers turned away older men on the grounds that they 'had come to expect higher wages'.[41] Older men might also be more subject to illness, or might be 'disinclined to learn new methods'.[42] In a small group of veterans who died between 1939 and 1956 at Downgate, Tidebrook, East Sussex, a residential facility run by a charity supporting homeless and destitute ex-servicemen, the Embankment Fellowship Centre, the absence of supportive family and sheer age appear to have been

---

35  S.R. Graubard, 'Military Demobilization in Great Britain', *Journal of Modern History*, pp.297-311.
36  TNA PIN15/722, cited in N. Barr, *The Lion and the Poppy*, p.81.
37  Bureau of Labor Statistics, 'Public Attitude Toward Ex-Servicemen after World War I', *Monthly Labor Review*, p.1060.
38  Bureau of Labor Statistics, op. cit. p.1060.
39  In 1936: 'The chances of a man of 62 getting back into employment once he had become unemployed were only a fifth of those of a youth of 19, a third of those of a man of 30, and a half of those of a man of 50'. (W. Temple, *Men Without Work*, p.22).
40  E. Butchart, 'Unemployment and Non-Employment in Inter-War Britain', *University of Oxford Discussion Papers in Economic and Social History*.
41  The average weekly wage dropped from 73.8 shillings a week in 1920 to a low of 53.7 shillings a week in 1933. (B. Eichengreen, 'Unemployment in Interwar Britain', *Refresh*, p.3).
42  Eichengreen, op. cit. p.3.

the key factors in the predicament of residents.[43] Unemployment in the longer term may have had rather less to do specifically with veteran status than might be expected.

Today's eagerness to get close to the experience of the Great War soldier, and the sentimental preoccupation with suffering has directed our focus in particular ways. It has not been the intention of this book to downplay the negative psychological impact of the war. Rather, the aim has been to widen the focus of understanding by addressing the issue of how men coped positively in the trenches. In doing so, it becomes clear that we have undervalued the ability of such individuals to have protected themselves against the stress of war. We have similarly accepted a presumption that continued psychological victimhood was widespread. Whatever the vagaries of the statistics, the evidence of long-lasting significant psychiatric damage is lower than might be imagined. The men who fought were clearly more hardy than some have given them credit for being. The thrust of this book is that this is not necessarily surprising. In contemplating whether their war experience jeopardised their adjustment to the peace, we may similarly have overestimated the pervasiveness of continuing problematic war-related personal effects. An individual might have coped well with the war, but poorly with the separate and very real challenges of post-war Britain. A focus on the wider context of this period suggests less unique long-lasting effects of war experience than we might have expected. The discussion of the Great Depression shows a complex relationship between veteran status and being out of work. In this, the veteran's age was a much greater issue than being a veteran *per se*, although the psychological issues stemming from war-experience no doubt played their part in unemployment. Alistair Thomson argues that at a certain point after the war, a number of health and social issues might come together to undermine the coping of a particular veteran. 'A range of physical and mental health problems' could reach a tipping point 'exacerbated by unemployment' and perhaps family instability.[44] The problem is that the number of individuals who fell foul of this equation is not known.

Michael Roper, in the Epilogue to his book *The Secret Battle*, describes his grandfather, a veteran of Gallipoli and the Western Front. He pursued a stable life in employment with a contented marriage. The war's mark on him included malaria, nightmares and a propensity to 'angry outbursts'.[45] He clearly suffered some continued psychological reactions, the irritability being a symptom of the now familiar post-traumatic increased arousal. The author's grandfather, who served from the Somme to the Armistice, had a similar explosive temper. He was returned to the UK within a week or two of the armistice with diphtheria, when a diagnosis of valvular disease of the heart was made. Whether this condition arose from war service or not, diph-

---

43  P.E. Hodgkinson, 'Veteran Unemployment, the Embankment Fellowship Centre, and the Downgate Twenty-One', *Stand To!* p.53.
44  https://www.futurelearn.com/courses/ww1-stories/steps/31768. See also A. Thomson, *Anzac Memories*.
45  M. Roper, *The Secret Battle*, p.318.

theria would not have improved it. Whilst VDH was viewed in many as a functional condition, in his case it proved fatal at the age of 64. He successfully remained in stable employment with the exception of a year or so prior to the Second World War, and in a marriage which produced two daughters. These two men, like a wide range of veterans, had coped with the war successfully. Yet they continued to be marked by their experience. They remained, as no doubt did many others, sometimes moody or irritable for the rest of their lives. The author's grandfather would not, however, have seen himself as a victim. Those who participated in the war could not have failed to have been changed. This does not mean that they were psychiatric casualties of any sort. Being changed by an experience self-evidently does not indicate a failure of coping.

As noted above, the values that sustained soldiers a century ago are now largely rejected. This change occurred rapidly in some cases in the post-war world. But was the war itself responsible? Society no longer subscribed to the same code of manliness. Firstly, the notion of 'domestic manliness' had to be revised. Women had ably demonstrated that they could do a 'man's work'. Whilst their presence immediately disappeared from traditional male jobs, as demobilised soldiers returned, the gendered nature of workplaces would not in the longer term be able to remain the same. This would have an inevitable effect on the male's position in the home. Secondly, the concept of 'heroic manliness' underwent even more dramatic revision – Malcolm Tozer claims that 'the ideal of manliness had evaporated' by the end of the war itself,[46] literally blown out of existence in the futile juxtaposition of man and high-explosives. Manliness had involved standing face-to-face with other men. This image had been crushed beneath the juggernaut that was the developing technology of war. Even the word itself virtually became extinct in the grimy reality of the economically depressed post-war world. The acceptance of the reality of shell-shock had posed a particular challenge. British psychiatrists came to accept its presentation as hysteria,[47] a condition previously viewed as the province of female patients. Whilst German and French psychiatrists had been quite willing to acknowledge the presence of hysteria in men, British doctors had not, exactly due to the 'weakness and emotionality' implied.[48] To acknowledge its occurrence in men served only to erode the core of manliness further.

---

46  Tozer, 'Manliness: The Evolution of a Victorian Ideal', p.476.
47  Forty-six high-ranking officers and psychiatrists gave evidence to the War Office Committee of Enquiry into 'Shell-Shock' in 1922. All dismissed the notion of shell shock as a unitary concept, recognised it as emotional in nature, and recognised the genuine nature of battle stress. Dr Henry Head, neurologist at the RAF Hospital, Hampstead, opined that 'fear may be transformed into either hysteria or anxiety neurosis'. Most experts believed the established diagnosis of hysteria to be the most appropriated diagnosis of shell shock behaviour. (RWOCESS, pp.43-68).
48  T. Loughran, 'Masculinity, Shell Shock, and Emotional Survival in the First World War', http://www.history.ac.uk/reviews/review/944). Hysteria is now known as conversion, indicating the process of an emotion being converted into a physical symptom.

The work of women during the war was ample demonstration that courage was not the sole prerogative of men. The universality of fear similarly presented another serious challenge to the traditional view of bravery. Many of the experts who gave evidence at the War Office Committee of Enquiry into 'Shell-Shock' regarded fear as the central cause of the condition. The comments of William Tyrrell will stand for all. He believed such breakdown to be: 'Born of fear. Its grandparents are self-preservation and the fear of being found afraid'.[49] In the face of these realities the heroic image of courage metamorphosed into a version based on endurance, the ability to sustain discomfort and fear. Wounded veterans began their journey to the forefront of the image of the hero, the place that such individuals hold today. The war thus cemented Stoic notions of endurance in the perception of what constituted courage, yet in post-war society, general Stoic principles drifted once more rapidly out of favour. The 'Bright Young Things' of the early 1920s and their *carpe diem* attitude to life in the post-war boom were the antithesis of the Stoic image. But as the economic struggles of the Great Depression took hold, endurance again underscored the coping of many, even if the beacon of Stoic manliness no longer burned. After a further cataclysmic war, the much vaunted 'Blitz spirit' passing into folk memory, British society no longer had a use for Stoicism.

The war thus participated in the destruction of the principles that had sustained the men who fought it. Michael Roper takes care not to suggest 'that a psychological attitude replaced unreflective belief in manliness as a normative standard'.[50] The Great War changed very little suddenly, rather it accelerated changes whose seeds had been present before the conflict. The psychologisation of society was a project for a later generation. Yet one indication of the increasing tendency to introspection is seen in the literature of the Great War itself. Many veteran memoirs, to a greater or lesser degree, examined the personal experience of war. Some famously expressed a sense of cynicism, as in the title of D.W.J. Cuddeford's *And All For What?* or Henry Russell's *Slaves of the War Lords*. Others applied acute self-analysis, as did Patrick Campbell in his memoir *In The Cannon's Mouth*. So many writers disclosed, as did Campbell, the experience of intense fear. Aubrey Herbert chose to put the experience of psychological breakdown into fiction, his work *The Secret Battle* emphasizing that reactions to fear were 'not only a matter of individual personality, but of circumstance'.[51] R.C. Sherriff's play, *Journey's End*, showing the emotional deterioration and reliance on alcohol of its central character Captain Denis Stanhope, became immensely popular. As Anthony Fletcher notes: 'No Edwardian audience could possibly have tolerated such a stage hero'.[52]

---

49  RWOCESS, p.31
50  M. Roper, 'Between Manliness and Masculinity', *Journal of British Studies*, p.359.
51  Roper, 'Between Manliness and Masculinity', p.356.
52  A. Fletcher, *Life, Death and Growing Up on the Western Front*, p.118.

Lord Moran took the view that 'men suffered more' in the First World War in comparison to preceding conflicts 'not because it was more terrible, but because they were more sensitive'.[53] He credited men with more imagination as the 19th century progressed, imagination which he viewed as undermining coping. Born in 1882 into the late heyday of Victorian manliness, Moran died in 1977, a decade after the 'Flower Power' of the so-called 'Summer of Love'. The events of the summer of 1967 demonstrate how much the attitudes of youth, who had contributed so much to the conscript armies of 1918 almost 50 years earlier, had changed. Those who self-select into the armed forces in the present day and who possess the characteristics of hardiness are no doubt imbued with many mechanisms that protect them against the stress of war. Moran's views on how 'sensitive' he believed a conscript army, assembled one hundred years on from the outbreak of the First World War might be, would have been interesting. He would no doubt have raised the question as to whether the modern world is disadvantaged by the loss of some of the values he cherished, and the coping skills they fostered.

---

53  Moran, *Anatomy of Courage*, p.29.

# Bibliography

**Unpublished Primary Sources**

J.W. Barnett, IWM Docs 666
F. Bloor, IWM Docs 7819
T. Brookbank, IWM Docs 8178
R.H. Bryan, IWM Docs 13953
E.R. Buckell, NAM 2002-09-9
H.R. Butt, IWM Docs 6771
E.F. Chapman, IWM Docs 1799
F.G. Chandler, IWM Docs 15460
H.H. Cooper, IWM Docs 10892
W. Clarke, IWM Docs 1377
H.T. Clements, IWM Docs 3413
W. Cobb, IWM Docs 10857
E.C. Crosse, IWM Docs 4772
H.M.B. de Sales la Terriere, IWM Docs 14737
R.G. Dixon, IWM Docs 2001
C.H. Dudley-Ward, IWM Docs 6374
R.C. Foot, IWM Docs 3354
G. Fortune, IWM Docs 12967
A. Griffin, IWM Sound 9101
R. Gwinnell, IWM Docs 11601
J.L. Hall, IWM Sound 14599
W.B. Henderson, IWM Docs 4592
A.J. Heraty, IWM Docs 4609
T.A. Jennings, IWM Docs 6596
H.J. Knee, IWM Docs 6972
J.T. Lawton, IWM Docs 2787
E.B. Lord, IWM Docs 6559
J. McCauley, IWM Docs 6434
J.B. MacKenzie, IWM Docs 926
C.K. McKerrow, IWM Docs 2386
T. Macmillan, IWM Docs 11149

E.L. Marchant, IWM Docs 12054
K.W. Mealing, IWM Docs 5514
M.W. Murray, IWM Docs 7097
L.J. Ounsworth, IWM Sound 332
F.E. Packe, IWM Docs 1653
H.S. Payne, IWM Docs 196
W.A. Quinton, IWM Docs 6705
S.H. Raggett, IWM Docs 1027
D. Railton, IWM Docs 4760
C.S. Rawlins, IWM Docs 7314
A.C. Razzell, IWM Sound 11952
B.A. Reader, IWM Docs 4127
H.C. Rees, IWM Docs 7166
J.R. Rodinson, Diaries (2 volumes), author's collection
W.B. St. Leger, IWM Docs 20504
W.D. Shanahan, IWM Docs 6312
W.J. Shewry, IWM Docs 508
E.E. Simeons, IWM Docs 2808
B.V. Sporton, IWM Docs 11731
H. Tansley, IWM Sound 13682
F. Ware, CWGC SDC 60/1 Box 2033
F. Whitham, Letters, author's collection
A.E. Wrench, IWM Docs 3834
H.W. Yoxall, IWM Docs 22290
War Diary, 1/19th Battalion London Regiment, TNA PRO WO/95/2738

**Printed Primary Sources**

A.M. Adam, *Arthur Innes Adam 1894-1914 – A Record Founded on his Letters*, Cambridge, Bowes & Bowes, 1920.
J.B.P. Adams, *Nothing of Importance: Eight Months at the Front with a Welsh Battalion*, New York, R.M. McBride, 1918.
An Amateur Officer, *After Victory*, London, A. Melrose, 1917.
W.L. Andrews, *Haunting Years*, London, Hutchinson, 1930.
Anonymous, *A Soldier of England*, Dumfries, J. Maxwell, 1920.
Anonymous, *Henry Dundas – Scots Guards*, Edinburgh, William Blackwood, 1921.
M. Arthur, *Forgotten Voices of the Great War*, London, Ebury Press, 2002.
G. Ashurst, *My Bit – A Lancashire Fusilier at War 1914-18*, Marlborough, Crowood Press, 1987.
B. Bairnsfather, *Bullets and Billets*, New York, G.P. Putnam, 1917.
A. Behrend, *Make Me a Soldier*, London, Eyre & Spottiswoode, 1961.
A. Behrend, *As From Kemmel Hill*, London, Eyre & Spottiswoode, 1963.
D.H. Bell, *A Soldier's Diary of the Great War*, London, Faber & Gwyer, 1929.

J. Bickersteth (ed.), *The Bickersteth Diaries 1914-1918*, Barnsley, Leo Cooper, 1998.
H.F. Bidder (Orex), *Three Chevrons*, London, John Lane, 1919.
R. Binding, *A Fatalist at War*, London, Allen & Unwin, 1928.
W.R. Bion (F. Bion, ed.), *War Memoirs 1917-19*, London, Karnac, 1997.
J. Blacker (ed.), *Have You Forgotten Yet?*, Barnsley, Leo Cooper, 2000.
E. Blunden, *Undertones of War*, London, Penguin, 1982 (originally published 1928).
F.A. Bolwell, *With a Reservist in France*, London, Routledge, 1918.
C.M. Bowra, *Memories 1898-1939*, London, Weidenfeld & Nicholson, 1966.
C.A.L. Brownlow, *The Breaking of the Storm*, London, Methuen, 1918.
F. Buckley, *Q.6.a and Other Places – Recollections of 1916, 1917 & 1918*, London, Spottiswoode Ballantyne, 1920.
A.M. Burrage (Ex-Private X), *War is War*, Barnsley, Pen & Sword, 2010 (originally published 1930).
E. Cadogan, (K. Charatan & C. Cecil, eds), *Under Fire in the Dardnelles*, Barnsley, Pen & Sword, 2006.
D. Campbell, *Forward the Rifles*, Dublin, Nonsuch, 2009.
P. J. Campbell, *In the Cannons Mouth*, London, Hamish Hamilton, 1979.
P.J. Campbell, *The Ebb and Flow of Battle*, Oxford, Oxford University Press, 1979.
J.A. Cardot, *Artilleurs de Campagne*, Paris, La Pensée Universelle, 1987.
C. Carrington, *Soldier From the Wars Returning*, London, Hutchinson, 1965.
A. Carton de Wiart, *Happy Odyssey*, London, Pan, 1950.
J. Cassells, *The Black Watch – A Record in Action*, New York, Doubleday Page, 1918.
H. Chapin, *One Man's War – Letters from a Soldier Killed at the Battle of Loos*, Kindle edition, n.d.
G. Chapman, *Vain Glory*, London, Cassell, 1937.
G. Chapman, *A Passionate Prodigality*, London, Mayflower-Dell, 1967 (originally published 1933).
C.P. Clayton, *The Hungry One*, Llandysul, Gomer Press, 1978.
H.S. Clapham, *Mud and Khaki*, London, Hutchinson, 1930.
S. Cloete, *A Victorian Son*, London, Collins, 1972.
B. Congeve, *Armageddon Road – A VC's Diary 1914-1916*, London, William Kimber, 1982.
J. Cooksey & D. Griffiths (eds), *Harry's War: The Great War Diary of Harry Drinkwater*, Croydon, Ebury Press, 2013.
G. Coppard, *With a Machine Gun to Cambrai*, London, HMSO, 1969.
J. Crawford (ed.), *No Better Death – The Great War Diaries and Letters of William G. Malone*, Titirangi, Exisle, 2014.
O. Creighton, *With the Twenty-Ninth Division in Gallipoli*, London, Longmans Green, 1916.
H.P. Croft, *Twenty Two Months Under Fire*, London, John Murray, 1917.
L.W. Crouch, *Letters from the Front*, privately printed, 1917.
D.W.J. Cuddeford, *And All for What?* London, Heath Cranton, 1933.
H. Dalton, *With British Guns in Italy*, London, Methuen, 1919.

G. Davidson, *The Incomparable 29th and the 'River Clyde'*, Aberdeen, James Gordon Bisset, 1920.
C. Davison, *The Burgoyne Diaries*, London, Thomas Harmsworth, 1985.
A.J. Dawson, *A 'Temporary Gentleman' in France*, London, G.P. Putnam, 1918.
C. Dawson, *Carry On – Letters in War-Time*, London, John Lane, 1917.
C. Dawson, *The Glory of the Trenches*, New York, John Lane, 1918.
C. Dawson, *Living Bayonets – A Record of the Last Push*, London, John Lane, 1919.
G.W. Devenish, *A Subaltern's Share in the War*, London, Constable, 1917.
M. Dide, *Ceux qui Combattent et Ceux qui Murent*, Paris, Payot, 1916.
M. Dide, *Les Émotions et la Guerre*, Paris, F. Alcan, 1918.
T. Donovan, *The Hazy Red Hell*, Staplehurst, Spellmount, 1999.
C. Douie, *The Weary Road – The Recollections of a Subaltern of Infantry*, London, John Murray, 1929.
W.E. Drury, *Camp Follower: A Padre's Recollections of Nile, Somme and Tigris during the First World War*, Dublin, Exchequer Printers, 1968.
G. Dugdale, *'Langemarck' and 'Cambrai'*, Shrewsbury, Wilding, 1932.
A.R. Dugmore, *When the Somme Ran Red*, New York, Grosset & Dunlap, 1918.
J.C. Dunn, *The War the Infantry Knew*, London, Times Warner, 1994 (originally published 1938).
A. Eden, *Another World 1897-1917*, London, Allen Lane, 1976.
C. Edmonds (C. Carrington), *A Subaltern's War*, London, Anthony Mott, 1984.
G.E.M. Eyre, *Somme Harvest: Memories of a PBI in the Summer of 1916*, London, Stamp Exchange, 1991 (originally published 1938).
R. Feilding, *War Letters to a Wife*, Staplehurst, Spellmount, 2001 (originally published 1929).
J.M. Findlay, *With the 8th Scottish Rifles*, London, Blackie, 1926.
H.T. Floyd, *At Ypres with Best-Dunkley*, Boston, Indypublish, n.d. (originally published 1920).
D. Fraser (ed.), *In Good Company*, Salisbury, Michael Russell, 1990.
N. Fraser-Tytler, *With Lancashire Lads and Field Guns in France*, Manchester, John Heywood, 1922.
E.R.M. Fryer, *Reminiscences of a Grenadier 1914-1919*, London, Digby Long, 1921.
R.N. Gale, *Call to Arms*, London, Hutchinson, 1968.
D. Garstin, *The Shilling Soldiers*, London, Hodder & Stoughton, 1918.
A.H. Gibbs, *Gun Fodder: The Diary of Four Years of War*, Boston, Little Brown, 1919.
J.G. Gillam, *Gallipoli Diary*, London, George Allen & Unwin, 1918.
A.D. Gillespie, *Letters from Flanders*, London, Smith Elder, 1916.
N. Gladden, *Ypres 1917*, London, Kimber, 1967.
P. Glenconner, *Edward Wyndham Tennant – A Memoir*, London, John Lane, 1919.
J. Glubb, *Into Battle*, London, Cassell, 1978.
H. Gordon, *The Unreturning Army*, London, Dent, 1967.
G.H. Greenwell, *An Infant in Arms*, London, Lovat Dickson & Thompson, 1935.
S. Graham, *A Private in the Guards*, London, Macmillan, 1919.

S. Graham, *The Challenge of the Dead*, London, Cassell, 1921.
R. Graves, *Goodbye to all That*, London, Folio Society, 1981 (originally published 1929).
W.H.A. Groom, *Poor Bloody Infantry*, London, Kimber, 1976.
R. Haigh, *Life in a Tank*, Boston, Houghton Mifflin, 1918.
R.G. Hamilton, *The War Diary of the Master of Belhaven 1914-1918*, Barnsley, Wharncliffe, 1990 (originally published 1924).
A.A.H. Hanbury-Sparrow, *The Land-locked Lake*, London, Arthur Barker, 1932.
D. Hankey, *A Student in Arms: Second Series*, New York, Dutton, 1917.
R.E. Harris, *Billie – The Nevill Letters: 1914-1916*, Uckfield, Naval & Military, 2003.
F. Hawkings, *From Ypres to Cambrai*, Morley, Elmfield, 1973.
A. Herbert *Mons, Anzac and Kut*, London, Edward Arnold, 1919.
S.H. Hewett, *A Scholar's Letters from the Front*, London, Longmans Green, 1918.
E Hiscock, *The Bells of Hell Go Ting-A-Ling-A-Ling: An Autobiographical Fragment Without Maps*, London, Arlington, 1976.
F.C. Hitchcock, *"Stand To" – A Diary of the Trenches 1915-1918*, Uckfield, Naval & Military, 1988 (originally published 1937).
E. Hodder-Williams, *One Young Man*, London, Hodder & Stoughton, 1917.
L. Housman, *War Letters of Fallen Englishmen*, New York, E.P. Dutton, 1930.
H.E.E. Howson, *Two Men – A Memoir*, Oxford, Oxford University Press, 1919.
E.H.W. Hulse, *Letters*, privately printed, 1916.
G.R. Husbands (J.M Bourne & B. Bushaway, eds), *Joffrey's War*, Beeston, Salient Books, 2011.
J.G.W. Hyndson, *From Mons to the First Battle of Ypres*, London, Wyman, 1932.
J.E. Jeffery, *Servants of the Guns*, London, Smith Elder, 1917.
R.G.B. Jeffreys (C. & L. Dodd, eds), *Collected Letters 1916-1918*, Dublin, Old Tough, 2007.
P. Jones, *War Letters of a Public Schoolboy*, London, Cassell, 1918.
E. Junger, *Storm of Steel*, London, Allen Lane, 2003 (originally published 1920).
F.H. Keeling, *Letters and Recollections*, New York, Macmillan, 1916.
A. Lambert, *Over the Top*, London, John Long, 1930.
G.B. Laurie, *Letters*, Aldershot, Gale & Polden, 1921.
E.G.D. Liveing, *Attack*, New York, Macmillan, 1918.
O.J. Lodge, *Raymond, or Life and Death*, London, Methuen, 1916.
I. Logan, *On the King's Service*, London, Hodder & Stoughton, 1917.
C.W. Longley ('Wagger'), *Battery Flashes*, London, John Murray, 1916.
J.F. Lucy, *There's a Devil in the Drum*, Uckfield, Naval & Military, 1993 (originally published 1938).
W. Ludwig, *Beiträge zur Psychologie des Krieges*, Leipzig, J.A. Barth, 1920.
J. Lusk, *Letters and Memories*, Oxford, Blackwell, 1917.
P. MacGill, *The Great Push – An Episode of the Great War*, London, Jenkins, 1916.
C. McKenzie, *Gallipoli Memories*, London, Cassell, 1929.
H. Macmillan, *Winds of Change 1914-1939*, London, Macmillan, 1966.

R.J. Manion, *A Surgeon in Arms*, Toronto, McLelland Goodchild & Stewart, 1918.
F. Manning, *The Middle Parts of Fortune*, Edinburgh, Peter Davies, 1929.
G.B. Manwaring, *If We Return*, London, John Lane, 1918.
'Mark VII' (M. Plowman), *A Subaltern on the Somme*, London, J.M. Dent, 1927.
A.A. Martin, *A Surgeon in Khaki*, London, Edward Arnold, 1917.
B. Martin, *Poor Bloody Infantry: A Subaltern on the Western Front*, London, Hutchinson, 1987.
R.M. Maxwell (ed.), *Villiers-Stuart Goes to War*, Kippilaw, Pentland Press, 1990.
P. Maze, *A Frenchman in Khaki*, London, William Heinneman, 1934.
H.E.L. Mellersh, *Schooboy into War*, London, William Kimber, 1978.
Lord Moran, *The Anatomy of Courage*, London, Sphere, 1968 (originally published 1945).
A.H. Mure, *With the Incomparable 29th*, Edinburgh, W.R. Chambers, 1919.
J. Murray, *Gallipoli as I Saw It*, London, William Kimber, 1965.
J. Murray, *Gallipoli 1915*, Bristol, Cerberus, 2004 (originally published as *Gallipoli as I Saw It*).
A. Nasson, *For Love and Courage*, London, Preface, 2008.
H. Ogle, *The Fateful Battle Line*, London, Michael Glover, 1993.
R. Palmer, *Letters from Mesopotamia*, privately printed, (n.d.).
E.W. Parker, *Into Battle – A Seventeen-Year-Old Joins Kitchener's Army*, London: Leo Cooper, 1994 (originally published 1964).
R.D. Pinkerton, *Ladies from Hell*, Toronto, McLelland Goodchild & Stewart, 1918.
C.D. Plater, *Catholic Soldiers: By Sixty Chaplains and Many Others*, London, Longmans Green, 1919.
A.O. Pollard, *Fire-Eater – The Memoirs of a VC*, London, Hutchinson, 1932.
D.J. Polley (A.C. Mott, ed.), *The Mudhook Machine Gunner*, Bromley, Glago, 1998.
M. Ponsonby, *Visions and Vignettes of War*, London, Longmans Green, 1917.
M. Pottle & J.G.G. Ledingham, *We Hope to Get Word Tomorrow*, Barnsley, Frontline, 2009.
E.B. Poulton, *The Life of Ronald Poulton*, London, Sidgwick & Jackson, 1919.
D. Priddey, *A Tommy at Ypres*, Stroud, Amberley, 2011.
C.B Purdom (ed.), *Everyman at War*, London, J.M. Dent, 1930.
T.W. Pym & G. Gordon, *Papers from Picardy*, London, Constable, 1917.
H. Quigley, *Passchendaele and the Somme – A Diary of 1917*, London, Methuen, 1928.
J. Reith, *Wearing Spurs*, London, Hutchinson, 1966.
F. Richards, *Old Soldiers Never Die*, Uckfield, Naval & Military, 2003 (originally published 1933).
S. Richardson, *Orders are Orders: A Manchester Pal on the Somme*, Manchester, Neil Richardson, 1987.
'A Rifleman' (A. Smith), *Four Years on the Western Front*, London, Odhams, 1922.
R. Roberts, *The Classic Slum: Salford Life in the First Quarter of the Century*, Manchester, Manchester University Press, 1971 (originally published 1902).

S. Rogerson, *Twelve Days on the Somme*, London, Greenhill, 2006, (originally published 1933).
D. Rorie, *A Medico's Luck in the War*, Aberdeen, Milne & Hutchinson, 1929.
R.B. Ross, *The Fifty-First in France*, London, Stodder & Houghton, 1919.
H. Russell, *Slaves of the War Lords*, London, Hutchinson, 1928.
F.M. St Helier Evans, *Going Across; or, With the 9th Welch in the Butterfly Division*, Newport, R.H. Johns, 1952.
S. Sassoon, *Counter-Attack and Other Poems*, New York, E.P.Dutton, 1918.
S. Sassoon, *The Complete Memoirs of George Sherston*, London, Faber & Faber, 1972.
R. Scott, *A Soldier's Diary*, London, Collins, 1923.
E. Shackleton, *South – The Story of Shackleton's 1914-17 Expedition*, London, William Heineman, 1919.
M. Shadbolt, *Voices of Gallipoli*, Auckland, Hodder & Stoughton, 1988.
E.H. Shears, *Active-Service Diary*, Liverpool, Henry Young, 1919.
G.A. Studdert Kennedy, *The Hardest Part*, London, Hodder & Stoughton, 1918.
M. Tanner (ed.), *War Letters 1914-1918, Volume 1, Wilbert Spencer*, Kindle edition (n.d.).
I. & A. Taylor (eds), *Those who Marched Away – An Anthology of the World's Greatest War Diaries*, Edinburgh, Cannongate, 2009.
J. Terraine (ed.), *General Jack's Diary*, London, Cassell, 2000 (originally published 1964).
J.-M. Tèzenas du Monteil, *L'Heure H. Etapes d'Infanterie*, Paris, S.N.E.V., 1960.
A. Thomas, *A Life Apart*, London, Victor Gollancz, 1968.
R. van Emden & S. Humphries (eds), *Veterans*, Barnsley, Leo Cooper, 1998.
P. Vansittart (ed.), *John Masefield's Letters from the Front 1915-1917*, London, Constable, 1984.
E.C. Vaughan, *Some Desperate Glory*, London, Macmillan, 1985.
'Vedette', *Adventures of an Ensign*, London, William Blackwood, 1917.
F.A. Voigt, *Combed Out*, London, Swarthmore, 1920.
A. Wade, *The War of the Guns*, London, Batsford, 1936.
L. M. Watt, *In France and Flanders with the Fighting Men*, London, Hodder & Stoughton, 1917.
A.G. West, *The Diary of a Dead Officer*, London, George Allen & Unwin, 1919.
T.L.B. Westerdale, *Messages from Mars: a Chaplain's Experiences at the Front*, London, C.H. Kelly, 1917.
M. Williams, *With Innocence and Hope*, Oxford, YouCaxton, 2014.
P. Witkop (translated by A.F. Wedd), *German Students' War Letters*, Philadelphia, Pine Street Books, 2002 (originally published 1928).

## Printed Secondary Sources

American Psychiatric Association, *Diagnostic and Statistical Manual of Mental Disorders – Third Edition*, Washington, American Psychiatric Association, 1980.
Aristotle, *Nicomachean Ethics*, n.d.
M. Arnold, *Poetical Works*, London, Macmillan, 1891.
Australian Bureau of Statistics, *Suicide in Australia*, Canberra, 1983.
R. Baden-Powell, *Scouting for Boys*, 1908.
P. Barham, *Forgotten Lunatics of the Great War*, Yale University Press, New Haven, 2004.
N. Barr, *The Lion and the Poppy: British Veterans, Politics and Society 1929-1939*, Westport, Praeger, 2005.
C.E.W. Bean, *The Official History of Australia in the War of 1914, 1918, Vol. II*, Sydney, Angus and Robertson, 1941.
R. Bellah, *Habits of the Heart*, New York, Harper & Row, 1985.
J. Benson, *The Working Class in Britain 1850-1939*, London, Taurus, 2003.
I.R. Bet-El, *Conscripts – Forgotten Men of the Great War*, Stroud, History Press, 1999.
A. Bishop & M. Bostridge, *Letters from a Lost Generation*, London, Little Brown, 1998.
Board of Education, *Annual Report of the Chief Medical Officer of the Board of Education, 1919* [Cmd. 995] 1920.
B. Bond (ed.), *The First World War and British Military History*, Oxford, Clarendon Press, 1991.
J. Bourke, *Dismembering the Male – Men's Bodies, Britain and the Great War*, London, Reaktion, 1996.
P.B. Boyden, *Tommy Atkins' Letters: The History of the British Army Postal Service from 1795*, London, National Army Museum, 1990.
C. G. Brown, *The Death of Christian Britain*, London, Routledge, 2001.
M. Brown, *Tommy Goes to War*, Stroud, Tempus, 1999.
C.D Bryant & D.L. Peck, *Encyclopaedia of Death and Human Experience*, Los Angeles, Sage, 2009.
J. Burnett, *Annals of Labour: Autobiographies of British Working Class People*, Bloomington, Indiana University Press, 1974.
B. Caine, *Friendship – A History*, Equinox, London, 2009.
D. Cairns, *The Army and Religion: an Enquiry and its Bearing on the Religious Life of the Nation*, London, Macmillan, 1919.
W.B. Cannon, *Bodily Changes in Pain, Hunger, Fear and Rage*, New York, Appleton, 1929.
J. Carey (ed.), *The Faber Book of Reportage*, London, Faber, 1989.
H. Carpenter, *J.R.R. Tolkien: A Biography*, London, George Allen & Unwin, 1977.
H. Carrington, *Psychical Phenomena and the War*, New York, American Universities Publishing Company, 1920.
N. Cave, *Vimy Ridge*, Barnsley, Pen & Sword, 1996.
N. Cave, *Hill 60*, Barnsley, Leo Cooper, 1998.

H. Cecil & P.H. Liddle (eds), *Facing Armageddon – The First World War Experience*, Barnsley, Pen & Sword, 1996.

W.S. Churchill, *Thoughts and Adventures*, London, Odhams Press, 1949.

S. Cole, *Modernism, Male Friendship, and the First World War*, Cambridge, Cambridge University Press, 2003.

W. Collins, *The Moonstone*, Ontario, Broadview, 1985 (first published 1868).

C.H. Cooley, *Social Organization: a Study of the Larger Mind*, New York, Charles Scribner, 1909.

C. Corns and J. Hughes-Wilson, *Blindfold and Alone – British Military Executions in the Great War*, London, Cassell, 2001.

J.G. Cotton Minchin, *Our Public Schools: Their Influence on English History; Charter House, Eton, Harrow, Merchant Taylors', Rugby, St. Paul's Westminster, Winchester*, London, Swan Sonnenschein, 1901.

H. Cunningham, *The Volunteer Force: A Social and Political History 1859-1908*, Connecticut, Archon Press, 1975.

S. Das, *Touch and Intimacy in First World War Literature*, Cambridge, Cambridge University Press, 2005.

O. Davies, *Witchcraft, Magic and Culture, 1736-1951*, Manchester, Manchester University Press, 1999.

P. Dennis and J. Grey (eds), *Defining Victory 1918*, Canberra, Army History Unit, Department of Defence, 1999.

E.T. Devine, *Disabled Soldiers and Sailors. Pensions and Training*, New York, Oxford University Press, 1919.

E. Durkheim, *Suicide*, Glencoe, Free Press, 1951.

J. Ellis, *Eye Deep in Hell*, Glasgow, William Collins, 1977.

N. Ferguson, *The Pity of War*, New York, Basic Books, 1999.

A. Fletcher, *Life, Death and Growing Up on the Western Front*, London, Yale University Press, 2013.

J.G. Fuller, *Troop Morale and Popular Culture in the British and Dominion Armies 1914-1918*, Oxford, Oxford University Press, 1991.

J. Greenwood ('One of the Crowd'), *Mysteries of Modern London*, 1883.

S. Grogan, *Shell Shocked Britain – The First World War's Legacy for Britain's Mental Health*, Barnsley, Pen & Sword History, 2014.

A.H. Halsey (ed.), *Trends in British Society Since 1900: A Guide to the Changing Social Structure of Britain*, London, Macmillan St. Martin's Press, 1972.

E. Hancock, *Bazentin Ridge*, Barnsley, Leo Cooper, 2001.

E. Hanna, *The Great War on the Small Screen*, Edinburgh, Edinburgh University Press, 2009.

N. Hanson *The Unknown Soldier*, London, Doubleday, 2005.

P. Hart, *The Somme*, London, Weidenfeld & Nicholson, 2005.

P. Hart, *Fire and Movement*, Oxford, Oxford University Press, 2015.

P. Heinl, *Splintered Innocence: An Intuitive Approach to Treating War Trauma*, Abingdon, Brunner-Routledge, 2001.

M. Hirschfeld, *The Sexual History of the World War*, New York, Falstaff Press, 1937.
HMSO, *Report of the War Office Committee of Enquiry into "Shell-Shock"*, London, Imperial War Museum, 2004 (originally published 1922).
P.E. Hodgkinson, *British Infantry Battalion Commanders in the First World War*, Farnham, Ashgate, 2015.
P.E. Hodgkinson & M. Stewart, *Coping with Catastrophe – A Handbook of Post-Disaster Psychosocial Aftercare*, (2nd Edition) London, Routledge, 1998.
R Holmes, *Firing Line*, London, Jonothan Cape, 1985.
R. Holmes, *Acts of War*, London, Cassell, 2003 (originally published as *Firing Line*).
R. Holmes, *Tommy*, London, Harper Collins, 2004.
R. Houlbrooke, *Death, Religion and the Family 1480-1750*, Oxford, Oxford University Press, 1998.
T. Hughes, *Tom Brown At Oxford*, 1861.
L. Huot & P. Voivenel, *Le Courage*, Paris, F. Alcan, 1918.
P. Jalland, *Death in the Victorian Family*, Oxford, Oxford University Press, 1996.
R.R. James, *Gallipoli*, London, Macmillan, 1989.
W.D. Jamieson (C. Housey, ed.), *Men of the High Peak: A History of the 1/6th Battalion the Sherwood Foresters 1914-1918*, Long Eaton, Millquest, n.d.
D. Jones (ed.), *Bullets and Bandsmen*, London, Owl Press, 1992.
E. Jones & S. Wessely, *Shell Shock to PTSD – Military Psychiatry from 1900 to the Gulf War*, Psychology Press, Hove, 2005.
L. Joubert, *Treatise on Laughter*, 1579.
J. Keegan, *The Face of Battle*, London, Pimlico, 1991.
C. Kingsley, *Two Years Ago*, 1857.
R. Kipling, *Rewards and Fairies*, New York, Doubleday Page, 1916.
R.G. Latham, *Dictionary of the English Language*, London, Longmans Green, 1870.
E.J. Leed, *No Man's Land: Combat and Identity in World War 1*, Cambridge, Cambridge University Press, 1979.
P. Leese, *Shell Shock*, Basingstoke, Palgrave Macmillan, 2002.
J. Lewis-Stempel, *Six Weeks*, London, Weidenfeld & Nicolson, 2010.
P.H. Liddle, *Men of Gallipoli*, Newton Abbott, David & Charles, 1976.
P.H. Liddle (ed.), *Passchendaele in Perspective*, London, Leo Cooper, 1997.
D.W. Lloyd, *Battlefield Tourism: Pilgrimage and the Commemoration of the Great War in Britain, Australia and Canada, 1919–1939*, Oxford, Berg, 1998.
T. Lutz, *Crying – The Natural & Cultural History of Tears*, New York, W.W. Norton, 1999.
B. MacArthur (ed.), *For King and Country – Voices from the First World War*, London, Abacus, 2008.
H.B. McCartney, *Citizen Soldiers – The Liverpool Territorials in the First World War*, Cambridge, Cambridge University Press, 2005.
L. MacDonald, *Somme*, London, Penguin, 1993.
L. MacDonald, *They Called it Passchendaele*, London, Penguin, 1993.
L. MacDonald, *Voices and Images of the Great War*, London, Penguin, 1991.

J.M. MacKenzie, *Popular Imperialism and the Military 1850-1950*, Manchester, Manchester University Press, 1992.
R. McKibbin, *Classes and Cultures – England 1918-1951*, Oxford, Oxford University Press, 1998.
J. MacLeod (ed.), *Uncovered Fields: Perspectives in First World War Studies*, Leiden, NLD, Brill N.H.E.J, N.V. Koninklijke, Boekhandel en Drukkerij, 2003.
J.M McPherson, *For Cause and Comrades: Why Men Fought in the Civil War*, New York, Oxford University Press, 1997.
W.G. MacPherson, W.P. Herringham, T.R. Elliot, & A. Balfour (eds), *Medical Diseases of War: Volume Two*, London, HMSO, 1923.
S.R. Maddi, *Hardiness – Turning Stressful Circumstances into Resilient Growth*, New York, Springer, 2013.
R.H. Malden, *Fatalism*, London, SPCK, 1917.
J.A. Mangan, *Athleticism in the Victorian and Edwardian Public School*, Cambridge, Cambridge University Press, 1981.
J.A. Mangan & J. Walvin (eds), *Manliness and Morality: Middle-Class Masculinity in Britain and America, 1800-1940*, Manchester, Manchester University Press, 1987.
S.L.A. Marshall, *Men Against Fire*, New York, Morrow, 1947.
H. Mayhew, *London Labour and the London Poor* (4 vols), London, Griffin, Bohn and Company, 1861-2.
D. Meichenbaum, *Stress Inoculation Training*, New York, Pergamon Press, 1985.
C. Messenger, *Call to Arms*, London, Weidenfeld & Nicholson, 2005.
J. Meyer, *Men of War: Masculinity and the First World War in Britain*, Basingstoke, Palgrave Macmillan, 2009.
M. Middlebrook, *The First Day on the Somme*, New York, Allen Lane, 1971.
B.R. Mitchell & P. Deane, *Abstract of British Historical Statistics*, Cambridge, Cambridge University Press, 1962.
T.J. Mitchell & G.M. Smith, *Official Medical History of the Great War, Casualties and Medical Statistics*, London, HMSO, 1931.
K.W. Mitchinson, *Gentlemen and Officers*, London, Imperial War Museum, 1995.
R. Mitchison, *British Population Change since 1860*, London, Macmillan, 1977.
M. de Montaigne, *Essais*, 1570-92.
C. Moore-Bick, *Playing the Game – The British Junior Infantry Officer on the Western Front 1914-18*, Solihull, Helion, 2011.
C.S. Myers, *Shell Shock in France 1914-18, Based on a War Diary*, Cambridge, Cambridge University Press, 1940.
D.C. Noonan, *Those We Forget – Recounting Australian Casualties of the First World War*, Carlton, Melbourne University Press, 2014.
R.A. Nye, *Masculinity and Male Codes of Honour in Modern France*, New York, Oxford University Press, 1993.
W. Orpen, *The Outline of Art*, London, George Newnes, n.d.
J. Price, *Everyday Heroism: Victorian Constructions of the Heroic Civilian*, London, Bloomsbury, 2014.

C. Pugsley, *On the Fringe of Hell*, Auckland, Hodder & Stoughton, 1991.
S.J. Rachman, *Fear and Courage* (2nd edition), New York, W.H. Freeman, 1990.
V.S. Ramachandaran (ed.), *Encyclopaedia of Human Behaviour*, New York, Academic Press, 1994.
E. Roberts, *A Woman's Place: An Oral History of Working-Class Women 1890-1940*, Basil Blackwell, Oxford, 1984.
J.M. Robson (ed.), *Collected Works of John Stuart Mill*, London, Routledge Kegan Paul, 1963-1991.
F.P. Roe, *Accidental Soldier*, London, 1981.
M. Roper, *The Secret Battle – Emotional Survival in the Great War*, Manchester, Manchester University Press, 2009.
N.L. Rosenblum (ed.), *Liberalism and the Moral Life*, Cambridge, Mass., Harvard University Press, 1989.
J.B. Rotter, *Social Learning and Clinical Psychology*, New York, Prentice-Hall, 1954.
W. Ruch (ed.), *The Sense of Humor: Explorations of a Personality Characteristic*, New York, Mouton de Gruyter, 1998.
L. de Sacy, *A Discourse of Friendship*, London, 1707.
T.W. Salmon, *The Care and Treatment of Mental Diseases and War Neuroses ('Shell Shock') in the British Army*, New York, National Committee for Mental Hygiene, 1917.
R.J. Schoeck, *Erasmus of Europe: The Making of a Humanist, 1467–1500, Volume One*, Edinburgh, University Press, 1990.
M.E.P. Seligman, *Helplessness: On Depression, Development, and Death*, San Francisco, W.H. Freeman, 1975.
Seneca, *On Benefits*.
G.D. Sheffield, *Leadership in the Trenches*, Basingstoke, Macmillan, 2000.
N. Sherman, *Stoic Warriors: The Ancient Philosophy Behind the Military Mind*, Oxford University Press, Oxford, 2005.
R.C. Sherriff, *Journey's End*, London, Gollancz, 1929.
A. Simpson, *Hot Blood and Cold Steel*, London, Tom Donovan, 1993.
W.J. Slim, *Defeat into Victory*, London, Cassell, 1956.
S. Smiles, *Duty*, London, John Murray, 1880.
S. Smiles, *Self-Help*, London, John Murray, 1907 (originally published 1859).
M.C. Smith, *Awarded for Valour – A History of the Victoria Cross and the Evolution of British Heroism*, Basingstoke, Palgrave Macmillan, 2008.
G.M. Smith and T.H. Mitchell, *History of the Great War Based on Official Statistics: Volume 7, Medical Services, Casualties, and Medical Statistics*, London, HMSO, 1923.
M. Snape, *God and the British Soldier*, Abingdon, Routledge, 2005.
N. Steel & P. Hart, *Passchendaele – The Sacrificial Ground*, London, Cassell, 2000.
D. Stevenson, *1914-1918 – The History of the First World War*, London, Allen Lane, 2004.
Stoicism Today, *Live Like a Stoic for a Week*, Exeter, Exeter University, 2013.

S.A. Stouffer (ed.), *The American Soldier: Combat and its Aftermath, Volume Two*, Princeton, Princeton University Press, 1949.

J.M. Strange, *Death, Grief and Poverty in Britain*, 1870-1914, Cambridge, Cambridge University Press, 2005.

S.K. Strange & J. Zupko, *Stoicism: Traditions & Transformations*, Cambridge University Press, Cambridge, 2004.

N. Tadmor, *Family and Friends in 18th-Century England: Household, Kinship, and Patronage*, Oxford, Oxford University Press, 2001.

W. Temple, *Men Without Work – A Report Made to The Pilgrim Trust*, Cambridge, Cambridge University Press, 1938.

P.R. Thompson, *The Edwardians: The Remaking of British Society*, London, Weidenfeld & Nicolson, 1975.

A. Thomson, *Anzac Memories: Living with the Legend*, Clayton, Monash University Publishing, 2013.

T. Travers, *Gallipoli 1915*, Stroud, Tempus, 2001.

H.A. Vachell, *The Hill*, London, John Murray, 1905.

T. Walter, *On Bereavement – The Culture of Grief*, Buckingham, Open University Press, 1999.

War Office, *Statistics of the Military Effort of the British Empire During the Great War*, London, HMSO, 1922.

A. Watson, *Enduring the Great War*, Cambridge, Cambridge University Press, 2008.

J.C. Weaver, *Sadly Troubled History: The Meanings of Suicide in the Modern Age*, Montreal and Kingston, McGill-Queen's Press, 2009.

J. Whaley, *Mirrors of Mortality*, London, Europa, 1981.

A. Wilkinson, *The Church of England and the First World War*, London, SPCK, 1978.

A. Williamson, *Henry Williams and the First World War*, Stroud, Sutton Publishing, 2004.

D. Winter, *Death's Men – Soldiers of the Great War*, London, Penguin, 1979.

J. Winter, *The Experience of World War I*, London, Greenwich Editions, 1988.

J. Winter, *Sites of Memory, Sites of Mourning*, Cambridge, Cambridge University Press, 1995.

Winter, J & Robert J.L., *Capital Cities at War, Volume One*, Cambridge, Cambridge University Press, 1997.

J. Winter (ed.), *The Cambridge History of the First World War*, (3 vols), Cambridge, Cambridge University Press, 2014.

A. Woolf, *Subalterns of the Foot – Thee World War I Diaries of Officers of the Cheshire Regiment*, Worcester, Square One, 1992.

T. Wright ('The Riverside Visitor'), *The Pinch of Poverty*, 1892.

M. Zeidner & N. Endler (eds), *Handbook of Coping: Theory, Research, Applications*, New York, John Wiley, 1996.

## Printed Articles

M.H. Abel, 'Humor, Stress and Coping Strategies', *Humor: International Journal of Humor Research*, 2002, (15) pp. 365-381.

C. Bird, 'From Home to the Charge: A Psychological Study of the Soldier', *American Journal of Psychology*, 1917, (28) pp.315-248.

M.A.S. Boksem, P.H. Mehta, B. Van den Bergh, V. van Son, S.T. Trautmann, K. Roelofs, A. Smidts, & A.G. Sanfey, 'Testosterone Inhibits Trust But Promotes Reciprocity', *Psychological Science*, 2013, (24) pp.2306-2314.

Bureau of Labor Statistics, U.S. Department of Labor, 'Public Attitude Toward Ex-Servicemen after World War I', *Monthly Labor Review*, 1943, (56) pp.1060-1073.

V. Burton, 'Review of M. Roper and J. Tosh, *Manful Assertions*', *Social History*, 1993, (25) pp.392-4.

E. Butchart, 'Unemployment and Non-Employment in Inter-War Britain', *University of Oxford Discussion Papers in Economic and Social History*, 1997, (16).

D. Clarke, 'Rumours of Angels: A Legend of the First World War', *Folklore*, 202, (113) pp.151-173.

D. Cox, R. Hallam, K. O'Connor, & S. Rachman, 'An Experimental Analysis of Fearlessness and Courage', *British Journal of Psychology*, 1983, (74) pp. 107-17.

M. P. Deahl, A.B. Gilham, J. Thomas, M.M. Searle, & M. Srinivasan, 'Psychological Sequelae Following the Gulf War', *British Journal of Psychiatry*, 1994, (165) pp.60-65.

J. Drewett, 'Diffused Christianity: Asset or Liability?', *Theology*, 1942, (45) pp.82-92.

R.I.M. Dunbar, 'Neocortex size as a constraint on group size in primates', *Journal of Human Evolution*, 1992, (22) pp.469–493.

B. Eichengreen, 'Unemployment in Interwar Britain', *Refresh*, 1989, (8) pp.1-4.

G. Field, 'Perspectives on the Working-Class Family in Wartime Britain, 1939-1945', *International Labor and Working-Class History*, 1990, (38) pp.3-28.

V. Florian, M. Milkulincer & O. Taubman, 'Does Hardiness Contribute to Mental Health During a Stressful Real Life Situation? The Roles of Appraisal and Coping', *Journal of Personality and Social Psychology*. 1995, (68) pp.687-695.

S. Freud, 'Mourning and Melancholia', *International Journal for Medical Psychoanalysis*, 1917, (4) pp.288-301.

C.T. Fryer, 'Psychological Aspects of the Welsh Revival: 1904-5', *Proceedings of the Society for Psychical Research*, 1905, (51) pp.196-199.

S.R. Graubard, 'Military Demobilization in Great Britain Following the First World War', *Journal of Modern History*, 1947, (19) pp.297-311.

A. Haggett, 'Looking Back: Masculinity and Mental Health – the Long View', *The Psychologist*, 2014, (27) pp.426-9.

B. Harrison, 'Oral History and Recent Political History,' *Oral History*, 1972, (3) pp.30-48.

P.E. Hodgkinson, N. Oatham & A. Caisley, 'Identity and Separation – The Letters of Private Frederick Whitham', *Stand To!*, 2015, (102) pp.7-10.

P.E. Hodgkinson, 'Veteran Unemployment, the Embankment Fellowship Centre, and the "Downgate Twenty One"', *Stand To!* (105) pp.50-4.

E. Jones & S. Wessely, 'Psychiatric Battle Casualties: An Intra- and Interwar Comparison', *British Journal of Psychiatry*, 2001, (178) pp.242-247.

E. Jones, I. Palmer & S. Wessely, 'War Pensions (1900-1945): Changing Models of Psychological Understanding', *British Journal of Psychiatry*, 2002, (180) pp.374-9.

E. Jones, R.H. Vermaas, H. McCartney, C. Beech, I. Palmer, K. Hyams, & S. Wessely, 'Flashbacks and Post-Traumatic Stress Disorder: The Genesis of a 20th-Century Diagnosis', *British Journal of Psychiatry*, 2003, (182) pp.158-163.

E. Jones & N. Greenberg, 'Long-term Psychological Consequences among Chemical Warfare Survivors of World War I and their Current Relevance', *Psychiatric Annals*, 2007, (37) pp.724-8.

G.S. Jones, 'Working Class Culture and Working Class Politics in London, 1879-1900: Notes on the Remaking of a Working Class', *Journal of Social History*, 1974, (7) pp.460-508.

P. Kerkkänen, N.A. Kuiper, & R.A. Martin, 'Sense of Humor, Physical Health, and Well-being at Work: A Three-year Longitudinal Study of Finnish Police Officers', *Humor: International Journal of Humor Research*, 2004, (17) pp.21-35.

S.C. Kobasa, 'Stressful Life Events, Personality, and Health – Inquiry into hardiness', *Journal of Personality and Social Psychology*, 1979, (37) pp.1–11.

N.A. Kuiper, R.A. Martin, & L.J. Olinger, 'Coping humour, stress, and cognitive appraisals', *Canadian Journal of Behavioural Science*, 1993, (25) pp.81-96.

J. E. McCarrol, R.J. Ursano, & C.S. Fullerton, 'Symptoms of PTSD Following Recovery of War Dead', *American Journal of Psychiatry*, 1995, (152) pp.939-941.

J. E. McCarrol, R.J. Ursano, C.S. Fullerton, X. Liu, & A. Lundy, 'Somatic Symptoms in Gulf War Mortuary Workers', *Psychosomatic Medicine*, 2002, (64) pp.29-33.

T.M. McMillan & S.J. Rachman, 'Fearlessness and Courage in Paratroop Veterans of the Falklands War,' *British Journal of Psychology*, 1987, (78) pp.375–383.

M.F. McTaggart, 'Danger Values', *Journal of the Royal United Services Institution*, 1921, (66) pp.284-292.

S.R. Maddi, M. Brow, D.M. Khoshaba, & M. Viatkus, 'Relationship of Hardiness and Religiousness to Depression and Anger', *Consulting Psychology Journal*, 2006, (58) pp.148-161.

E. Madigan, '"Sticking to a Hateful Task": Resilience, Humour, and British Understandings of Combatant Courage, 1914–1918', *War in History*, 2013, (20) pp.76-98.

A. Maslow, 'A Theory of Human Motivation', *Psychological Review*, 1943, (50) pp.370-96.

W.H.R. Rivers, 'An Address on the Repression of War Experience', *Lancet*, 1918, (1) pp.173-177.

A. Roddenberry & K. Renk, 'Locus of Control and Self-Efficacy: Potential Mediators of Stress, Illness, and Utilization of Health Services in College Students', *Child Psychiatry & Human Development*, 2010, (41) pp.353–370.

M. Roper, 'Between Manliness and Masculinity: The "War Generation" and the Psychology of Fear in Britain, 1914–1950', *Journal of British Studies*, 2005, (44) pp.343-362.

A.C. Samson & J.J. Gross, 'Humour as Emotion Regulation: The Differential Consequences of Negative Versus Positive Humour', *Cognition & Emotion*, 2012, (26) pp.375-384.

K. Schmid & O.T. Muldoon, 'Perceived Threat, Social Identification, and Psychological Well-Being, *Political Psychology*, 2013, (20) pp.1-18.

E. Shorter, 'Paralysis – The Rise and Fall of a Hysterical Symptom', *Journal of Social History*, 1986, (19) pp.549-582.

P.B. Sutker, M. Uddo, K. Brailey, A.N. Allain, & P. Erra, Psychological Symptoms and Psychiatric Diagnoses in Operation Desert Storm Troops Serving Graves Registration Duty, *Journal of Traumatic Stress*, 1994, (7) pp.159-171.

L. Tay & E. Diener, 'Needs and Subjective Well-Being Around the World', *Journal of Personality and Social Psychology*, 2011, (101) pp.354-365.

J. Tosh, 'Masculinities in an Industrializing Society: Britain, 1800-1914', *Journal of British Studies*, 205, (44) pp.330-342.

D. Vincent, 'Love and Death and the Nineteenth-Century Working Class', *Social History*, 1980, (5) pp.233-247.

A. Watson, 'Self-deception and Survival: Mental Coping Strategies on the Western Front, 1914-18', *Journal of Contemporary History*, 2006, (41) pp.247-268.

C.R. Williams, 'The Welsh Religious Revival 1904-5', *British Journal of Sociology*, 1952, (3) pp.242-259.

H.M. Williams, 'Letters From France, Vol.2', *The Monthly Review*, 1792, (10) pp.93-8.

N. Wilson, C. Clement, J.A. Summers, J. Bannister, & G. Harper, 'Mortality of First World War Military Personnel: Comparison of Two Military Cohorts', *British Medical Journal*, 2014, (349) p.7168.

## Theses

S.J. Bannerman, 'Manliness and the English Soldier in the Anglo-Boer War 1899-1902: The More Things Change The More They Stay The Same', unpublished BA thesis, University of British Columbia, 2000.

L. Behlman, 'Faithful Unto Death: The Postures of Victorian Stoicism', unpublished PhD thesis, University of Michigan, 2000.

K.C. Fielden, 'The Church of England in the First World War', unpublished MA thesis, East Tennessee State University, 2005.

P.E. Hodgkinson, 'Human Remains on the Great War Battlefield – Coping with Death in the Trenches', unpublished MA thesis, University of Birmingham, 2006.

P.E. Hodgkinson, 'British Infantry Battalion Commanders in the First World War', PhD thesis, University of Birmingham, 2013

C. Pividori, 'The Death and Birth of a Hero: The Search for Heroism in British World War One Literature', unpublished PhD thesis, University Autònoma de Barcelona, 2012.

M. Purdy, 'Roman Catholic Army Chaplains During the First World War', unpublished MA thesis, University of Central Lancashire, 2012.

M. Tozer, 'Manliness: The Evolution of a Victorian Ideal', unpublished PhD thesis, University of Leicester, 1978.

**Unpublished Papers**

G. Holmes, 'Report on the Conference on "Neuroses"', 1939.

**The Internet**

ActiveHistory.ca – History Matters, http://activehistory.ca/2014/03/soldier-suicide-after-the-great-war-a-first-look/ (accessed 8 April 2015).

G. Brame, Diary, http://www.firstworldwar.com/diaries/onthebelgiancoast.htm (accessed 1 September 2014).

British Legion, http://www.legion-memorabilia.org.uk/badges/numbers.htm (accessed 11 August 2015).

A.M. Burrage, Diary, http://www.firstworldwar.com/diaries/burrage_intro.htm (accessed 1 September 2014).

L. Buswell, 'With the American Ambulance Field Service in France', http://www.lib.byu.edu/~rdh/wwi/memoir/Buswell/AAFS1.htm (accessed 15 May 2006).

J. Couthamel, 'Sexuality, Sexual Relations, Homosexuality', http://encyclopedia.1914-1918-online.net/article/sexuality_sexual_relations_homosexuality (accessed 7 April 2015).

A. Crome, '"Mobilise the Nation for a Holy War" – Churches, Chaplains and British Religion in World War I', http://www.alc.manchester.ac.uk/abouttheschool/schoolsandcommunityengagement/wwi-centenary-events/podcasts/ (accessed 6 November 2014).

E. Cronier, 'Soldiers on Leave', http://podcasts.ox.ac.uk/series/first-world-war-new-perspectives (accessed 5 February 2015).

A.A. Dickson, Diary, http://www.firstworldwar.com/diaries/varietiesoftrenchlife.htm (accessed 6 November 2014).

F. Farley, http://www.artofmanliness.com/2011/02/14/the-art-of-manliness-podcast-34-the-attributes-of-a-hero-with-dr-frank-farley/ (accessed 18 October 2014).

A. Fell, 'Realities of Total War', https://www.futurelearn.com/courses/ww1-heroism/steps/15157/progress (accessed 3 November 2014).

C. Field, 'British Religion in Numbers', http://www.brin.ac.uk/news/2012/some-historical-religious-statistics/ (accessed 14 August 2015).

J. Grenfell, https://movehimintothesun.wordpress.com/2010/11/22/into-battle-julian-grenfell/ (accessed 20 January 2015).

L.W. Griffith, *Up to Mametz*, (1931), http://freepages.history.rootsweb.com/~alwyn/Mametz/ (accessed 1 April 2006).

Horniman Museum, London, http://www.horniman.ac.uk/collections/browse-our-collections/authority/event/identifier/event-36 (accessed 21 December 2014).

T. Loughran, 'Masculinity, Shell Shock, and Emotional Survival in the First World War', (review no. 944) http://www.history.ac.uk/reviews/review/944 (accessed 8 June 2015).

R.L. Mackay, Diary, http://www.firstworldwar.com/diaries/rlm1.htm (accessed 1 September 2014).

J. Meyer, 'Citizen Heroes', https://www.futurelearn.com/courses/ww1-heroism/steps/15161/progress (accessed 3 November 2014).

D.C. Noonan, http://www.theage.com.au/comment/why-the-numbers-of-our-wwi-dead-are-wrong-20140428-zr0v5.html (accessed 19 August 2105).

Harry Patch, http://www.bbc.co.uk/history/worldwars/wwone/last_tommy_gallery_03.shtml (accessed 26 April 2015).

Pitt Rivers Museum, http://web.prm.ox.ac.uk/amulets/index.php/museum-trail/15-resources/153-trail-bullet/ (accessed 21 December 2014).

J. Racine, 'Memoirs of the Great War', http://www.seaforthhighlanders.ca/museum/?p=540 (accessed 16 December 2014).

P. Reed, 'Arras Point du Jour Discovery of Remains June 2001', http://www.battlefields1418.com/point_du_jour.htm (accessed 7 April 2015).

Science Museum, London, www.sciencemuseum.org.uk/broughttolife/objects/display.aspx?id=6517 (accessed 21 December 2014).

J. Scotland, 'Soldier Suicide after the Great War: A First Look', http://activehistory.ca/2014/03/soldier-suicide-after-the-great-war-a-first-look/ (accessed 25 August 2015).

J. Sellars, 'Stoicism and its Legacy', https://podcasts.ox.ac.uk/stoicism-and-its-legacy (accessed 13 August 2015).

P. Shaw-Stewart, http://archives.balliol.ox.ac.uk/Past%20members/PHStewart.asp (accessed 28 October 2014).

The Great War Interviews, http://www.bbc.co.uk/iplayer/group/p01tbj6p (accessed 8 April 2015).

The Stiff Upper Lip, https://emotionsblog.history.qmul.ac.uk/2012/10/the-history-of-the-stiff-upper-lip-part-2/ (accessed 18 October 2014).

Swansea University, 'Disability in the South Wales Coalfield', http://www.swansea.ac.uk/media-centre/latest-news/disabilityinthesouthwalescoalfieldexhibitionrevealsanextraordinaryhiddenhistory.php (accessed 25 August 2015).

Victorian School, http://www.victorianschool.co.uk/school%20history%20lessons.html (accessed 26 August 2014).

Victorian Web, http://www.victorianweb.org/history/work/burnett6.html (accessed 18 October 2014).

W. Walker, Diary, http://www.firstworldwar.com/diaries/battleofloos.htm (accessed 1 September 2013).

A. Watson, http://www.inter-disciplinary.net/ptb/wvw/wvw1/Watson.pdf 'Fear in Combat and Combating Fear: British and German Troops in Endurance Warfare, 1914-1918' (accessed 27 August 2015).

F.W. Watts, Diary, http://www.firstworldwar.com/diaries/nightcounterattack.htm (accessed 6 November 2014).

G. F. Wear, Diary, http://www.firstworldwar.com/diaries/17-21.htm (accessed 6 November 2014).

# Index

12th Division  92
18th century  77, 224
19th century  78, 165, 224, 255
20th century  xvi, 76-78, 224
21st century  82, 245, 247
46th Division  110, 189
47th Division  220
51st Highland Division  218

Absence (of/from family and/or home)  54, 63-65, 68, 91, 243, 251
Adam, Second-Lieutenant Arthur  24, 157
Adams, Second-Lieutenant Bernard  26, 28, 40, 44-45, 111, 128, 194, 226, 231, 257
Adaptation (to conditions)  xviii, 104, 138, 143, 146-147, 152, 158, 163, 191, 195, 197, 202, 204-205, 213-215, 220-221, 225, 230, 234, 236, 245
Adrenalin  25, 28, 48, 138-139, 146, 153, 174, 177, 185
Afraid *see* Fear
Aisne, River  25, 32, 36, 47, 49, 56, 152, 189, 230-231
Albert Medal  165, 178
Alcohol  31-33, 37, 48-50, 89, 154, 162, 226, 230, 254
Allen, Lieutenant John  89, 114, 232
Aloneness  150, 152, 172
Amulets  132-134, 136
Andrews, Lance-Corporal William  21, 25, 35, 43, 68, 71, 88, 97, 170, 229
Anglo-Saxon  100, 166
Anticipation  24, 29, 100, 149, 151, 156, 174-175, 177

Anxiety  xvi, 25, 45, 48, 73, 104, 135, 140, 148, 174-175, 188, 248
ANZAC  196, 207
Argyll & Sutherland Highlanders  180
Army Post Office  54, 56
Army War Graves Service  190
Arousal (physical)  25-26, 28-29, 37, 146, 153, 158, 174-175, 251-252
Arras  xi-xii, 35, 37, 43, 87, 113, 148, 177, 181, 187, 195, 200, 210
Ashamed *see* Shame
Ashurst, Private (later Sergeant) George  113, 121, 127, 140, 142, 148, 197
Atheists  117, 119, 240
Athletics  97-98
Atrocities  39, 42, 109
Autonomic nervous system (ANS)  25, 138
Autonomy  30, 38
Avoidance (as coping strategy)  48, 51, 66, 104, 123, 190, 209-211, 213, 220, 245

Bailleul  37, 131
Bairnsfather, Lieutenant Bruce  47, 52, 70, 147
Balfour, Isaac Bayley  227, 266
Barnett, Lieutenant Denis  90, 229
Basic needs  30-32, 36-37, 51, 83, 91
Beaumont Hamel  142, 217-218
Beer *see* Alcohol
Bell, Captain Douglas  25, 69, 139
Belonging  xviii, 30, 37-38, 51, 53, 57-58, 68, 70, 74-76, 81, 91, 236, 245
Bethune  68, 73, 242

Bible 98, 134, 209
Bickersteth, Lieutenant Burgon 'Bishop' 42, 114, 117-118, 123, 226
Bickersteth, The Reverend Julian 43, 83, 108-109, 113, 115, 117-118, 131, 197, 211, 219, 232, 237-238
Bidder, Major Harold 84, 142, 151, 189
Bion, Captain Wilfred 26, 43, 155, 188
Blacker, Second-Lieutenant Carlos 38, 71, 74, 100, 109, 122, 133, 144, 188, 229
Bloor, Gunner Frank 195, 200
Blunden, Second-Lieutenant Edmund 26, 84, 142, 206, 232-233
Bois Grenier 241-242
Bolwell, Private Frederick 40, 196
Bombardment 34, 47, 115, 137, 141-143, 145-151, 156-160, 175, 179, 194
Bonding 63, 80-81, 86, 228
Bones 117, 193, 198, 205, 219
Book of Common Prayer 240
Border Regiment 216
Boredom 27-29, 37, 41, 47-48, 137
Bourke, Joanna 79, 91, 250
Bourne, John xii-xiv, 79
Bowra, Lieutenant Cecil 92, 203
Brame, Private George 87, 113, 123, 154
Bravery 22, 26, 62, 138, 140, 150, 152, 154, 159, 162, 164-165, 167, 169-170, 173, 177-185, 219, 234-235, 240, 254
Breakdown (nervous/psychological) 25, 181, 249, 254
Breeding 96, 99, 169-171, 225
Brent, Frank 43, 86
Brittain, Second-Lieutenant Edward 159, 162
Brittain, Vera 55, 61, 159
Broodseinde 37, 126
Brownlow, Captain Cecil 51, 142, 152, 155, 158
Buckley, Captain Francis 22-23, 40, 86, 126, 231
Bullying 82-83, 91, 168-169
Burgoyne, Captain Gerald 27-28, 43, 49-50, 58, 83, 124, 131, 147, 180, 188-189, 202, 207, 214, 239-240

Burial xi-xiii, 109, 117, 196, 206-208, 210-211, 213, 217-219, 222-223, 226, 235-243
Burrage, Private Alfred 89, 114, 116, 121, 126, 137, 152, 157, 168-170, 195, 232-235
Butt, Private Herbert 193, 203, 205

Cairns, David 108, 115
Callousness 24, 152, 191, 198, 202-203, 220, 227, 233, 235, 238
Calmness 159, 166, 233
Camaraderie 23, 84
Cambrai 27, 143, 164, 176, 179, 224, 232
Cambridge 110, 118
Cambrin 127, 217
Campbell, Second-Lieutenant (later Captain) David 41, 50, 153, 161
Campbell, Second-Lieutenant Patrick James 37-38, 55, 72, 74, 82, 88-89, 125, 141, 146, 150-151, 153, 158-159, 162, 175, 178, 181-182, 189, 201-202, 208, 254
Cannadine, David 191, 223
Carré, Captain Gilbert 114, 232
Carrington, Hereward 129, 185
Carrington, Second-Lieutenant Charles xx, 27, 30, 32, 36, 80-81, 120, 123, 126, 132, 136, 144-145, 151, 153-154, 175, 178, 206-207, 241
Cassells, Scout Joe 48, 113, 138, 175-176
Casualties xi-xii, 33, 38-39, 61, 121, 123, 128, 146, 158, 184, 194, 217, 227, 231, 246, 249
Casualties, psychiatric 246, 249, 253
Casualty Clearing Station 26, 184, 248
Caterpillar Valley 210
Catholicism 107-108, 114-116, 119, 133, 203
Caution 94, 137, 179
Cavell, Nurse Edith 43, 109
Cemeteries xiii, 205, 212, 223-224, 237-238, 242
Censorship 60, 62, 112
Channel 70, 74, 114

Chaplains  42, 48, 110, 115-116, 128, 134-135, 169, 203, 209, 220, 237, 240
Chapman, Captain Edward  59, 89
Chapman, Second-Lieutenant Guy  41, 44, 71, 89, 116, 133, 155, 184, 198-199, 207, 214, 228, 230, 232
Character  94, 101-102, 107, 167-170, 172-173
Charity  153, 155
Charms  132-135
Cheerfulness  45, 47, 52, 54, 74, 87-88, 92, 94, 99, 104, 126, 153-154, 157, 163, 180, 184
Children  40, 53, 57-58, 63-64, 66, 71, 91, 101, 165, 170, 178, 191-192, 250
Chivalry  97, 99, 165, 173
Chloride of lime  196-197, 217
Chocolate  56, 65
Christ  77, 111, 114, 131
Christianity  22, 77, 95-98, 102-103, 106-108, 110-111, 118-119, 134-136, 165, 192, 240, 244
Christianity, Muscular  98, 103, 110
Christmas  56, 60, 109
Chums  ix, xiii, xix, 38, 76, 83, 85, 87-88, 90, 227-228, 230, 238, 240
Church of England  107-109, 116, 119
Churchill, Winston  166, 183
Cigarettes  48, 50, 56, 65, 147, 205
Citizen heroes  182-183
Civilians  vi, xiv-xv, 52, 71-72, 109, 177, 193, 196, 214, 243, 249, 251
Clapham, Private Henry  26, 32, 35, 49, 54, 56, 94
Clarke, Trooper W.  33, 194, 232
Clayton, Captain Charles  127, 140, 162, 189, 217
Clearing the dead  217-220
Cloete, Lieutenant Stuart  22-23, 80-81, 125, 157, 178, 199-200, 218
Clothing  30-33, 57, 59, 66, 124, 194
Clubs  35, 62, 91, 102-103
Cognitive dissonance  110, 135
Cold  32-35, 42, 49, 59-60, 66, 81
Collins, Second-Lieutenant W.N.  218-219

Colour  198-199
Commonwealth War Graves Commission  205
Companionship  51, 80-82, 87, 90-91, 143, 150-152, 228
Comradeship  23-24, 27, 30, 38, 60, 76, 79-80, 82-87, 89-92, 168, 170, 172, 184, 245
Confidence  38, 111, 163, 173, 181
Congreve, Captain Billy  105, 208, 235, 238, 241
Connaught Rangers  115
Conscripts  xiv, 54, 83, 107, 121, 210, 255
Constancy  94-95, 97, 105
Control  xvii, xix, 25, 29, 36, 45, 94-97, 101, 103-105, 122, 132, 135-137, 146, 149-150, 155-158, 160, 162-163, 167-170, 172, 178, 182, 185, 203-204, 222, 224, 230-231, 245
Convalescence  25, 121
Coolness  142, 150, 158, 162, 180-182
Cooper, Private Herbert  196, 212
Coping  xvi-xx, 21, 25, 28-29, 30-31, 34, 36, 44-45, 48, 51-52, 54, 57, 70-71, 75, 85, 93, 104, 115, 126, 135-136, 141-142, 154-155, 159, 161-164, 182, 184-185, 189-190, 208-209, 211-212, 214-215, 218-219, 220-221, 243-250, 252-255
Coppard, Private George  23, 42, 44, 49, 73, 79-80, 82, 86, 92, 123, 141, 144-145, 151-152, 156-157, 182, 189, 195, 198, 200, 210, 213, 228, 237-238
Corns and Hughes-Wilson  170-172, 264
Corpses  see Dead bodies
Courage  xvii, xix-xx, 27, 34, 52, 54, 94, 99, 101, 105, 138, 152, 155, 159, 161, 163-169, 171-186, 224, 244, 254
Courageous actor  173, 177-180, 185
Cowardice  117, 141, 151, 160-161, 163-164, 166-172, 174, 185, 210
Craiglockhart  150, 215
Creighton, Reverend Oswin  116, 201
Cremation  197, 223, 239
Croft, Henry  170, 181
Crome, Andrew  108, 119, 128, 134
Cronier, Emmanuelle  69-71, 73

Crucifix xii, 65, 131, 242
Crying 27, 35, 47, 53, 80, 100, 141, 143, 153, 162, 170, 198, 222, 224-226, 233-235, 265
Cuddeford, Captain Douglas 33-34, 47, 49, 113, 120, 149, 187, 195, 210, 225, 254
Cuinchy 26, 194, 217
Cynicism 48, 254

Davidson, Major George 42, 151, 170, 205
Davis, Private Reginald 40, 85-87, 112, 115-116, 204, 228, 235, 238, 240
Dawson, Second-Lieutenant Alec 22, 45, 146, 175, 201
Dawson, Lieutenant Conningsby 32, 44, 69, 71, 90, 96, 116, 118-119, 131, 147, 159, 161, 164, 166, 168, 173, 177, 182, 184, 232, 236
Dead bodies xi-xiii, xix, 35, 39, 43-44, 50, 60-62, 113, 122, 129-131, 133-134, 151, 158, 187--223, 230-232, 235-243
Death viii, xi-xiv, xvi, xviii-xix, 24, 28, 34-35, 40-41, 43, 45, 48, 51, 60, 64-65, 72-73, 80, 85-87, 89-90, 96-97, 100-101, 108, 111-115, 117-130, 134, 136-137, 140, 146, 149, 151, 154-155, 157, 159, 165-166, 168, 173, 179-180, 187-189, 191-196, 200, 203, 207-209, 211-212, 215-216, 220, 222-224, 226-236, 238, 241, 243-244, 250
Depression xvi-xvii, 27, 29, 31, 33-34, 52, 55, 72, 87, 98, 104, 119-120, 136, 190, 217-218, 231,
Depression, economic 249-250, 252, 254
Desertion 170-172
Despair 26-27, 135, 146, 174
Despondency 127, 156, 249
Devenish, Second-Lieutenant George 154, 161
Diet 32, 34-35
Disability 121, 164, 189, 250-251, 273
Discipline xiv, 30, 69, 94-95, 97-99, 101-102, 105, 163, 173

Discomfort 34, 44-45, 48, 60, 62, 85, 95, 101, 104, 193, 245, 254
Disgust 42, 83, 110, 154, 172, 201-203, 209
Dismemberment 127, 188, 198, 212, 215, 233
Disordered Action of the Heart (DAH) 247-248
Dissonance 62, 70, 74-75, 110, 135
Distinguished Service Order 22, 181
Distraction 26, 29, 37, 48, 50, 55, 58, 72, 132, 147, 156-7, 163, 211, 232-3, 245
Distress 46, 56, 99, 150, 187-188, 210, 246
Dixon, Lieutenant Reginald 88, 90, 197-198
Dixon, Thomas 100-101
Douie, Second-Lieutenant Charles 26, 47, 51, 87, 90, 127-128, 142, 145, 180, 187, 193, 203
Dread 68, 148, 151, 155, 160, 176, 189, 202, 207, 233
Drink *see* Alcohol
Drinkwater, Private Harry 33, 37, 45, 68, 85, 88, 91, 120, 122-124, 143, 148, 168, 180, 197, 258
Dublin Fusiliers 231
Dugdale, Captain Geoffrey 27, 115, 148, 161, 175, 181, 224
Dugmore, Lieutenant Arthur 24, 51, 145, 148, 160, 210
Dundas, Captain Henry 80, 86, 139, 150, 161
Dunn, Captain James 209, 237, 241
Durham Light Infantry 235
Duty, sense of 30, 40-41, 43-45, 94-95, 98-99, 101-102, 105, 107, 119, 156, 164-165, 167-168, 171-173, 177-180, 184-185, 245
Dyett, Sub-Lieutenant Edwin 171-172
Dysentery 35, 60

East Lancashire Regiment (Accrington Pals) 192
Education xvii, 38, 57, 63, 97, 129, 178
Egypt 215, 226, 239

Emotion xii-xiv, xvi, xix, 29, 46, 51, 55, 58, 63-64, 69, 74, 77-79, 82, 84-86, 89-94, 96-97, 99-101, 103-105, 107, 117, 125, 130, 135-136, 149, 153, 156-158, 163, 169, 172, 176-177, 192, 204, 206-207, 222-227, 229, 231-233, 235, 241, 243-247, 253-254
Endurance viii, xiv, xvii-xix, 33-34, 44, 52, 86, 91, 94-95, 99, 101, 118, 135, 150, 159, 163, 173, 182-186, 188, 245, 247, 254
Engall, Second-Lieutenant John 40, 111
Enthusiasm xviii, 27, 33, 41, 43-44, 90, 102, 118, 174, 182, 207
Epictetus 93-94, 98, 137
Eton 22, 80
Euphoria 28, 48, 69, 174
Evolution 100, 138, 178
Example 96, 154, 165, 174, 180-182, 200
Excitement 21-22, 24, 139, 175-177
Execution 43, 108-109, 170, 172
Exhaustion 24, 27-29, 34, 37, 130, 145, 182, 211, 217, 231, 246
*Express and Star* 62
Eyre, Private Giles 48, 88, 121, 143, 147, 149, 163, 184, 194-195, 198, 200, 212, 217, 228, 232, 238-239

Faith xix, 43, 106-107, 109, 111-113, 115, 117-118, 129, 131, 133, 135-136, 181, 211, 224
Faith, loss of 117-118
Family xiv, xviii-xix, 30, 38, 40, 52-54, 56-58, 61-62, 64, 69-70, 74, 76-78, 84, 91, 93, 100, 103, 134, 172-173, 192-193, 213, 224, 237, 243, 251-252
Farley, Frank 172-173, 185
Fatalism 46, 48, 68, 101, 106, 119-125, 135-136, 230
Fear xvi, xviii-xix, 23, 27-28, 30, 36, 45, 48, 65, 68, 71, 73, 94, 99-100, 104, 115-116, 120, 126, 128-129, 131, 136-164, 166-169, 171-178, 180-182, 185, 188-189, 192, 201, 204, 206, 231, 233, 238, 244, 254
Fearlessness 139, 161, 173, 178, 180

Feelings 27, 31, 39, 51, 92, 94, 100-101, 150, 152, 188-189, 193, 198, 203, 224-225, 227, 231-232
Feilding, Captain (later Lieutenant-Colonel) Rowland 23-24, 42, 98, 115, 123, 125, 153, 157, 170, 178-179, 184, 193-194, 206, 217, 220, 241
Fellowship 79, 84, 86, 92
Festubert 59, 64, 67, 97, 112, 134
First Gulf War 190, 221
First movements 94-5, 137-8, 224
Flanders xv, 21, 33, 65-66, 96, 100, 129, 160, 223, 231
Fletcher, Anthony 59-60, 254
Folklore 107, 130
Food 30-34, 37, 51, 78, 130, 143, 197
Fortune, Private G. 192-193
Fortune-telling 128, 132, 136
France xv, 27-28, 34, 37, 41, 47, 64-66, 70-72, 74, 86, 96, 107-108, 126, 129, 140, 149, 154, 160, 163, 184, 188, 196, 223, 225, 228, 234, 248
Fraser, Lieutenant-Colonel William 70, 124
French Army 31, 168
Fricourt 151, 176, 236-237
Friendship xi-xiii, xix, 23, 30-31, 38, 76-78, 82, 84-87, 89-92, 243, 245
Fright 27, 66, 83, 138, 140, 142-143, 148, 151-154, 157, 160, 163, 170, 176, 210
Front line 27, 29, 31, 34, 36, 56, 60, 84, 113, 115, 125, 140-141, 146, 156, 159-160, 166, 171-172, 184, 195, 205-206, 238-239, 242, 245, 248
Fryer, Private (later Second-Lieutenant then Major) Evelyn 41, 49, 140, 143, 218, 230
Fuller, J.G. 30, 46, 52, 69, 74
Funeral 106, 222-224, 238-239, 241
Funk 98, 137, 142, 148, 153, 156, 158-159, 161-162, 168, 200, 244
Futility xii-xiii, 244

Gallantry 152, 182, 237
Gallipoli 25, 32, 35-36, 42, 47, 50, 55, 81, 86, 114, 116, 125, 139, 144, 148,

150-151, 153, 160-161, 164, 184, 189, 196-197, 199-201, 203-205, 207, 209, 212, 215-216, 227, 231, 235, 239, 243, 252
Gamble, Ralph 80, 86
Garstin, Second-Lieutenant Denis 28, 122, 160
Garvin, Second-Lieutenant Gerald ('Ged') 59, 61, 71, 96, 100
Garvin, James 96, 100
Gas 24, 27, 148-149, 194, 196, 199
German Spring Offensive 1918 121, 231
Gibbs, Major Arthur Hamilton 41, 72, 84-85, 123, 143, 149, 179, 230-231, 233, 238
Gillam, Major John 81, 144, 148, 150, 160-161, 196, 227, 239
Gillespie, Second-Lieutenant Douglas 23, 37, 41, 58, 70, 146, 160, 165, 227, 231, 236
Givenchy 59, 174, 194
Gladden, Private Norman 40, 50, 83, 151, 156, 162, 167, 175, 212, 227
Glendenning, Private Edward 189-190
God 40-41, 58, 64-67, 77, 101, 106, 108-114, 117-119, 128, 130-131, 134-136, 141, 161, 168, 200, 212, 218, 226, 234
Gohelle 63, 132
Gommecourt 153, 175, 236
Gordon Highlanders 70, 122, 180
Gordon, General Charles 165-166
Gordon, Reverend Geoffrey 128, 135
Gordon, Second-Lieutenant Huntly 27, 41, 44, 50, 72, 114, 138, 144, 146, 175, 179, 181, 184, 193, 197, 204, 206, 211, 233
Graham, Private Stephen 42, 44, 48, 107, 113, 117, 126, 144, 202, 206, 208, 213, 229, 237
Graves xi-xii, 110, 131, 190, 194, 208, 217, 223-224, 234, 236, 238-243
Graves, Second-Lieutenant (later Captain) Robert 27, 45, 50, 56, 106, 112, 127-129, 131, 133, 148, 199, 209, 211, 228-229

Green, Private Walter 233, 235, 243
Greenwell, Second-Lieutenant (later Captain) Graham 29, 33, 54, 68, 84, 147, 153, 195-196
Grenfell, Captain The Honourable Julian 21-22, 23-24, 39, 144
Grief xiii, xix, 87, 137, 190, 211, 222, 224-225, 227, 229, 234-235, 243
Griffith, Second-Lieutenant Llewellyn 29, 69, 74, 144, 198, 216, 229, 234, 236
Grimsby Chums xi-xii
Guards, The 218, 242
Gwinnell, Private Richard 229, 238

Haigh, Captain Richard 31, 47, 175-176, 231-232
Hamilton, Lieutenant-Colonel Ralph 43, 204, 229
Hampshire Regiment 184
Hanbury-Sparrow, Captain Allan 39, 181
Hankey, Donald 149, 157, 175-176
Hardened 191, 202, 219-220, 234
Hardiness xvii, 101, 135, 184, 255
Hardship xv, 33, 37, 45, 52, 86, 99, 180, 191, 244-245
Hardy, Second-Lieutenant Mark 118, 178
Hatred 30, 42-43, 167, 214
Health xvii, 21, 27, 33-5, 58, 63, 97-9, 102, 250-2
Helles 32, 204, 211, 216
Helplessness 36, 47, 104, 135-136, 143, 149-150, 163, 189, 236, 245
Herbert, Lieutenant Aubrey 113, 159, 196, 254
Hermon, Lieutenant-Colonel Robert 57-58
Heroism 39, 72, 102-103, 164-166, 168, 172-173, 177-178, 180-183, 185-186, 225-226, 244, 253-254
Hewett, Second-Lieutenant Stephen 24, 29, 84, 92, 136, 147
High Wood 100, 130, 190, 199, 219-220
Highland Light Infantry 50
Hill 60 126, 199, 204
Hitchcock, Captain Francis 132, 163, 182, 198, 201, 205, 210, 212-213, 234, 239

Hohenzollern Redoubt 110, 189
Holmes, Richard xv, 42, 102, 188-189, 191, 230
Holy Communion 111, 115, 134, 136
"Home world" 58, 60, 62-63, 68, 72
Home xv-xvi, xviii, 22-24, 27, 30, 32, 37, 41-42, 44, 47, 51, 53-65, 68-75, 79, 84-86, 89, 91, 100, 105, 112, 116-117, 129-131, 136, 144, 146-147, 150, 160-161, 165-166, 187, 202, 205, 210-211, 215, 227-229, 231, 235-236, 249, 253
Homosexuality 80-81
Honour 40, 73, 97, 99, 105, 109, 137, 171
Honourable Artillery Company 182
Hood Battalion 164
Hooge 196, 201
Horror xv, xvii, 21, 42, 48, 70, 143-144, 156, 162, 176, 198-199, 201-203, 207, 210-211, 214, 220, 244
Hospital 25, 34-35, 63, 69, 73, 83-84, 110, 129, 172, 188, 192, 239, 248
Hughes-Wilson 170-172, 264
Hulloch/Hulluch 130, 217
Human Remains *see* Dead Bodies
Humanity 212-213, 220
Humour 27, 33, 44-48, 52, 66, 84, 86, 104, 155, 157, 166, 184, 194, 208-209
Hunger 31-32, 123
Husbands, Private (later Corporal) Geoffrey 55, 60, 69, 88, 140-141, 150-151, 154-155, 162-163, 176, 181
Hyndson, Second-Lieutenant James 25, 36, 47, 140, 189
Hyperarousal *see* Arousal
Hysteria 100, 142, 145, 149, 156

Immortality 134, 230
Indifference 51, 94-95, 98, 104, 117, 126, 157, 160-161, 164, 180, 203, 209, 222, 226, 233
Individualism xii, xv-xvii, 79
Intimacy 58, 73, 76-82, 84, 89, 226, 232
Introspection xii, xv-xvi, 51, 92, 103, 152, 162, 245, 254
Intuition 125-127, 136

Inured 191, 193, 211-212, 220
Irritability, 25, 28, 219, 251, 252
Isolation 58, 70, 80, 85, 88, 233
Italy 37, 55, 153

Jack, Brigadier-General James 29, 35, 60, 196, 214, 229
Jalland, Pat 192, 224
Jeffreys, Major Richard 33, 47
*John Bull* 166-167, 172
Jokes *see* Humour
Jones, Lieutenant Paul 59, 61
*Journey's End* 105, 254
Junger, Ernst 199, 201, 203, 210
'Just enough' xviii, 36, 51, 245
Just War 40, 109

Keeling, Sergeant Ben 24, 43, 110, 144
Kennedy, Reverend G.A. Studdert, "Woodbine Willie" 114, 134
Killing 39, 42-43, 98, 109, 117, 135, 175, 183, 230,
King, Major Arthur 235-236
Kipling, Rudyard 98, 101
Kirkwood, Lieutenant G.N. 216-217
Krithia 53, 127

La Bassée 37, 60, 132, 155, 237
Lambert, Private Arthur 29, 34, 37, 42, 55, 89, 100, 121, 126, 150
Lancashire Fusiliers 52, 142, 148
Lane, Private (later Corporal) Clifford 84, 86, 199, 209, 212
Le Havre 66-67
Leadership 38, 87, 171, 173, 181-182
Leave xviii, 25-27, 31, 38, 53, 62-63, 65, 68-75, 88, 121, 128, 147, 214-215, 217, 228
Leed, Eric xvii, 52, 58, 74, 136
Leese, Peter 246, 249
Legends 50, 130-131, 136
Leighton, Second-Lieutenant Roland 55, 61-62
Letters xviii-xix, 21, 24, 27, 39-41, 51, 53-69, 71, 73-75, 80, 89, 100, 111-112, 172, 183, 211, 215, 237

Liddell Hart, Basil 79-80
Lincolnshire Regiment xi, 200, 206
Liverpool Scottish 61
Liverpool Territorials 60, 62
Living, Second-Lieutenant Edward 153, 175, 177
Lodge, Second-Lieutenant Raymond 24, 61, 71, 129, 142, 196, 229
Logan, Padre Innes 39-40, 117, 234
London Regiment 216, 219
London 71-72, 107, 133, 223, 242
Longley, Second-Lieutenant Cecil 32, 55-56, 69, 196
Loos 63, 67, 71, 122, 160, 163, 174, 182, 189, 195, 200, 213
Loss xvi, xviii-xix, 24, 29, 53-54, 56, 64, 66, 96, 100, 130, 137, 187, 193, 223, 226-229, 232-234, 243
Love xviii, 30-31, 37-38, 51, 53, 55, 57, 68, 74-75, 80-81, 84, 90-91, 167, 179, 193, 229, 236, 241-242, 245
Loved-ones 30, 40, 53-57, 59, 69, 71, 74, 129, 222, 236, 245
Loyalty xv, 30, 44, 52, 89, 167
Luck 59, 66, 114, 124-126, 128, 131-134, 136, 169, 231, 233
Lucy, Sergeant John 33-35, 37, 49, 56, 69-70, 115-116, 123, 132, 162, 187-188, 208, 230-231, 234
Ludwig, Walter 48, 54, 85, 115, 120, 124-126
Lusk, Captain James 112, 241

MacGill, Patrick 203, 211
Mackay, Lieutenant Robert 29, 125, 128, 180-181, 202, 242
Macmillan, Second-Lieutenant Harold 23, 151-152, 176, 182, 208-209
Magic 106, 124, 128, 134, 136
Malone, Lieutenant-Colonel William 47, 54-55, 64, 139, 184, 207, 211, 226, 235
Mametz Wood 176-177, 198, 229, 234
Managing 31, 67, 145, 147, 152, 156, 159, 163
Manchester Regiment 151, 176
Manhood 23, 96-97

Manion, Captain R.J. Robert 45, 68, 120, 124, 149, 167, 169-170
Manliness xix, 51, 54, 62-63, 93, 96-106, 137, 159-161, 163, 165, 180, 224-225, 244-245, 253-255
Manning, Private Frederic 29, 39, 45, 79-80, 87, 89-90, 127-128, 153, 155, 158, 177, 187, 203, 206, 229, 231
Manwaring, Captain G.B. 24, 68, 71, 86, 121, 169
Marchant, Private (later Lieutenant) Eric 54, 112
Marcus Aurelius 93, 96-97
Martin, Second-Lieutenant Bernard 40, 72, 82, 85, 107, 118, 141-143, 145, 161, 189, 201, 234
Masefield, John 193, 198, 206, 241
Maslow, Abraham xviii, 30-31, 37, 53, 78
Mastery 30, 38, 100, 138, 156, 163
Mates v, xix, 38, 43, 67, 75-76, 92, 202, 222, 226, 228-229, 232-233, 235, 238, 240, 245
Maxwell, Lieutenant-Colonel Frank 215, 234
McCartney, Helen 60, 62
McCauley, Private John 88, 210, 213, 219-220, 230, 233, 242
McKerrow, Captain Charles 199, 203
Mental health xvii, 27, 31, 48, 51, 122, 142, 225, 245, 249, 252
Mesopotamia 111, 161, 207
Messines 115, 175
Meyer, Jessica 59, 103-104, 182, 185
Middle-class 97, 101-103, 107, 192-193, 223
Militarism 98-99
Military Cross 110, 167, 178
Mines 26, 61, 148, 219
Ministry of Pensions 92
Misery 26, 32-35, 56, 162, 193
Modelling 180-182, 186
Money 58, 63-65, 223
Monotony 28-29, 32, 40, 42, 47
Mons 25, 34, 113, 116, 123, 140, 142, 159

Morale xviii, 30, 33, 38-39, 49, 54, 69, 74, 92, 115, 130, 146, 208, 216-218, 245, 264, 277
Morality 41, 58, 95-96, 102, 169-171, 225, 245
Moran, Lord 45, 68, 119, 141, 146, 149, 166-173, 175, 178, 208, 225, 230
Mortality 63, 66, 71, 175, 188, 206, 212, 219-220
Mothers xviii, 21, 27, 40-41, 53, 55, 57-58, 60-61, 69-72, 80, 91, 110-112, 121-122, 133-134, 161, 188, 211, 227, 237, 243
Motivation xviii, 30, 39-41, 43, 51, 62, 105, 137, 171, 174, 244
Mourning xiii, xix, 191, 222-223, 237
Murray, Seaman Joseph 35-36, 53, 97, 189, 201, 205, 243,
Music hall 46-47, 102
Mutuality xv, 79, 87

Negative thinking 31, 34, 42, 46, 104, 120, 135, 163, 175
Nerves 21, 24-29, 37, 49-51, 62, 83, 99, 132, 139, 141-142, 144-145, 147, 149, 153-154, 156-157, 160-163, 169-172, 174, 177, 213, 218-219, 225, 246, 248
Neurasthenia 70, 248
Neuve Chapelle 67, 114, 170, 210, 234
Nevill, Second-Lieutenant Billie 44, 56, 61, 202, 235
New Testament 109, 134
New Zealand 226, 250
Nightmares 140, 188, 215, 247, 252
No-man's land 36, 39, 60, 97, 110, 113, 130, 157-158, 166, 189, 197, 201, 213, 230, 235
Nonconformist 107-108
Noonan, David 249-250
Northumberland Fusiliers 83, 145
Numbness 175-177, 191

Officer class 91, 105
'Old Bill' 47, 147, 184-185
Old Comrades Association 91
Optimism 120, 126, 139

'Over the top' 49, 90, 127, 134, 153, 174-175, 177, 180, 183
Ovillers 32, 34, 153, 216
Owen, Lieutenant Wilfred xiii, 185
Oxford 22, 72, 84, 137, 227

Padres 39, 107-108, 112-113, 115-117, 231, 234, 236, 238-240
Pain 30, 35, 45, 96, 114, 155, 175, 184, 189, 202, 222, 247
Palmer, Captain The Honourable Robert 111, 207
Pals xi, xix, 22, 34, 38-39, 41, 76, 83-89, 113, 151, 161, 226-230, 232-234, 238-239, 242-243
Pals Battalions xii-xiii, 76, 85
Parcels 56-57, 64
Parker, Private Ernest 40, 82, 113, 140, 147, 155, 157, 195, 235
Passchendaele 34, 126, 234
Patriotism 30, 40-42, 97, 99, 102-103, 105-106, 108, 165, 225-226, 244
Pessimism 120, 124
Photographs 55, 63-65, 74, 133, 198, 213
Pilots 87, 150, 165
Pinkerton, Sergeant Douglas 86, 141, 145, 150, 174, 176, 187, 239, 242
Pity 65, 98, 176
Plowman, Second-Lieutenant Max 29, 33, 36, 44, 49, 161, 170, 178, 190, 199, 213
Pluck 99, 156, 159, 168, 171
Point du Jour xi, xiii, 206
Pollard, Captain (previously Private, Second-Lieutenant) Alfred 23, 39, 41, 54, 70, 97, 139, 174, 180, 182, 207
Polley, Private David 34, 119
Ponsonby, Chaplain Maurice 48, 134, 169
Post-traumatic stress xiii, xvi, 146, 190-191, 219, 247, 251
Posture (of the dead) 198-200
Poulton, Lieutenant Ronald 54, 122, 140, 142, 242
Pragmatism xi, 32, 80, 112, 205, 242
Prayers 58, 66, 113-114, 116, 118-119, 131, 149, 200, 239-241

284  Glum Heroes

Pride  30, 39, 97, 152, 159, 166-167, 233
Primary groups  38, 53-54, 75, 84, 245
Protestant  107, 133
Psychology  xvi-xvi, xviii, xx, 31, 94, 153
PTSD *see* Post-traumatic stress
Public school  86, 97-98, 101-103, 178, 244
Purpose (sense of)  22, 24, 39, 42-3, 52, 71, 74, 111, 135, 244,

Quigley, Private Hugh  28, 53, 58, 119-120, 143, 146, 149, 160, 174, 199, 210, 214

Racine, Private James  68, 71, 125
Raggett, Lieutenant Shallett  174, 176, 186
Railton, Reverend David  220, 240
Rain  33-34, 55, 60, 194, 205, 218
RAMC (Royal Army Medical Corps)  83, 166-167, 169
Rats  129-130, 198-199, 203, 218
Reader, Private Alec  59, 61
Reith, Lieutenant John  22, 69, 71, 74, 108, 115, 133-134, 152, 169
Relationships  xiv, xviii, 38, 54, 62, 64, 76-82, 84-91, 226, 234, 243, 245
Religion  xvi, 39, 49, 95, 102, 106-118, 130-136, 180, 200, 211, 224, 226, 239, 245
Religion, emergency  113, 115, 134, 136
Religion, folk  108, 130, 134-135
Religious iconography  131-132, 134
Resilience  xvii, 30, 101, 246
Rest  36-7
RFC (Royal Flying Corps)  87
Richards, Private Frank  33, 49, 129-130, 154, 200, 204, 208-209, 212, 217, 242
Richards, Sapper B.R.  143, 156
Rifle Brigade  92, 212, 214
Risk  50, 59, 62-63, 66, 99, 119-120, 122, 158, 166, 172, 177-179, 182, 192, 249
Ritual  xiv, xix, 132, 222-223, 225-226, 237, 239-240, 243-244
Rivers, Dr William  150, 215
Rodwell  228, 232, 239

Rogerson, Lieutenant Sidney  22-23, 27, 29, 34, 44, 47, 79, 84, 86, 92, 151, 154, 194, 203, 213, 218, 226, 231, 236, 238-239, 262
Roman  77, 93, 95-96, 164
Roper, Michael  xviii-xix, 54, 57, 61, 188, 252, 254
Ross, Captain Robert  37, 117, 139, 188, 203, 230
Rossiter, Corporal Eric  131-132
Roussy, Professor G.  31-32, 168
Royal Air Force Medical Service  171
Royal Artillery  203
Royal Berkshire Regiment  42, 68
Royal Engineers  217
Royal Fusiliers  166, 184
Royal Irish Rifles  50, 115, 141
Royal Naval Division  32, 90, 164, 171, 216
Royal Naval Volunteer Reserve  97
Royal Navy  171
Royal Scots  xi
Royal Welsh Fusiliers  177
Royal West Kent Regiment  182
Rum *see* Alcohol
Russell, Private Henry  44, 49-50, 58, 69, 72, 85, 115, 121, 141, 147, 159, 181, 254

Sadness  xi, 156, 224, 229, 233, 238, 243
Safety needs  xviii, 30-31, 35-36, 78, 245
Safety, personal  41, 51, 57, 59-60, 68, 88, 132, 145-146, 156, 175, 177
Salonika  41, 123, 143, 179, 229, 247, 249
Sanctuary Wood  49, 97, 208
Sanders, Lieutenant Leslie  121-122
Sang-froid  143, 179
Sassoon, Second-Lieutenant Siegfried  viii, xiii, 29, 43, 70, 74, 83, 166, 176, 202, 213, 229, 262
Scots Guards  139
Scott, Ralph  28, 122, 201
Scottish Rifles  29, 112, 241
Seaforth Highlanders  242
Second World War  xii, xvi, 46, 91, 166, 246, 253
Secularism  106, 133

Self-actualization xviii, 30-31, 38
Self-control 25, 101, 103, 169-170, 178, 185, 224
Self-deception xviii, 59-60, 126, 159, 245
Self-efficacy 173-174, 180
Self-esteem 30-31, 38-39, 41, 52, 105, 134, 245
Self-reliance 94, 104
Self-sacrifice 96, 99, 105, 164-166, 178
Seneca 93-94, 137-138, 163-164, 222, 224, 226
Sentimentality xi, xvi, xviii, 42, 78, 83-85, 92, 128, 206, 240, 242, 244, 252
Separation 54, 57, 67, 89, 103
Serre 80, 103, 237
Shackleton, Ernest 81-82
Shame 39, 80, 94, 146, 148, 160, 168-169, 181, 201, 225, 234
Sheffield City Battalion 41, 79, 103
Shell-shock 31, 146, 149, 153, 170, 172, 174, 216, 220, 246-249, 253
Shell-Shock, War Office Committee of Enquiry into (RWOCESS) 25, 29, 31, 139, 168, 171, 180, 254
Shelter 30, 32, 51, 150, 180
Sherriff, R.C. 105, 254
Sherwood Foresters 73, 110, 189
Sherwood-Kelly, Lieutenant-Colonel Jack 179-180
Shirking 70, 88, 167, 171-172, 218
Shock 28, 66, 85, 110, 153, 169, 172, 177, 192, 204, 210-211, 213, 226-228, 230-231
Sickness 33, 111, 172, 192, 216, 218
Sleep xv, 27, 31, 33-35, 37, 50, 61, 70-71, 79, 88, 140, 144, 158, 178, 211, 216, 218, 231, 251
Smell 142, 187, 190, 195-197, 210, 212, 216, 220
Smiles, Samuel 101-102
Smith, Rifleman Aubrey 25, 33, 35, 54, 74, 87-88, 105, 200, 214
Snape, Michael 115, 118-119, 132
Snipers 22, 36, 39, 61, 140, 150, 176, 227-228
Solidarity xv, 78-79

Somme 24, 26-29, 33-35, 47, 51-52, 54, 61, 69, 71, 83-84, 88-89, 98, 110, 115, 121, 123, 127, 136, 143, 149, 151, 154-157, 160-162, 166, 170, 175-176, 183-184, 188, 190, 193-195, 197-198, 200, 203-205, 209-210, 212-213, 216-218, 225-226, 231, 235-236, 238, 242, 252
South Staffordshire Regiment 62
Southwell, Captain Evelyn 24, 147, 176, 227
Spencer, Second-Lieutenant Wilbert 56, 60
Sport 37, 62, 78, 81, 97-98, 102, 110, 147
Sporton, Private Bertie 194, 214, 229, 232
St Eloi 105, 205, 235, 238
Stage-managing fear 156, 159, 163
'Stiff upper lip' 96, 100-101, 226
Stoicism xvii, xix, 33, 44-46, 74, 93-101, 103-106, 137-138, 145, 156-157, 159, 161, 163-164, 168, 171, 173, 183-185, 220, 222-226, 228, 243-245, 254
Strain 24-27, 29-30, 34, 47, 50, 72, 86, 99, 116, 122, 145, 156, 163, 170, 174, 188, 224, 231
Stress xvi-xviii, 24-29, 31, 37, 45-46, 48-51, 54, 81, 85-87, 93, 104-105, 135-136, 147, 156, 170-172, 174, 190, 208, 216-217, 246-249, 252, 255
Suffering xiii, 38, 40, 44, 71, 89, 94, 101, 162, 166, 183, 220, 244, 247, 252
Suffolk Regiment 159
Suicide 27, 29, 56, 249-250
Sumpter, Major 181, 184
Supernatural 129-131
Superstition 68, 107-108, 128, 130-132, 134-136
Survival xv, 41, 60, 101, 121-122, 124, 128, 245
Sussex Regiment 115
Sustainer 9hero) 173, 185
Sympathy 40, 79, 154-155, 169-170, 202, 213
Synge, Lieutenant William 32, 49

Tansley, Corporal James 35-36
Tears *see* Crying
Tennant, Lieutenant Edward 150, 160
Terraine, John xii, 106
Terror xv, 86, 137, 141, 144-145, 152, 157, 159, 161-162, 200, 203, 244
Thiepval 204, 212, 236
Thomas, Second-Lieutenant Alan 51, 114, 131, 145, 177, 182, 232
Thompson, Private L. 204, 208-209, 211
Threat xvi, xix, 21, 28, 30, 36, 40, 45, 48, 52, 54, 80, 90, 95, 97, 104-105, 120, 135, 138, 144, 146, 148, 157, 160-161, 163-164, 217, 228, 245
Thring, Edward 97-98
*Times, The* xii, 22
Tiredness 29, 31
Tobacco (smoking) 31-32, 46, 50, 56, 63, 65, 157, 179, 197, 229
Toc H 112, 119
Treffry, Second-Lieutenant Dormer 127, 188
Trench warfare xvii, 31, 43, 51, 59, 108, 141, 180, 244
Trench, Major Reggie 55, 58, 73
Trones Wood 208
Tyrrell, Squadron-Leader William 32, 139, 149, 152, 157, 171, 174, 254

Unburied dead 195, 197, 203, 213, 216-217
Unemployment xiv, 250-252
Upper-class 97, 101, 107, 192-193, 223-224, 244
Uppingham 97-98

Vann, Lieutenant-Colonel Bernard William 110-111, 135
Vaughan, Second-Lieutenant Edwin 86, 89, 133, 140, 143, 145, 154, 194, 199, 201, 206, 208, 210-211, 240
"Vedette', Second-Lieutenant 156, 160, 218, 242
Victoria Cross (VC) 105, 110-111, 165, 174, 179, 183, 267
Vietnam War xvi, 39

Vimy Ridge 110, 113, 209, 215
Virtue 77, 94-95, 97-101, 105, 164-165, 169, 177-178, 233
Vision 195, 198
Voigt, Private Frederick 72, 142
Volunteers xiv, 39-40, 54, 70, 85, 107, 137, 171

Wade, Gunner Aubrey 203, 208
Wade, Major C. 213, 220
Walker, Private W. 87, 174, 200
Walker's Ridge 47, 184
War Office Committee of Enquiry into 'Shell-Shock' 25, 139-140, 168, 171, 180, 254
"War world" 59-60, 62-63, 65, 68, 70, 72, 75
War-weariness 40-41
Water, drinking 30-33, 51, 130, 144, 190, 195
Watson, Alexander xiv, xviii, 30, 48, 59, 112, 119-120, 125-126, 132, 157, 245-246
Watt, Reverend Lauchlan 116, 118
Weakness 51, 99, 164, 225, 253
Weather 22, 31, 33, 35, 59-60, 80, 209
Wellbeing 30-31, 50, 104
Wellington Battalion 47
Welsh Division 237
West Yorkshire Regiment 47
West, Second-Lieutenant Arthur 43, 50-51, 117, 142, 155, 158, 160, 210, 229
Western Front xiv, 25, 32, 43, 59, 68-69, 72, 74, 88, 94, 96, 100, 108-109, 119, 121-122, 125, 128, 138, 141, 155, 166, 191, 202, 206, 226, 234, 252
White feather 137, 168
Whitham, Private Frederick 63-8, 73, 114, 132
Will-power 28, 169, 171
Williams, Helen Maria 99, 225
Williams, Private Walter 70, 86, 131, 140, 160-161, 176, 204, 207, 210, 214, 226, 230, 240
Williamson, Private Henry 49, 109-110, 138, 141, 157

Williamson, Private Walter 59-60, 132
Wilson, Captain Theodore 111, 146, 161, 211
Wiltshire Regiment 240
Windiness 140, 153-155, 162-163
Wives 47, 55-58, 60, 62-63, 65-68, 71, 73, 78, 91-92, 100-101, 114, 121, 141, 146, 161, 179, 194, 235, 243
Women xx, 38, 40, 48, 53, 63, 78, 80-81, 84, 91, 101, 103, 165, 168, 191-192, 223-224, 250, 253-254
"Woodbine Willie" *see* Kennedy, Reverend G.A. Studdert
Working-class xv-xvi, 52, 60, 77-79, 91, 97, 101-103, 106-107, 113, 115, 128, 165, 191-193, 223
Workingmen's clubs 77-78, 103
Worn-out 26, 28, 50, 64, 116, 231
Worry 23, 61, 73, 122, 135, 143, 155, 182
Wounds 22, 24-26, 30, 33-35, 38, 40, 48, 53-54, 56, 60-61, 63-65, 67, 69, 80, 84-85, 87-88, 109-111, 113-114, 116, 120-121, 126-128, 130, 134, 142, 151-152, 155, 158, 160, 162, 164, 166-167, 172, 177, 179, 181, 183-185, 187-192, 207, 210, 216-217, 219-220, 228-230, 232, 235, 239, 250, 254
Wrench, Private Arthur 68, 124, 134

York and Lancaster Regiment 35
*Yorkshire Evening Post* 59, 62
Yorkshire Regiment 63, 66
Yoxall, Captain Harry 51, 122-123
Ypres 28, 33-35, 37, 49, 82-83, 112, 115, 118, 120, 123, 125-126, 133, 141, 145-146, 156, 158, 162, 167, 174, 189, 199, 203, 205-208, 210, 234
Ypres, First 25, 36, 196
Ypres, Second 26, 56, 88, 148
Ypres, Third 27, 29-30, 34, 115, 117, 120, 123, 126, 132, 136, 148, 154, 159, 175, 180, 184, 197, 240, 248
Yser 51, 128

# Wolverhampton Military Studies
www.helion.co.uk/wolverhamptonmilitarystudies

## Editorial board

Professor Stephen Badsey
Wolverhampton University

Professor Michael Bechthold
Wilfred Laurier University

Professor John Buckley
Wolverhampton University

Major General (Retired) John Drewienkiewicz

Ashley Ekins
Australian War Memorial

Dr Howard Fuller
Wolverhampton University

Dr Spencer Jones
Wolverhampton University

Nigel de Lee
Norwegian War Academy

Major General (Retired) Mungo Melvin President of the British Commission for Military History

Dr Michael Neiberg
US Army War College

Dr Eamonn O'Kane
Wolverhampton University

Professor Fransjohan Pretorius
University of Pretoria

Dr Simon Robbins
Imperial War Museum

Professor Gary Sheffield
Wolverhampton University

Commander Steve Tatham PhD
Royal Navy
The Influence Advisory Panel

Professor Malcolm Wanklyn
Wolverhampton University

Professor Andrew Wiest
University of Southern Mississippi

## Submissions

The publishers would be pleased to receive submissions for this series. Please contact us via email (info@helion.co.uk), or in writing to Helion & Company Limited, 26 Willow Road, Solihull, West Midlands, B91 1UE.

## Titles

No.1 *Stemming the Tide. Officers and Leadership in the British Expeditionary Force 1914* Edited by Spencer Jones (ISBN 978-1-909384-45-3)

No.2 *'Theirs Not To Reason Why'. Horsing the British Army 1875–1925* Graham Winton (ISBN 978-1-909384-48-4)

No.3 *A Military Transformed? Adaptation and Innovation in the British Military, 1792–1945* Edited by Michael LoCicero, Ross Mahoney and Stuart Mitchell (ISBN 978-1-909384-46-0)

No.4 *Get Tough Stay Tough. Shaping the Canadian Corps, 1914–1918* Kenneth Radley (ISBN 978-1-909982-86-4)

No.5 *A Moonlight Massacre: The Night Operation on the Passchendaele Ridge, 2 December 1917. The Forgotten Last Act of the Third Battle of Ypres* Michael LoCicero (ISBN 978-1-909982-92-5)

No.6 *Shellshocked Prophets. Former Anglican Army Chaplains in Interwar Britain* Linda Parker (ISBN 978-1-909982-25-3)

No.7 *Flight Plan Africa: Portuguese Airpower in Counterinsurgency, 1961–1974* John P. Cann (ISBN 978-1-909982-06-2)

No.8 *Mud, Blood and Determination. The History of the 46th (North Midland) Division in the Great War* Simon Peaple (ISBN 978 1 910294 66 6)

No.9 *Commanding Far Eastern Skies. A Critical Analysis of the Royal Air Force Superiority Campaign in India, Burma and Malaya 1941–1945* Peter Preston-Hough (ISBN 978 1 910294 44 4)

No.10 *Courage Without Glory. The British Army on the Western Front 1915* Edited by Spencer Jones (ISBN 978 1 910777 18 3)

No.11 *The Airborne Forces Experimental Establishment: The Development of British Airborne Technology 1940–1950* Tim Jenkins (ISBN 978-1-910777-06-0)

No.12 *'Allies are a Tiresome Lot' – The British Army in Italy in the First World War* John Dillon (ISBN 978 1 910777 32 9)

No.13 *Monty's Functional Doctrine: Combined Arms Doctrine in British 21st Army Group in Northwest Europe, 1944–45* Charles Forrester (ISBN 978-1-910777-26-8)

No.14 *Early Modern Systems of Command: Queen Anne's Generals, Staff Officers and the Direction of Allied Warfare in the Low Countries and Germany, 1702–11* Stewart Stansfield (ISBN 978 1 910294 47 5)

No.15 *They Didn't Want To Die Virgins: Sex and Morale in the British Army on the Western Front 1914–1918* Bruce Cherry (ISBN 978-1-910777-70-1)

No.16 *From Tobruk to Tunis: The Impact of Terrain on British Operations and Doctrine in North Africa, 1940–1943* Neal Dando (ISBN 978-1-910294-00-0)

No.17 *Crossing No Man's Land: Experience and Learning with the Northumberland Fusiliers in the Great War* Tony Ball (ISBN 978-1-910777-73-2)

No.18 *"Everything worked like clockwork": The Mechanization of the British Cavalry between the Two World Wars* Roger E Salmon (ISBN 978-1-910777-96-1)

No.19 *Attack on the Somme: 1st Anzac Corps and the Battle of Pozières Ridge, 1916* Meleah Hampton (ISBN 978-1-910777-65-7)

No.20 *Operation Market Garden: The Campaign for the Low Countries, Autumn 1944: Seventy Years On* Edited by John Buckley & Peter Preston Hough (ISBN 978 1 910777 15 2)

No.21 *Enduring the Whirlwind: The German Army and the Russo-German War 1941-1943* Gregory Liedtke (ISBN 978-1-910777-75-6)

No.22 *'Glum Heroes': Hardship, fear and death – Resilience and Coping in the British Army on the Western Front 1914-1918* Peter E. Hodgkinson (ISBN 978-1-910777-78-7)

No.23 *Much Embarrassed: Civil War Intelligence and the Gettysburg Campaign* George Donne (ISBN 978-1-910777-86-2)

No.24 *They Called It Shell Shock: Combat Stress in the First World War* Stefanie Linden (ISBN 978-1-911096-35-1)

No. 25 *New Approaches to the Military History of the English Civil War. Proceedings of the First Helion & Company 'Century of the Soldier' Conference* Ismini Pells (editor) (ISBN 978-1-911096-44-3)

No.26 *Reconographers: Intelligence and Reconnaissance in British Tank Operations on the Western Front 1916-18* Colin Hardy (ISBN: 978-1-911096-28-3)

No.27 *Britain's Quest for Oil: The First World War and the Peace Conferences* Martin Gibson (ISBN: 978-1-911512-07-3)

No.28 *Unfailing Gallantry: 8th (Regular) Division in the Great War 1914-1919* Alun Thomas (ISBN: 978-1-910777-61-9)